Additional Praise for *The HIP Investor*

"As an investor, executive, and entrepreneur, I have seen first-hand how successful commercial models can be an effective method for solving human needs. Successful leaders usually manage organizations that focus on positively impacting society. This HIP book shows you how the Human Impact + Profit approach is a powerful combination that can create great value for your portfolio, your business, and your world."

— Alvaro Rodriguez Arregui, Co-founder and Managing Partner of IGNIA
    Partners LLC; Chair of the Board, Compartamos Banco

"Herman's book provides forward-looking investors with unique tools to help build a compelling portfolio."

— Robert Safian, Editor, *Fast Company* magazine

"For those who want to do good and make money, this HIP book shows you how to do so through your work, investments, and shopping."

— Liz Cutler Maw, Executive Director, Net Impact

"This book is a how-to manual for creating business ventures and investment portfolios that are both profitable and good for the world."

— David Bornstein, Author, *How to Change the World*

"This transformational book shows how investors and companies can find opportunities to profit and have a positive human impact. With vivid examples across different sectors, Herman demonstrates how a focus on human impact is beneficial financially and socially."

— Perla Ni, Founder, Stanford Social Innovation Review; CEO,
    GreatNonprofits.org

"The socially responsible investment field has been in a long period of stagnation, relying on outmoded metrics and methodologies that do not keep pace with the realities of business today. *The HIP Investor* provides a breath of fresh air. Herman builds on the established success of beneficial social- and positive eco-impact business strategies to create an innovative, flexible, and practical road guide that enables investors to get started."

— Brian Dunn, CEO, Growth Capital Services Inc.

"Better products, more engaged people, lower costs, and better market share— all benefits that can come from satisfying what Maslow called our need for self-actualization. R. Paul Herman says that leaders, companies, and investors who align their views to this approach can thrive and excel beyond their peers, and I know he's right. *The HIP Investor* is a great guide for a company looking to create positive 'human impact and profit.'"

— Ray Anderson, Chairman and Founder, Interface Inc.;
    Author, *Confessions of a Radical Industrialist*

"Leading companies everywhere are increasingly measuring not just their narrowly defined accounting profits, but also their social and environmental impacts. This book describes why these drivers of intangible asset value are fundamental in assessing a company's long-term profitability and market valuation. While this book is intended as a guide for investors, it is simultaneously an excellent overview for senior executives and board members of the challenges and potential rewards from linking sustainability metrics and strategies (the HI of HIP) to profits (the P of HIP)."

—Dr. Paul R. Kleindorfer, Paul Dubrule Professor of Sustainable Development, INSEAD

"As the world experiences population growth, water shortages, and poor health and sanitation services, Herman proves that major corporations and investors can benefit from an investment mentality. Herman shows that corporations have made strides in seeking to solve the world's leading problems—and profited handsomely—by expanding their mindset to deliver billion-customer markets and products that address pressing human problems."

—Rahilla Zafar, Contributing Writer and Editor, *Knowledge@Wharton* and INSEAD Knowledge

"The principles in *The HIP Investor*—focusing on both Human Impact and Profit—make sense for both investors and business leaders. The leading portfolios in the next century will improve lives and make attractive profits—resulting in a long-term, lower risk win-win."

—Dave Stangis, Vice President of Sustainability, Campbell's Soup Company

"*The HIP Investor* is recommended for individuals and institutions who want to combine tough-minded financial analysis with criteria of ethics and sustainability for the long-term growth of their portfolios. Herman makes the case, drawing on examples of leading companies, that doing good and doing well can often go together in the world of investing."

—Dr. Eric W. Orts, Guardsmark Professor and Director of the Initiative for Global Environmental Leadership, The Wharton School, University of Pennsylvania

"Herman challenges social investors, individuals and institutions, to broaden the scope of their investment criteria to incorporate the wider human impact that such companies have on society, and outlines how to measure that impact—and its relationship to profit."

—Bob Annibale, Global Director, Citi Microfinance

"Herman has done us all a big favor by constructing an innovative means for improving your whole life—including your portfolio, your workplace, and your impact on the community. I urge you to read *The HIP Investor* to find practical advice that you can use now to lead a richer life personally, professionally and financially."

—Dr. Stewart D. Friedman, Author, *Total Leadership: Be a Better Leader, Have a Richer Life*; Professor, Wharton School, University of Pennsylvania

THE HIP INVESTOR℠

Make Bigger Profits *by* Building *a* Better World

R. PAUL HERMAN

with Jessica Skylar and Gayle Keck

WILEY

John Wiley & Sons, Inc.

Published by John Wiley & Sons, Inc., Hoboken, New Jersey.
Published simultaneously in Canada.

For general information on our other products and services or for technical support, please
contact our Customer Care Department within the United States at (800) 762-2974, outside
the United States at (317) 572-3993 or fax (317) 572-4002.

Wiley also publishes its books in a variety of electronic formats. Some content that appears in
print may not be available in electronic books. For more information about Wiley products,
visit our Web site at www.wiley.com.

Library of Congress Cataloging-in-Publication Data:

Herman, R. Paul.
    The HIP Investor^{SM} : Make bigger profits by building a better world / R. Paul Herman ;
with Jessica Skylar and Gayle Keck.
        p. cm.
    Includes bibliographical references and index.
    ISBN 978-0-470-57512-3 (cloth)
    1. Investments—Social aspects.   2.   Investments—Environmental aspects.
    3.   Social responsibility of business.   I.   Skylar, Jessica.   II.   Keck, Gayle.   III.   Title.
    HG4515.13.H47 2010
    332.6—dc22   2009049437

Printed in the United States of America.

10   9   8   7   6   5   4   3   2   1

For all the strong women of the world, including
My wife and soulmate, Gayle
My mother, Alice
My sister, Mary
` My mother-in-law, Sue Ann
My business partners, Jessica and Joan
My grandmothers, Mary and Martha
And all the high-esteem men who respect them.

Contents

Disclosure and Disclaimer

The purpose of this book is to educate you about a new investment approach. As with any decisions about investing, you should consider the risks involved, including potentially losing your principal.

This book is not intended to provide personalized investment advice. Each investor has different goals, timelines, tolerance for risk, as well as unique tax situations. Therefore, you should consult an investment adviser, accountant, or tax expert.

This book does not recommend the specific stocks, bonds, or other investment vehicles described within. Instead, the descriptions are intended to be illustrative of the potential benefits and risks of this investment approach. The author may own public or private investments described in this book.

As always, evaluate your personal situation, goals and risks before making any investment decisions and consult the appropriate investment professional.

HIP Portfolio Calculations

The HIP results do not represent the results of actual trading using client assets but were achieved by means of the retroactive application of a model, assuming a $100,000 beginning portfolio. There are inherent limitations of showing composite portfolio performance based on model results. Unlike an actual performance record, model results cannot accurately reflect the effect of material economic or market factors on the price of the securities, and therefore, results may be over- or under-stated due to the impact of these factors. Since model results do not represent actual trading and may not accurately reflect the impact of material economic and market factors, it is unknown what effect these factors might have had on HIP's decision making if HIP Investor were actually managing client portfolios. During the period for which model results are shown, securities of U.S. companies have generally been rising, and the model returns are a function of this market environment. If this environment were to change materially, the model results portrayed in HIP's material would, in likelihood, reflect results different from those portrayed.

The HIP, S&P, and Treasuries results include reinvested dividends or interest, and results are net-of-fees as a client would have paid to HIP on a quarterly basis in advance for advisory fees and brokerage costs. During the period for which model results are shown, HIP has maintained the same investment strategies and advisory services as those that HIP offers to clients. There is potential for loss as well as for profits. It should not be assumed that the recommendations made in the future will be profitable or will equal the performance of the securities in the portfolio. The S&P index is shown as a general market indicator and is not available for direct investment. Tax consequences have not been considered. Investments are managed via separately managed accounts with HIP Investor Inc. as the investment adviser. This is not an offer of securities. Past performance is not indicative of future results.

Introduction: The New Fundamentals—Build a Better World, Make Bigger Profits

Capitalism used to be easy. Discover, acquire, and defend a unique resource. Pay people the least you can get away with. Off-load as many liabilities and risks to government as possible. And, of course, collect the profits in as short a time as possible. These captains of industry used to be called "robber barons"; today they are simply called "capitalists."

For most of the history of investing, capitalists have delivered the highest financial returns to shareholders, with a focus on maximizing short-term profits at almost any cost. Nobel Prize-winning economist Milton Friedman reinforced this view by asserting that "the business of business is business," and that any distraction from making money as quickly as possible must be avoided. But the pure capitalist path melted down again in the fall of 2008, eliminating its excess returns.

At the same time, "do-gooders" have pursued societal change through charities and nonprofits focused on individual problem areas that address environmental, social, and human challenges on an individual basis. Many of these problem solvers provide social services that treat the symptoms, missing an opportunity to go "upstream" to fix the root cause.

The majority of investors have focused on a capitalist approach and short-term financial gain. However, this traditional approach has accelerated the number and intensity of societal problems, creating a larger gap between a better world and the world of today. To counter this approach, some investors have selected a "socially responsible" investment approach, which typically excludes "bad" companies from their portfolios. This approach has relieved some consciences, but in most cases has failed to yield attractive long-term financial results.

Until now, an investor would need to choose between these two options: short-term gains that risk society's stability, or positive intentions that fail to deliver consistently attractive returns. Now, there is a new investment approach—one that realizes bigger profits that capitalists seek while building a better world that do-gooders desire. This approach generates human impact and profit, or what I call "HIP," simultaneously. It embraces a comprehensive view of society. It produces long-term results while also yielding short-term profits. It enables for-profit companies to solve human problems for customers, employees, and society. It combines "doing good" and "making money"—drawing from the best of both worlds. "HIP investing" can produce bigger profits for your portfolio and build a better world for you, your family, and society overall.

By revitalizing your portfolio with a HIP approach, you can practice a fundamentally new way of investing. How can you build a more HIP portfolio? This book will explain how to be more HIP in how you invest, where you work, and what you buy. (You may even start evaluating every daily decision with the question, "how HIP is it?") I wrote this book to show you the tools and process to build an investment portfolio designed to realize Human Impact + Profit.

The HIP Approach

A diversified portfolio is built up of stocks, bonds, real estate, and other financial assets. The HIP approach enables you to evaluate each of these investment types methodically. Every asset in your portfolio can be rated on its HIP-ness. Since 2006, HIP Investor Inc. has analyzed, rated, and ranked the HIP factor of large, publicly traded companies. By 2009, HIP evaluated the largest 500 U.S.-based companies in the standard benchmark, the Standard & Poor's® 500 index. HIP has observed that the best-managed companies, which deliver both short- and long-term value for shareholders, do the following:

- **Assess** the trends to identify risks and opportunities of the entire global society, including environmental and social challenges.
- **Bring** products and services to market that serve the needs of customers, shareholders, and stakeholders.

- **Count** the quantifiable data beyond traditional accounting and finance numbers, to include human, social, and environmental results.
- **Directly** integrate a new management approach into the way decisions are evaluated and implemented across the whole enterprise.
- **Equate** the quantifiable human impacts to financial success—across income statements, balance sheets, and cash flow.

Investors, too, can use this methodology to position their portfolios for success. Those who adopt this HIP approach and criteria can discover leading indicators that drive the financials before they happen, providing an advantage over those who solely use the old greedy capitalist or optimistic do-gooder approach.

HIP portfolios can produce significantly higher returns, even adjusting for risk. Over the five-year period from July 2004 to June 2009, the HIP 100 portfolio outperformed the S&P 100 by at least four percentage points per year, or what financial experts refer to as 400 basis points. (The HIP 100 represents the same companies in the S&P 100 but reweights each of them for quantifiable sustainability.) This HIP portfolio, which covered both up- and down-markets also out-gained the lowest-risk approach of three-month Treasury bills. In Figure I.1, you can see the cumulative returns of all three portfolios. Because of HIP's fundamentally sound approach of measuring the leading indicators of quantifiable human impact, a HIP investor expects to make bigger profits by building a better world.

The HIP fundamentals enable an investor like you to outperform by combining the best of both disciplines. This innovative approach mixes the hard-nosed, data-driven analytics of finance with the comprehensive end-to-end lifecycle view of society's nurturers. When combined, you can benefit from a breakthrough approach that can make more money by doing more good. HIP investors and their advisers are already recalibrating their portfolios and you can choose to do so, too.

Focusing on Impact Adds Business Value

In 2007, Dave Stangis was the director of sustainability at Intel Corp. When Stangis first learned of the HIP methodology and its focus on quantifiable results, it was an enlightening moment.

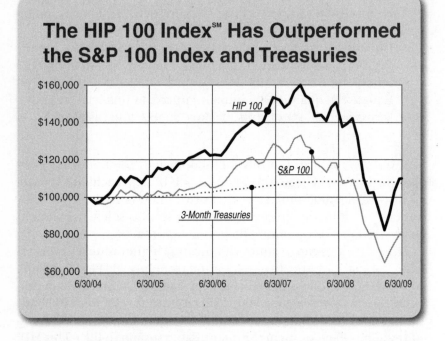

Figure I.1   The HIP 100 Index Outperforms the S&P 100 Index and Treasuries Historically

Source: HIP Investor; Standard & Poor's; Bloomberg Finance LP.

"Measuring results that focused on the outcomes of Health, Wealth, Earth, Equality, and Trust made sense business-wise," said Stangis. "You have to show real results to demonstrate how serious a player you are in delivering impact" (Stangis, interviews 2007–09).

Quantifiable results are one overarching element of the HIP methodology. Whereas capitalists focus on heaps of financial and operating ratios, many times they become disconnected from the true source of a company's growth: solutions for customers who have a human need. The benefits of that solution can be quantified—longer life from a medical device, more income from a savings account, or lower fuel usage (and emissions) from a hybrid car. Companies that quantify these values and understand how they drive financial value are well positioned for bigger profits and help to create a better world.

Intel Corp. historically has been rated as one of the 10 most HIP companies. It follows the five steps outlined above: (1) Assessing the global trends of billion-person markets and trillion-dollar opportunities instills a new mentality. (2) Bringing products to market to serve those customers positions Intel for new revenues, such as health care wireless products and home monitoring systems. (3) Counting the quantifiable impacts is possible by focusing on improved access to care and higher quality of life. (4) Directly embedding these criteria into management practices is easy for the company's engineering culture. (5) Equating those impacts to financial value has highlighted results of $50 million from overall resource conservation and efficiency initiatives—more than a 2-for-1 return on its investments in those areas (Intel CSR report 2008, 35).

Stangis has brought that thinking and approach to Campbell's Soup, where he is Vice President of Sustainability. He is energized by CEO Douglas Conant's drive to roll out the discipline of sustainability—a field that interconnects all the elements of company, customers, and society—into every business unit and employee. "Sustainable performance is one of the seven 'pillars' here," Stangis says of the company's goals and strategies. "And it is expected to drive business value across the whole enterprise."

Corporate leaders like Stangis, and others advocating similar initiatives (whom you will meet in this book) are helping to create new sources of shareholder value previously untapped, by improving the society around them. This HIP approach can be adopted by investors to select the best-managed companies for your portfolio—and by the companies seeking to be those leaders.

How HIP Is It? Three Questions to Ask of Any Investment

When evaluating a possible investment for your portfolio, you should ask "How HIP Is It?^{SM}" to understand the company's true commitment, measurements, and management of sustainability and how it drives profit. A company that is HIP will have compelling—and quantifiable—answers to the following three questions, also shown in Figure I.2.

1. **How HIP are the company's products?** What quantifiable impact do they have on the customer? How do they solve a human

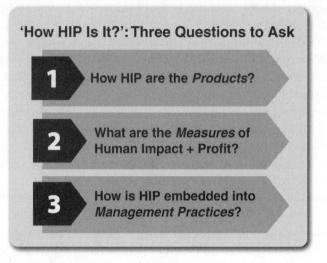

Figure I.2   Three Questions: How HIP Is It?

problem? What share of revenue do those HIP products provide?

2. **How is the company measuring its human, social, and environmental impacts?** Which are leading indicators for the business? How do those impacts drive profit and shareholder value?

3. **How do existing management practices reflect a HIP approach?** Do the vision and metrics support a long-term, comprehensive view of the company, customers, and society? Do all systems for accountability and all processes for making decisions include criteria for bigger profits and a better world?

Leading companies with a high HIP score systematically apply a strategic three-pronged approach. For the first category of **HIP products**, HIP leaders create revenue-generating products and services that have positive impact for their customers and society. SunChips, a product of PepsiCo, is made from organic corn that is converted to chips using solar power and sold in a compostable bag. PepsiCo classifies products that produce these benefits nutritionally and operationally as "good for you" or "better for you" and according to the company, these products total approximately 30 percent of its revenue (Morris 2008).

For the second category of **HIP measurements**, HIP leaders quantify their human, social, and environmental impacts. As we saw above with its $50 million savings, Intel Corp. aggressively pursues improvements in energy usage, water usage, and employee diversity, all of which can be enumerated and shown to directly link a more profitable bottom line. Data-driven approaches are critical, connecting easily to the manage-by-numbers of traditional business success, while also integrating a systematic view toward increasing stability and reducing future risk.

For the third category of **HIP management practices**, leading HIP firms embed a new type of thinking into every aspect of decision-making inside the organization. At General Electric, its "ecomagination" and now "healthy-magination" strategies are cross-company initiatives. Aspirational goals for reductions in greenhouse-gas emissions are integrated into executive and manager performance reviews, overall decision making, and pay and promotion decisions. This has led to new ways of governing the company. The proactive approach ensures that both profit and impact become recurring results. In 2008, GE generated $17 billion from "ecomagination" products, including wind turbines and fluorescent light bulbs, summing to nearly 10 percent of the company's nine-digit revenues (GE 2008 Ecomagination Fact Sheet).

This strategic three-pronged approach provides HIP investors the tools to evaluate the leaders and the laggards of an investable group of companies. With the HIP analysis, you can allocate more money to leaders and less money to laggards in your portfolio—or, you can consider excluding the laggards, but that may make for a riskier, less diversified portfolio. This book will explain what to look for when evaluating a company, and point to the leading indicators of more HIP companies that are poised to reap bigger profits while building a better world.

How Does HIP Make Bigger Profits?

The HIP approach has outperformed traditional and socially responsible investing because it focuses on sustainable business value. That value is counted in one of four ways. Three you can see on the financial statements: higher revenue, lower costs, and optimal taxes, all of which increase profit. The fourth is seen in valuation. The increased investor demand for a stock, by buyers willing to pay more for higher profits, drives the stock's value higher and enhances your financial return if you are a shareholder who buys in earlier. The combination of both can provide higher total return from both stock appreciation and dividends paid by the company, which can be reinvested for further gain.

> **Higher Revenue**. The highest-growth companies create value in three ways: identify new customers to buy existing products, invent new products, or acquire new products from other companies to sell to customers. Successful products solve a pressing human need. Population growth is fastest in lower-income economies. New customers from these economies are seeking out products reinvented for a lower-priced economy (e.g., the Tata automobile) or higher value (e.g., solar energy stove). Many times, a new version of an old product, like Procter and Gamble's single-use shampoo, is developed for sale in India. P&G customized the package size to be smaller so that prices would be affordable to everyday families in places like India. In this market, 70 percent of all shampoo used in India is from single-use sachets. For P&G and its industry-leading competitor Hindustan Lever, it is a multi-million dollar market (ENS Economic Bureau 2004). This product also increases the overall hygiene of these customers, which has a wellness benefit—a HIP solution. Chapter 3 will describe many more product examples that drive higher revenue.

> **Lower Costs**. Companies spend money on employees, benefits, outside services, energy, and materials. Finding savings typically requires either human ingenuity or technical innovation. Managing overall energy usage—which tends to be mostly fossil fuels—to be more efficient via motion sensors or staff action eliminates waste, lowers costs, and reduces carbon emissions. Interface Inc. has saved a cumulative $400 million in costs since embarking on its quest to be more sustainable through energy efficiency, materials reduction, and waste reuse and recycling (Interface Global EcoMetrics). Companies like Herman Miller and Salesforce.com also lower their costs from broad engagement of employees. In both cases, more than a fifth of the company is engaged in product development or operational initiatives that save money,

encourage innovation, and have a human benefit. In the case of the Aeron Chair by Herman Miller, it is 95 percent recyclable, generates higher profit despite higher costs because of higher pricing and attractive market share, and is motivating for employees due to its eco-design.

Optimal Taxes. Governments levy taxes at the federal, state, and local levels in order to deliver common benefit and services for their citizens. When seeking to create public good, governments can use tax incentives and rebates to stimulate private-sector action. Health care retailer Walgreens has adapted more than 100 of its California and New Jersey stores and at least two distribution centers to take advantage of renewable-energy state tax incentives, creating an accelerated return on investment for those projects. In those locations, this solar power will generate 20 to 50 percent of electrical needs and be a cleaner, less polluting, and more independent power source (FYPower 2001).

Investor Demand. The price of a stock is not just based on fundamentals like earnings and growth rate, but also on how many investors are seeking to purchase that stock. This may be tied to a particular company's prospects or competitive advantage, or to the industry as a whole (as when investors "rotate" in or out of a sector). The term "price-to-earnings ratio" is frequently used to assess the stock price relative to its profit potential. When companies are more transparent about their current and future plans, investors can more readily set a proper price. United Technologies is an industrial company that sells Otis elevators and Pratt and Whitney jet engines. When United Technologies started publicizing HIP products, like more eco-efficient buses and zero-energy building designs, its stock price moved up beyond the industry average (*BusinessWeek*, "What Price Reputation" 2007). Being transparent to stakeholders, including investors, is very HIP.

HIP Investor's research of more than 500 companies since 2006 shows that companies pursuing a HIP approach tend to drive more business value—through higher revenue, lower costs, optimal taxes, and higher investor demand. The HIP approach focuses on leading indicators—products solving a human need, quantifiable human impact, and comprehensive management practices—which tend to lead to higher profit and shareholder value, benefiting investor portfolios by up to 4 percent annually above the standard market benchmark.

Each chapter of this book will highlight HIP corporate innovations, case studies, and initiatives from this insightful research. You will also meet the leaders who are driving this business transformation to achieve higher human impact and profit. You will be able to evaluate "How HIP Is It?" for your purchases, your workplace, and your investments. You will learn how to incorporate these new fundamentals into your own portfolio and position yourself for a better world and bigger profits.

How Does HIP Build a Better World?

HIP investors realize bigger profits through a portfolio of companies that are actively building a better world. Those firms can create positive impact in a variety of ways:

- Innovating new products that improve quality of life
- Operating with higher environmental efficiency
- Offering new supply contracts to diverse suppliers

The HIP approach identifies more than 20 indicators whose values indicate positive results for society. These measures quantify the good that is created, allowing investors of all types to use this information to better design their portfolios. It also permits investors to gather a summary of human-impact results beyond pure financial returns. Typically, the better the human-impact performance, the bigger the profits.

HIP has defined five categories of human impact, which will be detailed in Chapter 1.

These areas are: Health, Wealth, Earth, Equality, and Trust.

1. **Health** refers to both physical and mental well-being, including quality of life.
2. **Wealth** encompasses ways for people to earn more, save more, or better secure their financial future.

3. **Earth** covers the water we drink, the air we breathe, and the overall ecosystem balance.
4. **Equality** seeks fair representation, whether classified by gender, ethnicity, or income class.
5. **Trust** includes open, transparent information and ethical and respectful behavior.

As a HIP investor, you can design your portfolio to equally weight each of the five, focus on only one of them, or blend them in any combination you desire. While some investors may focus on energy efficiency and choose to double up on Earth, others may hone in on ethical behavior and triple-up on Trust. The beauty of a HIP portfolio is you can choose among these five factors to match your specific desires for human impact. More specifically, as you will see in Chapter 7, you can set up face-offs among companies in the same industry, like Coke vs. Pepsi and Starbucks vs. McDonald's. Then, you can weight your portfolio to reflect those HIP results.

HIP offers a fundamentally new way of investing that gives each investor the power to choose what the most important leading indicators are, and to apply those preferences across multiple companies and industries. It is a more comprehensive approach than the financially-focused capitalists and a more inclusionary approach than the do-gooder investors. The HIP approach provides the foundation for a better world for you and bigger profits for your portfolio.

How HIP Are You?

There is a "generational shift" occurring in buying and investing right now. This force, which will also inherit $22 trillion of intergenerational wealth, is poised to have the highest economic impact since the baby boomers. The twenty-first century will see more active investors—and the financial advisers who serve them—seeking a broad range of "performance" indicators. This entire group will seek to apply their financial power to close today's large gaps and move toward more ecological balance and social stability, which would mitigate risk and increase potential profit.

This new generation of forward-thinking investors and fiduciaries, including a broad swath under the age of 45 (branded as Millenials and Generations Y and X), sees no division between the business, social, and government sectors. They realize that problems are multi-sector and the solutions are multi-disciplinary. They see the power of blending the best of the old capitalist and do-gooder investment approaches. Hence, these new investors will also reward those companies who see the world in the same way, and feel a shared accountability for improving the world.

These HIP investors and investment advisers—from all age groups and backgrounds—are seeking and investing in leading companies that pursue human impact and profit. Leaders like Procter and Gamble, Intel, and United Technologies are delivering great products that have a positive human impact, measuring them and embedding a HIP approach into their entire enterprises. These firms are driving the field with higher financial performance and greater social and eco-benefits.

You may be part of this movement already, or think in a similar direction. Have you determined how HIP you are? Will you apply this breakthrough approach to your investing and money management? Are you ready to be a HIP investor?

Are You Ready to Be a HIP Investor?

This book is written for investors of all types—you don't need to be rich or a financial whiz to build a HIP portfolio. This book also serves the investment advisers who seek fundamentally strong analytical approaches that deliver attractive financial returns and mitigate risks. Everyone can invest—and every aspect of your portfolio can pursue this new, transformational approach. Surveys show that the aspiration to "do good and make money" is mainstream, and if that is you, read on. Your guide is right here.

This book is designed to fully equip you as an investor to pursue a HIP approach for your entire portfolio. When you're done, not only will you know the HIP approach front to back, you will be in a position to work independently or with your financial adviser to capitalize on all the HIP opportunities you can find.

Chapter 2 is written to show you why here and why now. Growing populations, finite natural resources, a plethora of information, and a desire to "do good" are all changing the world and giving companies some of their greatest opportunities.

Chapter 3 evaluates how companies are responding to these opportunities. We'll review some of the leading products developing across Health, Wealth, Earth, Equality, and Trust. Their solutions will inspire you—and demonstrate how their new solutions are breaking down sector boundaries, serving human needs, and building top-line revenue.

Then we'll approach the meat of HIP's methodology. Chapter 4 will walk you through more than 20 factors, illustrating how it improves Human Impact and how it drives profit. The result: a full quantitative assessment of a company's Human Impact and Profit potential that goes beyond traditional surveys or blanket assessments, and instead gives a complete picture of the enterprise.

Chapter 5 approaches a company's management practices. Is the company structuring itself to become more sustainable? HIP's research shows that the highest performing innovators have a clear, measurable vision, a strong culture of accountability, integrated decision-making processes, and financial measures for each approach. This chapter will assess how to evaluate which companies are best structured to innovate and take advantage of Human Impact opportunities.

Next, Chapter 6 will show you how quantifiable impacts translate into a traditional income statement and balance sheet. It will also demonstrate how you assess and derive HIP value from standard accounting reports. You will also see how leading HIP companies are communicating their leadership to investors in the realm of human impact and profit.

After understanding how to fully evaluate a company's HIP score (incorporating its HIP products, Human Impact scores, and management practices), Chapter 7 will walk you through evaluating a company. You will also learn to build face-offs of competitive companies to evaluate their HIP factors, and how to weight the equities in your portfolio according to your preferences.

After rating all your findings, Chapter 8 provides the tools to construct a full HIP portfolio across stocks, bonds, real estate, and other types of investments. You *can* build a HIP portfolio that seeks to generate a better world and bigger profits in each asset class.

Finally, Chapter 9 shares a vision of what a more HIP world will be. Corporations will compete on human impact, and reinvent their businesses to deliver maximum results for society. Those results will better the bottom line and investors can use new tools to personalize their portfolios. The world will benefit from a fuller multidisciplinary approach, including what is taught in schools and academia. All

$175 trillion in global financial assets will be seeking human impact and profit—a very HIP world indeed.

This book is written for all investors and their fiduciaries—for everyone that is dissatisfied with the "robber baron" capitalist path and frustrated with the do-gooder philosophy. Each chapter provides you a basic overview of how and why HIP works, and for those who want to dive deeper, this book includes detailed metrics behind the results. The bottom line: if you're looking for a new way to invest that better reflects your goals and the world we live in, we'll give you the tools and process you need to take your investing to the next HIP level.

Are you ready to be a HIP investor? Let's get started and learn about the foundation of the HIP framework.

THE
HIP
INVESTOR^{SM}

PART

I

GETTING READY FOR YOUR HIP PORTFOLIO

The first step to developing your portfolio begins with a fresh perspective.

Let's start at the beginning. Being productive requires you to be healthy. Then you need to pay for your living expenses and accumulate some wealth. We would prefer to breathe crisp air and drink clean water from the earth. If you believe that every person can make a difference, then we need equality. Finally, for a community to grow, we need to trust each other.

Each of these five elements—Health, Wealth, Earth, Equality, and Trust—forms the foundation of the Human Impact + Profit (HIP) framework. It is inspired by Maslow's hierarchy of needs, and focuses on the human needs that each of us has.

Business is one provider of solutions to these everyday core needs. As a customer, you buy products that make your life easier or better. As an investor, you want to have companies that excel in the five elements in your portfolio.

While some may view solving social or environmental problems as the scope of government or nonprofits it is actually the leading companies today who view the world as a series of human problems to solve, and who do so profitably.

The global trends of our world line up with this new world view: that all of us want to live long, prosperous lives on an unpolluted earth that respects our individual potential and supports us working together ethically.

Companies that solve these problems will help the most people and make quantifiable human impacts on the world's seven billion citizens. These firms will also make the most money by assessing the global trends and designing their business strategies in response to these massive forces.

Chapter 1 shows you the foundation of the HIP framework that will be explored throughout the book. Chapter 2 outlines the trends that fit with this fresh perspective. By the conclusion of Part I, you will see the opportunity to be a more HIP investor—and discover how to realize more Human Impact + Profit for your portfolio and your world.

CHAPTER 1

The Importance of Human Impact to Investors

An innovative experiment on a holiday weekend by an entrepreneurial engineer led to a new form of business: one that created bigger profits and a better world.

Back in 1995, Pierre Omidyar sought to test how an Internet-based marketplace would price used goods. The first item up for bid: a broken laser pointer, which sold for $14 (Viegas 39). Omidyar then enabled this platform for individuals to buy and sell "collectibles," including a range of Pez candy dispensers, which he secured to surprise his college sweetheart, Pam, an avid collector (Cohen 83; eBay interview).

This experiment was so successful that it grew to become the premier online global auction site—eBay. People bid online to purchase products ranging from Beanie Babies to used computers, sending money to people they have never met, and wait for their purchase to arrive in the mail.

eBay's launch created a platform to support hundreds of thousands of entrepreneurs' businesses. IRS tax data shows that more than 700,000 people earn their primary income from eBay sales and for over a million others, eBay is a source of secondary income.

eBay generated a platform built on a shared need, to either buy or sell, that connects strangers and requires them to trust each other—building trust among strangers became one of eBay's core benefits. It also promotes the reusability of goods, empowers entrepreneurs globally, and generates healthy competition, which

3

consequently lowering prices. With the PayPal money-transfer and trust service, buying and selling over the Internet accelerated.

Essentially, eBay created a vibrant, interconnected, trusting marketplace that enabled customers to save and entrepreneurs to thrive by trading existing goods. It created positive human impact by design and was financially attractive for all involved—the buyers, the sellers, and eBay itself. The growth of the business produced natural benefits to society—human, social, and environmental. Today eBay serves 88 million customers, more than 1 in 100 people globally, who trade more than $10 billion worth of goods every three months (eBay Inc. Web site). Shareholders, entrepreneurs, and the company's founders profited as the site grew to a global audience and became a new mode of commerce.

The founder, Pierre Omidyar, and the first president, Jeff Skoll, made substantial profits from their venture and reinforced what they already knew: Businesses that build a better world perform better financially. Each has carried this lesson into their investing. Today, Pierre Omidyar—a fan of Adam Smith, markets, and self-sustaining systems—invests substantially in microfinance, the fast-growing financial industry that provides small loans to low-income entrepreneurs. Omidyar's portfolio includes $100 million of capital for institutions making these microloans, generating positive social benefits while earning a profit (Tufts e-news 2005).

Jeff Skoll has also pursued an impact-maximizing approach to investing. Skoll consistently seeks out for-profit investments that generate both societal good and financial gain. His investments include Generation Investment Management's global equity fund, founded by Al Gore and former Goldman Sachs banker David Blood.

Omidyar and Skoll both invest to generate Human Impact and Profit, also know as "HIP." As discussed in the introduction, a HIP investment approach yields higher financial returns while offering significant benefit to society. Thus, HIP investors earn bigger profits while building a better world.

How do you build a HIP portfolio? It's not as hard as you think, but first you need to start asking "How HIP Is This Investment?" Most investment funds and financial analysts ($8 out of every $9 of assets under management) tend to focus on short-term profits and traditional capitalist metrics. A small group of investment managers and their funds (about $1 out of every $9 of assets under management) seek to "do good" with "socially responsible" investing, but often underperform financially. Both ends of the spectrum need to consider Human Impact + Profit—the innovative investment approach that is designed to earn higher profits through improved human impact.

This book is written to help you evaluate your investments across asset classes for quantifiable human impact and profit, and build a portfolio that makes bigger profits by building a better world. To do this successfully, we first need to understand the building blocks of the HIP approach.

What Is Human Impact?

In the world of HIP, "human impact" describes what people need to be fulfilled, and what society needs to thrive. We all have basic needs and desires, and are seeking to achieve our highest potential, and in doing so, realize our lifelong goals.

To be able to think beyond the day-to-day, and work to realize our long-term goals, we first must address our core needs. Famed twentieth-century psychologist Abraham Maslow developed a framework to better describe what drives people's actions and guides their purpose. Maslow posited that higher-order goals could only be accomplished if more pressing human needs were solved first. His framework outlined five categories of human needs into a hierarchy (see Figure 1.1), starting with the most basic and progressing to the most fulfilling:

1. Physiological—breathing, eating, drinking, and sleeping.
2. Safety—physical security and financial security.
3. Social and Belonging—love, giving to others, group affiliation, and inclusion.
4. Ego and Esteem—self-respect, human worth, and confidence.
5. Self-Actualization—mission in life or personal destiny.

Maslow's hierarchy shows that people must have their basic survival needs met before being able to operate at the next level. While each level doesn't have to be complete to consider the others (you can be hungry yet still share love with your family), people do need to cover their basic needs to be fully focused on achieving the next higher level. If as a child, you don't eat well consistently, your body won't permit your brain to absorb new knowledge or study

Figure 1.1 Maslow's Hierarchy of Needs

Source: Maslow, Abraham, "A Theory of Human Motivation," *Psychological Review* 50 (1943):370–396.

effectively. If a lower-income family is desperate for money, students may not even have the chance to study, but may be required to work or farm instead of going to school. People who are not fulfilling their basic needs have difficulty advancing to the next stage of human aspiration (Maslow 1943).

HIP has built a unique methodology that builds upon Maslow's Hierarchy of Needs to construct a framework focused on measuring a company's total Human Impact and how it drives profitability.

How is serving these basic needs profitable? In India, citizens have a choice—spend up to 60 percent of their income for water or send the women and children to walk two hours a day to retrieve it (Global Giving Web site). Today, there are nearly one billion people without access to clean drinking water (Water.org). Entrepreneurs around the world are developing strategies to change this—from handheld water pumps, to community wells, to communities building their own pipelines—and all for a profit. These entrepreneurs are generating significant profits while realizing positive human impact for millions around the world. With access to water secured, individuals can now invest their money and time to more sustainable and profitable ventures for themselves and their families. In fact, in some communities with new clean water projects, 40 percent of families can now send their girls to school (Global Giving Web site).

Inspired by Maslow's hierarchy of needs, the HIP framework is designed to be a "scorecard" that hones in on five core human needs: Health, Wealth, Earth, Equality, and Trust (see Figure 1.2). This integrated view is structured to guide an organization to solve these human challenges by measuring results and tracking progress

HIP Companies Innovate to Answer Five Human Needs

- **Health**
  - Physical Health
  - Mental Agility
- **Wealth**
  - Income Growth
  - Asset Accumulation
- **Earth**
  - Carbon Neutrality
  - Reusable Products
- **Equality**
  - Gender Balance
  - Ethnic Diversity
- **Trust**
  - Transparent and Open
  - Credible and Ethical

Figure 1.2   HIP Companies Innovate to Answer Five Human Needs

toward the ultimate goals of providing long, healthy, and happy lives for the global population of over 6.8 billion people. In more detail, the five elements of the HIP framework are:

1. **Health** fundamentally covers physical health, mental agility, and overall satisfaction. Everyone needs to eat, drink, and fulfill basic needs as Maslow said. If you don't have your health, it's hard to do anything else.
2. **Wealth** encompasses income generation, accumulating assets, and achieving financial stability. Individuals and families need jobs to pay for food, drink, and health care, but also education, transportation, and supplies that support their human advancement.
3. **Earth** includes the air we breathe, the water we drink, and the land we cultivate. To derive benefit from our ecosystems in the future means to treat them properly today, managing natural resources to be clean, renewable, and available for future use. This also means minimizing pollution, like carbon emissions and effluent.
4. **Equality** is defined as the proportion and balance in society across gender, ethnicity, and class. As a society, we benefit most when all individuals are empowered to participate, contribute, lead, and innovate without bias or restrictions.
5. **Trust** comprises transparency of information, ethical actions, and credible decision processes. A group is most stable and durable when it shares openly how it operates, so that any decisions not consistent with the ethics, goals, and values can be constructively evaluated.

When all these goals are achieved, citizens can be happy and fulfilled; in the mind of Maslow, individuals can achieve their highest potential as all the barriers to "self-actualizing" have been removed (Maslow 1943). The HIP approach seeks to enable all people worldwide to participate in that journey and reach their highest potential, while empowering business to generate the highest returns.

A Leading Indicator: Quantifiable Human Impact

Today's commonly accepted performance measurement systems are often not sophisticated enough to look beyond financial results.

While measuring profits and earnings is critical, there are deeper human impact costs and returns to factor in.

While a healthy lifestyle is free, visiting the doctor costs money. Thus, illness increases traditional economic value. But what about the lost value in terms of an individual's productivity? The economic benefits for healthy people are not counted explicitly, missing an opportunity to focus on being well continuously. Instead, the measures focus on the aftermath, not the root cause. As Robert F. Kennedy remarked at the University of Kansas 1968, "Our gross national product (GNP) counts air pollution . . . and television programs which glorify violence in order to sell toys to our children. Yet the GNP does not allow for the health of our children, the quality of their education, or the joy of their play . . . it measures everything, in short, except that which makes life worthwhile."

Today, there is not yet a generally accepted scoring mechanism of "human impact"—how a company performs according to factors like health, wealth, earth, equality, and trust. To date, the most comprehensive and long-term view is designed into the Human Development Index (HDI), compiled by the United Nations. It ranks "human development" results by country—from health (e.g., infant mortality), to wealth (e.g., average income, savings rate), to earth (e.g., relative pollution, water use), to equality (e.g., gender balance, girls in school), and trust (e.g., labor rights, human rights). According to the UNDP Web site, the higher-performing countries are higher-income countries like Norway, Canada, and Iceland; while the lowest are lower-income countries like Zimbabwe, Botswana, and Congo. This happens for two reasons: one is that economic value is part of the equation for calculating HDI; the other is that higher impact requires financial capital to make improvements in quality of life.

HDI is compelling because it quantifies a more complete state of human conditions, not just the amount of money related to GDP. While higher-income countries tend to have higher human-development scores, and lower-income countries tend to have lower-development scores, there are exceptions to this general correlation. Let's examine an innovative measurement model that goes much further than traditional GDP to focus on multiple dimensions of quality of life.

Bhutan is a small, isolated country on the edge of the Himalayas in Asia, with a population of nearly 700,000. Throughout the twentieth century, Internet, and TV were banned and a tourist visa cost more than $100 per day. In 1972, Bhutan's former King Jigme Singye Wangchuck sought to ensure the country's long-term well-being. In contrast to traditional metrics, he developed the concept of "Gross National Happiness," which rates various measures of quality of life and personal satisfaction, including nine overall dimensions including health, psychological well-being, living standards, community vitality, and the use of time in a 24-hour day. In total, it assesses 72 indicators that add up to an indexed score of happiness. Despite Bhutan's low per capita income, Bhutan rates in the top 20 for "happiness" on a global scale (Seth 2009).

Other countries have started to follow in Bhutan's path in an effort to measure human impact beyond GDP. In 2009, France's President Nicholas Sarkozy appointed a 22-member commission, including Nobel Prize laureates Joseph Stiglitz and Amartya Sen, to understand the full scope of well-being and its multiple dimensions. The report recommended that economic indicators must look beyond production to overall wealth and income, including health, the environment, and inclusive political voice and governance. Sarkozy supported the conclusions enthusiastically: "We're living in one of those epochs where certitudes have vanished . . . we have to reinvent, to reconstruct everything. The central issue is [to pick] the way of development, the model of society, the civilization we want to live in" (*Wall Street Journal* 2009).

It is no longer just growing profit or accelerating GDP in a vacuum. The world needs a new, comprehensive view that measures how society will advance. This requires a redirected focus—a HIP framework for companies to evaluate their total potential for Human Impact + Profit.

Human Impact + Profit = Twenty-First-Century Measurement

The HIP Scorecard is designed to look beyond each of these approaches and to build a tool for companies to measure and manage their results across the five categories of Health, Wealth, Earth, Equality, and Trust, and for investors to gauge which companies are delivering the highest human impact and profit. HIP is essentially a Human Development Index for companies—with it, investors can determine the Human Impact + Profit of each firm in their portfolio.

This is not a subjective approach. As Maslow explains, by serving our most basic needs, we create a society that enables all of its members to achieve higher levels of fulfillment. By designing the systems that allow our society, including business, to align around those human needs, we all can achieve our maximum potential.

Profits, Profits, Profits

The crux of HIP's model is that each of HIP's factors is a leading indicator for shareholder value and profitability. When you evaluate a company by HIP's fundamentals, and build a portfolio that maximizes leaders and minimizes laggards, you can realize a higher return—even adjusted for risk—and an improved society. Now that's HIP.

Currently, investors tend to only measure and track the output of financial results: revenue, profit, and financial capital. That's the equivalent of only measuring GDP (the successor term to GNP). Because GDP is not a leading indicator, and hence has no predictive value of what's to come, its focus is to make the most money across a short time frame. But a short-term, profit-only approach has its downside—greed incurs excessive risks, and doesn't maximize long-term results. Financial statements provide a stark example: People are tracked as an expense on the income statement, not as an asset on the balance sheet. Yet innovation could not happen without the new ideas and management of the people who work in and manage the business. These systems lead to the mindset that staff is disposable, whereas in reality they create the value that allows the business to generate revenue and profit.

HIP's portfolios speak to the power of this approach—over the past five years, HIP portfolios have outperformed those weighted only by market values by 4 percent (or 400 basis points) on average, as seen in Figure 1.3.

Risk versus Reward

Recent financial volatility has been driven by several factors:

- Constrained supply of energy, oil, and natural resources leading to higher prices
- Population growth coupled with a desire to live well
- Excessive, double-digit inflation in providing health care
- Lack of equal access to opportunity
- Desire for an open society that is honest, ethical, and truthful

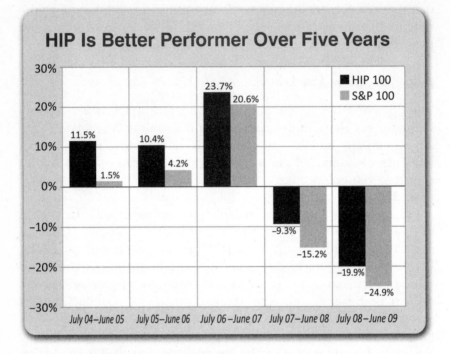

Figure 1.3   HIP Is Better Performer Over Five Years
Source: S&P, Bloomberg Financial L.P.; HIP Investor portfolios and analysis.

These factors and their resulting impacts on society and future profit are not accurately priced into current stock prices. While finance theory says that the market prices are perfect with all available information, the HIP methodology and academic studies show that leading indicators of performance are not incorporated on a timely basis. This gap between everyday market prices and the true valuation of forward-looking fundamentals creates an opportunity for HIP investors to profit, all by building a better world.

The new HIP fundamentals of investing focus on a long-term view, not just short-term profit maximization. Risks must be weighted as strongly as reward, especially those that are related to the environment or society. A more comprehensive, end-to-end view not only lowers risk but increases returns. The world of investing goes beyond pure financial ratios, but includes societal impacts. These have been previously discounted, not priced at their true value or seemingly have no worth at all.

In books on finance and economics, social and environmental factors are typically referred to as "externalities," or, in other words, something out of the company's control. But leading HIP companies view them as "internalities," critical to include the enterprise's mission and solved by its people. Eliminating water, air, or land pollution actually saves companies money, and avoids future liabilities and lawsuits. Even retraining and education of workers creates business benefits, forgoing the costs of firing and rehiring staff and potential culture clashes. When these "externalities" are assessed and counted as if they were internal costs, the cause of those factors and the ultimate results become more closely aligned. It's similar to the "total cost of ownership" concept, but adapted for a longer duration, and fuller view of the world.

Creating innovations and productivity in these markets for human needs enables the pioneers of those solutions to solve pressing problems and capture the rewards of the first mover: the trust of new customers, the pricing premiums of innovations, the branded recognition as a market leader, the magnet for the best talent to join that organization. As the rest of society purchases these HIP products, companies realize not only profits, but human impact, as well.

HIP's new investment approach is revolutionary in its potential. HIP shows that firms that quantify the difficult-but-not-impossible metrics of the human, social, and environmental factors across society can be rewarded with previously undiscovered business value.

The HIP Mindset Is Already Here

Until October 2008, capitalists were winning the argument that short-term profit maximization delivers the most value. The risks of that approach deeply drained the portfolio values of many investors. Many investors are now seeking something different, but haven't found it quite yet.

Today, there is broad support for a HIP mindset among consumers, employees, company leaders, investors, and their advisers. While the traditional belief espouses that seeking human, social, or environmental benefits in your portfolio requires an investor to give up financial returns, HIP's in-depth findings show that optimized businesses require a more multidisciplinary approach.

Nearly two in three (65 percent) consumers want to buy products and services from firms that deliver social good, which is determined by how the firm treats employees and the environment, not its charitable giving, according to a National Consumers League survey in 2006. Consulting firm McKinsey validates those numbers as well with its research, reporting that two in three consumers also report taking action in response to companies viewed as "against the best interests of society." Nearly half (49 percent) refused to buy socially irresponsible company products and 38 percent recommended that others not buy those firms' products. Nearly half (47 percent) of consumers are researching companies online to seek out their social and environmental performance.

The super-majority of Americans surveyed about their workplace feel strongly that benefiting society is important. More than 3 in 4, or 77 percent, people say that "commitment to social issues" affects where they work. This is up from nearly 1 in 2, or 48 percent, just a few years earlier. Today, more than 7 in 10, or 72 percent, also want their employer to do more for social causes. (See Figure 1.4.)

The good news is that 84 percent of global executives believe that their companies can deliver "both high social impact and above-average financial returns." However, only 3 percent reported that their firms are currently doing a great job.

This creates an opportunity for investors. Companies who act on these trends are well-positioned to tap new customer demand, attract talent, and deliver shareholder value. Companies who don't see this opportunity risk alienating about a fifth of individual investors (19 percent) who would refuse to invest in stocks of companies who avoid "doing good" (McKinsey).

While trusted financial brands have created unique indexes like the Dow Jones Sustainability Index and FTSE4Good, these indexes have not reliably outperformed the pure-profit capitalist approaches. Increasingly, large financial players are beginning to participate with a HIP view. The Carbon Disclosure Project, which measures environmental metrics including carbon emissions, has attracted the involvement of institutional investors managing $55 trillion in assets (CDP 2009 Global 500 Report). The Equator Principles, which specify social and environmental criteria for infrastructure projects around the world, has been adopted by global banks for about 80 percent of the capital financing of those projects (IFC blog).

Despite this prevalence of a HIP mindset, investment choices for individuals and advisors remain limited. Also, most large institutional investors are skeptical without years of data to show consistent

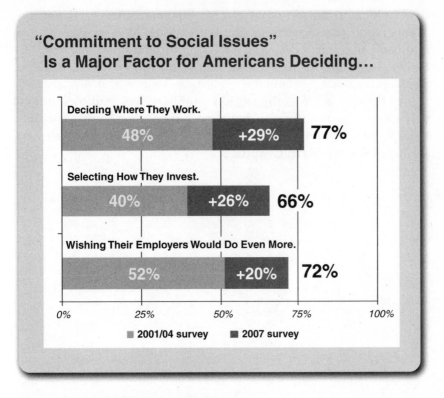

"Commitment to Social Issues"
Is a Major Factor for Americans Deciding...

Deciding Where They Work.
48% +29% **77%**

Selecting How They Invest.
40% +26% **66%**

Wishing Their Employers Would Do Even More.
52% +20% **72%**

0%   25%   50%   75%   100%

■ 2001/04 survey   ■ 2007 survey

Figure 1.4   Commitment to Social Issues
Source: Cone Inc.

outperformance. However, the proof of positive performance exists. This book will show you the essential HIP approach to tap into this potential. Now is your chance to become a HIP investor and transform your portfolio to capitalize on these trends: to make more money by doing more good.

Seeing the Light

By looking through a HIP lens, innovators capture new opportunities before others who are playing the old game. Businesses that look forward to assess all the global trends, bring products to market, count their human impact, directly link it to profit, and embed all of this in their approach—capture more financial benefit (on average, at lower risk) and help advance society. This results in happy shareholders, fulfilled employees, satisfied customers, and a strong supply chain (the ecosystem of job creation). Most investors know intuitively that this is the case, including sophisticated investors like Pierre Omidyar, Jeff Skoll, Leslie Christian, Nancy Pfund, Al Gore, and Vinod Khosla.

A HIP approach to the world's problems will lead to solutions that are financially attractive, lower overall risk, and improve society. Will you be a HIP investor? Let's start with the big picture—assessing the big global trends in Chapter 2.

2

Assessing the Global Trends: Why HIP and Why Now?

The time for a new approach to investing is now. Traditional approaches—the robber barons of capitalism and do-good underperformers—are stagnating and a new HIP way is here.

There are many problems in our world that need to be solved. Most of us are living longer, but the quality of our health is declining. More opportunities to make a living are appearing, from Chinese factories to Brazilian farmers. However, four billion people live on less than two dollars per day (Prahalad 2006). The earth's natural resources are being stretched to limits not tested before, but new technologies are paving new paths of undiscovered efficiency. Most of the world's women are not yet paid equally. As we learned with Maslow's framework, each of us can still realize even higher potential.

Human, social and environmental challenges surround us. In recent years, capitalists have treated them as nuisances for governments to debate or nonprofit organizations to address. However, leading businesses are finding that when they examine these trends using a HIP lens, they can solve human problems for profit.

Obesity and diabetes lead to innovations in health and wellness. Lack of access to capital markets opens up new opportunities for microloans to emerging entrepreneurs. The sun shines daily and the wind blows, creating markets for lower-cost renewable forms of energy. These are all trillion-dollar markets if calculated globally. As an investor, you want to understand these trends and evaluate who will profit from them. As a HIP investor, you can also help accelerate the reality of a better world by investing in those leaders who pursue higher human impact for their customers, employees, and suppliers. The world is changing rapidly and HIP offers a new approach to business that reflects these new realities, bringing with it bigger profits—and a better world.

What's different? And how do these differences make HIP the wave of the future? Let's take a closer look at how the world is shifting with a focus on the trends with the biggest impact:

- Nine Billion Customers with Many Unmet Human Needs
- Finite Natural Resources Running Out
- Everyone Knows Everything All the Time
- Demand for "Good" Is Growing

These trends are driving forces of a new, more HIP world.

Nine Billion Customers with Many Unmet Human Needs

The world is becoming more interconnected. Despite resistance and some denial, the world is linked tightly together and the decisions and actions of each and every person impact the larger world.

Businesses that are focused solely on their traditional markets are missing tremendous opportunities for growth. Every business is structured to think about its customer base—but now, the world demands a wider definition than ever before.

Traditionally, business has focused on middle- to high-income customers in key, developed countries (in other words, the United States and Western Europe). Today, target consumers represent many countries, income levels, and cultures.

First, businesses must expand their target customer base. Today's world has 220 countries with 6.8 billion citizens, and products that serve these billion-person markets can be trillion-dollar opportunities (Geodata Group). Hundreds of millions of customers across China, India, and Brazil are building their wealth and seeking out products that meet their unique needs. In 40 years, emerging economies are predicted to increase by nearly 3 billion people, equating to 40-percent growth in global population.

Companies that are thinking globally are positioning themselves for immediate and sustainable growth. After the 2008 global recession, China's economy is pursuing an aggressive comeback, and the International Monetary Fund (IMF) predicted economic growth of 9 percent in 2010. India's expansion is predicted to be 6.4 percent (Ito 2009). In comparison, the IMF projects the United States' growth at 1.5 percent (Alibaba 2009). Given these numbers, the greatest growth potential is outside of traditional markets.

The Fortune *at the Bottom of the Pyramid* by C.K. Prahalad brought the power of a new approach to global markets and consumers to the mainstream. Referring to the 4 billion people living on less than $2 per day, these markets are ripe and waiting for products. These individuals are consumers today and their purchasing power is growing. This prime market is calling for products that can be built for them—from the $199 computer produced by One Laptop per Child to the $2000 cars Tata is selling in India. Thinking of all human needs to be solved yields a wider market for products with a breakthrough advantage (OLPC and Murph 2009).

In 2008, seven or eight of every 1,000 people in India owned a car—with only 13 million private cars in existence. Compare this with the United States where more than 250 million cars are privately registered and, based on the numbers alone, 83 percent of the population owns a car (BTS Table 1-11 n.d). While cars will continue to be manufactured and sold in the United States, the larger growth potential is clearly in India—a country demanding affordably priced cars that fit their roads and needs.

Now, let's look within a traditional market. Who makes the purchasing decisions in your household? Did you know that, in the United States, women make 80 percent of household purchasing decisions and, by 2010, are expected to control $1 trillion, or 60 percent of the country's wealth, according to research from *BusinessWeek* and Gallup (Barletta 2007). The percentage of women-owned businesses and women-led households is increasing globally, while their purchasing power grows with it. It is imperative for companies to look beyond traditional markets, recognizing and responding to the power women have in the economy.

Life expectancy has doubled in the last century in the West, but we are not aging as well as we could be. This is an investment opportunity. Leading companies are revising their business strategies to include innovative health care and wellness products, including healthy food. General Electric has even launched an initiative called "healthymagination," to expand its health care products. Intel and

Qualcomm are adapting their technology products to serve billion-dollar markets for wireless health care awareness and patient monitoring. With one of every six dollars in the U.S. economy spent on health care that makes for a $2 trillion market. HIP investors are paying attention.

Is Colonel Sanders, the icon of Kentucky Fried Chicken (KFC), a vegetarian? He is in India, or at least some of the time. Yum! Brands, the owner of KFC, Taco Bell, and Pizza Hut, is the largest and fastest-growing restaurant company in India. Big brands are not accommodating local tastes on a global scale. You can eat Tandoori and Masala pizzas in Bombay, or vegetarian choices at KFC in Delhi. In Beijing, locals order fresh corn as well as locally flavored Gulao pork and chicken rolls. KFC restaurants in the United States now offer grilled chicken. Will they instead be called KGC for Kentucky Grilled Chicken (Yum! Brands, *CSR* 2008)?

Traditional markets and big brands can maintain their importance. However, the majority of future growth is expected to come from fast-growing populations seeking out a higher quality of life. Leading companies are already pursuing those opportunities and, more importantly, taking steps to meet diverse needs in innovative ways. These companies are embracing new consumers with human needs—from affordable nutrition and lower-cost health care to everyday products that fit the much lower annual incomes of most of the world. By designing for these markets, leading firms are positioning to gain more revenue and profit for shareholders—and more societal benefit overall.

Finite Natural Resources Running Out

As a society, we often consider natural resources to be boundless but the reality is becoming clearer—we are using (and abusing) the resources faster than they can be created. We are going to run out of these key resources, including oil, copper, and fresh water. Leading companies are beginning to recognize this and "dematerialize" their businesses.

Let's step away from the traditional example of oil, and focus on topsoil. Topsoil is created very, very slowly—think one inch every 300 to 500 years—and gains its fertile quality from millions of microorganisms living in the soil. With massive increases in agricultural output (and thus, the land it's being produced on), topsoil is subject to extensive tilling, frequent irrigation, and pollution. Today, topsoil is eroding, polluted with pesticides and fertilizer, and subject to the dangers of salinization.

If we continue to push topsoil to and beyond its limits, it will no longer be able to effectively produce the agriculture our society relies on. This is a scary predicament in more ways than one. The Green Revolution in 1970s India marked the introduction of chemical farming. This was a wildly successful movement; increasing productivity sufficiently enough to stave off a severe food shortage and propel India into grain exportation. But after 20 years, the approach took a turn for the worse, and the dangers of chemical farming became clear—the topsoil had been wholly depleted and polluted, losing its natural fertility at a rapid pace. Today, farmers can choose to purchase extensive quantities of fertilizer to make up for the damaged soil or, as many are choosing, to return to a more natural approach using organic compost with the goal of restoring their land (Organic Facts Web site).

Farmers around the world must choose between synthetic and natural fertilizer. While topsoil's productivity is initially enhanced by synthetics, it rapidly depletes the soil's fertility. If farmers do not embrace a more natural approach, topsoil's existence and rich productivity around the world is endangered.

Currently we both pollute and misuse our finite natural resources. Every time we burn fossil fuels, we emit carbon. That carbon lives on for at least a hundred years in the atmosphere. It has now accumulated to an increasingly dangerous level of more than 390 parts of carbon per million units of air becoming a health hazard for humans and the natural environment.

Since the age of industrialization, the world's use of fossil fuels has seen a dramatic increase. Between 1980 and 2006 alone, use increased by an average of 2 percent annually with fossil fuels supplying 86 percent of energy production (Green Planet Solar Energy Web site). The production of carbon is estimated to have risen 40 percent while the traditional outlets for carbon consumption have remained stable, leaving excess carbon throughout the atmosphere (Ravilious 2007). The result? Significant global warming that, with 90-percent probability, is presumed to be human caused (Roach 2007). If these emissions continue at such a high rate, Earth's temperature will continue to rise and scientists across the world predict large-scale food and water shortages that will have catastrophic effects on wildlife (National Geographic News, *Fast Facts* 2007).

The U.S. Environmental Protection Agency agrees and describes the need for transition clearly: "Heightened interest in global climate change, acid rain, respiratory ailments, and smog have raised concerns about emissions of carbon dioxide, sulfur dioxide, nitrogen oxides, mercury, methane, nitrous oxide, and particulate matter from burning fossil fuels. Concerns also exist about the other environmental impacts associated with traditional electricity generation fuel sources, such as the impacts of mining, drilling, processing, transporting, and disposing of fuels." (EPA *Green Power* n.d).

The 10 largest publicly listed energy companies are estimating $130 billion in capital spending—equivalent to the combined net worth of the three richest people in the world, Bill Gates, Warren Buffett, and Carlos Slim—but less than 5 percent of it is dedicated to renewable energy. However, governments, utilities, and forward-looking businesses recognize the gap. Capital spending on renewable energy could reach $27 trillion over 30 years. In 2008 alone, 40 percent of the new capacity additions for electricity were wind (see Figure 2.1).

The U.S. states of Minnesota and Iowa both get 7 percent of electric-utility generated power from wind farms. "I've made growing the wind industry in Iowa a top priority for my administration, and our investment is paying off for Iowans with hundreds of green collar jobs and hundreds of millions of dollars invested in our communities," said Iowa Governor Chet Culver (AWEA 2008). While General Electric is a leader in this market, there are worldwide competitors from Vestas in Denmark, to Siemens in Germany, to Gamesa in Spain, and Mitsubishi in Japan. Global corporations are not ignoring trillion-dollar markets of growth. Even the United Arab Emirate of Abu Dhabi is funding a $22 billion renewable-energy, zero-waste city called Masdar.

The Clean Air Act of 1970 has been amended several times since its initiation. The most recent in 1990 established an innovative approach to achieve the public benefit of reduced emissions through trading of "credits" by companies emitting pollution. Based on a concept introduced by Bill Drayton (then an EPA assistant administrator, today head of Ashoka), the source of acid rain (sulfur dioxide) had been drastically reduced with up to 90-percent lower capital spending by establishing a "cap-and-trade"-like system during the 1990s.

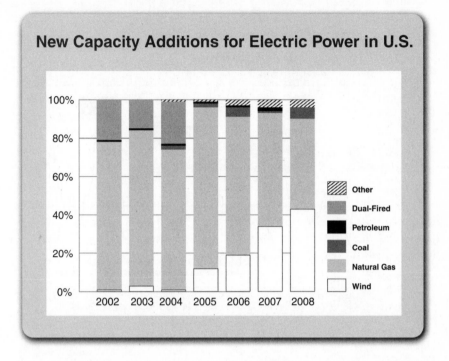

Figure 2.1   Percentage of New Capacity Additions for Electric Power in the United States

Source: AWEA.

Similarly, an emissions-trading approach for carbon is expected to reduce the cost of implementation by as much as 35 percent (Bornstein, 60).

Overall, the challenges are super-sized. The bottom line is well stated by Achim Stein, the executive director of the United Nations Environment Programme, "Fossil fuel use, agriculture, and land-use change are fundamentally affecting the systems on our planet" (Roach 2007).

So, what does this mean to businesses and investors? With rising demand for finite resources, and increasingly strained supply, the potential for spiking prices is high. In strained times, commodity prices all move in concert with each other (see Figure 2.2), as the world experienced in 2008.

Leading companies are looking forward, planning for volatile pricing of fuels and commodities, and inventing new products for

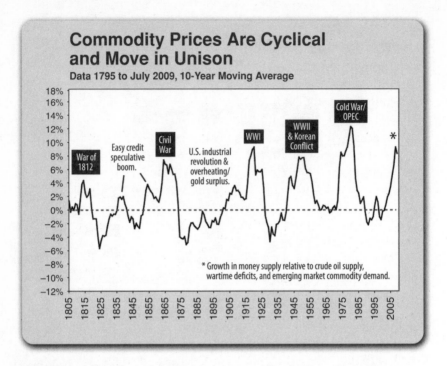

Figure 2.2 Commodity Prices Are Cyclical and Move in Unison (10-year moving average)

Source: Barry B. Bannister, CFA—Stifel Nicolaus & Co.

customers. Innovators are designing new operations that mitigate their risks of access to scarce supplies, and are planning for sustainable approaches environmentally and financially by expanding to include renewable resources and extending their use of finite resources.

Investors who understand where the capital will flow can make smart decisions about their portfolios. According to HSBC research, governments around the world have allocated U.S. $430 billion in fiscal stimulus to key climate change themes. Those financing the low-carbon solutions, like venture capitalist Vinod Khosla's $1 billion fund, are very well positioned to benefit, while those who ignore the risks gamble on being left behind (CDP *Global 500*, 13). This trend affects the Earth, disrupts the distribution of Wealth, exacerbates the Health impacts of pollution, and continues to disrupt to lower-income populations seeking the benefits of Equality.

Everyone Knows Everything All the Time

The quality and quantity of information available today is unparalleled. For nearly any question, there's an immediate answer available on the Internet. One billion people worldwide use mobile devices to talk, email, text, watch videos, and manage their livelihoods. Regular communication can be published to all of society—frequently and in deep detail.

Leading firms are becoming more open and transparent, using two-way forums and tools like Facebook, Twitter, LinkedIn, and blogs, on top of annual reports, shareholder meetings, shareholder calls, and Corporate Social Responsibility reporting.

With increased information comes increased expectations. Individuals now expect full disclosure and the real statistics behind, well, everything. The backlash against companies that hide things from their stakeholders is real, and the reward for transparency of information is high. The more information that is disclosed, the easier it is for outsiders to evaluate a company or product, and interestingly, the higher the performance and profit.

One of the most transparent companies is high-tech titan Infosys, a global company based in India. Its 200-page annual report shares everything from its financials calculated in six different countries' accounting formats and languages, the pay and experience of hundreds of managers, and even an estimate of the "human asset value" of its professional high-tech staff.

"A leader has to create hope, a plausible story about a better future for the organization. Everyone should be able to see the rainbow and catch a part of it. This means instilling trust, which requires adherence to a value system, that enhances the confidence, commitment, and enthusiasm of the people," says Chairman and Chief Mentor of Infosys, Narayana Murthy (Infosys *Annual Report* 2009). While this may feel "cloudy," let's look at the data.

According to the Carbon Disclosure Project, increasing disclosure correlates with higher performance, even when the information might include details that are negative (see Figure 2.3).

In 2009, the business value related to leading companies who participate in several modes of social networking tools was tracked by expert analysts at EngagementDB. The biggest brands, including BMW, Starbucks, and Sony, were rated by how many and at what intensity they used online platforms to communicate and interact with

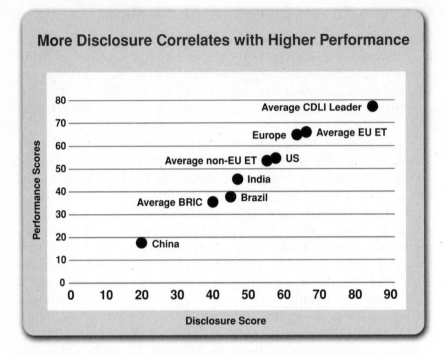

Figure 2.3 Analysis of Performance Scores versus Disclosure Scores—by Geographic and Leader Groups

Source: Carbon Disclosure Project.

their customers and stakeholders. What this compelling study found was that the more intensive communicators tended to have much higher growth in revenue, operating margin and net profit. Transparency was positively associated with financial gain. Companies who share more openly were better financial investments (see Figure 2.4).

Stakeholders—customers, shareholders, employees, and regulators—have come to expect corporate transparency in the twenty-first century. Companies that embrace this new approach are able to capture greater market share by building credibility and driving sales. Companies cloaked in secrecy do little to inspire confidence. They are often the riskiest investment and make stakeholders wary of working with them. These companies are often punished with lower valuations, diminishing their access to capital or increasing its cost, constraining their market potential, and discouraging an effective dialogue with a broader set of society. By reporting more information

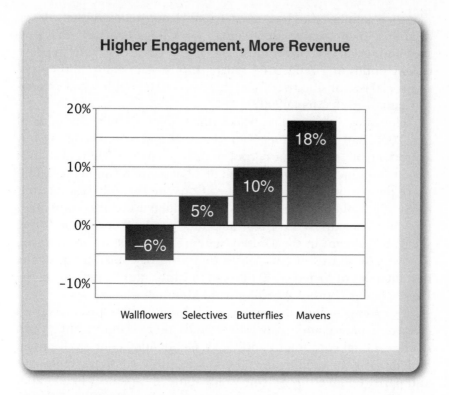

Figure 2.4 Higher Engagement, More Revenue: Revenue Growth Percentage Over Past 12 Months

Source: EngagementDB 2009 Report, Wetpaint, Altimeter Group.

and operating in a transparent manner, companies send the message that they are the leaders in their field, building credibility, market share, and earning a higher valuation.

Companies that are hopping onto the transparency bandwagon have a head start, both in measuring their results and in meeting expectations. Only time will tell the strength of customer loyalty they have built, but it is clear that transparency drives revenue.

Demand for Good Is Growing

In addition to demanding information, customers are seeking products that are good for them. Moms are buying healthy, sustainable products, like organic milk and fresh fruit. Children are demanding that their families purchase earth-friendly, nontoxic products. More than 9 in 10 new graduates want to work for a company that pursues both good and profit. Leading companies are seeking to prove this by publishing reports on citizenship, sustainability, and corporate social responsibility, to meet this demand through "CSR" reports (Sustainable Life Media 2007).

This quest for "good" is translating into consumer action. As of May 2007, half of consumers reported that they would refuse to buy a product or service if a corporation's behavior is detrimental to society. This includes a global high of 79 percent in China compared to 49 percent in the United States. Consumers would also actively discourage others from purchasing products from the companies they see as negatively affecting the public good, 68 percent in China versus 38 percent in the United States. Even investors are refusing to purchase shares in companies that are not contributing to the best interests of society at 49 percent in China and 19 percent in the United States (Bonini, McKillop, and Mendonca 2007).

To meet growing consumer demand to purchase products from more transparent and trustworthy brands, there is significant growth in educational consumer handbooks. GoodGuide.com was founded by University of California at Berkeley's professor Dara O'Rourke and partly financed by Silicon Valley venture capitalists like Draper Fisher Jurvetson. This online portal provides health, safety, and environmental ratings of consumer products, such as personal care items or groceries, to ensure that individuals are able to make informed decisions. Since its launch in 2008, it has now reviewed over 70,000 products, and has been recognized by *Time* magazine and *TechCrunch* in 2008. GoodGuide is connecting deeply with consumers demanding more detailed information on their purchases. Even macaroni and cheese (see Figure 2.5) can be analyzed and compared in depth by its nutritional value, environmental footprint, and social benefit (GoodGuide Amazon). Customers who use GoodGuide do more than browse the products—they actually follow through with an online purchase up to 20 times more often than the typical online consumer, according to Amazon.

Companies are striving to meet this demand for more information, juggling the call from multiple organizations with surveys testing company policies, practices, and performance. Leading companies, like Sun and Interface, are constructing interactive Web sites to update stakeholders.

Figure 2.5   GoodGuide Product Rating
Source: GoodGuide, Inc.

Table 2.1 Big Brands Buying High-Impact Growth Companies

High Impact Growth Co.'s	Acquisition Price	Big Brand Buyer
The Body Shop	$1.4 billion	L'Oreal
Burt's Bees	$913 million	Clorox
Ben and Jerry's	$326 million	Unilever
Odwalla	$181 million	Coca-Cola
Tom's of Maine	$100 million	Colgate-Palmolive
Republic of Tea	$43 million	Coca-Cola (43% share)
Stonyfield Farms	$? million (not disclosed)	Group Danone (82% share)
Honest Tea	$? million (not disclosed)	Coca-Cola (43% share)

Source: HIP research.

Over the past 10 years, high-impact, high-growth companies have been sought out—and bought out—by consumer-product conglomerate companies that want access to new consumers. They also want to learn the fundamentals of a HIP marketplace. Global cosmetics firm L'Oreal acquired the Body Shop for $1.4 billion, and Clorox bought Burt's Bees for more than $900 million. Interestingly, in the cases of Honest Tea and Burt's Bees, the new owner has not promoted its relationship externally or on the brand's packaging. (See Table 2.1.)

In recognition of the importance of this movement, executives and investors recognize the market value of "doing good" for example, 85 percent of executives rank corporate social responsibility (CSR) as a "central" or "important" consideration in investment decisions. This figure is almost double the 44 percent of five years ago, demonstrating the growth in CSR's significance (Fisman, Heal and Nair 2006).

The continued demand for companies and products that are "good" isn't going away—it's apparent to customers, employees, and investors that the current path is unsustainable. People are seeking to feel better from what they buy, where they work, and how they invest. The previous goals of only maximizing money are feeling hollow. The twenty-first century citizen wants to do "good" and make money but finds existing paths limiting. The time is ripe for a HIP way of buying, working, and investing.

How does a HIP investor adapt their portfolio to these trends?

Is Investing Keeping Pace?

These trends are happening now, and when you consider each of these forces on its own, it's a powerful call to change how you invest. When you consider them together, it is obvious that the time for a HIP approach is now.

Today, more than $22 trillion, or $8 out of $9 investment dollars managed professionally, is invested via traditional profit-only approaches (Social Investment Forum, ii). Since these portfolios have historically performed better, these investments are defined as the "core" of investing. The drawbacks? This system amplifies the focus on delivering short-term financial returns at the expense of long-term stability. This short-sightedness can result in an unexpected crash of economic risk, as well as environmental degradation and social costs. In October 2008, the risks of this approach were realized on a mass scale. By looking solely at profit, companies (and their investors) positioned themselves for a dramatic risk.

On the opposite end of the spectrum, two in three individual investors now see "commitment to social issues" as impacting how they invest, and 64 percent believe doing good is a positive indicator of an investment portfolio's future success (Cone Inc. 2007). Seven in ten financial advisers are seeking quantifiable information on this approach to answer their clients' questions, according to a SVT Group survey. These demands have led to $2.7 trillion under professional management, or $1 out of every $9 investment dollars being invested under the auspice of "doing good" (Social Investment Forum, ii). This approach is designed to make investors feel good about their portfolio investments, typically by screening out companies that sell "bad" products, like cigarettes, alcohol, and nuclear weapons. By restricting the investment vehicles available, this approach misses out on the positive benefits these "bad" companies provide, including job creation and wealth generation. While this investing taps into people's need to do "good," these funds typically offer lower returns.

So if doing "good" results in sub-par financial performance, and profit-only capitalism results in a shortsighted, high-risk approach, could there be a new path that achieves bigger profits and a better world? The HIP approach was designed to do just that—to outperform both do-gooders and profit-seeking capitalists in realizing higher financial returns with lower risk and real Human Impact for all investors. And HIP is working! Testing this approach back to mid-2004, HIP has outperformed the S&P 100 by 400 basis points, earning 4-percent more returns than the traditional approach.

An even more pointed example is pitting HIP against the two extremes—Socially Responsible Investing and the Vice Fund (ticker: VICEX), a fund composed solely of tobacco, alcohol, and defense companies, with the assumption that by focusing solely on profit, these industries will realize the highest shareholder returns. Over a five-year horizon (June 2004—June 2009), HIP delivered the best financial returns and measurable Human Impact. While the Vice Fund outperformed financially during much of the market upswing, HIP has outperformed since mid-2007 and experienced lower volatility. Over the long haul, HIP can generate bigger profits and a better world (see Figure 2.6).

A few leading investment analysts and fund managers have chosen this transformational approach. Today, strategies and financial

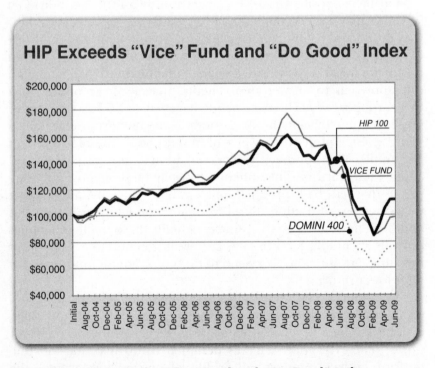

Figure 2.6   HIP Exceeds "Vice" Fund and "Do Good" Index

Source: Bloomberg Financial L.P.; HIP.

products similar to HIP exist for high-net-worth and institutional investors such as Generation Investment Management and Goldman Sachs' "Sustain" recommendations. Some venture capital funds are pursuing clean-tech approaches, like Khosla Ventures, TBL Capital and the Patient Capital Collaborative.

But there have been few options for the HIP investor until now. These four trends overlaid with the foundation of the HIP methodology can unlock the potential of your portfolio for bigger profits and a better world.

"The Trend Is Your Friend"

This chapter has shown you how these trends create exciting opportunities to solve human problems. They also map to the five HIP elements of Health, Wealth, Earth, Equality, and Trust.

Investing is slowly catching up with the trends but what are companies doing? Forward-looking businesses are developing new products to meet these new needs. They are also changing how they operate internally, and what they require from suppliers. The result of those changes is not only higher human impact, as you will learn in Part II, but also increased profitability. A better world can yield bigger profits.

HIP investors see the world in this way and seek out those companies that will solve these issues. A HIP Portfolio made up of these firms, and weighted according to their leadership, can be constructed for higher performance, lower risk, and increased impact. With a HIP view of the world, the trend is your friend.

Let's move forward and dive into the specific products forward-looking companies are developing in response to the world's new realities and the opportunities that come with them, aligning their approaches across the HIP factors of Health, Wealth, Earth, Equality, and Trust.

PART
II

RESEARCHING YOUR
HIP PORTFOLIO

Part II—Chapters 3, 4, 5, and 6—introduces HIP frameworks, including the scorecard of metrics and evaluations, and examples from the HIP research of 500 companies. By the end of Part II, you will have tools to evaluate how HIP a company is in its products, measures of impact, and management practices, and how those factors all link to financial value.

Chapter 3 explains the many ways that companies are already innovating with products that deliver human, social, and environmental value—while also generating revenue for those firms and growth for investors.

Chapter 4 showcases more than 20 metrics that you can use to evaluate each company to measure the Health, Wealth, Earth, Equality, and Trust across their customers, employees, and suppliers. These are leading indicators of both positive impact and profit.

Chapter 5 digs into management practices that keep companies HIP and sustainable over time, ensuring that decisions are made to increase both human impact and profit.

Chapter 6 outlines how products, metrics, and management practices tightly link with increases in value on the income statement, balance sheet, and even investor demand for a stock. The resulting effect provides a fundamental basis for higher shareholder value of more HIP firms.

When each investment in a portfolio is evaluated using the methodology above, then you can build a more HIP portfolio, which we will show you how to do in Part III.

Bringing Products to Market that Solve a Human Need

It is clear that the world is changing and companies are beginning to respond, shifting their realities and markets to solve what historically have been viewed as seemingly intractable human problems—for profit.

When General Electric's African-American affinity group gathered in 2003, they asked CEO Jeffrey Immelt, "What are we doing for Africa?" For the fourth year in a row, Immelt did not have an answer, so he improvised and offered up a $20 million charitable contribution" (Colborn and Heinrichs 2003).

In 2005, GE's products in the region (which combines Africa and the Middle East) generated about 3 percent of its world revenue (GE, *Annual Report 2008*, 31). To effectively deploy the $20 million in the continent, GE engineers traveled across Africa and were startled to find little to no GE technology in many health care facilities. By the end of their trip, they had determined not only how to invest their charitable contributions, but more importantly had identified new market opportunities that included affordable health care access for GE to explore (Colborn and Heinrichs 2003).

Previously GE's Healthcare products were built and priced for specific higher-income developed markets creating CAT scanners costing from $2 million to $5 million. These products had a high profit margin for GE, but were not affordable for the thousands of local hospitals globally, including Africa, where annual incomes for many citizens are only four digits (as in Kenya's $1600) (CIA).

This resulted in a limited number of customers who could afford health care. If GE could adapt their products for these markets, then a new source of customers—and human impact—would be possible.

"GE had the technology and know-how," says Frank Mantero of GE. "But we hadn't yet specifically designed, assembled and sold products for those markets. The affordable health devices market is one of those leading opportunities."

With an energy and focus on serving a new, untapped market, GE identified specific challenges including the continent's high infant mortality rate and lack of prenatal care. Those conditions were also prevalent in other regions of the world such as Central America and South Asia. The GE engineers invented a new product to increase health—a portable ultrasound machine that sold for 30 percent of the original cost. Using a rugged portable laptop and an ultrasound wand, the machine was built to be electronically reliable without continual technological support and to easily move from location to location, allowing for collective purchasing and efficient implementation (see Figure 3.1). The result—ultrasound machines were sold across the continent, generating $175 million in global revenue as of December 2007 and dramatically improving health care for millions across Africa (GE, *Healthcare* 2007).

Today, GE's sales to the Africa–Middle East region total more than $10 billion—or 5 percent of global revenue. GE is innovating a wider set of affordable products across the company that are designed to serve new consumers, rely on renewable resources, offer transparent information to their customers, and serve the demand for products that do "good." In addition, its Developing Health Globally program continues to deliver impact for nearly 5 million mothers, children, and citizens seeking care—a tremendous health benefit for approximately $8 per person. In total, this creates positive impact in Health and Equality.

What other companies are shifting to be in line with the world's new realities? What product is most dramatically improving health? What about Earth or Equality? Let's look at some of the impressive company responses to our world's changes, exploring innovations across HIP's Health, Wealth, Earth, Equality, and Trust categories.

Health

Walking down the aisles of a grocery store, shoppers are inundated with declarations of health. Many products make claims like "low fat"

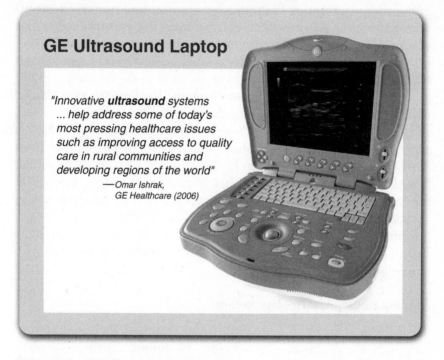

GE Ultrasound Laptop

*"Innovative **ultrasound** systems ... help address some of today's most pressing healthcare issues such as improving access to quality care in rural communities and developing regions of the world"*
—Omar Ishrak,
GE Healthcare (2006)

Figure 3.1   GE Ultrasound Laptop
Source: GE Corporation.

"heart healthy" or "lowers cholestorol," but how can consumers know which are true and which are simply advertising campaigns. Move out of the grocery store and into your home where you are focused on safeguarding the health of your aging parents. What innovations are out there to improve the well being of your family?

People are driven to make "good" decisions and are searching for healthier options. As the GoodGuide's rise to prominence has shown, consumers are seeking the information they need to make affordable, healthy choices.

HIP's Health category measures the impact a company has on their stakeholders' physical, mental, and emotional health. By investing in the health of its stakeholders, companies are positioned to increase their market share, command greater customer loyalty, and benefit from heightened employee productivity and retention.

Let's look at a less obvious Health factor—employee satisfaction. Employee satisfaction is a leading indicator that measures the involvement, engagement, and commitment of a company's staff. Satisfied employees offer better customer service, yielding increased profits through higher sales while also improving the mental health of a company's employees. This higher morale, less turnover, and lower training investments in retained staff can translate into higher shareholder returns.

Fortune magazine annually publishes its "100 Best Places to Work," which measures which companies rank the best in terms of employee satisfaction. Wharton Professor Alex Edmans analyzed these top-ranked firms alongside their shareholder performance from 1984–2005 and uncovered that by investing in the companies on the "100 Best Places to Work" list when they first appeared, a portfolio could generate an additional 4 percent per year in financial return (Wharton 2009).

Building from this health example, let's dive in to see specific health products companies are putting forward that generate financial returns.

Healthy Employees, Healthy Returns

To increase employee satisfaction and improve their employees' health, Bristol-Myers Squibb developed a unique approach combining its products and health education for their employees suffering from diabetes and rheumatoid arthritis. This approach not only improved the "health" of the workplace and increased employee satisfaction, it also produced direct health care savings of 34 percent and reduced absenteeism by 50 percent, saving $2,000 per person annually while simultaneously increasing business productivity and earnings (BMS, *Executive Summary* 2009).

Soup Wars

Throughout 2008, the *New York Times* featured dueling advertising campaigns between Campbell's Soup and Progresso Soup over which products had the lowest sodium and least MSG added (Elliott 2008). This war over health benefits was reminiscent of the "tastes great" versus "less filling" advertisements of Miller Lite beer ads in the 1980s, but with a significantly healthier message. The leading soup companies were vying to earn the "health" badge and attract the revenue for soup associated with 30 million American consumers weekly. In the past, soup brands focused on taste and pricing. Now, the companies were competing to share detailed information on the number, type, and nature of their ingredients to serve a "healthy" product.

Fast Food

The competition for being the "healthy choice" has even extended to quick-serve, commonly called fast food. McDonald's, which hosts two in three American fast-food eaters monthly for a meal, has shifted its menu to healthier options, including grilled chicken sandwiches, apple slices instead of fries for Happy Meals, and a range of salads. According to Bob Langert, the Vice President of Sustainability at McDonald's, the lunch salads are one of the healthiest options available when eating out and the top seller of available salads. With apples for sides and snacks, moms can take their kids out for a healthy meal at an affordable price. The salads are estimated to generate $600 million annually, or about 10 percent of domestic revenue (Interview, 2008).

Competitors like Subway have aggressively promoted the healthy eating of Jared, who lost weight by controlling how much he ate with the chain's small sandwiches. Wendy's is also offering healthier menu choices. As some cities begin to require disclosure about grams of fat and calories per serving, the quest for fast food that is also healthy can support positive impacts on health.

Healthy, Homestyle Eating

Grocery stores are also vying for these health-conscious shoppers. In 2005, grocery giant Safeway pioneered the "O" organics label for in-store offerings of healthier foods, offering 300 products at affordable prices. Safeway has extended the "O" brand successfully across 3000 stores, and rival grocery chains Albertsons and Price Chopper are now buying Safeway's "O" brand to try to benefit from its success (Supermarket & Retailer 2009). Building on "O's" success, Safeway has since expanded to include "Eating Right" products—225 products, including frozen entrees, soups, and salad dressings that are "better for you" (Safeway, Inc. *CSR* 2008). Eating Right products were estimated to sell $200 million in 2008 and Safeway's revenue grew after its introduction by an impressive 25 percent, jumping from $300 million in 2007 to an estimated $400 million in 2008 (Mininni 2009).

Healthy Snacks

PepsiCo, both a food and a beverage company, is gradually transforming its portfolio to meet the healthy demands of customers. Trans-fats are being removed from Frito-Lay products in North America, healthier oils are being substituted in the Walkers-brand crisps, and Omega-3 is being added to juices. For higher growth, lower income countries, PepsiCo is researching new nutrient-rich products, including oat-based cookies in Mexico by the Gamesa-Quaker business unit.

"We have seen growth in our 'better for you' and 'good for you' brands that relate directly to profitability," says Adriana Villasenor, Pepsi's director of sustainability. Pepsi claims that 30 percent of its overall revenue is from products that are "good for you" or "better for you," and is expected to grow to 50 percent.

With its Smart Spot labeling program, Pepsi labels products that contain at least 10 percent of the daily value of a target nutrient, and have limited fat, sodium, sugar, or calories. In 2008, 40 percent of PepsiCo revenue was derived from Smart Spot products including Tropicana juices, Naked Juice smoothies, Flat Earth fruit and veggie crisps, True North nuts, and Quaker oatmeal. "Our Smart Spot program in North America has positively educated consumers on how to make healthier choices in an easier fashion," says Villasenor.

As a trusted brand representing quality for families, The Walt Disney Company has set food guidelines aimed at healthier eating choices. Disney now requires its name, image, and characters to only be associated with kid-focused food products that meet specific nutritional guidelines. More than 600 million servings of Disney-branded fresh produce have been served since the program's launch in 2006 (IFT 2009).

Healthy Farming

Food production has positive-impact products as well. DuPont Qualicon creates products that enhance food safety including diagnostic tools for finding salmonella, listeria and e-coli in beef, sheep and pigs. Other products "fingerprint" bacteria through DNA testing with its RiboPrinter system (DuPont, *Sustainability*). Since the whole ecosystem benefits as well, then this is HIP in both Health and Earth.

CF Industries, a $4 billion nitrogen and phosphate producer, helps farming productivity (Google Finance). When used efficiently, its fertilizers increase crop yields of corn, cotton and wheat. These farming productivity products also enable strong root systems, support seed germination, and advance sugar development. Since 1950, these fertilizers have helped to contribute to increased crop yield of up to five times, reducing the amount of land required for food production. CF's market share in U.S. farm states is 28 percent for nitrogen and 18 percent for phosphates (CF Industries Web site, *Products*). Interestingly, nitrogen was used by weapons manufacturers in World War II, but became an agricultural input after the war (Michael Pollan, "From guns to plowshares"). However, nitrogen is overused by many farmers globally, causing unnecessary runoff into water sources and risking degraded soil by eliminating microbes. Using nitrogen smartly is a growth opportunity to be more HIP, producing both Health and Earth benefits.

Healthy Surfaces

Consumers spend about $1 billion annually fighting microbes, purchasing products from hand cleaners to mouthwash (AK Steel, *Markets*). So how does a producer of flat-rolled carbon, electrical, and stainless steel, tap into this market? AK Steel, a $7.6 billion company, has developed a silver-based compound that fits directly into steel surfaces and repels a wide range of bacteria, molds and fungi. This revolutionary steel creates cleaner surfaces and is used in appliances, air conditioners, medical devices, food preparation surfaces, deli scales, and salad bars. In 2008, health firm Baxter introduced the first needleless IV connector using this antimicrobial coating (Baxter, *Annual Report* 2008). AK Steel's innovation won a Popular Science award for "what's new," and is priced at a premium as over 60 percent of consumers are willing to pay higher prices for "clean" steel (AK Steel Web site).

Hospital Quality—Improved

In health care facilities across the United States, over 2 million patients contract infections, causing 88,000 deaths annually (Carpenter 2006). Hospital-related infections affect 1 in 20 patients in the United States. These infections not only have serious health implications for patients and visitors but also drastically reduce hospital profits—infections contracted while at a hospital are estimated to reduce operating profits by 63 percent (Carpenter 2006; RWJF 2004). Cardinal Health developed data mining technologies that are integrated into hospitals' existing systems to identify infections as they occur and to recommend changes in processes and practices to reduce future infections. The Alabama Hospital Quality Initiative's pilot across six medical centers realized a 19 percent drop in infections in 2002–2004, saved nearly $5 million and generated a 12x return on investment. If adopted on a large scale, this technology could not only offer a dramatic reduction in the number of infections but also has the potential to increase profits by 60 percent (Duggan 2006).

Wireless Health

As technology blends with health care, the industry is expected to spend $7 billion in wireless services by 2012 (Bigelow 2009). Qualcomm saw the market shifting with a demand for transparent medical records and global markets, and developed medical therapy implants, wireless controlled drug delivery, and even "smart Band Aids" (Qualcomm Web site). Figure 3.2 shows how your body can be the center of a wireless "body area network (BAN)" in the near future.

Texas Instruments is also focusing on wireless health care, developing low-power chips for use both inside and outside your body that can feed into a "personal area network system" which is tracked by a "body measurement system" (Texas Instruments, *2008 CSR*). Today, TI's digital light processing technology is licensed to companies creating products that project the location of the veins of all types of patients. From kids to seniors and cancer patients, this reduces the number of needle piercings, while also producing a revenue stream for TI (Coffey 2008). The medical electronics market was valued at $116.7 billion for 2008 (Databeans 2008).

Healthy products are attracting customer dollars, and thus driving investor value. The HIP framework crosses over each of these examples to measure the results and their link to profitability, for the company and your portfolio.

Wealth

Generating wealth isn't important just for your personal portfolio. Companies that produce wealth-generating products attract customers and improve economic vitality. This sets the stage for long-term growth and opportunity.

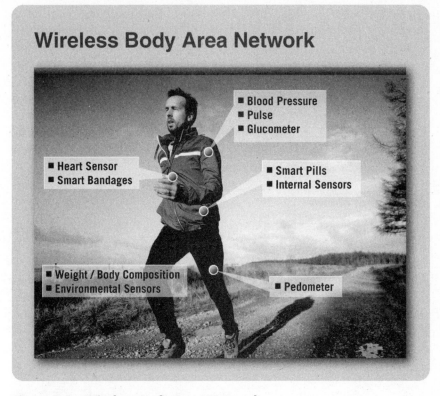

Figure 3.2   Wireless Body Area Network

HIP's Wealth category measures the economic benefits and welfare a company creates for its stakeholders. Companies are designed to generate wealth. However, when they expand their goal from just adding value for shareholders to adding value for their stakeholders—including their employees and customers—they expand the market and position themselves to reap the rewards.

Financial Services, Grocery Style

A compelling product in the HIP Wealth category is grocer Kroger's expansion into advancing economic benefits for customers. At $76 billion in revenue, Kroger's also owns food retailers Ralph's, Fred Meyer, and City Market, as well as Fry's electronics. Kroger's is also the fourth largest fine jewelry chain (Yahoo! Finance).

Kroger's Personal Finance Division, launched in 2004, offers a range of products including credit and debit cards, traditional insurance products (including life, home, trailer, and collector car insurance), mortgages, and equity loans. So what is the result of a grocery chain entering the finance game? Kroger has increased revenue per square foot per store for shareholders, while providing compelling financial deals and services for customers, and is in a position to leverage the combined buying power of its customers. Kroger's success and willingness to adapt to its markets has cemented it as a financial services innovator.

Control Your Money

Mint.com had over 550,000 active users tracking $174 billion in transactions and $47 billion in assets in September 2009 (Gross 2009). This free service was designed to give individuals better control and knowledge over their personal money management—Mint claims $600 in savings per active user, having identified over $300 million since its inception. Intuit acquired Mint.com, to tap into its earned revenue through referral fees on a marketplace designed to give customers better deals such as lower interest-rate credit cards or higher-rate deposits (Gross 2009; TechCrunch Web site).

Calling All Entrepreneurs

Financial services giant Citigroup has long focused on reaching individuals around the world with unique financial services. Recognizing the global microfinance opportunities, Citi Microfinance partnered with Citi's affiliate, Banamex, in Mexico to provide $50 million in financing for microfinance provider Compartamos (Citi, *Microfinance Banana Skins* 2009, 1). It also brokered a partnership with Overseas Private Investment Corporation to offer $100 million in financing for microfinance institutions, invested globally (Citi *Microfinance* 2009, 1). In 2009, Citi arranged another $250 million for MFIs in partnership with OPIC. Independently, Citi's global consumer unit in India serves the "under-banked" with a new micro-savings product named "Pragati" (Hindi for progress). The service uses money machines in microfinance institutions to provide customers access to their funds in six languages using fingerprints for access. (Citi, *Microfinance* 2009, 2). "There's an enormous need and a tremendous opportunity to provide services to people credit, but also insurance and savings," says Global Director of Microfinace Bob Annibale. "I hope one day we'll reach as clients many of today's unbanked people" (Citi, *Microfinance* 2009, 2).

Citigroup builds wealth for these customers from the earliest stages of their economic lifecycle, and in culturally and economically astute ways. This approach provides an important service by positioning Citigroup to serve the "under-banked" with access to capital to grow businesses and fund family education as their financial services provider while earning reasonable profits.

Healthy Dollars

The U.S. Census Bureau estimates that there are 45.7 million uninsured people in the United States (Bialik 2009). So what is the result? The country has a huge market of individuals who require care but are often hesitant to go to the emergency room until it is too late. This increases costs to the individual and the hospital. Pharmacy chain CVS is seeing this reality as an opportunity and has developed two products that not only improve the health of its customers but also the range of access across income and ethnic groups, boosting Equality as well as Health. These initiatives also generate substantial new job and revenue opportunities for the company:

- CVS launched a new health-savings pass for uninsured patients to obtain prescription drugs at affordable prices. This product is based on the pharmaceutical-industry consortium-led program called the "Together Rx Access Card," offered to 1.5 million citizens lacking Medicare or health insurance coverage (Bio Medicine 2008).
- CVS operates Minute Clinics, retail health providers, in its stores across the United States. Since their launch, Minute Clinics have served over four million patients. Staffed by family nurse practitioners and physician assistants, the clinics treat common illnesses, minor injuries, and administer health screenings and vaccinations. The clinics' treatments cost between $30 and $100, making them affordable for all. Today, they are "aggressively expanding" across the country to tap into the demand for reasonably priced, easy access health care (Minute Clinic Web site).

Pharmaceutical firms are also serving uninsured citizens. In 2008, more than 400,000 uninsured patients saved 25 to 40 percent at the counter as a result of Abbott programs, totaling $17 million on prescribed, brand name medicines (Abbott *CSR* 2008). This creates a boost to Wealth, Health, and Equality.

Eco-financing

With the heightened awareness of climate change, there has been a dramatic push toward renewable energy and managing climate change risks. From 2006 to 2008, Wells Fargo facilitated $4 billion of eco-related debt and equity, including large-scale wind and solar energy sites (Wells Fargo, *Annual Report* 2008). Simultaneously, Goldman Sachs, an early innovator in eco-finance markets, developed climate-related "catastrophe bonds" for companies wholly dependent on traditional energy resources, including hedging climate risk for insurance and re-insurance firms globally totaling $1.4 billion of hedged transactions. This results in financial Wealth for customers, and leads to Earth benefits—while increasing the bottom line for the companies.

From increasing access to offering new products, companies are helping individuals increase their personal wealth, giving them the financial resources they need to achieve their dreams for themselves and their families. Leading companies attract customers through tools that build the wealth and income of customers.

Earth

Green products are becoming more prevalent. Around the world, when a product can position itself as better for the environment, either using fewer finite resources or producing less waste, the product can be rewarded with preferential placement, highlighted advertising, increased purchases and loyal customers.

HIP's Earth factors evaluate both the short- and long-term impact a company has on the natural world. As many natural resources are becoming scarce, individuals consider environmental sustainability a top priority. Companies that increase efficiency and reduce their corporate footprint are poised to serve the market of eco-conscious consumers ahead of their competitors.

The Hybrid

While the word "hybrid" often brings to mind the Toyota Prius, the best-selling hybrid vehicle globally, Ford is a strong competitor and is closing in on Toyota's hybrid market share. However, while competing in the retail channel, the two companies have co-developed engine technologies that are used in both brand's vehicles. Ford offers a suite of hybrids including the Ford Escape, while Toyota produces the Highlander; both models feature an innovative technology co-developed jointly by Ford and Toyota (Takahashi 2004).

Ford, the only major U.S. automotive company to avoid government loans and bailout funds in 2008-09, has benefited from Chairman Bill Ford Jr. and CEO Alan Mullaly's ongoing commitment to sustainability. "It's not a separate condition, but an understanding if we get sustainability right, then we can have a competitive advantage, and customers will choose our products over the competition," says Thomas Niemann, of Ford's Sustainable Business Strategies group. Ford's forward-thinking approach changes the way they think about their business: "We are beyond targeting niche markets—we are targeting millions of customers."

Currently, Ford is augmenting its hybrid engine with fuel injection and turbo-boosting technologies designed to increase the hybrid's miles per gallon, lowering carbon emissions and reducing the environmental impact. "Our fuel economy advantages will translate to higher profitability," Niemann says.

Ford's commitment to hybrid technology has given them a distinct national and global advantage. It also has given the company a unique offering, significantly distinguishing them from their U.S. competitors.

In for the Long Haul

While automotive vehicles are dramatically improving their miles per gallon, many heavy- and medium-weight trucks stumble along, rarely even reaching 10 miles per gallon. Since trucks log the most hours and longest distances on the road, it is critical to create energy-efficient engines that not only reduce environmental emissions but are also positioned to save millions of dollars in fuel costs. Paccar, the $15 billion maker of Kenworth and Peterbilt trucks, has carved a path toward higher-efficiency, using a multi-tool approach that features hybrid engines, sculpted frames, and low-idle energy management systems that optimize electrical and fuel usage (Nasdaq and Peterbilt Web sites). In 2009, Kenworth's unique design became the first truck to earn the EPA's award for clean air excellence (Kenworth Truck Company Web site).

Fleet customers purchasing these new models, including Coca-Cola, have seen dramatic benefits to the bottom line. With 32 percent fuel efficiency improvement, 30 percent or more emissions reductions, and lower maintenance costs, CCE expects the investment in Kenworth hybrid trucks to generate a payback in less than four years, or an internal rate of return of more than 25 percent, says company spokesman Fred Roselli. Paccar's leadership and sustainable innovations like these have lead to seven decades of consistent profits and ongoing shareholder value outperformance (Katz 2008).

Natural Plastics

Renewable resources are everywhere—look no further than your garden to find resources that can be converted into packaging materials. Sealed Air, a $4.84 billion packaging innovator, has launched the "Nature Tray" (Yahoo! Finance). Designed as packaging for fresh beef, pork, chicken, and fish, the Nature Tray uses plant-derived products in place of traditional plastic and foam materials. This new packaging material reduces fossil fuel requirements by two thirds in comparison with traditional plastics—using dramatically fewer fossil fuels—and is compostable in specific facilities (though not wholly biodegradable). Figure 3.3 shows an improved product lifecycle; Natureworks is a joint venture of Cargill and Teijin.

Living, Sustainable Style

Are you looking to green your home? Home Depot launched an Eco Options label to identify products that save energy, are less toxic, and are produced in an environmentally friendly way. Today, there are over 3,000 products in the Eco Options label including low-flow shower heads, ceiling fans designed to replace air conditioning, and motion-sensor lighting, all of which reduce energy costs and create a healthier home.

The products labeled Eco Options typically outsell their counterparts and in 2007 totaled more than $3 billion, or about 4 percent of overall revenue. According to Ron Jarvis, Senior Vice President of Environmental Innovation, "On a long-term basis, I think sustainability

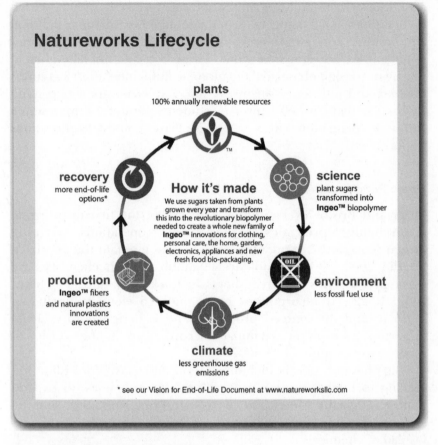

Figure 3.3 Natureworks Lifecycle

Source: Natureworks LLC, © 2009.

will be built into almost every product consumers buy." The goal for 2009 is to double the number of Eco Option products to 6000. Competitor Lowe's followed Home Depot's lead shortly after Eco Options was announced.

Green Building—Design with Style

Autodesk, a $2 billion design software company, describes its greatest opportunity as "influenc[ing] how our nine million users worldwide are designing and building, from buildings and cars to cities and shoes" (Autodesk 2008). In 2009 this goal was being realized.

Autodesk's Green Building Studio software and Web services is used by designers and architects to evaluate airflows, shading, lighting, and building configurations, to determine their impacts on energy, water, and carbon-emissions flows. These decisions are all evaluated during the design phase, making ultimate implementation less costly, timelier, and with fewer surprises. Autodesk's software is becoming so popular that Cornell University students are using it to design a 100 miles-per-gallon car for the X Prize contest (Innovations Report 2008).

Green Pharmaceuticals

Pfizer and Bristol-Myers Squibb were two of the first to integrate green chemistry principles into the company's operations, even using "green scorecards" to quantify, analyze, and evaluate the approach (Wedin 2006, 40-1). Bristol-Myers Squibb's bench chemists have developed a series of spreadsheets to track their impact (Thayer 2009, 13-22). It incorporates more than 16 elements including in-house and out-sourced processes, and is designed to evaluate opportunities to minimize impact, according to Stephen Taylor of Bristol-Myers Squibb (EPA 2007).

Big pharmaceuticals, including Merck and GlaxoSmithKline, are seeking to integrate these green chemistry principles, to expand impact and profit (Merck and GlaxoSmithKline Web sites). They include minimizing atoms, substituting solvents, and applying enzymes instead of chemicals.

Taxol, a drug designed to combat breast and ovarian cancer, is a dramatic breakthrough. The National Cancer Institute selected Bristol-Myers Squibb in 1991 to bring it to market (National Cancer Institute Web site). Initially, it was made from natural yew tree bark found in the U.S. Pacific Northwest, and the drug demand outweighed the available supply. Bristol-Myers Squibb cultivated yew shrub twigs and needles to reduce pressure on the available bark, increasing the available supply, and consuming less material for the drug's production (American Society of Pharmacognosy). The result—reduced costs, less environmental degradation, and increased quality of life for cancer patients. Today, Taxol is produced in cultures with isolated plant cells for fermentation thus reducing waste and pollutants. Since its inception, Taxol has generated $200 million in licensing revenues for the scientists of Florida State

University (FSU) who helped in its synthesis (Bristol-Myers Squibb Web site).

HIP's Earth element clearly covers a wide range of categories. Companies that are focused on saving the environment become eligible for tax incentives, increased consumer attention, premium pricing, lower energy costs, and a leg up against their competitors.

Equality

The world is diverse—are companies positioned to tap into potential consumers from across the globe? Or even within their region or locale? It is becoming imperative to expand your target market—let's dive in and see how companies are viewing customers in a new way.

HIP's Equality is the representation of gender, ethnicity, and income classes; and how the share of customers, employees, and suppliers match those proportions. Companies with higher levels of diversity are poised to tap into new markets and are better positioned to meet the needs of their customers.

Going to Growth

Forms of payment in a market dominated by youth are the lynch-pin for tapping online music purchasing market. Online music store iLike has 50 million registered users and there are unknown millions on iTunes. Since many users are under 18 and may not have access to credit cards (without their parents' approval), Apple has an opportunity to tap into the almost $200 billion dollar U.S. teenage market by utilizing innovative payment options (Virtual World News 2009).

Hispanics in the United States now account for 17 percent of the population—or one in every six people. This market has tremendous purchasing power (U.S. Census Bureau 2006). To attract this market, Walmart has launched a more economical bulk store (modeled after Sam's Clubs) called "The *Mas* Store." By creating a store that in name, brand, and inventory focuses on the $800 billion of Hispanic spending in the market, Walmart is positioning itself for dramatic growth.

Other companies have caught on—medical insurer United-Health has created "Plan Bien" (good plan) for Spanish speaking customers, and "Medicare Explicado" (Medicare explained) advises seniors on how to access government health benefits offering Spanish as one of the suite of languages (The National Health Plan Collaborative, n.d.).

By offering culturally adept and language-specific products for the growing Hispanic market, each of these companies is positioning themselves to serve consumers across the United States instead of limiting their reach to traditional markets.

Fashion or Function?

Shifting our focus to women and the trillions of dollars of purchasing power they influence, here's an example of what to avoid. Dell Computer nicknamed a part of their Web site "Della," in 2009. The section featured women crowded around their color-coordinated laptops seeking recipes and yoga mats. The goal—to be more accessible to women. The result—angry backlash and the site's removal.

"Let's market PCs like it's 1959," was the title of the critique written by MSNBC reporter Suzanne Choney in May 2009. "Want to market netbooks as a fashion statement? Fine," wrote Choney. "Just don't create a silo . . . that depicts females as poolside-lounging, latte-sipping ladies with little else to do than decide how to match their outfits to a computer" (Choney 2009).

As news spread, other women wrote in: "Come on Dell! Treat us like intelligent consumers and not like trained monkeys. Give us useful advice that actually helps us to better navigate and contribute to the Web. Show women how to start blogs, how to upload images and create galleries on Flickr, how to start e-commerce businesses, etc."

The Della campaign (and link) was abolished shortly thereafter.

The lesson—while it is important to adapt and serve specific markets, it must be done in a way (and by people) that shows an understanding of the core needs of the audience and focuses on solving the human need, not on stereotypes.

Affordable Health Care

Every country around the world struggles to provide affordable health care, and the tension for fair pricing between higher-income countries and lower-income countries is high. To address this head-on, Gilead Sciences, a $5.3 billion biotech firm known for its HIV and AIDS treatments, has developed an innovative pricing approach that results in better health, affordable products, and improved access to medicine (*BusinessWeek*, n.d.).

Gilead built partnerships with 13 companies in India to produce lower cost generic versions of its medications. Distributed in 95 countries where partners can price according to the market, Gilead collects a 5 percent royalty on purchases (Gilead Web site).

Merck, a $24 billion pharmaceutical firm, formulates prices for each country based on its income level and the pervasiveness of the disease. Merck then adapts the pricing of drugs, like retroviral treatments, to be affordable for each nation's local market (*BusinessWeek*, Merck n.d.).

Abbott, a $29 billion pharmaceutical firm that sells HIV treatments, has agreed to price its product at $1,000 per person per year for middle-income economies like Brazil, and $500 annually in low-income countries, including serving 110,000 patients in Africa. Currently, Abbott's HIV tablet medicine is approved in 161 countries globally (*BusinessWeek*; Abbott CSR, n.d.).

By asking the question—is the company poised to reach a variety of markets and is it effectively considering how to generate more equitable access?—HIP assesses the company's Equality rating by looking at diversification and market growth potential. The more diverse a company's product market, the more sustainable it is over the long term.

Trust

Customers are demanding more information—and companies that provide it are being rewarded. From connecting parents and teens to labels that certify performance to open-information marketplaces that facilitate great deals for customers, there are innovative HIP products focused on Trust.

HIP's Trust category measures the level of transparency and the consistency of ethical performance. Companies who behave in an ethical manner and report transparently attract market share as leaders of their markets. Their high levels of credibility leave them poised to take advantage of new opportunities.

Sustainable Forests

Plum Creek Timber is the largest private landholder across the United States and has demonstrated a commitment to ensuring that all of its land is independently certified to the standards of the Sustainable Forestry Initiative (SFI). Evolving consumer preferences for low-carbon impact products and emerging green building standards and practices has dramatically increased the demand for sustainably produced and sourced wood products. For example, since 2000, Home Depot has required all wood in its stores to be sustainable, even broom handles. This means avoiding endangered tree species and purchasing solely from certified and well-managed forestry suppliers.

Plum Creek Timber is committed to having independent third parties certify its sustainable forest management practices and procurement of wood. This approach helps connect with a broader range of consumers and retailers such as Home Depot (Plum Creek Web site).

Transparent Pricing

Progressive, one of the largest insurance providers in the United States, currently has more than 10 million policies in force with the goal of becoming consumers' number one choice for auto insurance. What makes their sales model innovative enough to reach that goal? When customers ask for policy quotes, Progressive automatically gives them its rates alongside those of its competitors. By providing transparent pricing across the industry and increasing ease of use for the customer, the company is establishing a reputation for customer service, honesty, and trust, as well as demonstrating an extraordinary amount of confidence in its product (Progressive Web site).

The Energy Marketplace

The Intercontinental Exchange (ICE), by the firm of the same name, was launched to represent the world's largest energy companies and global banks by transforming over-the-counter energy markets with an open, accessible, around-the-clock electronic energy marketplace. This offered a huge transition from the previously fragmented and opaque market. ICE gave energy price transparency, offering greater efficiency, liquidity, and lower costs. In 2008, ICE's revenues totaled $813 million, and it continues to push forward electronic marketplaces for energy. ICE has also expanded into commodities including sugar, cotton, and coffee (Yahoo! Finance). ICE's products facilitate increased transparency which leads to trust, as well as more efficient pricing for customers buying and selling materials and commodities- a combination of positive impact and higher profit.

Jewels—From Mine to Body

Do you know where your jewelry comes from? Were the metals mined sustainably? Or are your adornments the product of strip mining?

Walmart's Love, Earth® jewelry was designed to give consumers the ability to trace their jewelry's trek, from mining to purchase, online. The brand not only gives the customers tracking power but Walmart also ensures that all jewelry will be purchased responsibly from producers with strong environmental, human rights, and labor track records. The jewelry's transparency was made possible via a partnership across the supply chain, from sourcing to production to sales.

Long-term, the partners plan to work together to certify that 100 percent of the gold, silver, and diamonds used in the jewelry sold in Walmart will meet Walmart's responsible sourcing criteria. By 2010, Walmart will be tracing 10 percent of the gold and silver it sells and will have "made considerable progress towards traceability of diamonds" (Love Earth Web site).

HIP's Trust and transparency metrics are critical today. People demand quantitative information on a wide spread of topics and information—companies that are more forthcoming with information attract more consumers, establish customer loyalty and, depending on the information, charge premium pricing. The more honest and upfront with information that a company is, the lower the risk and the higher the potential return.

Next Step: Counting the Impacts

Companies are innovating products to meet the changing patterns of demand—and seeing new opportunities around every corner. Continuing to build from the trends and the products that solve specific human needs, let's move forward in Chapter 4, and review the specific, quantifiable impacts each company has across all of their stakeholders. The result—each company's Human Impact score to measure their specific impacts across the areas of Health, Wealth, Earth, Equality, and Trust.

CHAPTER 4

Count the Quantifiable Human, Social, and Environmental Impacts

What gets measured gets managed. That's one of the main contributing factors to the short-term profit orientation of robber-baron capitalists and investors. But the measures tend to be short-term and financial-only, which creates added risk because it does not properly account for leading indicators of performance that ultimately drive financials. When investors and leading companies look comprehensively and to the long term, more profit is possible—and so is a better world.

The world's largest retailer, Walmart provides an excellent example of the benefits of looking beyond pure short-term financial metrics. Walmart's efforts began in the fall of 2004 when executives including then CEO Lee Scott, asked BluSkye Consulting to develop a sustainability strategy, according to Walmart's Web site. Co-developed with front-line staff, managers, and executives, the approach identified opportunities to eliminate waste and attract new customers interested in health and environmental benefits—which naturally resulted in reduced costs and increased efficiency. In October 2005, Scott declared that "being a good steward of the environment and being profitable are not mutually exclusive. They are one and the same." The company also set three long-term goals (without a deadline at the time): "To be supplied 100 percent by renewable energy; to create zero waste; and to sell products that sustain our resources and the environment." (Plambeck 2007) Walmart kick-started this mission by launching 12 *sustainable value networks* that focused on specific product lines and cross-cutting issues, including:

- Packaging (e.g. no more toothpaste boxes, just sell the tube)
- Cleaning products (e.g. eliminate 70 percent of phosphates)
- Agriculture (e.g. facilitate the re-capture of methane from cows to fuel energy plants)
- Jewelry (e.g. track the gold and metals back to the source)

These initiatives created new products and revenue (like the Love Earth brand of jewelry which rejuvenated a lower growth category); decreased costs (with innovations such as cube-like milk containers that save shipping costs); and tapped into tax incentives for energy efficiency (spurring initiatives of solar panels on stores) (Walmart Stores Inc, Web site).

Its program was showing signs of success. Walmart found significant markets for 200 sustainable products, half of the 400 products it had tested in the summer of 2007 did well and were restocked. (*Wall Street Journal* 2007/08). Indeed, during Earth Month 2008, the sustainable products offered by Walmart sold so swiftly, that many were sold out before the month-long promotion ended. This customer demand accelerated Walmart's push for more sustainable products—and highlighted a way to showcase it to consumers. (Walmart Sustainability Milestone Meeting, July 2008). Walmart's program therefore tapped into a new market: consumers seeking products to make them healthier and that are better for the environment.

When Walmart turned to calculating its global environmental footprint, it discovered that 90 percent of its carbon emissions (from transportation to manufacturing to farming) were from its suppliers, and only 10 percent from its own stores, staff, and transportation. So, with more than 60,000 suppliers, Walmart and its buyers had the ability to pre-select its mix of products toward those suppliers with practices consistent with its sustainability goals. By intentionally choosing such suppliers, it could then measure and manage the process. Products with a nutrition label (like that adopted by Timberland in 2006) that quantifiably calculated these new elements would provide these consumers with additional information beyond just brand and price (and potentially increase demand).

Thus, the concept of a comprehensive, methodical Sustainability Index applicable to all products was launched. Walmart and BluSkye organized a team that included non-profits like Environmental Defense Fund, leading academics in lifecycle analysis and sustainability, internal Walmart leaders, and external experts like my firm, HIP Investor Inc. The challenge was to design a quantifiable scorecard to be used by 100 million customers covering products across 100,000+ suppliers.

During several all-day sessions in Bentonville, Arkansas, and multiple conference calls during 2008, the initial version of the Sustainability Index was developed by a cross-section of Walmart, its suppliers, and outside experts, which included me. The index was circulated internally for review and feedback from all those already working on sustainability, and many who were new to it. The process also included a 200-person summit in Bentonville over three days, convening suppliers, non-profit specialists, measurement experts, and Walmart staff. This highly engaging process, intended to be inclusive and to strengthen the ultimate outcome, resulted in a Sustainability Index covering four categories and intended benefits, both financial and societal:

1. Energy and Climate—using less fuel and saving greenhouse gas emissions.
2. Material Efficiency—consuming less, processing less, reusing and recycling, and ultimately moving to zero waste.
3. Natural Resources—higher quality production with fewer inputs (like water), which could be certified according to standards.
4. People and Community—open communication and increased transparency about sourcing and its impact in the local community.

These four categories are designed to serve customers with sustainable products, result in lower costs to companies and less negative impact on society, and deliver value for both shareholders and stakeholders. An initial survey of 15 questions was constructed to kick off the process for all suppliers worldwide, including those based in China, to quantify baseline information in 2009 (Walmart Stores, Inc. Web site).

Walmart's approach is indicative of the leaders in sustainability: Bring an increasing range of products to market that solve a human need, and measure the quantifiable results for how they drive impact and profit. This measurement approach for products was pioneered by Timberland, the footwear company.

Ultimately, a nutrition label of Walmart could emulate the example launched by Timberland back in 2006. Timberland replaced its 30 million old clay-coated, glued-together boxes with a 100 percent recycled post-consumer fiber-based box that was printed with soy-based inks and die-cut to fit together. That box, wrapped around Timberland's boots, now disclosed in quantifiable terms some of the environmental and community impacts, as well as the place of manufacture. In spring 2007, Timberland added a *green index* that quantifies three aspects of the manufacture of its boots and sandals—the climate impact, chemicals used, and resource consumption—as seen in Figure 4.1 (Butschli 2006, 11). Consumers can then judge the relative impacts across different shoe types, as Timberland expects all of its shoes to carry this green index by 2010, which complements the goal it has set to be carbon neutral.

This chapter will show how each of the five HIP elements—Health, Wealth, Earth, Equality, and Trust—is measurable across customers, employees, and suppliers. This comprehensive value-chain approach ensures that a company is appropriately measuring the impact on overall society, including the environment, and how it relates to the bottom line. In addition, we will demonstrate the power of measured results, or outcomes that correlate with true performance. Do-gooder investment approaches of the past tended to focus on policies and practices, which are not methodically followed and do not create a consistent output. HIP values actual "walk" over promised "talk."

The HIP approach also prioritizes outcomes and results over inputs and process. For example, in the case of Frito's corn chips, the input is the amount of corn to be made into chips. A process measure would be efficiency of chip production. An output measure would be the change in customer health and nutrition from eating those chips. HIP seeks to maximize the number of output measures to gauge quantifiable results.

Now that HIP's research has analyzed more than 500 public companies, you can more easily learn where to look for this information (e.g., from the company, third-party sources, government tracking), how to compare across companies (e.g., standardizing by unit of

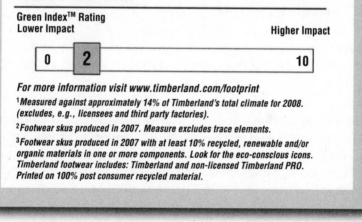

Timberland's Nutrition Label and Green Index

OUR FOOTPRINT

Climate Impact[1]	
Use of renewable energy	6.36%
Chemicals Used[2]	
PVC-free	81.14%
Resource Consumption	
Eco-conscious materials[3]	5.27%
Recycled content of shoebox	100%
Trees planted through 2007	668,225

PRODUCT FOOTPRINT

Green Index™ Rating
Lower Impact   Higher Impact

| 0 | 2 | | 10 |

For more information visit www.timberland.com/footprint

[1]*Measured against approximately 14% of Timberland's total climate for 2008. (excludes, e.g., licensees and third party factories).*

[2]*Footwear skus produced in 2007. Measure excludes trace elements.*

[3]*Footwear skus produced in 2007 with at least 10% recycled, renewable and/or organic materials in one or more components. Look for the eco-conscious icons. Timberland footwear includes: Timberland and non-licensed Timberland PRO. Printed on 100% post consumer recycled material.*

Figure 4.1   Timberland's Nutrition Label and Green Index
Source: The Timberland Company.

revenue or number of staff), and how it can be useful for your own portfolio. This chapter will also demonstrate the wide disparities in performance (measured in this manner) among companies by industry, leading investors to consider weighting the leaders higher and the laggards lower, contributing to a portfolio positioned for bigger profits and a better world.

Health

The first element to evaluate is health, and refers to core human needs—both physical and mental. As with each of the five HIP elements, we will evaluate this from a customer, employee, community, and supplier perspective.

HIP Health Metrics

There are six groups of quantifiable metrics a HIP investor can use to evaluate companies on Health:

1. Customer satisfaction
2. Employee satisfaction and retention
3. Wellness programs for all stakeholders
4. Employee safety
5. Supplier safety
6. Stakeholder and community health

Some are already considered business metrics by leaders. They are already benefiting from the positive human impact that results from them.

Customer Satisfaction   It seems so obvious: satisfying customers who buy your products and services is smart business. Customers who are happy return to buy more, and tell others about their positive experience. They could be satisfied by the innovative applications that run on the Apple iPhone and AT&T network, the always accommodating customer service at Nordstrom's, or the breakthrough eco-efficiency of a Toyota Prius. HIP investors should look for reported measures of high customer satisfaction. For companies with HIP products and revenues, these customers' human needs are being solved.

As consulting firm Bain has measured, the most profitable customers are a firm's repeat customers (Reichheld and Allen 2004). Once a customer finds a product that solves a problem, they tend to buy again, as long as the company keeps them happy. And when customers become *net promoters* (i.e., willing to recommend a company to others), those firms experience the highest revenue growth. As we saw earlier, customers are willing to recommend products that are good for society.

The customer satisfaction gurus at J.D. Power (who are now owned by McGraw-Hill) have proven how satisfaction consistently drives higher revenues, increased market share, and boosted profits—all of which lead to higher shareholder value. According to J.D. Power IV's book with Chris Denove, shareholder value increased by 52 percent for the automotive industry in years 1999 to 2004 for firms with rising satisfaction. Over that time, car companies with no change in satisfaction lost 21 percent in shareholder value, and those with declining customer satisfaction lost 28 percent of shareholder value. The correlation also held for increases in sales as automotive companies with the highest satisfaction ratings experienced revenue growth of 44 percent while those firms with the lowest satisfaction ratings experienced sales declines of 4 percent.

Interestingly, when companies are successful and customers are highly satisfied, those customers share that with three to four people on average. However, if a company creates a terrible customer experience and a very dissatisfied customer, those customers will tell six to seven people on average. Interestingly, in between those two extremes, there is little for customers to talk about, according to J.D. Power (Denove and Power 2006).

A customer's referral value can be a high multiplier, even when the actual customer may not be highly profitable. An October 2007 *Harvard Business Review* feature (Kumar, Petersen and Leone) reported on a survey of 9,900 telecom customers and 6,700 financial services clients that found that the highest-value customers can generate profit for companies not by buying more, but by spreading referrals to potential customers. It's a much more expansive view of customer profitability that values "customer referral value" as part of "customer lifetime value" (Kumar, Petersen and Leone 2007).

Revenue derives from customers—how much they buy, how much they pay, and who else they tell. How does this fit with the HIP approach? As we saw in Chapter 3, every customer has a core need to be fulfilled. The more in-depth a company goes to discover unmet needs, the more likely it is to build a path to continued expansion of products and services that generate revenue and profit. Thus, emphasis on customers and customer happiness is an important evaluation metric for a HIP investor.

As an investor you can access customer satisfaction information from The American Customer Satisfaction Index (ACSI), generated by the University of Michigan and its Ross School of Business (at www.TheACSI.org). Updates are published throughout the year, rotating industries by quarter (The American Customer Satisfaction Index Web site). Some of these ratings date back to 1996.

For 2008, the top three industries by overall satisfaction on the ACSI are: Personal Care & Cleaning Products (85 percent), Pet Food (84 percent), and Credit Unions (84 percent). The least-satisfied customers by industry are: Airlines (62 percent), Newspapers (64 percent), Cable & Satellite TV (64 percent), and Wireless Phone Service (68 percent) (The ACSI Web site).

The ACSI tracks subindustries within large sectors. In the financial sector, you see that the industry average for credit unions (84 percent) outranks property and casualty insurance (81 percent), big banks (75 percent) and Internet brokerages (74 percent) (The ACSI Web site) It is important to note that companies rated by ACSI tend to be consumer-facing; those selling to businesses, like materials and industrial companies, tend not to have numerical ratings at this source. According to Professors Don O'Sullivan of Melbourne (Australia) Business School and John McCallig of Smurfit Business School in Dublin, the ACSI's customer satisfaction indexes correlate with higher shareholder value, and are a reliable signal of future firm performance. These ratings also positively influence investors' expectations about the likelihood and level of future profit. Earlier studies on ACSI in 2004 pointed to a lag of up to three quarters, or nine months, for the increased value to be reflected (O'Sullivan and McCallig 2009).

In addition companies often self-report customer satisfaction scores in their own annual reports, sustainability reports, press releases, or Web sites. For example, a survey of Agilent's customers by an independent firm says 98 percent of customers are satisfied (Agilent Technologies Web site). Compuware, a provider of corporate IT services including mainframes, claims 97 percent customer renewal rates. Salesforce.com declares its 94 percent loyalty from customers expecting to continue using its online customer-management software (Salesforce Web site). Jacobs Engineering reports a 90.5 percent quality approval rating from its customers (Jacobs Engineering Group Inc. Web site). And Medco Health Solutions trumpets that it was ranked number one as a mail-in pharmacy, in addition to its "most admired" ratings (Medco.com® Web site). As a HIP investor, you want to seek out quantifiable results like these, but be conscious that companies' self-reports can be selective about descriptions.

The government also can sometimes be a source of information. For example, see the U.S. Department of Transportation's tabulation of complaints about airlines, where you can find out that Southwest Airlines typically has the fewest complaints (such as its 2008 record of 0.25 complaints per 100,000 passenger equivalents, or approximately one complaint for every 400,000 customers) (Office of Aviation Enforcement and Proceedings 2008, 49).

Since customers directly generate top-line revenue, tracking this metric in your investment evaluation can be highly valuable. In half of the largest 500 firms, there is some source of third-party or self-reported information regarding how well a firm is serving its customers.

Employee Satisfaction (Engagement) and Retention   Employee satisfaction is linked with good customer relations and with overall increased productivity—again, factors that seem obvious as smart business. HIP investors should look for measures of employee satisfaction such as high employee retention rates (also reported as low turnover rates).

Daniel Goleman, the driver behind the emotional intelligence movement, outlined in his book *Primal Leadership* that optimistic, enthusiastic leaders more easily retain their people, compared with those bosses who tend toward negative moods. Employees who feel upbeat please customers and therefore improve your bottom line. Research finds that an increase of 1 percent in service to customers triggers a 2 percent increase in revenues. When employees are not happy or fulfilled, they leave faster, which again affects customers (sometimes for up to three years). As you might surmise, the research also indicates that 50 percent to 70 percent of employee satisfaction is tied to their direct manager. Hence, some companies look at employee engagement to surface which managers are performing or not.

The additional link to shareholder value is shown in Wharton finance professor Alex Edmans's discovery of shareholder value outperformance of 4 percent annually by the firms in *Fortune*'s annual listing of "The Best Companies to Work For." Employee retention in the energy, materials, and utilities industries is very high, which in turn builds up collective corporate expertise and ensures long-term stability. Leaders include Ball Corp with a global retention rate of 94 percent (ranging from 85 percent in Asia, to 97 percent in

North America). Energy firms like Hess and Marathon (with 95 percent and 94 percent retention rates respectively), and utilities like Duke (95 percent) (Duke Energy 2009) and Constellation Energy (91 percent of graduates stay five years or more) treat employees as long-term assets that contribute to higher customer satisfaction and financial results.

Meanwhile, in the much lower paid retail sector, companies like Best Buy contend with staff turnover rates as high as 64 percent (Best Buy CSR 2009, 15). The Apple stores and their "genius bars" claim a significantly higher 80 percent retention (Apple Store Web site). Family Dollar stores have brought their manager retention rates up to 70 percent-plus, an improvement of another one in ten leaders, according to investor relations manager Kiley Rawlins (phone interview, Jan. 26, 2009). The leaders have found that high retention rates boost customer service and hence revenue, while keeping turnover costs low, yielding a profit advantage.

To head off employee turnover and to promote high staff engagement and retention, financial software company Intuit proactively addresses employee engagement and managerial competence. Intuit comprehensively surveys its 8,000+ staff annually in November about overall satisfaction with the work environment and managers (*Fortune* 2008). Intuit typically gathers a phenomenal 92 percent+ response rate with its online survey. The results scores are then used by managers to start a dialogue with employees about ways to improve the workplace. Sometimes this leads to clearer manager communication or improved focus to address important issues. For the manager's senior leaders the scores can also indicate opportunities for leadership development, coaching, or a role change. Intuit's investment in high retention has kept turnover—and the associated costs—lower than competitors.

A HIP portfolio that rates both customer and employee satisfaction highly is a major factor in portfolio outperformance. Unfortunately, only one in five of the largest 500 companies reveal their employee satisfaction or retention scores. The companies that do report such scores tend to attract the best talent and, when factored into an overall quantitative evaluation, rank as top performers financially as well. However, it should be noted that during times of economic distress (or a recession), employees tend to stick it out under less than tolerable situations, so retention rates should be looked at carefully.

Table 4.1   General Mills "TriHealthAlon"
Health Improvements

Lifestyle Risk Factor	1985	2005	Change
Smoking	21%	8%	−13%
Use a seat belt	44%	84%	+40%
Know cholesterol	9%	51%	+42%
Know blood pressure	35%	54%	+19%

Source: General Mills via Academy of Industrial Hygiene newsletter,
Fall 2006; http://www.aiha.org/1documents/aih/Diplo06-3.pdf.

Employee Health and Wellness (Access + Programs)   Employee
health and well-being has a direct effect on company well-being and
profitability. HIP investors should look for companies that provide
health insurance coverage for the majority of its employees. Higher
HIP scores flow from companies that go further and invest in wellness
programs that promote healthy lifestyles.

A quarter-century ago, General Mills recognized that its sales
force needed to get healthier. The sales staff spent much of their time
on the road or working from home where it was difficult to exercise
regularly, eat well, and maintain a healthy lifestyle. The company
initiated a pilot program called "TriHealthAlon" (like triathlon races
for health) to improve three aspects: their physical, social, and mental
well-being.

After its launch in 1986, the results for its 1,500-strong sales staff
across North America were impressive. Table 4.1 shows the improvements in "Lifestyle Risk Factors."

Gary Olmstead, director of safety and environmental management for General Mills, wrote about these results and the concept
of this pioneering wellness program in the *Academy of Industrial Hygiene* in Fall 2006 (Olmstead 2006). Olmstead advocates for wellness
programs that can improve health, leading to a staff that is more
productive and absent less, gets injured less frequently, and recov-
ers more quickly if injured. Therefore, the employee wins and the
company wins.

Safeway Inc. has blended employee engagement with wellness
initiatives. At Safeway's headquarters in Pleasanton, California, corporate staff compete against each other to get more fit and lose
weight, just like the TV reality show "The Biggest Loser." Friendly

competition to get healthier, has emerged. Safeway has even helped convert retail space nearby into fitness centers (Supermarket News Web site). Overall wellness initiatives at Safeway have kept health care costs for the company flat on a per capita basis, according to its CEO Steve Burd. In addition, employees with a Body Mass Index (BMI) of less than 30—the definition of obese—can pay $318 per year less for health insurance Those who reduce their weight can also get paid to do so. Overall, this is very HIP: healthier staff leads to longer life, more savings, and lower costs for Safeway (NPR radio).

Since these initiatives improve employee productivity and reduce future health or insurance expenses, companies invest in them. A number of top companies, across a wide variety of industries, have initiated wellness initiatives and increased health care coverage, for example:

- Whirlpool offers health coaches to advise on weight loss and stress reduction (Definity Health, n.d).
- John Deere, in addition to similar programs described above, offers tobacco-cessation programs that are effective in helping employees quit smoking (John Deere 2003).
- EcoLab started covering 100 percent of preventive care for associates and families covered by the U.S. medical plans (Eco-Lab 2007).
- KLA-Tencor funds 100 percent of preventative health expenses (KLA-Tencor 2006).
- Starbucks pays for health care for part-time workers (over 20 hours) as well as full-timers (Starbucks Web site).
- JC Penney and Macy's offer subsidized coverage for part-timers.
- Whole Foods Market provides health care at no cost to eligible full-time team members (working more than 30 hours weekly) (Whole Foods Market Web site).
- Industrial firm Monsanto's Canada unit cover 100 percent of health premiums for 100 percent of employees (Yerema 2009) and provides parental leave benefits for up to 26 weeks.
- Financial firm Invesco in the UK also offers employees access to legal advice, financial management, and even beauty therapists. (Invesco Web site)
- Walmart uses its scale of nearly 2 million employees to keep health care premiums affordable. In the United States,

employees can pay as little as $11 a month for coverage, with low premiums for dependent children (as little as 30 cents more). While one in 10 staff has no health care coverage from any source, nearly half get coverage from Walmart, with the remainder through other sources like a spouse or Medicare (Walmart, *Healthcare Benefits*, n.d).

As a HIP investor, you will find that four in five of the 500 largest companies have enough details that explain the benefits, and some details of health care coverage. One quarter of them typically have descriptions of the amounts or share the company or employee pays. The more staff covered, and the more a company pays, the higher the HIP score on wellness and health for employees. These companies realize higher staff productivity, and retention and thereby lower expenses in the long term, thereby contributing to financial success and human impact.

Employee Safety   Like employee health and wellness, a safe work environment has many financial benefits to companies—more consistent productivity, high staff morale, lower medical expenses or insurance premiums—and it produces a positive return on investment for a group of the company's most valuable assets: its employees.

When former Secretary of the Treasury and now health care process and measurement innovator Paul O'Neill took over as CEO of Alcoa in 1987, employee morale was extremely low. O'Neill saw that employees needed to feel respected, supported and valued: "A bedrock, non-negotiable pre-condition was safety: every employee in the world, in every Alcoa operation, in every country, will go home safe at the end of the workday" (O'Neill 2002).

O'Neill's initiative to build a safety culture drastically reduced injuries in the high-risk work environment of aluminum refining and can production factories. CEO O'Neill saw it as people-focused first, cultivating trust among the employees by focusing on their welfare first, and ensuring that "employees would prosper" along with management, not at the expense of management.

What resulted was a compelling transformation. Total reportable incidents dropped from 1.87 per hundred workers to 0.11 from 1987 to 2000. (Manufacturing costs per unit stabilized, and profitability returned to Alcoa.) O'Neill's health-focused initiative, measurable in its results, created a profitable environment because of its focus on employees (which through acquisitions grew another 100,000 employees during O'Neill's tenure). Job safety became the core metric on which senior executives were measured (Carlson School of Management 2002). For shareholders, his focus on human impact and profit multiplied Alcoa's shareholder value by 10 times from $2.9 billion in 1987 when he started, to $29.9 billion when he retired in 2000 (Krause 2005, 3).

Most industrial and energy companies treat safety seriously. For example, Valero Energy, who is as opaque as you can get in the energy industry (see Fast Company feature on Big Oil, 2008), has been a consistent leader in Occupational Safety and Health Administration's (OSHA) refinery safety program. As Amy Feldman, Sara Olsen and I wrote in February 2008 in our Fast Company feature on Oil "[e]leven of its 17 refineries have achieved 'star site' status in OSHA's prestigious Voluntary Protection Programs, a level achieved by only 23 of the 149 refineries in the country. This means Valero's refineries have continually maintained an injury and illness rate at least 33 percent below the industry average" (Fast Company 2008). Until the recent erosion in oil prices, Valero also produced strong financial results.

You would imagine that industrial companies might experience the highest rates of injury. Yet while they are dangerous, safety is closely managed and measured. For example,

- Agricultural equipment maker John Deere won 77 awards in 2007 from the U.S. National Safety Council for low injuries (0.25 lost time injuries per 100 workers, or 200,000 hours worked), including its heavy-manufacturing plant in Waterloo, Iowa for the best safety record in that class (John Deere 2007).
- Engineering and construction firm Fluor aggressively managed to a 0.28 safety case rate that also included subcontractors.
- Oil services leader Cameron had no lost-time incidents in 2007.

Within an industry, performance can vary widely. In aerospace and defense, while Northrop Grumman has dropped its safety "case rate" from 5.28 in 2004 to 3.39 in 2007, a 30 percent drop (Northrop Grumman Annual Report 2007, 11), its competitor Rockwell Collins has a "case rate" of 1.2 injuries per 100 workers in 2008, a major reduction from its 3.9 rate in 1993.

Surprisingly, retail presents a more physically dangerous work environment:

- Workers at The Gap (both manufacturing and stores) experienced 4.29 injuries per 200,000 hours worked in 2008, reduced from 5.66 in 2004 (Gap Inc. Web site).
- Starbucks (stores only) experienced 5.46 injuries per hundred workers in 2007, down from 7.19 in 2005.
- Best Buy's workers in distribution centers had an 8.6 percent case rate in 2007, with a 5.0 percent rate in delivery distribution, and 4.4 percent in the retail stores (Best Buy 2009).

More than half of the largest 500 companies do not report job safety information, while 3 in 10 report some form of comprehensive quantifiable performance, with the remainder sharing anecdotes, goals for reduction, or specifics about smaller units of the public company. In some cases, OSHA statistics may be available. When looking at these job safety statistics note that some companies report total injuries per 100 workers and others report total injuries per 100 workers which result in lost days of work (which is much lower than total injuries). In 2008, average injuries across all industries was 4.2 per 100 workers, while injuries resulting in days of work lost was 1.2 per 100 workers (BLS Web site). HIP investors should look for companies that do report statistics (particularly in sectors or industries with higher rates and for trends that reflect continued improvements in safety related statistics). The OSHA Web site publishes a "watch list" for companies with higher safety risks.

Supplier Safety Outsourcing of manufacturing has become the norm for many companies. Manufacturing's share of the U.S. economy has dropped from 27 percent of U.S. GDP in 1950 to 11.5 percent in 2008. Well-managed companies tend to have codes of conduct for positive treatment of a supplier's workforce, and track performance in safety and health. This practice will tend to yield higher quality and more consistency among the products and services sourced outside the company. Likewise, some of the same benefits that flow from those practices for in-house programs will accrue when applied to suppliers.

When work is outsourced, there is the risk that standards for how the work is performed may not be closely managed. For example, Royal Dutch Shell experienced 37 workplace fatalities in 2006, many related to violence in Nigeria. We know that because Shell does track its injury rates for not only its 100,000 employees, but also for its 300,000 contractors. ENI, Italy's leading oil producer, provides access to health care for both its staff and its contractors worldwide. ENI supports 300 health clinics globally, helping to keep its accident rate for all staff near an all-time low in 2006 (ENI CSR 2006, 41).

HIP investors should look for those companies that proactively measure and manage their suppliers.

Stakeholder and Community Health   Corporations can both benefit their bottom line and reduce their overall operating risk by engaging the communities in which they operate. Many non-U.S. markets (think India, China and Brazil) provide high-growth opportunities for creative corporate approaches.

For example, in Rio de Janeiro, the health care firm Johnson and Johnson (J&J) has partnered with Mobile Metrix, a nonprofit, to investigate the needs of the low income, base-of-the-pyramid communities. Mobile Metrix provides quantitative numbers about how many people live there, what their health needs are, and how much income is available for products that improve life and health. The nonprofit pays locals to collect the information with handheld digital devices, which create jobs as well (Katz 2009). "We can help increase access to health care, boost income for those collecting the data, and create a new market for corporations," says Melanie Edwards, founder of Mobile Metrix. J&J can then target the right products to the right customers—something not possible without this census-type data. It also generates new revenues and profits while the community's health profile increases with access to affordable health care products, the wealth from income-paying jobs goes up, and more Equality is realized.

Company investments in local infrastructure both improve the manufacturing and distribution of their products and benefit the members of the community overall. The Manual Distribution Centers created by Coca-Cola in Africa are an example of improved infrastructure. Coca-Cola has helped employ individuals who deliver products by bicycle or pushcart in areas with unstable roads, which can benefit the overall community (Coca-Cola CSR 2008, 50). How's this HIP? More infrastructure improves the local community, through jobs and higher incomes for locals, while higher revenue and market share benefits Coca-Cola. According to an estimate by the UN's International Fund for Agricultural Development, towns and villages in Africa with smooth roads and easier access produce one-third more crops per hectare than those with poor infrastructure. In addition, the farmers pay 14 percent less for fertilizing their production and collect incomes that are 12 percent higher. Another study has shown that $1 in road maintenance in Africa lowers annual maintenance costs on vehicles by at least $2, a payback of 2 to 1 or more (The Economist 2002).

Savvy corporations like Marathon Oil, Dow, and DuPont regularly invest in infrastructure in the course of their normal international operations. Big energy companies have learned to be proactive about evaluating the environmental impacts of new projects and adapting their plans to minimize damage. Companies describing tangible results in these types of initiatives tend to be better managed, and result in higher shareholder value over time.

HIP investors should look for companies that describe value-adding investment in local infrastructure. Typically, investment in local communities helps establish relationships to expanding global markets.

Wealth

Creating wealth—for customers, employees, and shareholders—is a HIP practice.

Some companies focus on creating wealth for customers. At the entrance to a very famous corporate headquarters there is a sign that calculates the march toward that goal: "So far this year, we've saved families: $260,000,000,000." (City Data) That sign, as you might guess, is in Bentonville, Arkansas at Walmart's home office, where I visited in July 2008. Founder Sam Walton said years ago, "If we work together, we'll lower the cost of living for everyone . . . we'll give the world an opportunity to see what it's like to have a better life" (Live Better Index Web site).

That $260 billion is a cumulative savings in the cost of living to all customers over more than 20 years (1985 to 2006). It counts not only the lower prices at Walmart, but also the prices lowered by competitors when Walmart enters their market. Depending on the product, some prices can be 5 percent to 25 percent lower for similar goods compared to other outlets. The overall impact of this savings is estimated at $2,500 per household in the United States. For example, since September 2006, Walmart's $4 generic pharmaceutical program has saved consumers more than $1 billion (Business Planning Solutions 2007).

Yet HIP investors should note that emphasis on low prices is a dangerous sole metric. In fact, Walmart's historical focus on "always low prices" also led to episodes of social inequality and less environmentally friendly materials, like toxic paint on toy trains and other negative impacts detailed in movies like *The High Cost of Low Prices*. HIP investors should be looking for ideas like Walmart's new mission, "Save money, live better," which brings to the forefront additional criteria beyond "buying just on brand or on price," says Rand Waddoups, Walmart's senior director of sustainability. "We see a long-term and more comprehensive approach to valuing sustainability, which serves the customer and society, with benefits for the shareholder, too."

Other leading firms have focused on increasing customer wealth, as well. Financial firm Discover Card has introduced tools to better manage your finances showing how to best manage your credit card payments. Intuit acquired Mint.com, which helps more than 550,000 users reduce their interest payments on student loans, credit cards and other liabilities, and find higher interest rates on their bank accounts (Finkle 2009). Saving customers' money cultivates repeat purchases and word of mouth referrals. Customers build trust in the brands that "help them find the best prices," like Progressive Insurance does with its online comparison engine.

Industry-wide price comparisons are not easy—particularly if you are interested in factoring in other elements. For example, the HIP Scorecard on Big Oil in February 2008, attempted to do an industry-wide price comparison of which gasoline sellers are the "best deals" for customers. The tools are not yet available to do this comprehensively, but in the California market, Valero tended to be priced the least versus its competitors Chevron and BP. So, while Valero's HIP score was the lowest, this customer savings brought them higher market share and revenues, while creating economic benefit for the customer.

HIP Wealth Metrics

A HIP investor should also examine how companies build wealth for employees. The following metrics can be useful in evaluating which companies are top performers. Leading companies boost the income and assets of their employees, resulting in stronger financials for everyday employees and for their long-term bottom line.

Four metrics relating to growing employee and community income and assets provide good insight into wealth creation—for shareholders and for a firm's stakeholders. They include:

1. How a firm provides for employees' future savings and retirement.
2. The level of employee pay relative to industry peers.
3. The CEO's compensation relative to average staff pay.
4. The cash amounts charitably "invested" in the community.

Employee Wealth Matching (Retirement, Options, Pensions)   As described above, for customers to be truly satisfied, employees need to consistently perform well; and to achieve that, employees must be satisfied with their employers. HIP companies seek to align their goals with employee goals through wealth-matching programs. These programs can vary from pensions, to 401(k) matching, to access to company stock, and options to buy that stock. Offering ownership in the company is an excellent tool for aligning employee and employer interests. For example, financial software company Intuit promises to grant stock options to all employees—it also earns very high employee engagement scores, a likely indicator of satisfied and returning customers (Intuit Web site).

It is not easy to compare wealth-matching programs across companies. They vary not only by investment type (pension, 401(k), stock grant) but also by the rate of matching employee contributions. The best plans typically match 6 percent of employee contributions, which in simplest form can be a dollar-for-dollar approach. A sample of the various wealth-creating methods is shown below:

- National Semiconductor matches 150 percent for the first 4 percent, which equates to a net 6 percent contribution by the company (National Semiconductor Annual Report 2008, 86).
- Sherwin-Williams, in addition to its 6 percent matching for employee savings, also contributes 7 percent of an employee's salary to a pension plan that vests over three years (Sherwin-Williams Web site).

- First Energy's savings plans let employees deduct up to a maximum of 75 percent of base pay to stock it away for the future (First Energy Corp. Web site).
- Intuitive Surgical and Patterson both offer half-time employees access to stock ownership and wealth matching (Equity Market Partners 2009, 70). They can also buy company stock through payroll deductions at a 15 percent discount.
- At Whole Foods, more than 13,000 staff received stock options from the company (Whole Foods 2007 10-K, 13). Leadership grants recognize team member performance, and service hour grants recognize employee actions in the community (these totaled nearly half of the stock grants in 2007). In addition, more than 2,000 staff choose to buy Whole Foods stock quarterly at a 5 percent discount, collected through payroll deductions.

Companies applying an inclusive approach, like Whole Foods Markets, cultivate strong staff loyalty and lower turnover, leading to higher customer satisfaction. Whole Foods shareholder value consistently grew until its erosion in 2006 to 2008 from competitive pressures. Whole Foods commitment to employees' compensation and benefits may have helped contribute to its 2009 out-performance against the S&P 500.

HIP investors can look at three main metrics for employee wealth matching:

1. How many employees benefit from wealth matching? The best are 100 percent, all eligible employees, including part timers.
2. How much pay is matched? Six percent matched at 100 percent is top tier; energy and utility firms can be even higher.
3. Is there a discount for buying company stock? Up to 15 percent discounts are offered by the most generous companies, typically in high-tech.

Employee Pay (Relative to Industry Peers) If people flock to the highest pay, then why doesn't everyone work in financial services, health care, or technology sectors that exhibit the highest pay rates? And why would anyone work in retail or food service sectors characterized by the lowest pay rates? In fact, absolute pay levels do not alone provide the necessary information. Indeed, leaders in each sector may not necessarily pay the highest. For example, Disney historically pays under the average compensation for the opportunity to work with the "Magic Kingdom." Top-paying firms, especially in investment banking, typically want staff to put in extraordinarily long hours. But the level of relative pay within an industry or sector does tend to be a contributing factor for a HIP portfolio.

HIP investors don't have an easy job figuring out pay levels. Despite the detailed financial statements issued by companies, it is rare to find a total compensation number to divide by the total number of staff to calculate an average pay per employee.

There are some sources of limited compensation information. Employees self-report pay at Web sites like PayScale, SimplyHired and JobNob. Yet these are not very reliable—the number of respondents is a small fraction of the entire company, and the pay rates reported tend to be those of higher paid managers, scientists, and executives. Some of the Web sites have features to adjust for geography, years of experience, and role, which can help yield a more reliable estimate.

For a HIP portfolio, proceed with caution. Check to make sure there are enough respondents to make the information comparable. Be careful in calculating averages, as the number of employees who reply varies by years of experience, job type, and geography. A HIP investor can calculate a weighted average adjusting for those factors to make the numbers more comparable. This research can help set the stage for identifying companies with pay policies consistent with balanced wealth creation for employees, not just executives.

CEO Compensation Relative to Average Staff Pay   How is the ratio of CEO compensation to average staff pay useful to a HIP investor? One expects higher levels of CEO compensation to correlate to increased shareholder value. But how does the ratio of CEO-to-worker pay correlate with higher financial performance? For an overall portfolio, we have calculated that a lower ratio correlates to higher levels of financial performance. However, results for individual companies may vary widely. HIP investors realize that CEOs can be paid relative to increases in long-term shareholder value, but that overall lower CEO-to-worker pay ratios connote more employees sharing in the wealth, which fosters higher employee dedication and productivity resulting in financial success—for the CEO, the workers, and you as an investor.

Each year the *Wall Street Journal* runs a special section on executive pay. In 2008, in conjunction with The Hay Group, a compensation consultant, they calculated the total amount of executive compensation, including salary, benefits, and grants of stock and options.

According to The Corporate Library, the average compensation for an S&P 500 CEO was $10.4 million in 2008. The average worker's compensation is just over $40,000, according to the Bureau of Labor Statistics, based on a 40-hour work week and median employee wages of $20.62 per hour in 2008. Therefore, the average CEO makes more than 300 times the average worker's pay. Figure 4.2 shows the historical averages of this ratio, which peaked in the year 2000 at more than 500 times or just over 40 times in 1980.

As a HIP investor, you can research these figures easily at the Web site for the AFL-CIO (http://www.aflcio.org/corporatewatch/ paywatch/), the largest union organization in the United States. You can also view the differences in calculations compared to the

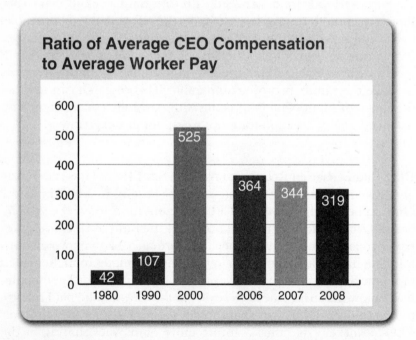

Figure 4.2   Ratio of Average CEO Compensation to Average Worker Pay

Source: Institute for Policy Studies; United for a Fair Economy.

Securities and Exchange Commission (SEC). The AFL-CIO calculates what the stock and option grants are worth at fair value.

To calculate a score, take the CEO compensation from the AFL-CIO database, and divide by an estimate of the average workers pay. About one-sixth of the S&P 500 score under 100 for this ratio. Some include CEOs who already own plenty of stock like Steve Jobs of Apple, Jerry Yang of Yahoo!, and Marc Benioff of salesforce.com. Highest ratio companies score over 500, many of who are in the financial industry. Some even score over 1000, like Bob Simpson of XTO Energy and Eugene Isenberg of Nabors Industries, whose companies beat the S&P 500 during years of rising oil prices, but have been more at parity as energy prices have stabilized.

Community Development Investment (Including Cash to Charity)
While charity investments do not directly create business value (and indeed cannot for the foundation to retain tax-free status), it is a leading indicator of how the corporation engages with the community. Our research indicates that the most HIP companies engage in community development investments, which many categorize as charity or foundation grants. While this is the only non-profit measure in the HIP metrics, the business value is that the best programs foster employee involvement in society, which three in four employees want their company to do. (Cone survey, 2007). It also improves relationships with communities (which are made up of consumers) and benefits the corporate brand, which in turn can lead to higher market share.

Tax law prohibits corporations from getting a direct benefit from their charitable giving. But that doesn't restrict the corporation from seeking to solve a core human problem effectively, especially if the giving is in the same field of expertise. Financial firm Charles Schwab's foundation seeks to boost the "financial fitness" and economic literacy of youth and adults, so they better manage savings, spending, and investing. Executive director Carrie Schwab-Pomerantz writes a syndicated column on managing money better.

A company who takes seriously the opportunity to generate human impact, using their products and people, is salesforce.com Inc. The business value translates into higher employee engagement (from volunteering), which boosts productivity. It also can lead to innovations in product features, like those from non-profit customers that it serves with free software.

Before salesforce.com's first-year anniversary in 2001, CEO Marc Benioff created the Salesforce.com Foundation with a unique "1-1-1" model, covering 1 percent each of equity, time and product. One percent of founding equity stock would be used for charitable grants, which in 2008 funded $4.7 million in grants focused on youth and technology. One percent of paid employee time (or 20 hours) is available yearly for volunteering, (the current policy is actually six paid days, or 2.4 percent of staff time or 38,000 employee hours in 2008). One percent of product translates into "in kind" donations of software-seats to nonprofits to help them achieve their social missions more efficiently. Of the nonprofits surveyed, 22 percent reported decreases in the costs of fundraising, and 28 percent increased their productivity in fundraising or earning income (Salesforce Foundation 2008).

In addition, "we have used our own salesforce.com technology to closely monitor and measure the success of our employee volunteer programs and product donations," says Suzanne di Bianca, executive director of the Salesforce.com Foundation. "For example, we can click a dashboard and see at a glance how many of the nonprofits we have donated product to are logging into the system on a regular basis, adding custom fields." This provides metrics on usage to generate more innovation, and hence where the organization can focus its resources efficiently.

Another great example of corporate giving directly flowing from its business is GE's Developing Health Globally program. GE Healthcare business unit's "base of the pyramid" strategy markets medical products to middle-income economies, like China and India. At the same time, low-income economies like Cambodia, Ghana and Honduras are in need of life-saving equipment, which they cannot afford. Top GE engineers and managers, many of whom work on ecomagination or healthymagination products, are rewarded with opportunities to implement new hospital technologies in these regions.

Project director Krista Bauer says GE manages product-based donations in a sustainable manner. "If you put it in the field, you need to have a positive impact, and need to own the results," Bauer says. The goal is to increase the people impacted per dollar spent, which Developing Health Globally estimates at 4.8 million, based on a charitable "investment" of $40 million, or about $8 per person.

Unfortunately, most corporate foundations are not systematic about tracking their quantifiable impacts. The disciplined management of the rest of the corporation doesn't regularly flow over to how charitable "investments" are made. The donations, whether dollars or in-kind, are tracked—but how does a HIP investor gauge a "return on charitable investment"? Even the rankings of top corporate foundation philanthropy by *BusinessWeek* or *Chronicle of Philanthropy* do not yet track these resulting impacts.

A HIP investor can examine both the cash donated and the in-kind product contributions comparatively across companies. Since product donations are difficult to compare, especially with high-margin products like pharmaceuticals and software, a more consistent measure is cash donated as a percent of revenue. (Reported profits are a volatile measure as a denominator for this metric, as they can vary widely from year to year.) Overall, community investments create value in the community and benefit the business, especially where employees are engaged more deeply. This benefits the bottom line because staff are happier in their work and feel more fulfilled, and that leads to great service for customers and innovations from staff.

Earth

How much is the earth worth to you? If you had to pay for the formation of soil, addition of nutrients, or pollination of flowers, how much would it total? Back in 1997, several scientists estimated the total value of "ecosystem services" at $14 to $54 trillion—the average, $33 trillion, was almost twice the worldwide GDP that year (Staff of World Resources Program 1998).

Companies are now realizing the value to be gained by optimizing earth's resources, not just extracting or mining them. One leader is Kohlberg Kravis Roberts (KKR), the famed private equity firm, which owns over 45 companies including Toys 'R' Us and mattress maker Sealy (Environmental Leader 2008). Since May 2008, KKR has partnered with the Environmental Defense Fund (EDF) on a Green Portfolio Project to develop metrics and test which eco-efficient initiatives are most valuable to the business. As of February 2009, their collaborative initiatives at Sealy realized $16 million in bottom-line benefit and saved 25,000 metric tons of greenhouse gas emission, including reduced mattress scrap and advanced trucking efficiency. EDF is taking the lessons learned from these initiatives to other firms in the KKR portfolio, constructing a "how-to" guide and Web site (Environmental Defense Fund 2009; Kohlberg Kravis Roberts & Co. Web site).

Public companies are increasingly tracking these types of earth-related metrics, from waste to water to carbon and energy. As a HIP investor, you will see improvements in reporting these metrics over time, and will be better prepared to identify leading companies who will have higher profits and shareholder value.

HIP Earth Metrics

Companies focused on optimizing earth's resources can benefit from lower material, energy, and water bills, as well as earn tax savings for renewable energy investments and spur innovation of new revenue from customers seeking eco-efficient products as well as enhancing the value of the brand. As Innovest's *carbon beta* analysis, TruCost's *profit at risk* evaluation and HIP Investor's own calculations have shown, a portfolio of these top performers in Earth impacts yield higher returns and are positioned for lower financial risk.

In September 2009, Hewlett Packard earned the top spot on Newsweek's Green Rankings (*Newsweek*). HP is also a top-rated company in the Earth category of HIP metrics. How are they achieving this top performance?

"We are de-materializing our products' businesses," says Bonnie Nixon, Director of Environmental Sustainability for HP, "and trans-materializing our company to provide more services." What does that mean? Instead of computers, HP is selling computing services. Instead of printers, it seeks to sell more printing services. "We will manage a whole fleet of printers and do it responsibly." HP expects this strategic shift to generate higher margins and a more stable future (Nixon 2009).

When it does build printers, HP is now designing for disassembly as well. The result of this new design has reduced the production cost by 8 percent. It also helps to meet the European mandate for re-capturing and "taking back" technology from customers at the end of the useful life.

Cummins Engine, United Technologies, Eastman Kodak and Pfizer pharmaceuticals are among the top companies benefiting from efforts to optimize earth resources.

A HIP investor can track four main drivers of Earth impacts:

1. Waste Re-usage
2. Water Efficiency
3. Energy Efficiency
4. Greenhouse Gas Emissions

How can a HIP investor discover this very meaningful information? Leading companies disclose this information willingly as they increase transparency about these ecological factors. The Carbon Disclosure Project Web site collects emissions and energy-related data from firms globally. Further detail on leaks, spillage, and accidents can sometimes be found through the U.S. EPA. A more HIP firm offers more disclosure and typically more efficient performance in these Earth metrics. As these leading indicators both signify increased risks and likely higher costs, firms that measure them, manage them, and communicate transparently outside the company tend to be better managed. Hence a HIP investor can use them to identify companies for a more HIP portfolio.

Waste Re-usage, Re-cycle, and Re-sale; Resource Efficiency   Limiting waste is an obvious benefit: it can reduce costs and lessen the amount of resources used. So, how are we doing? About 6 percent of all the material inputs going into a manufacturing process come out the other end as a finished product while 94 percent can be un-used or wasted, according to INSEAD professor Robert Underwood Ayres.

Ten tons of active mass raw materials, not including construction materials, per person is extracted from U.S. territory by the economy, Ayres estimated in 1989. "Roughly 75 percent is mineral and non-renewable while 25 percent is, in principle, from renewable sources," Ayres wrote back then. "Six percent of the total is embodied in durable products. The other 94 percent is converted into waste residuals as fast as it is extracted. The tonnages of waste residuals are actually greater than the tonnages of crops, timber, fuels and minerals (because air and water contribute mass to the residuals)" (Ayres and Kneese 1989, 109–117).

Is that still true two decades later? "We ran numbers for a number of sectors, based on company-reported data a few years ago, and found numbers in similar range with some variation by sector of course," says Gil Friend, president of Natural Logic consulting, and author of *The Truth About Green Business*. "In my experience it's a very rare CEO who even has a guess of what the ratio is for his or her company. And the guess is usually very, very wrong" (Friend 2009).

Yet a number of firms are directly addressing the issue:

- DuPont now tracks "shareholder value per pound of product" as a metric of material efficiency relative to financials.

- Goodyear focuses on "zero waste to landfills." In 2007 all Goodyear manufacturing facilities in the United States fulfilled this goal (Environmental Leader 2008). Goodyear engineers also innovated a method of retreading without the use of organic solvents (Goodyear Web site).
- Hasbro has reduced 90 percent of waste related to manufacturing its U.S. game products in less than five years. At year-end 2007, 88 percent of that remaining waste was recycled (Hasbro Web site).
- General Mills recycles 88 percent of its waste. While 12 percent went to landfills in 2008, the goal is to reduce that by another 15 percent in the next five years (General Mills, CSR 2009).

It's obvious how eliminating waste eliminates cost and increases profit. It sometimes can even boost the top line revenue through what can be called "trash to cash." Waste Management Inc., a traditional garbage removal company, now considers itself a materials manager—it seeks out innovative ways to generate revenue from collecting and moving garbage. Today, it operates almost 300 landfills with associated collections and transfer points across North America, serving 20 million customers. Those landfills gestate gases like methane that can be recaptured and turned into energy. Since methane is also equivalent to 21 units of carbon emissions, capturing it can both power new energy-generation and reduce emissions. Waste Management's recycling revenues account for nearly 10 percent of its total revenue, as well. Cost centers, like trash, are becoming revenue centers for cash (Waste Management Social Responsibility Report 2006).

Re-manufacturing products and parts is another strategy for revenue generation with high resource efficiency. Cummins' subsidiary ReCon sells certified re-manufactured items that use 85 percent less energy than that of new products (Hromadka 2008). This results in savings for the customer through lower energy bills, reduces affiliated emissions, and grows that business unit's revenue.

HIP investors can find quantifiable information from the companies, as about a third of the largest companies disclose sufficient information, but more than half do not report any waste metrics, and only a fifth have anecdotal information. Currently 10 companies are leaders in recycling, reusing, or reselling waste, and keeping input costs lower, leading to financial benefits.

Water Efficiency, Re-capture and Re-use   Water is a precious resource that is increasingly strained. The planet is 70 percent water, but most of it is salt water. Fresh water is increasingly at risk and becoming scarce, which was evidenced in the Southeast United States in 2008. New products like Procter & Gamble's Coldwater Tide help customers reduce water at the point of use. Innovations like GE's desalinization equipment and Dow's water treatment membranes may help but these processes can be highly energy intensive and potentially expensive. Companies with water efficiency practices (particularly in industries or sectors that are heavily dependent on water) will be much better positioned for future growth and earnings. Some of the programs to look for include:

- Ball Corp. (46 percent water recycling) (Ball Corporation Web site) and Devon Energy (80 percent water recycling) (Tronche 2008) report water re-use in manufacturing and production processes which avoids taking new water from river systems and instead re-uses existing water in the ongoing processing.
- Micron Technology won an Environmental Excellence award in 2008 for using cold river water from an existing aquifer recharge system to cool its computer chip production (Micron Web site).
- Industrial companies like Parker Hannifin have set specific "water index" goals, calculated as water volume per million dollars of revenue. For Parker Hannifin, that rate in 2008 is 355 cubic meters of water per US$ million sales (Parker Hannifin 2008).
- On that water efficiency metric, leaders are realizing aggressive efficiency improvements such as Caterpillar (11 percent reduction), United Technologies (14 percent), and Abbott (21 percent). Citigroup and JP Morgan Chase also calculate total water usage per employee (Citigroup and JP Morgan Chase company reports).

Another factor to evaluate relates to water misuse. The U.S. Environmental Protection Agency (EPA) monitors wastewater discharges and other spills into water systems. While companies can report spills and cleanups as Occidental Petroleum and Chevron do, a HIP investor should be aware that these occurrences can create potential legal liabilities as well as negative earth impacts.

Like other Earth metrics, more than half of the S&P 500 companies are not yet reporting water, and about one in six are sharing partial information about specific sites or pilot programs recently initiated. For those firms that do report publicly and are efficient, a HIP investor can weight those with high reuse and recycling ratios for a portfolio seeking higher human impact and profit.

Energy Efficiency and Renewable Power   Energy efficiency clearly contributes to lower costs and lower environmental impact. A HIP investor will recognize that the power of eco-efficient initiatives amplifies when companies design for more than one goal. For example, cosmetics maker Estee Lauder converted 54 percent of its disposable waste to energy in 2007, saving costs in hauling waste and purchasing new energy. Estee Lauder has also become a renewable energy leader by partnering with DomeTech to install 3,200 solar panels at a fragrance factory, which supplies half of the plant's daytime energy needs—at a projected savings of 10,000 tons of carbon emissions over the life of the system. This installation is one of the largest solar energy systems in the United States outside a utility (Estee Lauder CSR 2007).

A HIP investor can estimate energy intensity and compare among industry peers. Some companies report energy usage (in gigajoules); others report kilowatt-hours of electric purchases—dividing either measure (usage or purchases) by revenue, you can compare energy intensity. You can then use that measure to compare across companies within a sector or to look at trends over time. Leading companies like Eastman Kodak report cutting energy usage by 36 percent from 2002 to 2007, representing consecutive annual reductions of 5 percent per year (Kodak Annual Report 2008).

Renewable energy eliminates the need for fossil fuels, their pollution, and the risks associated with volatile price swings—one of the most eco-efficient initiatives. A HIP investor may choose to value highly firms with on-site production, as shown in Table 4.2.

Another category of renewable energy initiatives includes renewable energy certificates (RECs), which like carbon offsets, allow a company to claim the benefit of "green energy purchases" for that produced by others. The EPA's Green Power Partnership recognizes the top purchasers of on-site renewable energy as well as RECs. Within that list, the top corporate renewable energy leaders by kilowatt-hours as of July 2009 are: Intel, PepsiCo, Whole Foods, Kohl's and Dell. An

Table 4.2   Top Renewable Energy On-Site

Company (on-site renewable kWh)	Share of Total Electricity	Type of Renewable Energy
Kimberly Clark (192mm)	7% of total	BioMass
Kohl's (19mm)	2%	Solar
Walmart (17mm)	1%	Solar
Johnson & Johnson (11.6mm)	1%	Biogas, Solar
Macy's (10.4mm)	3%	Solar
Safeway (4.5mm)	<1%	Solar

Source: Environmental Protection Agency, http://www.epa.gov/greenpower/toplists/top20onsite.htm.

investment in RECs supports production of renewable energy to the grid, but certificate purchasers still need to use nonrenewable energy to run their facilities. So, a REC purchaser gets positive branding and supports the advancement of renewable energy but does not necessarily benefit from the lower costs of that renewable energy.

In sectors like utilities, HIP investors can evaluate the mix of renewable power as an indicator of future financial risk. Higher proportions of fossil-based fuel, especially those relying on coal, can put those utilities' profits at risk when carbon legislation is implemented. Utilities like PG&E in California already generate 25 percent of their power from a mix of hydro, solar, wind, and geothermal sources. PG&E also generates nuclear power, which also reduces their carbon risk, though there are potential risks with disposal of nuclear fuel (PG&E, *Renewables* 2008). TruCost has estimated the highest impact of a carbon tax on potential profits to be utilities.

Greenhouse Gas Emissions, Intensity, and Reductions   By now we all have heard about the dangers posed by greenhouse gases, which are the summation of carbon and other emissions that pollute the earth. When any form of fossil energy is used, carbon is a natural byproduct. Thus as fuels like oil, natural gas, and coal are used to power planes, trains, and automobiles; generate electricity and heat; and as a feedstock for chemicals and plastics; carbon is quite embedded in our global economy.

HIP investors will recognize that companies that better manage their carbon intensity and accomplish reductions in emissions tend to outperform. These leaders realize lower costs, better manage risks, position for fewer liabilities, and generate revenue from customers seeking products with zero- or low-emissions products.

Tracking carbon is an emerging discipline. It has sprouted into a new field of managerial accounting. Companies that track their overall carbon emissions, from GE to Dow to Walmart, understand their carbon "footprint" and consequently know how to manage it. Reducing carbon leads to reductions of energy, cost and pollution.

The Carbon Disclosure Project (CDP), a nonprofit based in London with operations in New York through Rockefeller Philanthropy Advisors, is a clearinghouse of information on these greenhouse gas (GHG) emissions. The CDP involves 475 institutional investors representing $55 trillion of assets (CDP 2008). These include banks like HSBC, JP Morgan Chase, and Goldman Sachs.

The CDP is a reliable source of information on more than 2,000 organizations (corporations and governments) across 66 countries reporting emissions (CDP Web site). Each organization that reports to the CDP quantifies its overall emissions (tons of GHGs emitted by year), its goals for reduction, and its related operational and management processes. A HIP investor will want to know if a company is tracking its emissions and reporting that data. To date, two in three companies of the largest 500 in the United States have neither declared carbon reduction goals, nor time frames for potential reductions. While some companies may still be calculating them, others may still be ignoring the potential risks. HIP investors value the companies that disclose their emissions, set specific time tables for reductions, and benefit from the lower costs and risks associated with this path.

Table 4.3 shows U.S. corporations noted as leaders in carbon disclosure by CDP (note that their emissions intensity varies and that performance is not rated here).

Using either the CDP or a company's own disclosures, a HIP investor can compare levels of emissions in tons, divide them by either revenue or employee base of the company (or, where available, pounds or tons of product made), and evaluate who are leaders and laggards.

HIP investors should be aware that companies that do not report (about half of the largest 500 firms) or just report anecdotes (about 1 in 7) may not be reaping the benefits outlined above, or at least not communicating with investors about it, lowering their stock price and shareholder value.

HIP's analysis indicates that a portfolio that highly weights the leaders in emissions reduction can generate both a positive earth

Table 4.3   U.S. Companies Recognized by CDP as Leaders in Carbon Disclosure

Consumer and Health Care	Energy and Utilities	Materials and Industrials	Information Technology	Financials
Carnival	PG&E	Boeing	Cisco	Simon Property
Walmart	PSEG	Burlington	Hewlett Packard	Group
Schering-Plough	Con Ed	Northern	EMC	Allstate
J&J	FPL Group	UPS		
GlaxoSmithKline	Chevron	Praxair		
Biogen Idec	Spectra	DuPont		
	Hess			
	Anadarko			
	Transocean			

Source: Carbon Disclosure Project, 2009 report, page 19.

impact (fewer emissions) and increased opportunities for higher profit. Innovest's "Carbon Beta" analyses (now operated by RiskMetrics) and TruCost's index with the S&P 500 have found a positive relationship between emissions reduction and financial outperformance.

Equality

Global economics demand an understanding of the diversity of customers, employees and suppliers. As confirmed by Catalyst.org data, a HIP approach recognizes that the more diverse a company, the higher financial performance.

Alan Lafley, the former CEO of Procter & Gamble, the top-rated company in the HIP 100 Index in 2007 and 2008, is on the record for equality enabling even more innovation and competitive advantage. P&G is one of the most diverse enterprises in the United States and worldwide—a contributing factor to its 100+ year history of consumer products leadership. According to Lafley, "Diversity is a key business strategy that enables P&G to be 'in touch.' Diverse organizations will out-think, out-innovate and outperform a homogeneous organization every single time" (Diversity Inc Web site).

HIP Equality Metrics

The HIP metrics in Equality look across the spectrum of customers, employees, and suppliers. So, let's examine how to count quantifiable metrics in equality that create competitive advantage and drive business performance. HIP investors should look at:

1. Customer diversity
2. Board diversity
3. Employee diversity
4. Supplier diversity

Customer Diversity   A core HIP metric that every company can count is revenue by geography. It's easy enough to imagine the diversity of the world and how we are different. Successful companies discover what makes their product unique to customers, and can then build on that to grow revenue and income in new markets.

International revenue helps to diversify financial performance across countries with varying growth rates, currency values, and business cycles. International diversification stabilizes revenue variations. An added value of selling in another country is that it typically provides new jobs there—in sales, service, and accounting. These jobs create local wealth and begin a path to being more inclusive of the local society.

Firms with strong international revenue typically understand more about diversity than ones that are just serving local markets. With a world that will soon total 7 billion people, there is tremendous opportunity for growth, if you understand what human problems you can solve.

In fact, the 500 largest companies based in the United States do this very well. Approximately half of the total revenue generated by S&P 500 firms is outside their home country. In addition, some U.S.-based firms have more than 80 percent of their revenue generated internationally (see Table 4.4).

However, there is tremendous customer diversity without expanding outside your home country. Here in the United States, the business value of customer diversity can show up in top-line revenue as well. Procter & Gamble's global head of purchasing, Rick Hughes, says that ethnic consumers are often more brand loyal than some other groups, and "what we want to do is capture and capitalize on that brand loyalty" (Greene 2008, 138).

To evaluate how HIP a company is, look at its percentage of revenue in international markets—which is typically organized by continent (e.g., South America, Europe), region (e.g., Latin

Table 4.4   International Revenue Share, 2008

S&P 500 Firm	International Share of Revenue
Philip Morris International (consumer)	100%
Newmont Mining Corp. (energy)	95%
NVidia (tech)	92%
AMD (tech)	87%
Texas Instruments (tech)	87%
Qualcomm (tech)	87%
Intel Corp. (tech)	84%
Applied Materials (tech)	84%
AES Corp (energy)	81%
Colgate Palmolive (consumer)	80%

Source: Bespoke Investment Group.

America, Middle East, and Africa), and sometimes by large country (China is typically called out, like in the Yum! Brands example).

The higher rates of international revenue, as shown in Table 4.4, typically translate into more opportunities for growth, based on a wider view and understanding of customer needs worldwide. This builds on the trends that you read about in Chapter 2.

Board Diversity   Directors of Boards are intended to represent the interests of the investors in the company. In addition, directors are fiduciaries of the long-term interests of the company, which include how best to serve customers and employees.

Most consumer-focused companies serve a wide variety of customers across gender and ethnicity. However, the management of those companies is not always representative of the customer base that it serves, nor the workforce it represents. Individual investors are less diverse than the overall population and workforce.

According to the 2005 Census Report, the overall population of the United States is 51 percent women and 49 percent men, and ethnically it is 12.5 percent Hispanic, 12.3 percent African-American, 3.6 percent Asian-American, 0.9 percent Native American, and 75.1 percent Caucasian. In the United States, the workforce is nearly a 50-50 split among women and men, as the 2008–2009 recession's job losses have affected men four times more than women.

The HIP Equality metrics quantify diversity and analyze the proportion of human diversity at every level of the company. Since customers are the source of revenue, the HIP approach rates companies more highly for matching their leadership and workforce to the customer base diversity. Also, since the company purchases materials and services from suppliers, and creates jobs and entrepreneurial wealth, the HIP approach seeks to match that up to the population distribution of the societies where the company operates.

When evaluating a company on equality metrics, start at the top. The Board is intended to represent you as a shareholder, and to position the company for future customer and revenue growth. Does the company reflect those values in its Board composition?

In counting diversity at the Board level, we examine the total number of women and nonwhite males and divide by the total number on the Board. The higher that percentage, the more diverse. (In Table 4.5, we list the total number of woman and ethnic minorities—ethnic women are counted only once when calculating the diversity percentage.)

In our HIP analysis of the largest 500 companies based in the United States, there are only 10 firms (or 2 percent of the largest 500) with a Board diversity of 50 percent or above. Who are they? The list in Table 4.5 might surprise you:

Table 4.5   Most Diverse Boards, 2009

Company/Industry	Board Diversity	Board Diversity Composition
Pepsi Bottling Grp/Consumer (being acquired by PepsiCo)	60%	4 women, 3 ethnic (1 woman) on Board of 10
Archer Daniels Midland/ Agriculture	56%	3 women, 2 ethnic on Board of 9
Ryder System/Trucking	55%	4 women and 2 ethnic men of 11 total
Aetna/Insurance	54%	4 women, 3 ethnic men on Board of 13
Coach Inc./Consumer retail	50%	2 women, 2 ethnic men on Board of 8
Estee Lauder/Consumer retail	50%	6 women and 3 ethnic (2 are women) on Board of 14
Eastman Kodak/Consumer	50%	2 women, 5 ethnic (1 woman) on Board of 12
Pacific Gas & Electric/Utilities	50%	3 women, 3 ethnic (1 woman) on Board of 10
McKesson/Health care	44%	3 women, 1 ethnic, on Board of 9

Composition as of August 2009.
Source: Company Web sites; HIP analysis.

Why is this statistic valuable? An analysis by the Catalyst Inc. indicates that, when a Board has more women, it tends to have higher financial performance, whether return on equity, return on invested capital, or return on sales (profit). A second reason is that more diverse Boards beget more diverse executive teams and managers. This increased diversity strengthens the organization through a wider variety of new ideas to consider. Just like ecosystems, which require diversity and variation to ensure species survival, human diversity strengthens the long-term prospects of a company—and increases its likelihood of attractive financial results.

As HIP is an inclusive approach, you should also evaluate the least diverse Board—we see it as a leading indicator to weight the laggards lower on this criteria.

This may be difficult to believe, but there are more companies with no women or ethnic minorities on their Board than there are in our "best" category. These least-diverse Boards, shown in Table 4.6, are concentrated mostly in six industries.

Table 4.6   Least Diverse Boards, 2009

Industry	Companies
Consumer	Monster.com
	Philip Morris International
	L-3 Communications
Industrials	Allied Waste
	Equifax
	Expeditors
	Stericycle
	Republic
Materials	Titanium Metal Corp.
Energy	National Oilwell Varco
	Nabors Industries
	Pioneer Natural Resources
	Smith International
	XTO Energy
Info Tech	National Semiconductor
	Fidelity National Information Services
Financials	Invesco
	Kimco Realty

Composition as of August 2009.
Source: Company reports; HIP analysis.

These companies neither exclusively serve men as customers, nor do they have no ethnicities in their workforce. Thus, the governing Board of the company is not reflective of its own organization. This tends to increase the risk of "surprise" issues that can arise and creates the potential to miss new trends that may be evolving. While many of these companies are in technical specialties, they do face competitors who are more diverse.

A recognizable name on the least-diverse Board list is Philip Morris International (PMI). PMI was split from Phillip Morris Cos. in 2008 as the international "growth" company.

It is surprising that a consumer-focused company seeking to serve billions of consumers would not have a woman on its Board. While the first strength listed in its 2008 annual report is "the quality of our employees, represented by an experienced management team, strong organizational depth and a highly motivated and diverse professional workforce," that diversity is not well represented at the highest levels (Altria Group Web site). There is not a woman among its top 18 executives listed in the annual report. The only instance of the word "women" is a reference to charitable support for an anti-domestic violence organization. There are women employees in photographs of company staff in the last two pages of the online version of the report. A HIP investor might ask if a lack of women Board and executive team members is representative of a lack of interest by qualified women leaders to PMI's product, or a lack of invitation by the Board?

While men are more prevalent smokers in every country of the world (except Sweden), women still smoke—albeit at much lower rates. According to the World Bank, the male-to-female ratios of smokers tend to be closer in higher-income countries, with many fewer women smoking in lower-income countries. Maybe Philip Morris International has evaluated this and seen men as the core buyer of its cigarettes, but there are certainly women customers and staff whose interests may not be fully represented.

A HIP tenet is that the leadership, and especially the fiduciaries, of an organization should be representative of those it serves and is accountable to. With a comprehensive viewpoint, the Board of a company seeks to understand its customers and where future growth will come from, connect with employees as to how the company operates, and obtain multiple stakeholders' perspectives that highlight new opportunities or challenges for the enterprise. The

HIP measure of Board Diversity is a first step in balancing the multicultural nature of society. Leaders with high Board diversity tend to be well managed, open to new innovations, and producers of increased shareholder value beyond those that lag in this metric. Plus, it's 100 percent transparent to anyone who seeks to research it.

Employee Diversity   HIP investors know that diversity in the workforce adds great value. A HIP portfolio will give weight to those companies that intentionally build a workforce that reflects its underlying customer base (both actual and potential).

"We are not the old-fashioned manufacturing company my friend works for," says Ann H.S. Nicholson, the director of investor relations for Corning, a materials company that has pioneered innovations like heat shields for spaceflight, optical wires that run under the ocean to carry Internet traffic, and ceramic bakeware for your oven (Nicholson 2009).

Nicholson is referring to two elements of its equality results. First, Corning's overall diversity in terms of gender and ethnicity is highly global, covering over 27,000 staff across 70 locations worldwide (Corning Web site). Second, the systematic approach that Corning takes to ensure it is reflective of the societies it operates in and the customers to whom it sells. Both are reflective of a very HIP approach, because as the Catalyst.org data shows, the more diverse a company, the higher financial performance it realizes.

"We track ethnic minorities—from African-American to Asian-American—especially in the scientific communities we operate in, as well as gender diversity across payrolls and locations," says Nicholson. This is a unique practice amongst even the largest of companies, who are not as systematic as Corning around the world. One financial firm told HIP it was "illegal" to track in that way (but never provided the specific law or rule that applied). Many other firms have not prioritized it and thus have not built the tracking into their human resource systems. If it is not measured, then it cannot be easily managed.

Corning's methodical tracking of its diversity applies to all roles in the enterprise, from front-line worker to middle manager to senior executive. It also tracks equality metrics by each location and business division, before rolling it up to corporate-wide numbers. These metrics are then color-coded like a stoplight (red is big gap, yellow is small gap, green is on target) to visually see where there are deficiencies to the ultimate goals.

"We are 'green' in all categories," says Nicholson, fulfilling the goal of "striving to reflect the available workforce" especially for technical specialties. Corning's analysis compares its employee workforce to overall census sources from government tracking, though accurate information about population segments can lag by 18 months or more.

Corning pays attention to employee turnover and retention in each diversity category across gender and ethnicity, as well as the distribution of new hires into each unit of the company. Corning admits they are not "leading edge" but not a laggard either. The resulting positive environment for diverse talent has earned it recognition on *Fortune*'s "Best Places to Work" list and *Working Mothers* magazine.

There are several areas of diversity within the workforce that deserve special attention:

- Women staff and managers
- Ethnic staff and managers
- Gay and lesbian diversity

Women Staff and Managers   Twenty-five (or 5 percent) of the largest U.S.-based 500 companies have a workforce that is more than 40 percent women. The 40 percent benchmark has been the recent average of women in the full-time workforce. However, the recent recession has led to the elimination of more manufacturing and construction jobs, which tend to be heavily male. Thus, the male-female workforce balance is verging on an equally balanced 50 percent to 50 percent.

Catalyst Inc. has found that corporate Boards with higher gender diversity also lead to executive teams and managers with more gender diversity. This helps to strengthen the organization to meet the needs of its customers and its staff, helping to discover new markets and product innovations more attuned to the emerging trends.

Some may question whether financial performance improves for firms with higher women employees and managers as women are sometimes paid less for similar jobs. While this would be illegal in the United States, the leading companies are more diverse and outperform financially. Companies with the higher proportions of women tend to be in the consumer, financial, and health care industries, *which also have higher margins.* Hess Corporation is a stand-out in the energy industry, with 41 percent of its workforce comprised of women (Hess CSR 2007, 7) as is EOG Resources (39 percent) (*Fortune* 2008). Competitors like Chevron (29 percent) and ExxonMobil (25 percent) (CSR 2007, 15) had much lower proportions (Company Reports).

Yet in management, women leaders are consistently prevalent in the retail, media, and financial industries. Retail firms with the highest ratios of women managers are Nordstrom (73 percent), Liz Claiborne (65 percent of senior managers, one third of direct reports to the CEO), and Gap (61 percent of senior managers, more than half of direct reports to the CEO). In media, 50 percent of the top corporate officers are women at the Washington Post Cos. In the financial sector, Aetna (64 percent), Pitney Bowes (54 percent), XL Capital (44 percent), and SunTrust Banks (44 percent) are comfortable with high proportions of women executives and managers (Company Reports).

Surprises for low women manager representation include media conglomerate Meredith Corp., which reaches more than 30 million readers through 150 titles, including publishing *Family Circle*, *Ladies Home Journal*, and *Better Homes and Gardens*, and which has no women leaders listed on the Executive Committee of the management team (Meredith Web site). Online, Meredith's Women's Network has 15 million unique monthly visitors, so the lack of women managers becomes even more curious.

What is also surprising is that firms with very HIP products like Hospira's compostable IV bag, Stericycle's eco-friendly equipment, and Danaher's motion-control products, all lack women on their senior executive teams.

Based on the data, utilities and high-tech companies have fewer women in their workforces. Some of the lowest proportions are reported by Southern Company (24 percent) in utilities and Texas Instruments (23 percent) in high-tech. There are likely companies that are much further behind, but only one in five companies we evaluated report this type of quantitative information comprehensively. Another one in five communicate only incomplete anecdotes that pertain to one part of their business.

The HIP approach gives credit to companies who report numbers, even if they may not be the most positive relative to peers. We see this transparency as helpful to shareholders, employees, and customers—creating an environment of open information, just as financial information is shared for traditional investors. Implicit too is that measurement of these factors signals that the company may likely be seeking to improve its performance in these categories.

Ethnic Staff and Managers As you read in Chapter 2 about global trends, there is tremendous diversity worldwide. There is also deep diversity in the United States, attracting citizens from all nations and backgrounds pursuing a path to a future that may not be as easily achieved in their native country.

As previously discussed, both the United States and the rest of the world have a rich diversity of cultures, ethnicities and traditions. The markets that evolve to serve citizens from each of these backgrounds can provide large financial opportunities, like the billion-plus populations of China and India. In addition, HIP investors will look for global corporations that also recognize the rich pool of talent available in the global marketplace—companies that recognize that innovative new ideas are not limited to one country—just as Nobel Prizes in chemistry, physics and medicine, peace, literature, and economics, have been awarded to pioneers from more than 50 countries.

For example, Marriott Corp. certainly has a global reach—its hotels are in 66 countries, employing 146,000 people speaking more than 50 languages. In addition, more than 500 Marriott hotels are owned or franchised by ethnic minorities or women (Marriott International web site).

Marriott sees inclusive diversity as core to operating as a leading, global corporation. Marriott pledged in 2005 to double its ethnic and women ownership by 2010, creating more wealth and entrepreneurship (Marriott *Committed* n.d). In the United States, domestic employees comprise 61 percent ethnic minorities and 55 percent women. Marriott is cultivating that talent with its Thirst for Knowledge (*Sed de Saber*) education program to teach language and life skills to its Spanish-speaking employees. The company also states that it works closely with magazines across the spectrum: *Black Enterprise, Black MBA, Careers and the Disabled, Diversity Inc., Hispanic Business,* and *Working Mother*. These efforts contribute to Marriott being recognized as a "Best Company to Work For" by *Fortune* for 11 years in a row (Marriott International Web site). Talent is attracted to opportunity, and Marriott maximizes that path for employees of all backgrounds.

Global companies recruit talent where it exists.

- Of Colgate Palmolive's general managers, three in four are not American.
- Energy equipment companies Cameron International Corp. (58 percent of staff) and Schlumberger (46 percent of managers) value the leadership of local talent.
- Utility Edison International (of Southern California, 35 percent) have been able to recruit and retain high-quality ethnic managers and executives, reflective of the demographics of their service areas.

High-tech companies vary in their reported percentages. The results seem to depend both on whether the company does physical manufacturing versus virtual production of software, and on its geographic location in the United States. For example, employees with ethnic minority backgrounds comprise 45 percent of the workforce at Yahoo! and 39 percent at Autodesk—both are primarily located in Silicon Valley, California, which has above average diversity (Company reports and *Fortune*). Whereas Xerox (over 30 percent) and HP (24 percent of staff, 17 percent of managers) have slightly lower numbers but offer a wider variety of computer hardware and consulting services, and have a much larger geographic footprint with slightly less diversity than California (Company reports).

Some companies do not report systematically, but do offer some anecdotal information regarding ethnicity. For example, beer titan Anheuser-Busch (now owned by European beverage company InBev) highlighted that its information technology group was ethnic, at 4 percent of managers and 12 percent of staff (Computerworld Inc 2008). We expect that over time, this anecdotal reporting will lead to more systematic approaches.

HIP values transparency highly, which is why low quantitative scores get more weight than anecdotes or partial information, or no information at all (four in five large companies do not report). Again, the systematic data reporting is all voluntarily provided by the companies—they are not yet required to be released.

Gay and Lesbian Diversity   The Corporate Equality Index, developed and managed by the Human Rights Campaign (HRC), based in Washington, D.C. (Corporate Equality Index 2009) rates and ranks corporations, both public and private, as well as government sector employers, on the policies and processes that support inclusiveness of gay, lesbian, bisexual, and transgender employees. While the HIP framework tends to focus on quantitative results and outcomes versus policy checkboxes of the traditional method of socially responsible investing, the HRC's index results in high correlations with financial performance for shareholders.

This is an area of very divergent practices across industries and companies. As of August 2009, six states have voted, legislated or judicially decided that gay marriage is legal (Vestal 2009). While energy company Chevron is based in California, where the majority of citizens voted down gay marriage in 2008, it is the largest company by revenue in the United States to offer health benefits to domestic partners who are gay, lesbian or transgender. Chevron has earned a "perfect 100" score from the Corporate Equality Index.

On the other hand, in 1999, Texas-based Exxon acquired Virginia-based Mobil to become the largest U.S.-based energy company (CNN Money 1999). After the acquisition, ExxonMobil eliminated access to health benefits for any newly hired gay employees, or for new partners of existing employees, a benefit previously offered by Mobil. Exxon's explanation was that the partnerships were not "legally valid" or common-law marriages. ExxonMobil has not yet changed its policies.

That same year, London-based British Petroleum merged with Chicago-based Amoco. While BP did not have a policy to provide health benefits for domestic partners, Amoco did—and in 2000, it was adopted as the policy for all U.S. employees.

Of the *Fortune* 1000 companies, which are ranked by revenue, only 137 firms have realized a perfect HRC score of 100 in 2009. These include American Airlines, GM and Ford, Citigroup and Bank of America, Deloitte and Ernst and Young, and Harrah's (Corporate Equality Index 2009).

The index was created in 2002 to formalize the comparison of varying gay-friendly health policies, to provide encouragement for positive support structures in corporations (like Caterpillar's Lambda Network), and as a check and balance on anti-gay behavior in the workplace (Solmonese 2009). The first year's results recognized 13 firms with perfect scores (Corporate Equality Index 2002). The index evolved in 2006 to reward the increase of the number and type of health benefits available for domestic partnerships, which grew to

138 companies as top performers (Corporate Equality Index 2006). The latest enhancement to the HRC index is scheduled for 2011, so that there are no exclusions in the health plans for employees who are gay or transgender (HRC Foundation Web site). The total number of perfect scores in 2009 totaled 260 firms.

HIP investors value a high HRC score as it indicates companies that recognize the full diversity of society and the talents within all people. Again, high HRC scores correlated very highly with financial outperformance, a sign of great long-term leadership.

Supplier Diversity   Supplier diversity can be a source of innovation for large corporations. A Kaufmann Foundation report found that in two-thirds of new jobs, two-thirds of the innovations come from mid-size and small ventures. This entrepreneurial force also accounts for two-thirds of the differences in economic growth rates among industrialized countries (National Commission on Entrepreneurship 2002). These enterprises are started and owned by the increasingly diverse population in the United States that we saw in the chapter on trends. A HIP investor will look for companies that foster and encourage supplier diversity. This is good business that leads to creating the path for jobs and wealth creation for communities as well.

When growing up in the South, a certain young African-American woman sold ear piercings to her friends for $2 per person, which included three follow-up visits. Her passion for people led to her tremendous business success. Today, she employs thousands of people.

You are likely thinking it's Oprah Winfrey, right? No, it's Janice Bryant Howroyd. Her company, ACT-1, has revenues of $750 million, according to *Black Enterprise* magazine, twice as much as Oprah's Harpo Inc. Though you may not have heard of her, many *Fortune* 1000 corporations have—ACT-1 provides a wide range of corporate services: temporary and direct staffing, including technologists, pre-screening and background checks for employers' job candidates, accredited distance learning, electronic document management, and a travel agency.

Howroyd's original entrepreneurial goal was very HIP. "I enjoyed helping people get temporary and permanent jobs," she said in a 2009 interview. "I wanted to keep the humanity in human resources" (ACT-1 Web site).

Table 4.7   Top Five African-American Owned Businesses, 2008

Company (HQ in State)	Business	Revenue ($ billion)	Staff	Corporate Customers
World Wide Technology (MO)	Technology systems, supply chain services	$2.53 B	1138	US Dept of Defense, Cisco
CAMAC Int'l (TX)	Oil & gas services, trading	$2.43 B	300	Energy companies
Bridgewater Interiors (MI)	Automotive systems	$1.18 B	1508	Ford
TAG Holdings (MI)	Automotive supplies	$0.75 B	400	Chrysler, Kohler, Honda, Samsung
ACT-1 (CA)	Staffing services	$0.75 B	336	Several *Fortune* 1000 firms

Source: Black Enterprise 100 (2008),
http://blackenterprise.com/wp-content/themes/b-e/img/be100s/pdfs/industrial-service.pdf.

Howroyd is not alone. African-American owned businesses are big business. The top 10 African-American owned companies range from $455 million in revenues to more than $2.5 billion, and employ from 59 to over 12,000 staff each. Table 4.7 shows the top five firms ranked by revenue.

This experience extends worldwide. IBM sees great business value, from innovation to security of supply. IBM's chair Sam Palmisano views the advantages as a quite compelling business case—he recognized minority-owned business as the "mainstream of the global economy . . . driving global growth." He went further to acknowledge that IBM's decision to work with those suppliers comes from the opinion that "Such companies bring a new dynamism and spirit, and offer new ideas and points of view—providing innovative alternatives and aggressively filling niches being abandoned by larger suppliers" (Palmisano 2007).

In the United States, government contractors tend to have some of the highest rates of supplier spending with small business, women-, minority- and veteran-owned companies, as well as government-certified hubZone companies (in areas targeting domestic economic development). Due to their large share of government contracts that give preference and high decision weightings to diversity in the supply base, Northrop Grumman's defense and electronics services and ITT report larger than expected shares of diverse supply chain spending, which can support both human impact (wealth creation, equal opportunity) as well as profit for these companies (Company Reports).

As a HIP investor, it can be challenging to surface and analyze this information. Nearly half of the 500 largest firms do not report any supplier diversity information, and another one in four highlight only anecdotes. Despite this gap, a HIP investor can use the available information to select high-performing companies that do well financially and for society. In addition, a HIP investor should be aware that there are intermediary companies with an ethnic or woman ownership whose core purpose is to satisfy the requirements for diversity. While some profits are earned by the ethnic and women owners, it may not be in the true spirit of the goal.

We have completed four of the five elements of HIP—Health, Wealth, Earth, and Equality. The final quantifiable element is Trust.

Trust

When HIP was first conceived, there were four elements: Health, Wealth, Earth, and Equality. The first *Fast Company* scorecard covering 21 of the 100 largest companies rated quantifiable metrics in each of those categories. However, when editor Bob Safian of *Fast Company* agreed to look more deeply into one industry, Big Oil, the HIP analyst team in conjunction with Sara Olsen and Brett Galimidi of SVT Group, discovered the need for a fifth element: Trust.

For Big Oil, one metric that was particularly insightful was analyzed by Jenny Harms, then an MBA at the Fuqua School of Business at Duke University. We created a measure of "riskiness" for each companies' oil investments. We first documented all the countries that were the source of oil production for the top 10. While we sought to weight the production by volume for each country, we found that information was not publicly available. The intent was to test the correlation of risk and return with the openness of the governing approach. Second, we evaluated the "openness" of each political system—from democracy to dictatorship. We relied on the Corruption Perceptions Index by Transparency International for ranking. Somalia, Myanmar, and Iraq were the lowest rated in 2008, while Denmark, Sweden, and New Zealand were the highest rated. Third, we then created a weighted average of

Table 4.8   Global Energy Firms and Political Risk, 2006

Global Energy Co.	Countries Which Supply Oil & Gas	High Political Risk Countries	Share of Highly Risky Countries
ExxonMobil	22	9	41% Lowest
Marathon	10	5	50%
Shell	32	17	53%
ConocoPhillips	21	12	57%
Groupe Total	42	24	57%
Chevron	37	22	59%
Repsol YPF	29	19	66%
ENI	20	14	70% Highest
Valero	No reporting	No reporting	No reporting

As originally calculated for "Oil" Fast Company, April 2008, using 2006 data.
Source: Company reports; Transparency International; HIP Investor and SVT Group analysis.

the level of participation by each Big Oil company and ranked them.

Which global firm was the least exposed? The answer, in Table 4.8, will surprise you: ExxonMobil. Yes, the same ExxonMobil who does not rate very high on equality did seem to be mitigating its business risk by avoiding oil and gas sources in nations that had more political volatility. On the other hand, BP's joint-venture investment in Russia's oil and gas ventures has experienced lawsuits by oligarch billionaires, the ejection of BP's country leader, and negotiation over control of the entity—all since 2003 (Reed and Elder 2008). The dollars at risk are almost half a billion. Mitigating political risk is essential for future stable returns.

The positive response to the fifth element of Trust ensured its place in the evolution of the HIP Scorecard. The beauty of the HIP approach is that it can morph over time as you discover new fundamentals that become leading indicators of higher shareholder value or lower risk.

HIP Trust Metrics

In HIP's research of 500 companies, the following metrics indicate levels of trust:

- Agreeing to be interviewed
- Third-party certifications

- Legal actions
- Lobbying

Agreeing to Be Interviewed   In general, public companies do not lie, especially to the media. That foundation made the HIP Scorecard analysis published by *Fast Company* in both 2007 and 2008 even more powerful.

However, on rare occasions, public companies do lie. ExxonMobil is one of those companies. One example of purposeful obfuscation is Exxon's initiative to dispute climate change, including luring academics with at least $20 million to support "junk science."

When the *Fast Company* feature on Big Oil was released in February 2008, both Sara Olsen of SVT and I were in Bangkok to judge the Global Social Venture Competition for South-East Asia at Thammasat University. The good news was that CNBC's Squawk on the Street wanted to interview us; the bad news was that we could not get patched in from Asia. However, Brett Galimidi of SVT, and Amy Feldman, our co-writer, were interviewed for a short segment called "How Green is Big Oil?" interviewed by Mark Haines.

After reviewing some highlights of the HIP quantitative analysis, CNBC asked ExxonMobil what they thought of being ranked in the middle. ExxonMobil spokesperson Alan Jeffers asserted:

"It is unfortunate and curious that *Fast Company* did not contact ExxonMobil for information on the company's activities or operations in the development of its report. As a result, the report contains many glaring inaccuracies." Continuing, ". . . world energy demand will increase by as much as 40 percent over the next 25 years. Exxon-Mobil is working hard every day to help meet that demand in an environmentally responsible, reliable, and efficient way."

"Exxon was never invited to participate?!" I exclaimed at the TV screen. That of course was a lie since I e-mailed and called them directly. At 11 P.M. in Cambodia, I immediately went to the computer to pull up the ExxonMobil original denial of wanting to be interviewed.

The truth was clearly laid out, but ignored by ExxonMobil. Media coordinator Gantt H. Walton's e-mail reply dated October 3, 2007 wrote: "Paul, we appreciate your interest in ExxonMobil but unfortunately we will have to decline your request. As you can imagine, ExxonMobil receives a lot of requests and it is impossible for us to accept them all. Again, we appreciate your interest in our company." Luckily, Brett disputed ExxonMobil's falsehood on-air live, which was also captured in the transcripts online. But that episode revealed to me that even though most public companies are honest and ethical, not all are.

On the other hand, BP, who was top-rated in the HIP Scorecard for 2006 data, had a much different on-air reply. Company spokesperson Scott Dean said: "BP is pleased that it is the top ranked oil company in the survey. We think that it reflects our investment in alternative energy and commitment to sustainability."

The discussion on each quarterly earnings call is captured and transcribed for public companies. You can use SeekingAlpha.com as a resource. Be aware that not every shareholder or investment analyst can ask questions. Some public companies have been known to exclude analysts known to be critical from the process. So, as a HIP investor, remember these words from the nuclear détente of the early 1980s when you read public information: "trust but verify."

Exercise your right to speak up at annual shareholder meetings. Be in contact with companies as you discover facts that are not transparent. Participate in social networks such as Companies LikeMe.com and JustMeans.com to make your voice heard. If you are a shareholder in a public company, you own a real share in that firm. Let the company know what you think, how you feel, and what solutions they should consider to build a more HIP future.

Third Party Certifications   Third party certifications can help build trust and signal an independent third-party judgment that tends to be fair and impartial. But HIP investors also check the source and the methodology. Positive certifications reduce the likelihood of subpar returns, either because of the product's higher quality or its increased telegraphing of expectations to the customer. Both increase business value.

If you bought a washing machine or electric iron a century ago, you might have been influenced by *Good Housekeeping* magazine's seal of approval, which initially endorsed 21 products (*Good Housekeeping* Web site). The magazine's research lab, which *Consumer Reports* emulated, tested products for consumers. Since 1941, Good Housekeeping has offered a replacement or reimbursement if the products certified are found to be defective. In addition, many products that advertise in *Good Housekeeping* are also covered by its pledge to replace or reimburse (although there are some exclusions, like contraceptives, diet plans and financial services) (Barron 2009).

More recently, certification programs have arisen to help evaluate environmental claims like "natural" or "biodegradable" for products. Currently there are more than 270 certification programs active worldwide, according to EcoLabelling.org. The top categories covered are food (74 certifications), retail goods (72), and buildings (45). The top regions for these certifications are Europe (96), North America (78), and global (51).

The quality of certifications is (and should be) important to customers and investors. According to Scot Case of TerraChoice, 98 percent of 2,219 products surveyed in North America making eco-claims "commit at least one of 'seven sins of green-washing.'" False claims tend to be most prevalent in cleaning products, cosmetics, and products for kids, says Case. Since "green" products per store almost doubled from 2007 to 2008, and "green" advertising has tripled from 2006 to 2008, the need for clear standards is pressing, Case advocates.

How can an investor value these certifications? A HIP investor selects the certifications that encourage top-line revenue without risking the brand reputation or legal actions. The Malcolm Baldridge Quality Award is presented annually to those companies with top process excellence. The ISO 9001 standard for managing quality added a designation for environmental and energy management systems in 1996 called ISO 14001. Ford Motor Company was an early adopter for itself, saving 1 million gallons per day of water at one of its truck factories. Subsequently, it mandated all suppliers to be certified as ISO 14001 as well. This commitment was another contributing factor in avoiding bankruptcy, unlike GM, which took several years to follow Ford's lead (Fielding 2000).

Legal Actions　Being in business invites lawsuits. Companies find that people they never heard from seek out reasons to file lawsuits in order to obtain a settlement. Many ambulance-chasing lawyers earn fees just from companies making a cost-benefit calculation about the nuisance value and opportunity cost of settling versus fighting.

Corporations are obliged to disclose material risks to you, the shareholder. To learn more about all the legal actions corporations face, you can read the annual report and its footnotes. The section can be called "Legal Proceedings," "Potential Liabilities," or "Pending Lawsuits." Energy and industrial companies will have environmental lawsuits, like GE's dumping of toxins in the Hudson River in the 1980s, or Chevron's gas additive MTBE leakages. Retailers may have class action lawsuits by employees for disputes about overtime, promotions and/or discrimination, as Walmart or Yum! Brands have experienced in the past. Financial companies will face suits related to lack of disclosure, or misrepresenting investment risks, like Citigroup and AIG's overexposure to derivatives. Product failure lawsuits are common, especially for well-known companies like Apple and Dell. Intellectual property battles are even fought over products like low-cost laptops for billion-person markets in emerging regions, like AMD and Intel.

The annual report's footnotes are essential to understanding the potential risks of the company's current and past actions. The lawsuits listed here are not frivolous, and many times quite serious and costly. A HIP investor reads the details closely to evaluate the total exposure of the company in financial and reputation risk. An astute reader can also surmise a pattern of un-HIP behavior, like class action lawsuits by retailers skimping on pay or promotions for certain staff.

The legal actions disclosures are some of the most important revealed by the company. According to HIP's research, the best-managed companies that manage their businesses proactively to consider human impact also tend to avoid legal actions and conflicts, and tend to deliver financial outperformance and lower risk.

Lobbying   In 2006, a new investment product launched called The Blue Fund. Founded by a former McKinsey & Co. consultant, Daniel Adamson, it was based on the amount and proportion of political contributions from the corporation and its top three executives (Baue 2006). The contribution data is public information provided by the U.S. Federal Elections Committee (FEC) and can be searched online by name, city, state, zip code, employer, or amount at http://www.fec.gov/finance/disclosure/advindsea.shtml.

Analysis underlying the Blue Fund revealed of the S&P 500 that 80 companies committed to neutrality and did not give to either of the two largest political parties; 80 gave more to Democrats and 360 gave more to Republicans. Then, the Blue Fund evaluated the financial performance of each group. Overall, looking back over the past 5 years, the Blue Fund found that the Democratic-giving companies outperformed the Republican-giving companies overall, and in every industry (except energy, which had no large companies with political giving to Democrats).

This "blue" mutual fund (named for the Democratic color) launched in 2007, and despite positive consumer testing did not attract enough assets (less than $10 million) to stay in business, and closed as of June 2008. The important lesson is that quantitative data on political contributions led to a unique investment strategy.

A HIP investor seeks to be inclusive and value high "human impact," which is supported by politicians of all parties (except maybe libertarian). The FEC data on political contributions we mentioned earlier is collected and organized by Open Secrets, a nonprofit based in Washington, D.C. When you go to www.OpenSecrets.org, you can find the dollar value of political contributions by the company as far back as the year 1990. You can evaluate contributions for political candidates or re-election campaigns, the political action committees and 527 organizations, and fees paid for lobbying.

HIP investors should examine lobbying, as it may reveal a company strategy/policy vis-à-vis a fair playing field. Two aspects of this metric are important. First, the lobbying amounts overall tend to advocate for narrow corporate interests rather than a balance with society as a whole. Second, calculating the amount spent relative to revenue, and comparing to industry competitors, may be indicative of a firm that is seeking special conditions, which could create unfair advantages relative to competition. Table 4.9 shows the highest lobbying expenses by company in 2008.

Table 4.9   Highest Lobbying Expenses by Public Companies, 2008

Public company	2008 Lobbying	Business Units Affected
ExxonMobil	$29.0 mm	Energy
PG&E	$27.3 mm	Renewable energy
Northrop Grumman	$20.7 mm	Defense contracts
GE	$19.4 mm	Defense; health care
Verizon	$18.0 mm	Telecom; Internet; cable
Boeing	$16.6 mm	Aerospace; defense; satellites
Lockheed Martin	$16.0 mm	Defense; aerospace
AT&T	$15.1 mm	Telecom; Internet; cable
Southern Co.	$14.1 mm	Energy
Altria Group	$13.8 mm	Cigarettes
General Motors	$13.8 mm	Automotive

Source: OpenSecrets.org.

Mid-size companies in growth mode typically contribute very little, like Paccar ($200,000) or Ecolab ($30,000), or not at all, such as Air Products and Chemicals or Pall Corp. Fast-growing Google Inc., founded in 1998, did not spend on lobbying until one year before going public (2002), when it expensed $80,000, but grew to $2.84 million in 2008. Oracle, a tech-industry titan, spent $5 million on lobbying in 2008.

The numbers don't always tell the whole story, though. For example, Halliburton only spent $620,000 on lobbying in 2008, but also had its former chief executive Dick Cheney operating as Vice President of the United States. Many claims of favoritism for Halliburton as a preferred contractor with no-bid contracts disguise the quantitative comparisons of lobbying-to-revenue ratios. Meanwhile, the numbers don't hide extreme lobbying, like Peabody Energy's $8.4 million on lobbying in 2008, mainly related to the mining industry (Open Secrets).

Finally, it is important to note that political contributions come from large organizations of workers, as well. Those workers are seeking to protect or advocate for their interests. As the table below shows, these groups can include government employees, realtors and the electrical trade. These "investments" in influence do not solely come from corporations. The political "ecosystem" crosses sectors in seeking to achieve varying outcomes, some related to human impact like health care or employee pay. Table 4.10 shows the top five companies donating politically from 1989 to 2009.

Table 4.10   Top Five Political Donors, Cumulative 1989 to 2009

Organization	Total Dollars (annual rate)	Political Party Receipts
AT&T Inc.	$43.5 million ($2.2 mm)	44% Democratic, 55% Republican
AFSCME – government staff	$41.0 million ($2.0 mm)	98% Democratic, 1% Republican
Nat'l Assn. of Realtors	$35.2 million ($1.7 mm)	48% Democratic, 51% Republican
Goldman Sachs	$31.2 million ($1.5 mm)	64% Democratic, 35% Republican
Int'l Brotherhood of Electrical Workers	$31.0 million ($1.5 mm)	97% Democratic, 2% Republican

Source: OpenSecrets.org, http://www.opensecrets.org/orgs/index.php.

Overall, lobbying is an important indicator as it has the possibility to undermine the trust of consumers. Lobbying can also erode trust with stakeholders whose protests or boycotts can immediately impact the stock value of the company. Our analyses of total shareholder return show that leading companies have higher trust scores—and a low lobbying ratio versus its competitors is a main metric in that calculation.

Putting It All Together

Across five elements of HIP—Health, Wealth, Earth, Equality, and Trust—we have reviewed more than 20 data-driven metrics for you to evaluate as an investor. Each leads to quantifiable business value—from higher revenues to lower costs, from optimal taxes to premium pricing from investors. This financial value can lead to building a portfolio that supports higher human impact and profit.

Integrating a HIP approach into the day-to-day management practices of the company is critical to embedding them into each decision the company makes, from product development to manufacturing to capital spending.

In the next chapter, we show how leading companies embed HIP management practices in five ways. These practices are leading indicators of future performance, as companies fully integrate HIP thinking, action, and ongoing improvements into everyday business. (Chapter 6 shows how HIP metrics link to higher profits and lower risk for the bottom line and investment portfolios). HIP investors who observe these characteristics can better position their portfolios to seek future outperformance.

CHAPTER

Directly Embed HIP Criteria into Decision Making

Now that you understand how human needs can be solved for profit, and the range of human impacts to measure numerically, you want to ensure that the companies in your portfolio embed HIP management practices.

During the design of the HIP Scorecard magazine feature for *Fast Company* late in 2006, Keith Hammonds, then managing editor, asked a critical question: "How can an investor be assured that these quantifiable human impacts have any chance of recurring?" His skeptical, yet savvy question, helped take the early HIP framework to the next level.

The first version of the draft HIP management-practices list encompassed 10 possible categories, and was inspired by the 7-S framework (shared values and strategy; structure and systems; staff, skills, and style) that McKinsey strategy consultants constructed in the 1980s (Mind Tools Web site). As we prepared to send it to companies, it was winnowed down to the five highest-impact, results-oriented categories. If companies did well on those primary five, we realized, then the remaining five (like training programs) would naturally follow.

From mid-January to mid-February of 2007, we contacted the 100 largest and most innovative companies. With earnings season underway—and this being the inaugural HIP Scorecard—we managed to interview 21 companies in less than four weeks.

Three CEOs made the time to dive deeper and explain how they managed to generate human impact and profit in a systematic way that was outlined in the HIP Scorecard: Ray Anderson of Interface, Brian Walker of Herman Miller, and Thomas King of Pacific Gas & Electric's regulated utility business unit. Other interviewees were heading up corporate sustainability as SVPs, VPs, directors or internal advocates.

As founder of carpet maker Interface, Ray Anderson empowered staff to design a plan to respond to customer feedback it received early in the 1990s from architects and designers concerned about Interface's environmental impacts. In the mid-1990s, Interface set a goal of having a zero carbon footprint by the year 2020, something that is now called Mission Zero™. After 2020, Interface is seeking to be restorative, or having only positive impacts and no net negative impacts on the environment as the Paul Hawken book *Ecology of Commerce* details. Over the past 15 years, Interface's management systems have yielded more than $400 million in cumulative avoided costs, and kept the company alive in a very difficult industry.

Brian Walker, CEO of office furniture and chair maker Herman Miller, outlined how the culture of the company embraced not only innovation but a long-term view that the needs of the environment and employees were balanced with a growing business. More than 1000 employees, or one in every five staff, were involved in a company "green team," both formally and informally as volunteers, to create, manufacture, or deliver products that minimized materials usage, were recyclable, utilized green energy in their manufacture, and were produced and sold in sustainable facilities. Walker credited Herman Miller's accomplishments to its long-term culture supporting active employee engagement and a world view that saw its larger mission as creating "a better world," an approach that enabled it to operate as a very HIP enterprise.

Bill McDonough, in his book *Cradle to Cradle*, hypothesized that parts of Herman Miller branded chairs could be "edible" since it was mostly made of compostable natural materials, like its Kira fabric derived from corn. ("You might be able to eat it," joked the eco-leaders at the company, "but it wouldn't taste so good and it might take you a while.")

When we interviewed Thomas King, the CEO of PG&E utility (under the PG&E holding company), he described their systematic implementation of an integrated scorecard, with 10 metrics tracking customer satisfaction, employee feedback, environmental performance, and financial stability. As a regulated energy provider,

PG&E is required to report on all the elements it touches in society.

The highest-rated companies on HIP Management Practices were a mix of systematic engineering cultures passionate about quantifying results, like United Technologies and Alcoa, as well as more creative business innovators who saw a new future to develop, like Herman Miller and Liberty Property Trust. At the end of these interviews, we reflected on Keith Hammonds' provocative question, which was quite prescient—"how will this be recurring?" The resulting Management Practices, which are embedded in companies' DNA and decision-making, correlated with higher human impacts. I also strongly believe they could be a predictor of future human impact, as product development takes months—or even years—and processes inside a company evolve to be more efficient.

As we designed the layout of the first HIP Scorecard for the April 2007 issue of *Fast Company*, our estimates of leading management practices correlated closely with increased human impact (see Figure 5.1).

While the "profitable and sustainable" line implied a one-to-one relationship, the actual results as plotted showed the difficult reality of realizing extraordinary HIP results. Overall Human Impact scores were below the one-to-one line, despite the firms' having earned higher Management Practice ratings. We interpreted that to mean that increases in impacts have a "lag factor," taking time to show up in quantitative performance. Also, we posited that recurring impact would not persist without strong management practices.

This HIP Scorecard *version one* encompassed 21 leading companies willing to open themselves up to deeper evaluation and scrutiny. But this led to push-back from some participating companies, particularly InfoSys. Company representatives felt snubbed because InfoSys's lower-left position on the HIP grid made it appear to be the "loser" in our analysis. We explained that all 21 participants were likely top performers through the mere act of agreeing to be interviewed and at that time, the HIP Scorecard did not yet display all 100 candidates considered nor provide the comprehensive view of the entire S&P 500 that we have now.

"You are likely the most HIP company in Asia," I offered to InfoSys's executives. "We are a global company," they retorted. "We expect to perform well against our global competitors." True enough, I

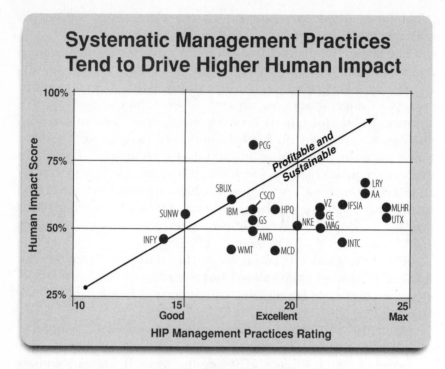

Figure 5.1   Driving Profit Through Impact

Source: HIP Investor and SVT Group analysis, published in *Fast Company*, April 2007.

replied, and said that our work in the future would no doubt indicate that these first 21 companies were leaders among a broader pool. In the end, Infosys did admit that the HIP Scorecard and ratings were "tough yet fair."

How do leading, well-managed companies consistently deliver top performance in human impact and profit? These five categories have proven to be a solid foundation of how a very HIP organization operates:

1. Paints a compelling business *vision* that integrates sustainability, complete with deadlines and quantifiable success.
2. Manages performance with a balanced scorecard of five to 10 *measures*, including human impact.
3. Aligns all impact measures to the *financial* implications and reporting.

4. Establishes *accountability* and rewards with successes in sustainable, profitable growth.
5. Embeds HIP criteria into corporate *decision-making* systems.

The HIP Quiz, at the HIPinvestor.com website, provides multiple-choice answers to these five questions, rated on a five-point scale. The most HIP practices total a top score of 25; the least HIP, a mere 5 (of 25 maximum points).

Let's examine how leading companies implement these management practices.

Paint a Compelling Business Vision Integrating Human Impact

"I believe that this nation should commit itself to achieving the goal, before this decade is out, of landing a man on the moon and returning him safely to earth."
—U.S. President John F. Kennedy, May 1961

A compelling vision is inspirational, measurable, and has a deadline. The United States rallied behind President Kennedy's unifying aspiration. A compelling vision is specific in expected result and timing—"man on the moon," returned safely to earth, by the end of the decade—which makes it easy to judge success or failure.

Ray Anderson, founder and Chair of Interface Inc., approved of his team's compelling vision recommended back in the mid-1990s: Interface will be "100 percent environmentally sustainable by 2020" and "environmentally restorative" (as the book *The Ecology of Commerce* defines it) starting in 2021 (Interface Global Web site and Hawken 1993).

Twenty-five years is a longer lead-time than the 8.5 years Kennedy gave the United States and NASA. Yet eliminating the waste stream from a firm manufacturing carpets and office furniture is no small task either. While the Manhattan Project yielded an atomic bomb in less than five years, what to do with the nuclear waste from the by-products of processed uranium and plutonium continues to vex our country (Richmond Times Dispatch, *Nuclear Sites* 2009).

Interface Inc.'s continuous implementation toward this goal has yielded more than $400 million to date in total cost savings, in addition to its much-reduced waste and dramatically lower environmental pollution (Interface Global, *Climate Change* 2007). The company has also survived industry shakeouts and is better positioned over the longer term.

For example, one of the engineers at Interface's LaGrange, Georgia facility designed a system for recapturing methane emissions (which are 21 times more destructive to the environment than carbon) and using them as an energy source, thereby lowering both pollution and energy cost. In addition, this methane-capture energy-reuse facility is a public-private partnership with the local municipality, which has a positive financial return both for Interface and the city.

Just as the moon shot inspired young scientists to dream, so does a maker of computer chips, semiconductor producer AMD. Because engineers, by nature, consistently seek to solve the world's toughest problems, AMD's executive team laid out this challenge for the company's product developers back in 2004: "50×15" (AMD, *The Future*, 3).

Or to put it less cryptically, half ("50" percent) of the world's population, (3.3 billion people today) should have access to the Internet by the year 2015 ("15"). Since approximately 1 billion people have mobile phones (not all of which are Internet-enabled) and fewer than 300 million have computers, AMD engineers would need to think creatively about which devices (mini smart phones powered by AMD chips?) as well as which types of wireless transmission technology (innovations like Intel's WiMax broadband towers?) could serve another two billion people. Now, *that's* a compelling HIP vision: providing increased information access for another third of the world would likely lead to more human impact—such as better health, increased wealth, and more equality. Of course, if the engineers could create this innovation at the right price, it would also boost AMD's profits.

Recall, from Chapter 3's discussion of Wealth and Equality products, that both AMD and Intel see this base-of-the-pyramid market (poorest four billion making under $2 per day) as central to their next wave of growth—and inspiration for innovating new products, which will improve quality-of-life for citizens in places like Senegal, Cambodia, or Bolivia (Prahalad 2006, 187).

Still, today many companies' visions are to "increase shareholder value" or to "boost cash flow per share" or "maximize return on invested capital (ROIC)." These visions are only inspiring to narrow-minded profiteers. To truly inspire employees, suppliers, and customers requires a compelling vision of Human Impact AND Profit—especially as 72 percent of employees want their employers to address social issues in the course of doing company business (Cone Inc., *Survey* 2007).

Honeywell is a company of several businesses—from aerospace systems, to turbochargers for vehicles, to building-control systems. Honeywell is also a company of engineers who seek to be systematic in solving problems. Chairman and CEO David Cote, in the 2006 annual report, declared boldly: "Nearly 50 percent of our product portfolio company-wide is linked to energy efficiency. We estimate the global economy could operate on 10 to 25 percent less energy just by using today's existing Honeywell technologies" (Honeywell 2006 annual report).

One-tenth to one-quarter less energy usage, worldwide, just by using half of Honeywell's technologies in existence today—wow! To be clear, while this statement was published with large type in the CEO's annual letter, it was not yet Honeywell's business vision; the letter's early pages still talked about "financial performance" and "cash deployment," as well as "one Honeywell culture."

While 2007's report did not mention an update to the CEO's assertion the year before, David Cote declared in Honeywell's 2008 annual report in his typical folksy language:

"The energy efficiency drive is extremely beneficial for us because with our existing product line-up (i.e., stuff we already have) if, for example, the United States could just immediately and comprehensively adopt the products we have already designed and that are in the marketplace today, the country's energy consumption could be reduced by 15 to 20 percent."

Interestingly, this is not yet a formal, public goal for the company. To be compelling, it would need a stated deadline (by 2010 or 2020, for example). But it is a gauntlet that appeals to today's need for more efficient energy usage—and it would simultaneously boost Honeywell's profits. Stay tuned to see if this statement finally becomes a rallying cry, like AMD's "50×15."

The world's largest retailer is always subject to scrutiny. But Walmart initiated a massive overhaul of its business in the mid-2000s, resulting in an extended tagline: "Save money. *Live better*." Walmart's legacy of driving down costs to offer the lowest possible prices is legendary. But this company-wide reinvention has three specific goals:

1. To be supplied 100 percent by renewable energy.
2. To create zero waste.
3. To sell products that sustain our resources and the environment (Little 2006).

Each of these goals has very specific and measurable targets, with timelines, which we will revisit in the next section on Performance Measures. At a high level, for Walmart's stores in the United States, 2025 is the target date for zero waste (Walmart, *Stores Fact Sheet* 2009), while in its UK subsidiary ASDA, it is 2010, because that chain is already at 65 percent reuse or recycling (Rushe 2009). Walmart's "Save money. Live better." mantra is integrated into all advertisements and communications. It is the new promise to deliver both Human Impact + Profit, and that is a HIP vision.

Visions focused on positive impacts, but not specific to goals or timing include those of Intel, United Technologies, Johnson Controls, and 3M (all engineering cultures, by the way). In 2007, Intel's Gary Niekirk talked of its "sand to sand" vision. Since chips are made from silica, which comes from sand, the company's goal is to have the end of the lifecycle result in sand as well. At United Technologies, "successful businesses improve the human condition," say Chair George David and CEO Louis Chênevert, in the annual report (United Technologies Annual Report 2008). Johnson Controls seeks "a more comfortable, safe and sustainable world" (Johnson Controls Web site). Innovator 3M, building on a constant stream of new products, expresses a "singular commitment to make life easier and better for people around the world." Each of these visions gets some HIP credit for their aspiration to solve human problems. However, to earn the best score requires a more specific outcome and time frame for achieving it, like Interface and Herman Miller did with Carbon Neutral by 2020.

An Anti-HIP Vision?

What visions are anti-HIP? Though no corporation publicly states they will "destroy the earth," or "take advantage of people," most traditional profit-making opportunities are predicated on finding a cheaper source of labor, transforming materials that nature has produced for free, or exploiting another's intellectual property—the domain of robber-baron capitalism.

While the cigarettes that Altria (Philip Morris's spin-off of its United States business) sells create the risk of massive health problems—and ultimately death—the company calls out "aligning with society" as one of its four major goals. Yet, the human impact strategies listed are still generic, including "meet compliance requirements," "reduce environmental impact," and "help reasonable tobacco regulation succeed."

In addition, one of Altria's other major goals, "create substantial value of shareholders," lists sub-strategies like "responsibly maximize cigarette profitability," and "build substantial share and profitability in other tobacco products." As we mentioned back in Chapter 3, the essential nature of these products is harmful to health—recognized by the public and regulators alike—and they are also produced in ways that harm the environment. To make money according to these legacy products necessitates negative human impact—and hence is very un-HIP (Altria Group Web site).

Once you understand how HIP a company's vision actually is, then you can evaluate how a corporation applies a "balanced scorecard" of metrics that incorporate both Human Impact and Profit.

Manage All Performance with a Comprehensive Balanced Scorecard

Every business measures profits, but that is a lagging indicator. To be predictive, you need to look at leading indicators. What measures might be predictive of financial success?

Obviously, customer satisfaction is one such measure. If customers are happy, they will return to buy more, and really happy customers will refer new customers to the business. JD Power, a customer-satisfaction measurement firm, built its business on showcasing the linkages between customer delight and profits (McGraw Hill Companies Web site). JD Power's book *Satisfaction* (2006), reveals how highly satisfied customers drive increasing top-line revenue, which translates to bottom-line profit and ultimately to shareholder value.

Since customers are served by employees, keeping staff satisfied is critical to long-term success as well. *Fortune*'s annual list of Best Companies To Work For, created by The Great Places to Work Institute in

San Francisco, provides regular ratings and rankings. When Wharton Professor Alex Edmans back-tested the financial performance of these employee-friendly firms, he found a positive correlation between high employee ratings and shareholder value outperformance (Edmans 2009).

Sustainability factors—including human, social and environmental impacts—are also leading indicators of profitability and financial outperformance, which was demonstrated in the previous chapter. Thus, when companies integrate customer, employee, and impact metrics into a cohesive scorecard that managers can easily use, they benefit from a more HIP management system.

A common measurement system called the "balanced scorecard" was popularized by Harvard professors Robert Kaplan and David Norton during the 1990s, based on General Electric's performance management systems in the 1950s as well as early 20th-century French process engineers (Norton and Kaplan 1996). This approach looks beyond mere financial profits, which tend to be lagging indicators of results that have already occurred. Kaplan's and Norton's Balanced Scorecard included perspectives like "Customer," "Process," and "Learning" in addition to "Profit." This typically produces a more comprehensive and proactive view of the business and requires "leading indicators."

According to the HIP methodology, a leading company quantifies the results of impacts in each of the five HIP categories: Health, Wealth, Earth, Equality, and Trust. For large companies, the HIP methodology captures more than 20 metrics. Start-up companies might only have three to five in total.

How Many Is Too Many Metrics?

In addition, a scorecard of metrics must not just be measurable, but also meaningful to business executives and managers. The GRI (Global Reporting Initiative), originated by CERES.org, lays out an encyclopedia of 100-plus measures and descriptors across 10 categories. Approximately 1000 companies worldwide report to some level of GRI standards, mostly corporations with very large staffs and large-cap valuations (Ceres Web site).

These measures seek to capture that which is quantifiable, but do not necessarily focus on what is meaningful. Businesses can have positive or negative contributions to all aspects of human impact.

Certainly they need to understand which areas they can influence the most—and the results of those actions. However, it is difficult for a manager to juggle more than a handful or two (literally, five to 10) of performance measures. Thus, the GRI, while helpful in its comprehensiveness, falls short of being a practical tool for managing the business.

A HIP company seeks to implement a manageable set of performance measures that are quantitative leading indicators, covering both Human Impact and Profit, which can be rolled out from the front-line to the Board of Directors. While the HIP Scorecard for investors can track 20 or more metrics, leading companies select the most meaningful measures to track. With accountability, this small handful can drive increasing business value based on positive impact.

Creating a Balanced Scorecard

Bonnie Nixon, Director of Environmental Sustainability, told me everyone at Hewlett Packard says: "If you want to change something here at HP, get a scorecard." Engineers love to quantify changes in their world, and a consistent way to track that is through numerical counts of impacts and profit.

Scorecards show how HP is consolidating 85 data centers to six, and going from 6000 technology application systems to 1500. HP also indicated that 80 percent of all enterprise customer Requests For Proposal (RFP's) now have eco-factors in them, and that 79 percent of consumers would choose more eco-efficient products if all other aspects are the same.

NIKE looks at its product development with a wide-ranging scorecard. The "NIKE Considered Index" evaluates new creations for their total life-cycle impact, from solvent use to waste volume, the use of materials and how those might be treated with chemicals. By looking end-to-end, NIKE can select the most optimal product design for performance, cost, and sustainability.

Based on the 10 measures of its Balanced Scorecard (CEO interview), which included the environmental lifecycle costs, Herman Miller evaluated products like its Aeron chair in the early 2000s. It even decided to add a long-life material to the chair for durability. Rather than reject that higher-cost material, it re-evaluated what customers would pay, and increased the price and profit margin of the chair for its overall appeal.

A balanced scorecard of measures examines multiple stakeholders and what they value. For Starbucks, it is six categories:

1. Product, the coffee mainly.
2. Partners, the suppliers and farmers.
3. Customers, who generate revenue.
4. Stores, and the employees who work in them.
5. Neighborhood, and the communities the company facilitates.
6. Shareholders, the co-owners of the company (Starbucks Coffee Company Web site).

As Ben Packard, VP of Sustainability, explains, Starbucks sees business value in a multi-stakeholder approach. The best coffee is grown and picked when the farmers are paid a fair price and operate high-quality farming techniques. Customers are enamored of the premium quality, willing to pay higher prices and return to stores more often, not only for the product but for the friendly baristas, who are also dedicated because of Starbucks's generous benefits, including health care coverage. The neighborhood benefits from the close connection of customers to employees, and shareholders benefit from the virtuous cycle of all stakeholders pulling together (Starbucks Coffee Company Web site).

One leading example of a balanced scorecard to measure and manage the business is Pacific Gas & Electric, the regulated utility in northern California. Working with regulators, the company created 10 core metrics, which cover all aspects of its energy business, from customer and employee satisfaction to environmental performance and safety. Of course, it also includes financial results. In this case, as a regulated entity, PG&E is also reporting these to the Public Utilities Commission, and its executives, managers, and supervisors have monthly and quarterly goals to realize. It also creates a positive dialogue with the regulators, who are looking out for managing the risks to society. This common approach then provides a unified approach that is a more integrated view of the business and its potential to create value not only in profit but also for all elements of society.

Can balanced scorecards be used in traditional manufacturing businesses? Definitely. In 2000, Alcoa, the aluminum company, organized around six core areas, with goals for 2020, as well as shorter term. "Providing this clear measurement of our progress both internally and externally," the company's Web site says, "will lead to stronger tactical planning for businesses through an integrated approach" (Alcoa, *Sustainability Approach*).

Here's an example of specific goals Alcoa has set under one of its six categories, "Safe and Sustainable Products and Processes." According to Alcoa, one-third of all aluminum ever produced is still in use. About one-quarter of the company's final products are currently made from reprocessed scrap metal, while more than half of the aluminum cans it produces in North America are remanufactured from recycled cans. Alcoa seeks to increase the scrap-to-product conversion to 50 percent by 2020, and North American can recycling to 75 percent by 2015.

For Alcoa's managers and executives, each of the company's six sustainability-performance categories has a quantitative performance metric shown in Table 5.1—which coincidentally also maps to a HIP element.

As outlined above, Alcoa's performance measures, and associated management systems, end up operating in a very HIP way. These metrics are strategic to creating customer value, employee

Table 5.1 Alcoa's Sustainable Scorecard

Category	Targets and Metrics	HIP Element
Economic Benefit	Strong balance sheet	Profit
Respect and protect people (employees)	Physical health	Health
	Culture of safety	Health
	Diversity	Equality
	Employee engagement	Health
Respect and protect people (communities)	Community engagement	Equality
	Volunteer service	Wealth
Safe and sustainable products and processes	Recycling (fabricated products and end-use cans)	Earth
Meet the needs of current and future generations through efficient resource use	Material use	Earth
	Landfill waste	Earth
	Energy intensity	Earth
	Water use	Earth
	Greenhouse gas emissions	Earth
	Toxic emissions and discharges	Earth
Accountability and governance	Audit integrity	Trust
	Swift resolution to complaints and compliance	Trust

Source: Alcoa, Inc.

engagement, environmental balance, a trust-based organization, and overall shareholder value. The company even makes it easy to track success via its Web site. Alcoa sees that Human Impact leads to Profit—and that's very HIP.

Alcoa isn't the only company that lets you track its performance goals online. Sun Microsystems' Web site (www.sun.com/aboutsun/csr/) also provides the latest updates on its comprehensive performance goals and timelines.

Interface Inc. breaks down each metric by facility, from Australia and Thailand, to Canada and Georgia (U.S.). Go to the company's Web site and you can track each facility by "eco-metric" or "socio-metric" data, along with a summary rollup. The total savings are counted and you can see how these metrics drive business value (Interface, *Ecometrics*).

Just as the economy has leading and lagging indicators, so do companies. The challenge is to understand which companies are managing proactively using leading indicators of performance. These firms then tend to outperform by looking ahead rather than into the rearview mirror for financial results.

Align Human Impact Metrics with Financials

Land, labor, and capital—these three factors of production form the basis of economics theory, as well as the basis for debates over which economic system is most appropriate. Without land, we could not grow food or timber or harvest other resources. Without labor, there would be no one to do the work. Without capital, there would be no financing for equipment or facilities to get the work done.

In today's economy, the land's resources are becoming more stretched, labor is becoming overworked, and capital is seeking more transparency about how it will be used. Therefore, new constraints on how an economic system functions are emerging.

Just as technology, at different points in time, has meant a mainframe computer, a desktop computer, a laptop computer and now mobile devices like iPhones and PalmPres, so must the traditional factors of production morph as society innovates and advances. Each element of the economy, whether agricultural, industrial or information-based, can be more HIP. Napoleon Wallace, an MBA at UNC's Kenan-Flagler School sees "land, labor and capital" equating to a triple bottom line of "planet, people and profit."

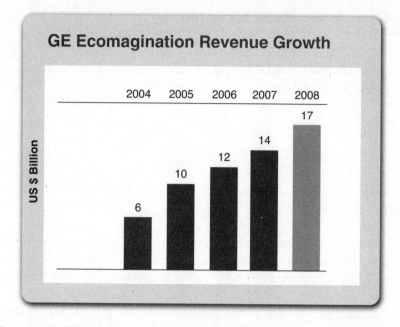

Figure 5.2   GE's Ecomagination Revenue Growth
Source: GE Corporation.

For example, GE has multiple business units encompassing 80 ecomagination products, which totaled $17 billion of revenue in 2008 (see Figure 5.2). That is nearly one in ten dollars of corporate revenue. Those products, which have grown from 17 products representing $6 billion in revenue in 2004, realize both incremental human impact and profit. CEO Jeff Immelt has set a goal of $25 billion by 2010 (Schmid 2009).

GE's more recent "healthy-magination" strategy for solving human problems is launching new products that increase access to, and affordability of, health care. Both strategies yield business value from quantifiable improvements, either in Earth factors, like energy and water efficiency, or from Health factors, like longer duration and better quality of life.

"Ecomagination is a business initiative to help meet customers' demand for more energy-efficient products and to drive reliable growth," says GE's annual report. It also reflects the company's commitment to "invest in a future that creates innovative solutions to environmental challenges and delivers valuable products

Table 5.2   GE Revenue by Business Group

Business Group	2008 Revenue by Group	2008 Profit by Group	Gross Profit Margin by Group
Energy infrastructure	$38.6 billion	$6.1 billion	15.8%
Technology infrastructure	$46.3 billion	$8.1 billion	17.5%
NBC Universal	$17.0 billion	$3.1 billion	18.2%
Capital finance	$67.0 billion	$8.6 billion	12.8%
Consumer and industrial	$11.7 billion	$0.4 billion	3.4%

Source: General Electric 2008 Annual Report.

and services to customers while generating profitable growth for the Company" (GE Ecomagination Report 2008, 1). This connection between human impact and profit makes it easy to see how HIP creates shareholder value.

For GE, this is also dimensionalized in its growth by business unit. Growth rates are higher in its health and infrastructure business units, and lower in financials and entertainment groups, as seen in Table 5.2.

Businesses that reframe their market share, customer segmentation and managerial accounting systems in terms that go beyond mere financials can better understand how drivers of human impact link to financial value. In PepsiCo's case, products are classified as "good for you," "better for you," and "fun for you" (Morris 2008). While 70 percent of products today are *fun* like Doritos, the *good* and *better* categories, currently at 30 percent of revenue have goals to move to 50 percent of revenue. Manufacturer DuPont says that revenues generated from "nondepletable resources" will double to $8 billion (DuPont 2008).

At Campbell's Soup, the company has highlighted growth categories for its soups, segmented by "mg per serving of sodium." Interestingly, the revenue split is 30 percent "healthy" (less than 480mg/serving), 20 percent "mid-range" and 50 percent the remainder (above 700mg/serving). Grouping products by salt levels shows how a key driver of health relates to the top-line financials (Campbell's, *CAGNY Presentation* 2009).

Enhancing overall understanding of both the financial statements and the leading-indicator impacts allows staff, managers, and executives to better operate and innovate to be more HIP. Procter

& Gamble is already repositioning its market evaluations to be integrated with traditional financial metrics, according to Clifford Henry, Associate Director of Global Sustainability.

In 2008, Office Depot, a $14 billion retailer, sold more than 6100 products with green attributes across its 1600 North American stores, up from 5200 the year before and 4000 in 2006 (Environmental Leader 2009; Office Depot Web site). It is now rolling out a *Shades of Green* labeling systems for customers, says Melissa Perlman, Manager of Public Relations. Each "green" product attribute will be rated *dark green* for the most eco-friendly, *bright green* for the middle ground, or *light green* for a slight positive impact. The attribute will also explain the benefit to customers, such as "diverting materials from landfills." The Office Depot customer portal shows how customers can identify the proportion of their spending in each of the *dark*, *bright*, and *light* categories (Environmental Leader 2009).

With this online tool, Office Depot will be able to calculate the aggregate customer purchases and growth rates that comprise its own revenue, potentially on a day-by-day basis. Thus, executives and managers can also monitor and manage green revenues and profits, as well as the customers who buy the products (Environmental Leader 2009).

Similarly, Interface Inc. has live tracking of costs related to energy, waste, water, and other *ecometrics* and *sociometrics*. On its Web site, the company enables anyone to check on the results by facility, and in total (as shown in Figure 5.3).

Interface proactively manages the inputs and processes that contribute to higher human impact, and the subsequent financial results—improvements directly aligned with increased profitability.

Leading companies using these tools can consistently outperform those which are not taking advantage of these impact-to-profit relationships. They can more easily report on progress, as well as decentralize accountability throughout the organization. The next management practice category describes how that accountability must be embedded in the organization.

Establish Accountability for HIP Across the Entire Enterprise

In June 2009, sustainability reporting and consulting firm Framework:CR published the results of a survey identifying the accountability structures most associated with recognition for HIP-like

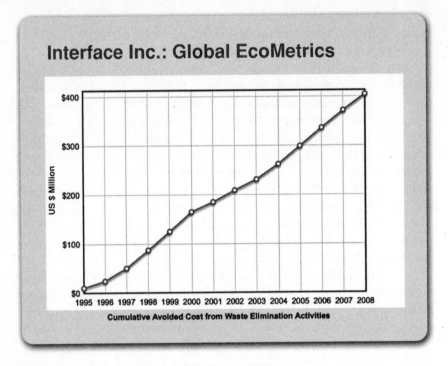

Figure 5.3   Interface Inc.: Global EcoMetrics

Source: Interface Inc.

practices. As Kathee Rebernak and Aleksandra Dobkowski-Joy explained, sustainability leaders exhibited three characteristics. First, managers in charge of sustainability were of a higher rank, one or two levels away from the CEO. Second, leaders housed the sustainability function in an externally facing group, the most typical being Corporate Affairs, Legal, or a dedicated department. Third, leaders presented to—and interacted more frequently with—the Board of Directors (Framework: CR 2008).

These findings are consistent with the success of any new business initiatives, from a new product (think how Steve Jobs innovates at Apple), to successful merger integrations, to business reengineering. Executive leadership with focused management structures, visible and accountable to the Board, is a common factor for success in traditional business initiatives—and also in sustainability.

Executive Leadership

Let's start with the leadership role. At Procter and Gamble, the VP of Global Sustainability, Len Sauers reports directly to the CEO. It's the same at NIKE with Vice President of Corporate Responsibility, Hannah Jones; DuPont's Chief Sustainability Officer Linda Fisher; and Campbell's Soup VP of Sustainability Dave Stangis. Leading companies give a HIP approach the executive heft it needs to succeed in rolling out new initiatives or pushing back against resistance.

Next, this leader can build a department of staff or create a discipline across the enterprise. Dave Stangis of Campbell's Soup prefers the "discipline" approach. "It's the highest leverage," Stangis explains. "Our small team of three can more easily accomplish systemic change when each business group and employee feel like it's part of their job every day, rather than that of a specific department." This is consistent with leading companies that aggregate a small band of experts who help spread expertise across the organization, not unlike Human Resources might or a Safety Director does in regular business operations.

While NIKE has a small group of about a dozen staff, and Starbucks more than 20 in their sustainability or CSR department, decentralized companies seek to spread responsibility into the multiple business units they operate. Medical firm Johnson & Johnson, which has more than 200 business units comprising $63.7 billion in revenue, says, "In keeping with our decentralized organization, primary accountability rests with each franchise Group Operating Committee" (Yahoo! Finance; Johnson & Johnson, *Sustainability Report* 2007). At Wells Fargo, Pat Callahan is the executive-level leader of sustainability, as well as the merger integration of Wachovia. Its Environmental Affairs Council is composed of 19 executives from the business units, as well as corporate groups. In addition, 25 "green teams" have emerged from staff networks focused on advancing eco-efficiency. Wells also involves an external advisory board to anticipate new environmental-related opportunities (Wells Fargo Web site).

Board Engagement

Whether centralized or decentralized, it's essential for all levels of the company across business units to integrate a HIP discipline. This is reinforced when boards of directors are accountable, as well. NIKE has a specific committee on Corporate Responsibility, composed of five Board members. Toy maker Mattel has blended it into the Governance committee (Nikebiz Web site). At retailer Gap Inc., it's combined with the *Governance, Nominating and Social Responsibility Committee* (Gap, Inc. Web site). The most HIP firms typically describe quarterly updates to Board Committees and sometimes twice-annual presentations on specific initiatives—from renewable energy expansion that reduces emissions, carbon, and energy costs, to wellness initiatives for employees that boost health and manage health care costs.

External experts are engaged through Sustainability Advisory Boards, as at Kimberly-Clark, which draws from cutting-edge designers, socially responsible investors, industry innovators, and experts in engaging stakeholders and nonprofits. This external Board reports to the CEO (Kimberly-Clark Sustainability Report 2007, 3).

Cross-Discipline Accountability

In October 2006, Cisco Systems, a $36 billion provider of networks and systems, vastly expanded the organization's responsibility for implementing its environmental goals (Google Finance; Cisco Systems, *CSR* 2008). Did it appoint a new executive? Set up a large department? Nope. Chair and CEO John Chambers instead applied a new multidisciplinary and cross-functional approach: the EcoBoard, which would report to the Board of Directors and CEO on a quarterly basis. Co-led by three executives (Laura Ipsen, John McCool, and Ron Ricci) and comprising a dozen senior executives overall, the EcoBoard was a network of leaders, empowered to seek out, review, and approve a vast set of eco-opportunities.

Cisco's goals were bold. Its operations needed to reduce greenhouse gases. New products were required to reduce power consumption. Also, network architectures and solutions must help customers achieve their environmental goals (Cisco EcoBoard Web site). Cisco's new collaboration technologies, like TelePresence videoconferencing and WebEx online meeting software, were applied internally to reduce the company's own GHG emissions from travel by 10 percent (Cisco Systems Annual Report 2008 and Web site). The new "wisdom of the crowd" approach was embedded in the EcoBoard, so as to benefit from expertise across the group while not bogging down in the perils of too much consensus.

"The EcoBoard was a new approach," says Angel Mendez, SVP of Facilities and Operations, "but enabled us to more quickly find new ways to team together, and benefit from each others' ideas and avoid mistakes." The EcoBoard was consistent with Cisco's overall evolution toward more group decision-making, now known internally as the "collaborative management model."

Cisco has formalized this approach based on three elements: *working groups* with start- and end-points, which focus on a new business idea; *councils*, which review the designs and ensure they fit across disciplines, and *Boards*, which keep the whole effort strategic and focused on $1 billion opportunities. The EcoBoard, as the first implementation of this approach, can also evaluate opportunities below $1 billion if they have environmental benefits.

Within a company of more than 38,000 staff, this horizontal approach helps to avoid traditional vertical silo-driven thinking, eliminate redundancies and encourage an integrated approach from the entire company (*Fortune, Cisco Systems* 2006). Some of Cisco's Boards are even focused specifically on geographies like Mexico, China, Russia, and overall "Emerging Countries," which link to global high-growth markets, noted in Chapter 2 on HIP trends.

Top-to-Bottom, Inside-Out Responsibility

Ensuring that accountability takes place across the entire enterprise requires multiple teams, sponsors, and networks. At Walmart, teams working on topics like reducing packaging are composed of representatives from inside staff, linkages to suppliers, and external experts, like academics and environmental nonprofits. These teams are lead by "network captains," who are directors or VPs who help break down barriers to success. A higher level "executive network sponsor" and an enterprise-wide "sustainability team" oversee multiple teams and help provide alignment among multiple goals. On a quarterly basis, the entire company's staff is connected through a videoconference update to review progress toward goals, and celebrate the success of the past three months (Walmart Stores, *Sustainability Report* 2009).

Accountability is reinforced through the pay and performance system. For example, the Walmart buyers have a share of their bonus now tied to the core goals of lowering waste, increasing renewable energy and putting more sustainable products on the shelves for customers to buy. Those products still need to meet the goals of "sell-through" and profit margin, but also must integrate HIP criteria.

Impact Tied to Pay, Promotion, and Recognition

GE's CEO Jeff Immelt is serious about reducing greenhouse gas emissions. He has set a reduction target for each of the business unit leaders at the company. If a business unit meets the profit target but not the GHG emissions target, those executives will not earn their full bonuses. This is similar to GE's efforts in the 1990s when implementing a new culture. If a manager "hit the numbers," but did not live up to the new values, then that person could not receive their full bonus.

Similarly at Alcoa and Intel, performance reviews, promotions, pay raises, and recognition are tied to improvements in HIP-like measures. Managers and executives have numerical targets for environmental metrics and for diversity. At Bristol Myers Squibb, "employees must perform effectively in many areas that are not measured specifically by financial or operational results" (Bristol Myers Squibb Sustainability, *Employees*).

Top-Down versus Bottom-Up Leadership?

Is it possible to initiate change deep inside the organization? Ask Sue Amar of salesforce.com, the $1 billion software services company (Google Finance). As a senior business analyst seeking more environmental leadership by the company, Amar stood up at a company meeting in 2006 and said, "We want to be a responsible company, but haven't aligned to do that for the earth or sustainability. What are we doing for the environment?" (Salesforce Foundation Web site). CEO Marc Benioff asked her to take the initiative, and Amar organized an Earth Council focused on sustainability. More than 200 employees applied to be on the council, feeling energized about this purposeful mission. Amar was recognized as one of salesforce.com's top 12 volunteers of the year in 2007, since in this case, her work was in addition to her regular day job. Now, working full-time as the company's Sustainability Program Manager, Amar shows how individuals can "be the magnet" and initiate the changes they envision from the bottom up.

Top-performing HIP organizations have committed CEO leadership, frequent Board interaction, cross-discipline collaboration, and responsibility across the entire organization, and link their pay and performance systems to HIP results. But less than 5 percent of the 500 largest U.S. companies have set up accountability in this systematic way. That's right, fewer than 25 out of 500.

Embed HIP Criteria into Every Decision-Making Process

This last management practice category focuses on including HIP criteria in every decision-making process. Alcoa provides the perfect example.

Despite its heavy industrial processes, Alcoa is actually one of the few companies to implement a triple-bottom-line evaluation in its decision-making. This analysis of financial profit, environmental aspects, and social factors is the immediate next step after defining a project at Alcoa. Figure 5.4 shows how the company systematically evaluates all capital projects and operational improvements according to a HIP type of framework.

Let's walk though an example of Alcoa's triple-bottom-line thinking. For years, the spent lining of aluminum smelting pots was regarded as industrial waste. But by looking at this "waste" in a

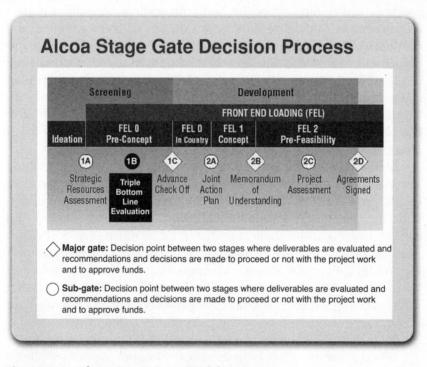

Figure 5.4   Alcoa Stage Gate Decision Process

Source: Alcoa, Inc.

different way, Alcoa developed the ability to turn the smelting pot linings—which include carbon—into a raw material for other industries. At year-end 2005, 28 percent of the spent linings were no longer waste but raw material for new products, and Alcoa had turned trash into cash. What used to be cost turned into new revenues and profits—and Alcoa was two years ahead of its seven-year goal to reduce landfill waste by 50 percent (Alcoa Group Web site).

This systematic approach of reviewing criteria beyond pure financials is also used by United Technologies for its product designs and capital spending reviews. This forward-looking approach systematically evaluates all types of risks, including the volatile prices of oil and pollution pricing regulations.

"Environmental criteria are integrated with capital projects here at Ford," says Thomas Niemann, of Ford Motor Company's sustainable business strategies group. "If you are only altruistic, then you might go out of business." But a lifecycle analysis that includes the long-term costs of all the materials and labor required contributes to a deeper understanding of the best course for both human impact and profit. In Michigan, Ford's 10.4 acres of "green roofing" did cost up to 25 percent more to install, but it will cost 50 percent to 65 percent less over its full life when compared to the maintenance required for a soft-membrane tar roof. The green roof also reduces water runoff, recaptures gray-water and contributes to lower costs. "Mr. Ford is focused on the human impact," Niemann says. "Environmental and economic responsibility are not exclusive from each other, but supportive of each other."

At Shell Oil and Marathon Oil, the planning and capital spending processes have included a forward-looking estimate for a range of potential carbon prices. These influence the prospective designs of new and refurbished plants, pipelines and infrastructure. At Chevron, all capital projects and enhancements valued at more than $5 million must be evaluated for environmental and social concerns, according to Maria Pica (Chevron). "We must evaluate the emissions profile, seek to reduce it and how we can use carbon credit to offset the remaining profile," she says. All projects over $50 million have mandatory considerations of the risks and benefits of sustainability issues.

While investment banks have typically financed whatever clients request, the Equator Principles developed by the World Bank have set environmental and social guidelines that have taken hold because they also address and mitigate investment risk. For project finance, which includes $315 billion of annual debt and equity going to new energy or infrastructure developments worldwide, the Equator Principles are applied in nearly 75 percent of those transactions, many of which happen in emerging economies (Project Finance; Environmental Data Services 2008). These principles have gradually spilled over into the everyday financings of some investment banks. Morgan Stanley says it has "adopted explicit limitations on financing or investing in projects that would, among other things: significantly degrade a critical habitat; support companies engaged in illegal logging; support extraction or logging projects in World Heritage sites; or violate local and World Bank pollution standards" (Morgan Stanley Web site).

At Kraft Foods, the package developers must evaluate every new design according to an eco-calculator, says Steve Yucknut, the VP of Sustainability. Numeric values assess the product-to-package ratio, the number of layers of packaging, and the impact on landfills. For larger projects, energy costs are tested for a range of scenarios. While low-energy inflation makes some sustainable projects less obvious compared to Kraft's traditional 14 percent ROI hurdle rate, if energy prices jump as they did in 2008, return on investment can jump to more than 25 percent. Yucknut says, "We tend to be open-minded and generous if sustainability is included in the project."

Less than 10 companies of the top 500 have reported systematically integrating HIP criteria into their decision-making processes. This long-term, lifecycle approach can add business value to a range of decisions. Product development could yield more innovative products. Capital spending would evaluate more risk factors—and factor in the cost of unexpected energy and environmental scenarios. Managerial reporting would include a broader set of measures beyond just financials.

These leading management practices can be embedded in the DNA of the company, and can be clear predictors of future positive impact, leading to higher financial performance.

HIP Management Practices: A Predictor of Impact?

It is surprising that companies like Coach, the maker of leather accessories, dispute that environmental factors affect their businesses. Here's how Coach spokesperson Andrea Shaw Resnick responded to a 2007 request from the Carbon Disclosure Project, a not-for-profit organization that collects corporate climate change information: "Upon review of the document, we have decided not to complete the questionnaire given the fact that it really has nothing to do with our type of business and unlike the Gap, we do not have the internal capability to complete it." Coach has declined to participate in the 2008 and 2009 CDP surveys as well.

What doubters need to recognize is that these factors affect every company. Leaders who seize the opportunity and initiate programs to increase human, social, and environmental impacts, realize higher financial performance.

Earlier in the chapter, we showed how the HIP Scorecard published in *Fast Company* in April 2007 demonstrated higher HIP management practices correlated with higher human impacts. Does the relationship hold for the S&P 100 and the S&P 500? A HIP analysis of both indexes (see Figure 5.5 and Figure 5.6) shows that integrating

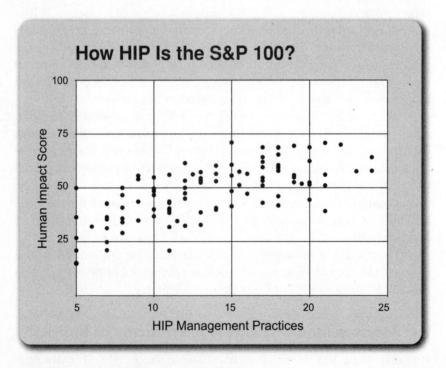

Figure 5.5   How HIP Is the S&P 100?

Source: HIP Investor analysis.

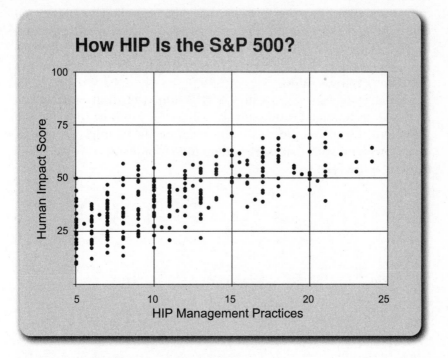

Figure 5.6   How HIP Is the S&P 500?

Source: HIP Investor Analysis.

sustainability more deeply into how companies are run (management practices) leads to a higher level of quantifiable Human Impact.

Evaluating management practices shows how companies can ensure a more HIP approach over time, and embed a higher likelihood of financial outperformance. As a HIP investor, you can evaluate companies by researching and interviewing them. Leading companies, like Alcoa and Walmart, are becoming more transparent about how they make decisions. Encourage other companies to follow their lead—because as you now know, it can also benefit their bottom line.

Linking Impact and Practices to Profit

Leading companies are very systematic about being sustainable and seeking human impact and profit. A compelling vision with a timeline and a target focuses the enterprise. Then, a scorecard of leading indicators quantifies the impacts that can be linked to profit. Accountability is ingrained in the enterprise and decisions are judged by HIP criteria. Leaders who embed these management practices tend to correlate with, and drive, higher impact. These impacts link to higher business value.

In Chapter 6, we show how a HIP approach that equates impacts to the financial statements can increase profit on the income statement, boost net worth on the balance sheet, improve overall cash flows, and stimulate higher demand from investors—especially those that are HIP.

CHAPTER

Equate Impacts to Profit and Valuation

Now that you have evaluated a company's products, operating metrics, and management practices, the fun part starts—mapping it to profit and valuation. The exciting news is: Building a better world generates bigger profits and higher shareholder value.

About half of customers globally say they will refuse to buy a product or service if a corporation's behavior is detrimental to society (49 percent in the United States; 44 percent in France; 79 percent in China). Consumers also dissuade friends from buying products made by companies negatively affecting the public good, though it varies by country (38 percent in United States; 12 percent in Japan; 66 percent in China). Even as investors, some individuals refuse to buy the stock of companies that they believe, don't act in the best interests of society (19 percent in the United States, 5 percent in Japan, 49 percent in China) (Bonini, McKillop and Mendonca 2007).

Are corporate executives aware of this, or are they biased against linking human impact and profit? Overall, traditional corporate executives say that human impact and profit can coexist and generate attractive value. In December 2005, management consulting firm McKinsey & Company surveyed 4,238 executives globally about the role that large corporations, both public and private, should play in society. While about one of six executives said corporations should "focus solely on providing the highest possible returns to investors while obeying all laws and regulations," the super-majority-five-out-of-six executives agreed the goal should be "generate high returns to investors but balance with contributions to the broader public good." In this case, "good" was defined as jobs, donations, pursuing the intent not just the letter of the law, and avoiding other societal detriments, like pollution. More than two in three believed corporations, in general, contributed to that good, and three in four (76 percent) claimed their own corporations made a positive contribution. The top three industries recognized for "good" were health care (49 percent), pharmaceuticals (29 percent), and agriculture (28 percent), all aspects of the Health element of human impact (McKinsey 2006, "Global Survey of Business Executives").

A survey by *The Economist* in 2009 also demonstrates the shifting priorities toward a more HIP world. Of the 136 executives and 65 investors who responded, 85 percent said corporate social responsibility (CSR) was now a "central" or "important" consideration in investment decisions. This figure is almost double the 44 percent who said CSR was "central" or "important" five years ago, demonstrating the growth in CSR's significance. Similar findings were also reported by the Global CEO Survey conducted by PriceWaterhouseCoopers (Fisman 2006).

How do human, social and environmental benefits translate into profit and valuation? In December 2008, McKinsey and Boston College's Center for Corporate Citizenship asked chief financial officers, investment professionals who track sustainability and corporate social responsibility leaders, for their views. More than half of both CFOs and investment pros saw that social, environmental and governance improvements typically added shareholder value. However, 53 percent of those in corporate social responsibility roles reported they had no idea of how shareholder value creation related to these initiatives—and they are in charge of them! Also, while 85 percent of the entire group saw long-term financial value from environmental initiatives, only 29 percent replied that they expected short-term financial value from those eco-projects.

One of the most shocking numbers from this survey was that charitable giving was ranked "more important" than creating new revenue growth by the CSR corporate leaders group. In other words, they believed it was better to simply give money away than to innovate new products that both improved the customer's quality of life and grew the business. This lazy thinking should be a red flag to investors; it's the mark of a company that's stagnant or departmentally "siloed"—not one poised to innovate and grow (Boston College and McKinsey Company).

So, how does human impact equate to profit? Let's go to the numbers.

The Higher Valuation of Positive Human Impact

Two in three individual investors view a company's doing good as a positive indicator of expected investment performance. Do well-managed companies achieving high human impact realize higher profits or valuations? The HIP methodology tracks more than 20 indicators of positive human impact. Let's take a look at three examples covering the HIP categories of Health, Earth, and Equality.

Employee satisfaction is a leading indicator that measures the involvement, engagement, and commitment of a company's staff. As you read in Chapter 4, employee satisfaction is a HIP Health metric. Happy employees serve customers better than unhappy employees, which results in higher repeat business and referrals. These recurring and additional sales lead to revenue growth, and hence, higher profits. In addition, higher employee satisfaction leads to lower turnover and increased productivity. An annual list of these high employee-satisfaction companies is published every year in *Fortune* magazine. Wharton Professor Alex Edmans analyzed these top-rated firms and their shareholder performance for the period 1984 to 2005. Edmans found that if you had invested in these companies when they were first put on the list, then rebalanced your portfolio for every annual update, you would have made an additional 4 percent (or 400 bps) per year in financial return relative to the general market.

In the HIP Earth category, a subsidiary of RiskMetrics called Innovest analyzed the quantifiable environmental performance of corporations. From greenhouse gas emissions to energy efficiency, the firm estimated the "carbon beta" or coefficient. Over several years in the 2000s, a portfolio of these companies that weighted eco-leaders higher and eco-laggards lower, outperformed the standard benchmarks by up to 20 percent.

Now, in Equality, these results are impressive. My wife has always made it a practice to vote against Board of Directors slates that contain no women. She says it's the principle of the matter, but recent analysis shows that principle and good business sense directly coincide. A study by non-profit research organization Catalyst Inc. demonstrates that female representation on large companies' corporate Boards is a leading indicator of financial performance As seen in Figure 6.1, top-quartile *Fortune* 500 companies—those with

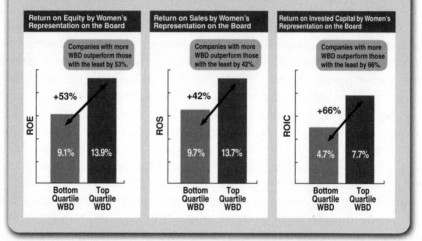

Figure 6.1   Women Board Directors (WBD) Align with Strong Performance at *Fortune* 500 Companies

Source: Catalyst, Inc 2007.

more than two women on a Board—outperform the bottom quartile (those with typically no or only one woman) by 53 percent for return on equity, by 42 percent on profit margin (return on sales), and by 66 percent for return on invested capital.

As large-company Boards typically range in size from 8 to 16 people, two women translates into a proportional ratio of 12 percent to 25 percent of all members. Catalyst Inc. upped the ante by showing the financial performance value of having three women on a large company Board. As seen in Figure 6.2, financial returns proved even higher for those firms edging toward more gender equality.

In addition, research by Catalyst Inc. has found that, at firms with more women Board members the gender equality ratios of executive teams and managerial ranks increase as well. Furthermore, HIP's own analysis has proved that high scores at the board, managerial, and staff levels for both gender equality and ethnic balance can deliver a portfolio with higher financial performance.

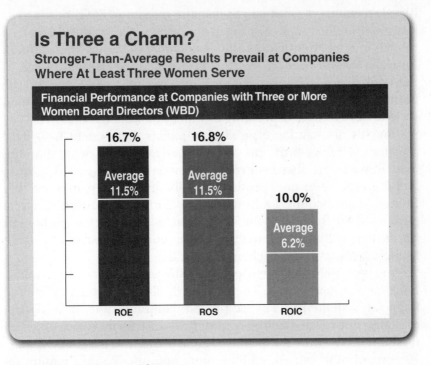

Figure 6.2   Is Three a Charm?

Source: Catalyst.org.

Happy, healthy employees are invested in their company's success. Eco-efficiency drives lower costs by requiring fewer inputs and creating less waste to haul away—as well as reducing pollution and emissions that would need to be cleaned up later. Increased diversity adds value through identifying customer groups with unique needs, desires, cultures, or traditions, and improving the quality of ideas, decisions, and actions that are taken in a company. These factors link directly to top-line revenue and bottom-line profit

Integrating several of these key human impact factors together as investment criteria also yields portfolios that have outperformed benchmarks. Goldman Sachs's Sustain index, which includes Enviromental, Social, and Governance factors (ESG) in its portfolio selection, outperformed the global benchmark MSCI by 25 percent from Fall 2005 to Spring 2007 (Goldman Sachs 2007). Generation Investment Management's fund for high net-worth and institutional investors is led by former U.S. Vice President Al Gore and David

Blood (formerly of Goldman Sachs) also integrates ESG criteria in its investment selection. Its approach has delivered annualized financial returns much better than its MSCI benchmark (Money Management Australia 2008; *Fortune*, Nov. 12, 2007). Of course, you have seen in this book how a HIP approach positions your portfolio to exceed the traditional benchmarks by focusing on the long term, taking a total societal view, and incorporating a strategy of sustainability.

But it's not just large public companies that benefit from HIP practices. High-growth, privately owned ventures delivering human impact can also be profitable investments—just ask Clorox and L'Oreal. Consumer-product conglomerate companies, or "Big Brands," have acquired a host of compelling HIP upstarts. L'Oreal purchased the Body Shop for $1.4 billion in 2000, and Clorox bought Burt's Bees in 2007 for more than $900 million. (Remember the table listing these purchases back in Chapter 2).

You see that HIP metrics correlate with higher shareholder value and appreciation. These metrics also map directly to the financial statements. This approach combines the best of the capitalist approach—being quantitative and focused on financial fundamentals—with the positive impacts that the do-gooders seek, 70 percent of whom are seeking more quantifiable information on sustainable investing (SVT Group survey of financial advisers, 2006).

Mapping Impact to the Financial Statements

Why do HIP portfolios, indexes, and valuations climb higher? They are focused on counting the leading indicators of impact and their ultimate financial result. On the income statement, these factors drive higher revenues and lower costs. On the balance sheet, they contribute to higher asset values and lower liability exposure. The result is higher profit, higher net worth, lower risk, and overall increased valuation once they are realized.

In the remainder of this chapter we'll explore how human impact leads to profit in three categories of financial calculations and reporting:

1. The income statement (higher revenues, lower costs)
2. The balance sheet (higher assets, lower liabilities)
3. The investor demand for the stock (hence, the likely higher price and valuation)

Note: For a deeper explanation of how accounting statements work, read *Crash Course in Accounting and Financial Statement Analysis* (Feldman and Libman 2007).

After we discuss these three areas of profit, I will show you the various ways in which leading companies—and their CEOs and CFOs—communicate all of these aspects to investors and financial fiduciaries, from Wall Street to Main Street. The insights from this chapter can be applied by companies seeking to be more HIP—and observed by investors seeking out those leading firms for their portfolios.

Translating Human Impact to the Income Statement

Income statements report the inflows of cash from customer sales and monetary outflows for the costs of materials, people, and taxes. Sales of HIP products boost revenue, and HIP operations manage costs more effectively.

Higher Sales from HIP Products

HIP investors first examine what a company sells and how HIP it might be. GE highlights its definition for customers and investors with its Ecomagination designation for some products, while PepsiCo highlights its "Good for You" category. You should dig deeper to confirm that they meet high standards. Given world trends toward greater Health, Wealth, Earth, Equality, and Trust, companies selling HIP products tend to experience higher sales growth. This can result from selling higher volumes of product, charging higher prices, or both.

Hannaford Brothers, founded in 1883, is a food retailer operating 170 stores across 5 states in New England, including its home state of Maine. Hannaford instituted a "Guiding Stars" program for rating food quality (including natural, organic, and healthy choices), which they describe as "nutritious shopping made simple." One star is for Good, two is for Better, and three is for Best. The ratings value whole grains, dietary fiber, minerals, and vitamins higher, but rank products with added sugars, sodium, cholesterol, trans-fat, and saturated fat lower. Each product is evaluated with the same criteria to maintain consistency. Hannaford has applied for a patent on its rating system (Hannaford Web site).

Table 6.1   Changes in Volume Based on Food Quality Ratings

Food Category	Sales Increase for "Starred" Foods	Sales Decrease for "Unstarred" Foods
Whole milk	+1% (fat-free milk, 3 stars)	−4% (whole milk, no stars)
Ground beef	+5% (90% or more fat-free)	−5% (no stars)
Chicken	+5%	−3%

Source: Hannaford Brothers; NewsInfusion TV.

More than 25,500 products have been rated so far (Sept. 2009), including all produce, 51 percent of cereals, 41 percent of seafood, over 20 percent of dairy and meat, and under 10 percent of soups and bakery. More than one in four products evaluated (28 percent) have earned one or more Stars (Hannaford Web site). Only five categories are excluded from ratings: bottled water, alcoholic beverages, coffee, tea, and spices and this system has helped customers identify more beneficial food items quickly and easily. With this information, customers are now buying differently, shifting market share from less-healthy products to more-healthy ones, listed in Table 6.1.

Consumers bought 4 percent less whole milk, which received no Stars, while increasing their purchases of fat-free milk by 1 percent, as it received the top rating of three stars. Sales of low-fat ground beef (90 percent or more fat-free) with Stars increased by 5 percent, while ground beef without Stars dropped by 5 percent. Healthier chicken preparations with Star ratings grew at 5 percent, while chicken products without Stars decreased by 3 percent (Hannaford *Grocery Shoppers Follow*).

On a relative basis, the sales volumes of several products with positive ratings moved faster: Yogurts and breakfast cereals with Stars grew more than 3.5 times faster than their no-Star counterparts. Packaged goods—including crackers, pasta, cereals, breads, canned and jarred foods, snacks, and beverages—with Stars grew at 2.5 times the rate of those with no Stars. Movement of Starred frozen dinners and entrees outpaced frozen no-Stars, growing about 4.5 times faster than those without Stars (Hannaford *Grocery Shoppers Follow*).

While the common perception is that healthier food costs more, Hannaford Brothers also suggests menus that increase both Health and Wealth, by saving customers money. The Hannaford Guiding Stars menu is essentially healthier, aside from a possible debate over the lunchtime choice of tuna versus a burger. Tuna, being high on the food chain, can accumulate more mercury. Meanwhile, hamburger meat tends to incur more Earth intensity, with a high level of water usage to produce it, from farm to store.

Customers short on time show high interest in these rating systems, and the increase in volume and sales reflect that for both the retailer and the food manufacturer.

Of course, any ratings system needs to be legitimate and valid. Several food ratings systems recently developed by manufacturers have been called into question. As both a consumer and investor, you should ensure that any ratings system is verified or developed by independent sources, as Hannaford's is.

Price premium is another driver of increased revenue. Organic milk is sometimes priced at up to double that of conventional milk (Dimitri and Venezia 2007, 9). Sales continue to grow for organic milk, especially with moms seeking healthier foods for home consumption. Organic milk purchases have tended to displace market share of conventional milk among higher-income households, purchasers with college degrees, and younger buyers (Dimitri and Venezia 2007, 16). Here's a personal example: At home, my wife and I pay the premium for organic, because we view it as a low-cost investment in our long-term health. We drink one gallon a week, so that amounts to an incremental $3 per week. At 52 weeks a year, this $156 investment seems to be a "healthy" return for the added benefits resulting from organic and natural dairy products, especially when compared to the $1000 per month that we can spend on health care insurance.

In some cases, price premiums can combine with higher usage. In green real estate, buildings that are energy-efficient or have other eco-improvements have tended to earn more per square foot, with lower vacancy rates. According to CoStar, even after the real estate meltdown, landlords of LEED-certified buildings can command an additional $10 per square foot per year, and owners can tack on another $150 per square foot when they sell a LEED-certified building. Occupancy rates of LEED- and Energy Star-rated buildings can run 4 percent higher, with higher tenant retention. (CoStar report 2008)

As corporations begin to track the value of more HIP products, they will start reporting more specific revenue numbers. For example, Corning estimated $500 million from its environmental-related products, such as gas/diesel engine technologies (Interview April 2009). Office Depot was able to report that, for 2007, its green products revenues were \$1.3 billion, flat from the previous year and totaling less than 10 percent of its overall revenue for that year (Office Depot 2009).

At Scotts Miracle-Gro, a \$3 billion lawn products company, natural products are a fast-growing segment of its business, already totaling \$100 million in revenue, or about 3 percent, according to CEO Jim Hagedorn. The *natural* approach, which focuses on fewer ingredients, is also dropping inputs, costs, and waste. Weed and bug killers in this line are using soybean oil and bio-herbicides, all of which have a green Earth impact and a green profit contribution (Wall Street Journal, *Grass is Made Greener*, 2009).

Recycling waste can generate top-line revenue, too. Trash-hauler Republic Services, Inc., is shifting its revenue mix toward recycling, which in 2008 totaled 7 percent of revenue. Profits can be enhanced when the waste streams feed renewable energy sources as well (Republic Services, Inc., *Credit Suisse*, 2009).

The future growth from emerging economies can help drive future revenue growth too. Chair Craig Barrett of Intel Corp. energized and challenged the Intel Developer Forum in 2008 to help expand the products that can deliver health, wealth and equality. For example, Intel's WiMax technology, which wirelessly connects people to the Internet over long distances, was accessible by 50 million people in 2008, and is targeted for 1 billion by 2011. That availability can increase access to education in Africa, with low-cost whiteboards using Wii remote controls. Access to capital via the Internet and microfinance sites like Kiva.org help local entrepreneurs make money, improve their family's lives, and benefit from Intel technology (Connors, *IDF*, 2008).

Higher revenues show up on the income statement through HIP products, metrics and management practices. In addition, these HIP practices can lead to an improvement in a company's brand which can lead to higher market share and brand loyalty. Let's look at how a HIP approach facilitates lower costs.

Lower Costs from HIP Operations

An income statement captures the costs of doing business, from people to materials, from fuel to real estate. A HIP company experiences higher productivity from staff and lower costs from efficient operations. Both lead to better productivity and increased cash flow.

Labor Productivity and Savings Highly satisfied employees are more engaged with their work, resulting in more innovation and better service to customers, which can generate revenue. It also helps reduce staff turnover and the associated retraining costs.

When companies become more HIP, they also benefit from boosted employee morale. Lauralee Martin, CFO of real estate firm Jones Lang LaSalle, says "employees feel more positive and more engaged around programs that benefit the environment and the workplace, especially during a downturn." The company also encourages at-home sustainability programs, which engages the excitement of employees and creates a more fulfilling job (phone interview, July 2009).

For Toyota, a new customer-service center in Southern California with natural lighting and low-toxic paint and furniture resulted in a 14 percent reduction in absentee days, as employees enjoyed a healthier work environment (Melaver, *Green Building*, 2008). This higher productivity helped Toyota avoid the incremental costs of replacement staff and maintain trained staff for customer inquiries.

In some cases, exciting roles in sustainability may attract talent willing to work for less, just as nonprofits do. In a 2008 survey of top MBAs from 11 top business schools, graduating students reported they would be willing to accept $14,000 (or 14 percent) less in pay if they felt their workplace did more for communities, the environment, and other employees, and acted more ethically (Montgomery 2007).

Materials, Energy, Waste, and Water Savings In the late 1990s, the Global Environmental Management Initiative (GEMI) sought to quantify the financial value of eco-improvements. Comprised of leading environmental, health, and safety (EHS) managers from large corporations, the group created documents like *Environment: Value to Business* in 1998, *Value to the Top Line* in 2001 and *Value to the Investor* in 2004, showing how these programs grew revenue, saved costs, and enhanced overall shareholder value (GEMI Publications Web site).

Jim Thomas, currently the first Vice President of Corporate Social Responsibility at retailer JC Penney, was a sustainability leader at Novartis. At that time, he co-chaired GEMI and sought to help fellow eco-initiative leaders better communicate internally to CEOs, CFOs, and investor relations staffs, as well as to Wall Street.

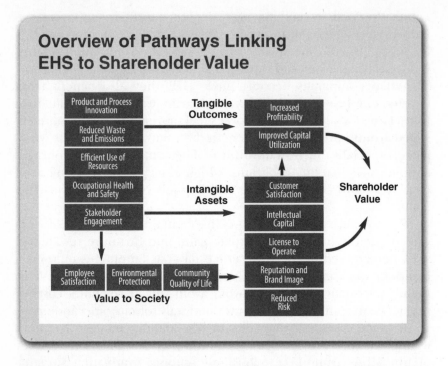

Figure 6.3   Overview of Pathways Linking EHS to Shareholder Value
Source: Global Environmental Management Initiative (GEMI).

"Sustainability can enhance and protect the market value of corporations," says Thomas. The model in the 2004 report outlined many components of overall sustainability—including "EHS" for environmental, health, and safety—that are still in place today, as seen in Figure 6.3.

A good example is found at PepsiCo, where partnership initiatives with retailers like Walmart and Tesco, evaluate ways to reduce the operational environmental footprint of the entire value chain. According to Adriana Villaseñor, PepsiCo's Sustainability Director, this not only enhances customer perceptions of PepsiCo products, but has a real bottom-line impact on profitability by reducing costs to operations. For instance, in the past year Frito-Lay North America experienced a $55 million savings due to conserving water, gas, and electricity.

At Hewlett Packard, driven by the European Union regulatory requirement for mandatory take-backs of technology equipment from customers at the end of its lease or useful life, HP engineers designed printers for easier disassembly and reuse. This resulted in lowering costs as much as 10 percent due to simplifying both the manufacturing process and the printer's components. Looking forward, HP is seeking more dramatic cost reductions through its EcoSolutions products. Now in development, flexible electronic displays are designed to take advantage of new manufacturing methods so that the products will contain 90 percent less materials by volume (HP, *Extends Environmental Leadership,* 2009). "We are de-materializing the business," says Bonnie Nixon, Director of Environmental Sustainability.

For companies seeking to eliminate waste streams, to find new uses for old materials, and to remarket recyclables, Waste Management's Upstream business unit is advising business customers on how they can cash in on items that used to be destined for landfills. Customer cost savings drop to the bottom-line profit. Waste Management also optimizes natural resources—and profits—while converting municipal solid waste to "clean" electricity by burning trash or recapturing the gases from landfills.

At energy company Ashland, "instead of disposing, we are recycling," says their Integrated Resource Management Sheet. Reusing sulfur and phosphorous has led to $240,000 of savings in inputs, and generated $155,000 in profit. Recapturing the energy from burned solvents has contributed $600,000 (Ashland 2009).

Water, sewage, electricity, and waste-hauling expenses can all be reduced to help conserve natural resource intensity. Hobart, a company of Illinois Tool Works, sells food waste pulping equipment and hyper-efficient dishwashing machines to create dramatic savings in customer expenses, while also benefiting the environment. Figure 6.4 shows how super-efficient equipment leads to fewer wasted resources and lower costs.

Lower Facilities Costs in Green Real Estate   Let's move from operations to real estate. A survey of commercial real estate management in 2008 by Jones Lang LaSalle found that 76 percent of managers now think, "sustainability is a critical business issue." Energy-related projects had been implemented by more than half the survey respondents because those types of initiatives were seen to yield the fastest payback. Office recycling programs were even more

Fewer Resources and Lower Costs with Hyper-Efficient Hobart Equipment

Expense Item	Usage in Disposer System	Usage in WastePro	Cost per Unit	Total Annual Saving
Water (gal.)	1,314,000	262,800	$0.002/gal	$2,102
Sewage (gal.)	1,314,000	262,800	$0.002/gal	$2,102
Electrical (kWhr)	8,169	19,601	$0.075/kWhr	($857)
Plastic liners	18,250	3,650	$0.25 each	$3,650
Labor (hrs.)	1,095	365	$7.80/hr.	$5,694
Hauling (per mo.)*	$450	$90	Reduced 80%	$4,320
Total Saving				$17,011

*Based on volume reduction.

Figure 6.4   Fewer Resources and Lower Costs with Hyper-Efficient Hobart Equipment

Source: Courtesy of Hobart Corporation.

prevalent, though, generating higher awareness because employees found it easy to participate (Jones Lang LaSalle, *Perspectives,* 2008).

The Chief Financial Officer of real estate property manager Jones Lang LaSalle (JLL) is a renegade. CFO/COO Lauralee Martin has spearheaded the effort to communicate the benefits to investors. "We are seeking to educate traditional investors that sustainability directly links to profitability," she says. Which investors are interested? "Mainly the European ones," Martin replies.

By the end of 2009, JLL was targeting to have 500 accredited LEED professionals on staff, including building managers, project managers, and expert advisers. One of their key roles is managing to reduce costs—saving energy, water, and waste. JLL's projects have included taking McDonald's headquarters to LEED "Gold" status and Bank of America to "Platinum" in the LEED certification for real estate eco-efficiency standards.

JLL's CEO, Colin Dyer, described the company's efforts in the first-quarter 2009 quarterly earnings call: "In sustainability and in a ground-breaking contract, we were named project manager for the multi-year retrofit program at the Empire State Building (ESB). The aim of this project is to cut energy consumption by 38 percent to reduce the landmark building's carbon emissions by 100,000 metric tons over the next 15 years." Stakeholders in the ESB project seek to inspire managers of other large buildings to follow in their footsteps. "With increasing government regulation of carbon emissions and with older inefficient buildings far outnumbering newer energy efficient properties," Dyer said, "we see growth in this work for our market-leading energy and sustainability services worldwide" (Jones Lang LaSalle, *Q1 Earnings*, 2009).

How does that ambitious, big-picture goal translate into immediate improvements? Old-style radiators running on steam are pulled out, the wall is lined with insulation, and then the radiators are replaced. Windows are popped out and sealer is injected between layers of glass, which saves energy from escaping. Efficient lighting with sensors is another fast payback initiative. In fact, CFO Martin says many of these early initiatives yield very quick paybacks.

The lessons from this building are also being published on the Internet at www.ESBsustainability.com. "Everything is geared to be an educational tool," Martin adds, so others can learn from the experience. Certainly a far cry from the secretive robber-baron days, when common wisdom held that corporate knowledge should never be shared.

The move toward more open, comparable information about life-cycle solutions is also found at the Durability Doctor Web site, hosted at the Partnership for Advancing Technology in Housing (Durability Doctor Web site). Companies supplying improved housing materials include DuPont, Masco, GE, Honeywell, and Interface. Pilot houses showcase the benefits in Omaha, Nebraska, and Charleston, South Carolina.

Facilities lessons can be learned from AIMCO, which rents to 1 million residents across 250,000 apartments nationwide. One-time SVP at AIMCO, Robert de Grasse initiated a movement to increased efficiency, with a 25 + percent ROI through lighting improvements and an attractive ROI from boiler replacements. Even bigger opportunities can be found in expenses that customers themselves pay, de Grasse says, but it's difficult since the investment would need to be coordinated across multiple users. Today, de Grasse is an independent consultant for facilities optimization. "Sustainability is something we infuse into it," he says, "as it's not yet fully valued unless you understand the details" (Wood 2007).

Eaton Corp, a $15 billion provider of power management, makes it easy to understand. On its Web site, the company lists two primary benefits: "save money" and "protect the environment." Eaton offers five categories of solutions, including indoor environmental quality, energy and atmosphere, and sustainable sites (see Figure 6.5). For sites seeking LEED certification, Eaton promises its products can help earn 40 percent of the required certification points. Lighting improvements, in particular, can save 10 percent to 30 percent of electricity costs (Eaton Corporation Web site).

Lower energy usage also positions a company financially for lower liabilities, as we will see later in the balance sheet discussion. Lower regulatory risk is likely, too, as climate-change legislation and carbon taxes evolve.

But if financial results are enhanced by a new fundamental, wouldn't that be of keen attention interest to the investing world? Apparently not. The mindset of "anything environmental or social must require a financial sacrifice" is old school. Tradition-minded capitalists who do not see the light on this leading indicator are missing out on new profit opportunities.

The Coming Cost of Carbon   "Businesses at large don't yet understand their 'lifecycle carbon footprints' of services they provide," says Mitch Jackson of Federal Express. "You might think that transportation is a big part of your carbon footprint, but many times it is much lower, depending on what you make and how your customers use it."

At FedEx, though, transportation is the largest component of the company's carbon footprint, as well as the largest piece of its variable cost structure. Fuel for airplanes and ground vehicles is 82 percent of expenses, in addition to creating greenhouse gas emissions. To reduce both factors requires large-scale replacement of planes. FedEx is in the process of changing out its Boeing 727s for more fuel-efficient, longer-distance and larger-payload 757s, resulting in a 47 percent reduction in fuel used per ton carried (and a 47 percent greenhouse gas reduction, too). With 777 freighters coming into the fleet in 2010, landings and takeoffs related to refueling stopovers can be eliminated, saving fuel, costs, and time. "It will be a service

Eaton's Green Products and Services

Eaton Solution	SS Sustainable Sites	EA Energy and Atmosphere	MR Materials and Resources	EQ Indoor Environmental Quality	ID Innovation and Design
Save Energy					
Automatic transfer switch		🍃			
Energy audits		🍃			🍃
Variable frequency drives and soft starters	🍃	🍃		🍃	
Paralleling switchgear		🍃			🍃
Power factor correction capacitors and filters		🍃			
Power Xpert® software and meters		🍃			🍃
Pow-R-Command lighting controls	🍃	🍃		🍃	🍃
Energy efficient and harmonic mitigating transformers		🍃			
Uninterruptible power systems (UPS)	🍃	🍃			🍃
Protect the Environment					
Busway		🍃			
Circuit breakers	🍃	🍃			
Integrated facilities systems (IFS)	🍃				
Medium voltage (MV) switchgear				🍃	
Pre-fabricated product assemblies (IPA)	🍃	🍃			
Refurbishing services			🍃		
Maximum Credits	2	15 + prerequisites	1	4 + prerequisites	5

Figure 6.5   Eaton's Green Products and Services

Source: Courtesy of Eaton Corporation 2009.

enhancement and a sustainability enhancement," Jackson says. FedEx Chair Fred Smith has also called for the company's aircraft fuel to be 30 percent bio-based by 2030.

How can companies easily calculate their carbon footprint? A savvy solution is offered by Climate Earth, a software company based in San Francisco. By using the manufacturing and financial accounting systems that track costs of materials and resources, Climate Earth can calculate a company's carbon profile in about 30 days. Its information tools help find savings in costs and carbon, even among a company's suppliers. Construction company Webcor is using these tools to find savings in multimillion dollar construction projects. It's also winning new projects by incorporating the savings in costs and carbon into its bids. "Carbon dioxide equivalence is a strategic metric," says Webcor's President and CEO Andy Ball (Rental Equipment Register 2009).

We've covered revenue and expenses. Now let's look at the third major driver of profit on the income statement—taxes. A reduced tax bill is also possible through initiatives creating positive human impact.

Tax Incentives, Rebates, and Credits Add Profit   Taxes on business cover income, payroll, assets and property, and sales of goods and services. As of this book's writing, health-care benefits were not taxed, though this has been under reconsideration to pay for aspects of health-care reform.

The American Recovery and Reinvestment Act provides for tax credits, rebates, and incentives for energy efficiency across vehicles, buildings, and industrial equipment. In some cases, the U.S. Treasury is cutting a check for 30 percent of the investment in renewable energy facilities that began operations in 2009 and 2010. This creates an attractive return-on-investment opportunity, as well as accelerating the move toward more renewable energy (IRS 2009).

The states of California and New Jersey have been two early movers in creating tax incentives for increased energy independence and efficiency. Walgreens took advantage of this by implementing renewable-energy projects in 100 stores across those two states in the past few years. They're not alone. Federal Express has also installed solar power generators at several sites in California and New Jersey, including solar panels at its Oakland airport hub (FedEx, *Sun Shines*). By year-end 2009, a super-size solar rooftop

installation of 2.42 megawatts will be installed at a FedEx facility in
New Jersey—though it will be owned by energy company BP Solar
(Cheyney 2009). FedEx leases most of its retail space, which makes
improvements a bit more difficult. Solar-power paybacks can take 10
to 15 years while retail leases are typically only five years, says Mitch
Jackson, the company's sustainability VP. But still, with an additional
1.4 megawatts in Cologne, Germany, FedEx's eastern European hub,
solar will total 5 megawatts by 2010. Tax rebates on renewable energy
will have benefited the bottom line in all locations—however, tenants
and landlords need to agree who pockets the savings.

"We want to use renewable energy and create the market for it,"
Jackson says. FedEx Office (formerly Kinko's) is a long-time member
of a green power development group, through the World Resources
Institute. Both FedEx Express and Office are part of the EPA's Green
Power program, and FedEx Office is rated #1 on green printers,
according to Jackson.

Yum! Brands, which owns KFC and Taco Bell, encourages their
outlets to hire economically disadvantaged and disabled workers,
earning a Work Opportunity Tax Credit while creating jobs, advancing equality and enhancing profit (Yum! Brands CSR 2008).

Calculating the Full Benefits for Return on Investment   Before we
finish the income statement mapping, let's dig into two detailed examples of return on investment. The first is data centers. In 2006
it was estimated that data center and server energy consumption
was 1.5 percent of all electricity consumed in the United States (Energy Star, *Congress*, 18). Some say the infrastructure costs to support servers over their lifecycle actually exceeds the server's initial
equipment cost. Tech companies like Amazon, Google, and Yahoo!
are now locating new data centers on the Columbia River in the
Pacific Northwest to benefit from lower-priced hydro-electricity (Katz
2009). Interesting when you consider that, a few hundred years ago,
water-powered enterprises were all the rage.

To optimize its Silicon Valley data centers, Sun Microsystems unified the server operations through "virtualization" software, enabling
the same applications to use multiple servers. After consolidating
2177 servers to 1240, the remaining equipment was arranged for energy efficiency. Then, energy sensors were placed in the data center to
manage air flow and cooling. (Some data centers at Cisco and Yahoo!
even use cooler outside air at night to minimize air conditioning

expenses.) These improvements resulted in a payback time of less than 3 years, from lower energy usage, smaller amounts of working capital for equipment, avoidance of a new data center construction project estimated at $9.3 million, and a utility energy-reduction incentive payment of $1 million. Also, the energy savings reduced pollution, saving 4100 tons of carbon annually (Fontecchio 2007).

Another example brings together all the savings from green buildings. Capital E analysts estimated the typical savings from energy, emissions, water, and operations and maintenance improvements over the 20-year life of green structures. Those benefits easily exceeded the estimated incremental costs of those improvements (see Figure 6.6). In addition, because of the "health" of the building, its open design and natural materials, fewer employees would get sick, and productivity would increase for staff. The inclusion of these employee-related benefits generated a net value that was three to five times higher, with a very attractive return on investment.

Financial Benefits of Green Buildings

Value per Square Foot	20-year NPV
Energy value	$5.79
Emissions value	$1.18
Water value	$0.51
Waste value (construction only)—1 year	$0.03
Commissioning O&M value	$8.47
Productivity and health value (certified and silver)	$36.89
Productivity and health value (gold and platinum)	$55.33
Less green cost premium	($4.00)
Total 20-year NPV (certified and silver)	**$48.87**
Total 20-year NPV (gold and platinum)	**$67.31**

Figure 6.6   Financial Benefits of Green Buildings
Source: Capital E analysis.

So you can see how companies can increase profit through higher income, lower costs and optimizing taxes, while also creating positive human impact. Next, we will examine the balance sheet.

Capturing Human Impact on the Balance Sheet

The balance sheet includes the value of assets, liabilities, and resulting equity or net worth. New assets, like bankable carbon credits, and new liabilities, such as lawsuits related to negative social or eco-performance, are currently considered "intangibles" but can affect net worth and company valuations.

The Hidden Asset

Only 30 percent of a company's market value can be found on the balance sheet categories of tangible assets: cash, inventory, plant, real estate, and equipment. More than two-thirds of market value is "intangible," according to a 2006 Ocean Tomo analysis. But would you call yourself intangible? Accounting principles do. Despite the traditional economic inputs of "land, labor, and capital," labor in accounting is treated an expense, not an asset. Yet technology-, financial-, and science-based companies are highly valued because of their talent and the innovations they create. Every night, the major asset of those companies walks out the door—an asset that is not quantified on the balance sheet.

One high-tech company realizes this quandary: the global firm Infosys, based in India. Read its annual report and you'll find many interesting aspects. It reports its financial statements in different formats and languages to accommodate shareholders in India, Australia, Canada, France, Germany, Japan, and the UK. In addition to its world-class transparency about nearly every possible number, it goes one further than any other annual report we've encountered. It calculates the asset value of its people.

Infosys properly identifies its employees as a source of wealth. "The definition of wealth as a source of income inevitably leads to the recognition of human capital as one of the several forms of wealth, such as money, securities, and physical capital," the company says. Infosys could not create value without its people, and they could disappear quickly, unlike physical assets. In its 2009 annual report, Infosys counts 104,850 employees, of which 97,349 are software professionals, and the remainder are "support" (Infosys, *Annual*

Report, 125). While physical assets on Infosys's accounting statements net out to $3.75 billion, Infosys calculates its "human resources value" at $21.5 billion, nearly five times larger. Return on traditional assets equaled 33.6 percent for Infosys, yet the company's return on human assets would be 5.9 percent (Infosys, *Annual Report,* 51 and 139). The point here is that traditional financial accounting has yet to properly account for the sources of competitive advantage, like those intangible people in a company. New ideas do not come from a machine, factory or even a computer. Innovations are produced by people. Trained talent appreciates over time, becoming more valuable. These fundamentals contribute to the driving forces behind a HIP company: Maximizing human impact internally, along with the factors that solve human needs, can lead to higher profitability and valuations.

Emerging Assets: Carbon Value

Another asset not yet captured on the balance sheet is the value of carbon. Today, much pollution incurs no cost to companies. Some air and water pollution is monitored, regulated, and occasionally fined. In two instances, cap-and-trade systems are already in place—for sulfur dioxide and nitrous oxide emissions. But we expect carbon taxes or cap-and-trade systems will eventually be the norm. When these systems are implemented, companies will need to scramble to systematically account for their emissions. A "credit" for carbon will be created for low-polluting companies that beat the standard. These carbon credits can then be traded from more efficient companies to less efficient companies. According to Bart Chilton, a commissioner of the Commodities Futures Trading Commission, the future market could be valued at $2 trillion (Reuters UK 2008). Imagine the future value for forward-thinking companies.

Today, the value of a "carbon credit" varies widely. In September 2009, the European Climate Exchange listed one ton of tradeable carbon equivalents at €10 to €12, or about $14 to $17. At the peak of the financial market, values were close to $45 per ton. In the United States, prices have run the gamut. The Chicago Climate Exchange, a voluntary platform, requires member companies that sign up to make significant reductions; in summer 2009, carbon prices remained under $1 per ton (Chicago ClimateX Web site). In the

Northeast and New York State, the Regional Greenhouse Gas Initiative (RGGI) covers utilities, which have committed to a 10 percent emissions reduction by 2018; the price per ton in Sept. 2009 was about $3 per ton (RGGI Web site).

Devon Energy, a $15 billion firm, is holding onto the carbon credits it's generating (Google Finance). "We are concerned about the future value and likely to hold onto them," says David Templet of Devon's environmental, health and safety group. Devon is investing in projects to reduce its emissions, including carbon sequestration, selling the gases trapped in the wells, and improvements from upgraded gaskets and valves. "If the price of GHGs rise to $60 to $80 per ton; then those credits will be valuable for our competitive advantage," says Templet.

The value of carbon reductions is a tradable asset. Companies that are more carbon-efficient today could accumulate higher asset values on their balance sheet when more comprehensive carbon-reduction policies are approved and implemented. Leading firms are investing in carbon efficiency now to reduce costs, earn attractive return on investment, and prepare for a future that includes tradeable carbon reductions.

Surprise Liabilities: Lawsuits

New liabilities can emerge when businesses ignore the true costs of their actions. Gun manufacturers have been sued for lack of safety controls on weapons. Tobacco manufacturers lost a $206 billion lawsuit related to the health impacts of their products. Auto manufacturers creating unsafe vehicles, like the Ford Pinto, also are pursued in court (NAAG, *Master Settlement*).

The chance of new legal liabilities increases when a company ignores human impacts and lifecycle costs. For example, future lawsuits might emerge around high-fructose corn syrup, which can contribute to obesity and diseases like diabetes.

Leading companies think ahead about the full impact of their products, operations, and ultimate actions. Well-managed firms engage customers early on to address their concerns about products and navigate potential hurdles with care. The least-HIP companies tend to have higher-than-average liabilities, in dollar value and gravity of offense. Judgments against companies can deplete accumulated cash; hurt the brand image, affecting sales; and distract top management from looking forward instead of backward—all of which affect profit and valuation.

New Liabilities: Payment for EcoServices?

In 1997, environmental economists from Argentina, Netherlands, and the United States estimated the value of Nature's services. Since many of these services, like soil formation and nutrient recycling are free, some companies treat them as having no cost. The total annual value of ecosystem services at that time was set at $22 to 37 trillion, or nearly double the global GDP of $18 trillion.

Since nature can manage natural resources more effectively than humans, preservation of ecosystems can be worth more than the human-made approaches. For example, the City of New York calculated that it could avoid building new water treatment plants for $6 to $8 billion, and instead protect the upstate New York watershed that purified the natural water systems at a cost of only $1.5 billion (Staff of World Resources Program 2009).

Will companies have to pay for Nature's services in the future? Governments can institute limits in usage or set a market-pricing mechanism to ration resources for the common good. Companies that proactively manage their Earth metrics and look ahead long-term will better manage the risk of new liabilities or expenses.

The last element of the balance sheet is equity, how a company calculates its net worth, or book value.

Equity: Spread It Around

Companies that share equity and ownership with employees more readily benefit from staff loyalty and productivity. Hewlett Packard, Google and Whole Foods all spread the equity ownership across all levels of the firm. This tends to not only increase employee satisfaction but also creates a more stable shareholder base, whose decisions on behalf of the company are vested with the long-term appreciation of the stock.

Companies that match employees' savings for the future (an excellent example of a HIP Wealth metric), particularly with discounts in company stock, contribute to longer-term stability and less volatility related to trading. Well-managed companies have broad-based ownership and make it easy for employees to contribute as co-owners.

Communicating with investors of all types is important in linking impact to profit. Investor education can occur in several ways, explained in the next section.

How Human Impact Can Alter Demand for—and Pricing of—Share Value

Investing success is strongly tied to understanding the future. Whether it is stocks, bonds, options, or real estate, the price of an investable asset is tied to the expectation of what the future holds. Expectations of the future influence the demand for, supply of, and hence price of that investment. In order to buy low you need to see the future before the general market does, and to sell high you need to understand that the future of a particular investment has realized its full potential.

Prices change as new information is revealed, but that doesn't mean you need "insider" information to build a profitable portfolio. More frequently, the determining factor is how many other investors believe that information to be relevant to the future earnings of a company, who also then incorporate it into the price they are willing to pay for a stock.

In this section, you will see how companies are communicating to shareholders the benefits of sustainability—from advertising to analyst briefings to shareholder meetings to their investor relations communications. This is HIP, as it builds Trust through more openness and transparency. It also leads to a higher demand of the stock of these companies by sustainable investors. Leading firms earn recognition from several sources—as you will see in the ProLogis example below. All of this attention can lead to higher prices, as the demand for the stock of leaders grows. When share prices rise, so does the total return to shareholders

Commercial real estate is shaking out as a sustainability battleground. Liberty Property Trust (LRY), Jones Lang LaSalle (JLL), CB Richard Ellis (CBG), and ProLogis (PLD) are all competing to be the most sustainable. How do you know which company is most serious? One way to tell is by going to the firm's Web site tab marked "investor relations." That is where everyone, from traditional capitalists to HIP investors, goes for more detailed information. In most corporate Web sites, there is also a separate tab for "sustainability" or "corporate social responsibility" information, stories or even metrics.

I asked GE about this distinction in 2007. While the company earned a high HIP Score for pursuing ecomagination and including financial information in its citizenship reporting, it was still producing two separate documents at the time. "We see two separate audiences for the information," said Frank Mantero, GE's Director of Corporate Citizenship Programs. "While ecomagination readers appreciate the financials, many GE investors are not yet appreciating the ecomagination information."

For most companies, that is certainly the case. However, click on Investor Relations at ProLogis, a real estate builder, co-owner and manager, and you find something striking. In the middle of the Investor Relations page, you can see both the annual report and the sustainability report, together. When you click on the Fact Sheet in that same section, you find the following three self-reported Company Strengths:

1. Superior global platform across 18 countries in North America, Europe, and Asia allows us to quickly respond to the needs of our customers.
2. Strong customer relationships built on a foundation of quality facilities and backed by unparalleled service
3. An unwavering commitment to sustainability.

In plain English and for all investors, there are three clear priorities, with a HIP goal as one of the three (Prologis, *Investor Fact Sheet*, 2009).

Right below, under Stock Information, the document lists share prices, market values, and memberships in various indexes. Shown in Figure 6.7, ProLogis proudly lists its inclusion not only in the traditional capitalist clubs of S&P 500 and *Fortune* 500, but also in the "do-gooder" indexes of Domini 400, FTSE4Good and Dow Jones Sustainability Index, as well as the recently established S&P U.S. Carbon Efficient Index.

On the flip side of the fact sheet for all investors, ProLogis highlights its straightforward sustainability strategy to lead the industry in distribution centers that are also sustainable in their operations, and to "create an optimal balance between shareholder value, the environment, and corporate social responsibility." The company also highlights its investments in 11 solar installations and 3 wind turbines.

ProLogis Investor Fact Sheet

Stock Information (as of June 30, 2009)	NYSE:PLD
Common share price	$8.06
Common share dividend projected rate for 2009	$0.70/yr
Dividend yield	8.7%
Equity market capitalization	$3.8B
Total debt	$7.9B
Total market capitalization	$11.7B

Member: S&P since July 2003

FTSE4Good since October 2005

Fortune 500 since April 2008

Domini 400 since August 2008

Dow Jones Sustainability Index since September 2008

S&P U.S. Carbon Efficient Index since January 2009

Figure 6.7   ProLogis Investor Fact Sheet
Source: ProLogis.com, Investor Relations, Fact Sheet (Second Quarter, 2009).

Essentially, ProLogis sees sustainability as a positive aspect for all investor types. Who is driving this? "We would not be there today unless the CEO was 100 percent supportive and behind us," says Jack Rizzo, the Chief Sustainability Officer at ProLogis. The Chief Sustainability Officer role was created as a top executive position, alongside the COO and CFO. What's more, the person to fill this role was cofounder Robert Watson, with two decades at the company. Establishing a Sustainability Board formalized high-level executive commitment to all of the company's goals.

As ProLogis pursues new construction, any new internally designed buildings are built to the regionally appropriate eco-qualified standards: LEED in the United States, BREAMM in the UK, and CASBEE in Japan. Achieving high scores didn't require much change and didn't take much effort, Rizzo says, because eco-standards are in line with principles of great design. Any incremental costs were typically certification costs from external consultants, while the building design itself substituted materials or equipment, or applied smart design principles.

Since it owns the buildings it builds, ProLogis applies a "lifecycle" approach to managing its assets. The result? Roof systems that last 18 to 25 years instead of just 15 years, due to closer monitoring and maintenance, along with innovatively designed flashing to reduce wear and tear. "We have a 25-year view instead of a 2-year view," says Rizzo. ProLogis also realizes 30 percent to 70 percent savings on electricity consumption related to lighting, thanks to motion sensors, fluorescent technologies, and using daylight in lieu of lighting, where appropriate. These savings directly map into the income statement and ultimately, profitability. Depending on contracts, some savings also flow to the client's bottom line, increasing customer satisfaction.

Before the economic meltdown, ProLogis's clients were leasing these properties faster than noncertified ones, retaining them longer, incurring fewer operating costs, and benefiting from enhanced branding as customers wanted to showcase spaces certified to high environmental standards. In addition, according to a 2007 ProLogis report, the higher-performance buildings delivered 7 percent to 9 percent more on resale value than nonrated ones. Since the recession, it's been harder to see similar financial results, but part of that is because ProLogis now co-owns its facilities with institutional investors like Fidelity and Vanguard.

Strategically Communicating with Investors

A company's valuation depends not only on the fundamentals of sales, costs, and taxes, but also on the supply and demand for the firm's stock. When more investors demand that stock, the price can rise. Investors might desire a particular stock for increased expectations of growth, such as from a new product, like Apple's iPod. Investors are also looking for new sources of competitive leadership, and sustainability is one of those themes.

Companies communicate with investors in a variety of ways to keep them informed. Quarterly earnings calls update the latest financials and expectations, but are typically only attended by Wall Street analysts and those with large institutional holdings. Shareholder meetings invite all investors, big and small. Special meetings just for analysts dig deeper into a company's strategic plans.

Sometimes, even mass-media advertising is a strategy. Let's explore how companies communicate with investors to increase transparency about their organizations and their initiatives that deliver both human impact and profit—which can also lead to increased demand for their stock.

Advertising for Investors

Back in 2005, one of the more HIP industrial companies, United Technologies Corp (UTC), the maker of Otis elevators and Pratt & Whitney engines, sensed investors were not fully aware of all the innovative products and initiatives the holding company conglomerate was pioneering (*BusinessWeek* 2007). UTC had solutions like buses that ran on renewable-energy fuel cells and building systems that used low volumes of water and energy. While engineering-driven firms are frequently shy to brag, UTC decided investor awareness was lower than it should be.

In 2006, United Technologies launched an advertising campaign in major newspapers and business magazines to communicate its latest innovative products currently available, as well as those on the horizon (DDB 2007). The advertisements showed detailed blueprint-like representations of helicopters, outlining 40 percent lower maintenance costs and "more rescues per gallon" of fuel. One theme asked, "Can the right thing and the profitable thing be the same thing?" The answer was "yes," and UTC positioned itself as the leader for those solutions and growing markets. (See Figure 6.8.)

By also posting these advertisements where investment analysts traveled—the trains from Manhattan to the suburbs of New York, New Jersey, and Connecticut—they targeted the desired audience: institutional investors and Wall Street analysts. After the launch, UTC's reputation with financiers as a leader in innovation jumped by 10 percent, according to Lippincott Mercer. In general, increased investor awareness of strong fundamental performance and innovative business strategies should lead to higher demand for a stock, especially among long-term investors, which can result in higher price-to-earnings multiples (*BusinessWeek*, 2007).

Shareholder Meetings

Shareholder meetings are a popular place to inform investors, especially since many consumer brand companies are owned by

Figure 6.8   Trust: Tell Your Story (UTX)
Source: Used with permission. © United Technologies Corporation.

individual investors. At Heinz's annual meeting in August 2009, the Chair, President, and CEO, William R. Johnson, showcased the company's integrated approach to sustainability—linking it to overall quality standards, which have proved to reduce cost, mitigate risk, and increase stability.

"Our commitment to quality also extends to other important areas like food safety, sustainability, and social responsibility," Johnson said. He highlighted specific profit-enhancing initiatives driven by creating positive impact in the areas of Health and Earth:

- "In food safety, our HeinzSeed program ensures virtually 100 percent traceability from the tomato seed to the finished product."
- "In the area of sustainability, we have a global initiative underway to achieve a 20 percent reduction in Greenhouse gas emissions, energy consumption, solid waste, and water consumption by 2015."
- "We are also focused on reducing the weight and size of packaging and increasing our use of recycled materials (Heinz Annual Meeting 2009)."

"Sustainability is smart business," summarizes one slide from the shareholder meeting, seen in Figure 6.9. Heinz is reaping the results for its 2009 fiscal year: $10 billion in revenue, 9 percent increase in net income, and a higher dividend for the sixth year in a row—all in recessionary times (Heinz Annual Meeting 2009). Johnson attributes customer loyalty to Heinz's leading brands around the world—in places like India, Indonesia, Russia, Poland, and Mexico—to its focus on "quality, nutrition, innovation, convenience, and value." While nutrition is highlighted second, and linked to quality overall, Heinz sees that the HIP trends in Health, Wealth, Earth, and Equality are positive drivers of a profitable business.

At the Hewlett Packard shareholder meetings, employees are fully engaged as most are co-owners of the company. Director of Environmental Sustainability Bonnie Nixon says that employee engagement on HIP issues is high at HP, from ideas in daily work, the blogs employees write for internal and external audiences, and as long-time investors holding company stock. HP is one of the top 10 HIP companies by quantifiable impact. "HP has more than 40 Global Sustainability Chapters and the Live Green program seeks to help employees change their behaviors at home, at work and in the community."

HIP investors may find some discussion of these topics at shareholder meetings—for example, Intel's CEO highlighting socially

Figure 6.9 Reducing Packaging Impacts
Source: H.J. Heinz Company © 2009.

responsible indexes, such as the Dow Jones Sustainability Index, where the firm has been listed. However, most companies—even if they are HIP leaders—are not communicating widely to investors about the profitable benefits resulting from their sustainability initiatives. As a shareholder, you can contact a company's Investor Relations department to recommend these topics be added to the next annual shareholder meeting. The more who do, the more the company will receive the signal that it's important to both act *and* communicate.

Shareholder Resolutions

One initiative investors sometimes pursue is the shareholder resolution. Like an election, it calls for a vote by shareholders of the company on a particular policy or practice. These initiatives are also called proxies. Capitalist investors have used them in corporate takeovers to force a sale. Do-good investors have used them to protest social or environmental policies, or lack thereof. Proxies tend to have a negative association, as they are often intended to force managers or boards to do something they have already decided against.

However, an interesting case of a shareholder proxy fight occurred at Federal Express. The citizenship mission of the company aspires to "connect the world responsibly and resourcefully," and FedEx's core mission is "People, Service, Profit"—as it has been for decades. Mitch Jackson, VP of Sustainability, says it follows that if you treat employees right, they provide superior service to customers, which increases profitability. Environment is part of all three aspects, Jackson says.

FedEx highlights its eco-performance in both the annual report and citizenship reports. "It has come up in annual shareholder meetings and stockholder proposals in the past," says Elizabeth Allen, Director of Investor Relations. "We have found there is a difference globally in the level of interest. European investors ask more questions about it than any other investors."

FedEx's founder and Chair Fred Smith has incorporated sustainability themes in his remarks at the shareholders meeting. The FedEx Board advocates for reduced greenhouse gas emissions, acknowledging that the company's main variable operating expense is fossil fuel costs. Increasing fuel efficiency and reducing GHG is strategic for FedEx to remain competitive. The company has 264 hybrid vehicles and would invest in more if the price premiums were lower, Jackson says.

Companies not pursuing eco-efficiencies typically have proxies filed by small groups of shareholders, a good example being Exxon-Mobil's ongoing battle with environmentalists. For FedEx, it was just the opposite. Stephen Malloy, of the Free Enterprise Action Fund, filed multiple proxies in consecutive years against FedEx, saying that it was "doing too much" by investing in renewable energy and hybrid electric vehicles, which Malloy felt did not increase shareholder value. FedEx's Board replied, says Jackson, that greenhouse gases were a proxy for fuel consumption, and the company needed to reduce fuel costs, hence supporting profits. The Malloy proxies collected less than 5 percent support and FedEx has continued initiatives that boost Earth metrics and profit at the same time. "It's a good illustration that environmental sustainability is good for your business," Jackson says.

Investment Analyst Meetings

Educating analysts at conferences about corporate strategies and directions is a common practice. To comply with SEC "fair disclosure" regulations to keep a level playing field for all investors, companies must also make public the presentations and transcripts, which you can typically find on the Investor Relations section of their corporate Web sites.

Campbell's Soup presented in February, 2009, to the Consumer Analyst Group of New York conference, which featured food, beverage, tobacco, and household products. Aware of the ongoing customer trend toward healthier, more HIP products, Campbell's is strongly highlighting the wellness profile of its condensed soups. Reduced-sodium products had net sales of $500 million in 2008, 10 times higher than five years earlier. Campbell's market share in these low- and reduced-sodium soups is one in six retail sales of this healthy category in the United States.

Campbell's CEO Douglas Conant described its switch to lower-sodium sea salt for its Select Harvest products, which gained five million new consumers by 2009. The company also launched lower-sodium, "all-natural" Swanson cooking stock and eliminated MSG from all kids' soups—which also have lowered sodium. Even Campbell's Tomato Soup, first sold in 1897 with a rope-jumping cartoon kid, is targeted to have 32 percent lower sodium in 2010, benefiting the 25 million soup eaters in the world who slurp a bowl at least once a week. On the acquisition side, Campbell's recently purchased Wolfgang Puck's organic soup business.

Campbell's and soup are synonymous, but health and wellness trends are changing the nature of consumer preferences and overall sales. To help educate the investment analyst community, Conant showed a chart segmenting the expected fiscal year 2010 net sales of its U.S. soup portfolio by sodium per serving (see Figure 6.10). About one-third of sales were expected to be "heart healthy," with less than 480 mg of sodium per serving. Half were expected to be above 700 mg per serving—much less HIP. And one-fifth were in between.

Conant also showed how Campbell's is positioning for HIP-style wealth trends. More than half of soup eaters worldwide are in Russia and China, according to Campbell's, with consumption in the city of

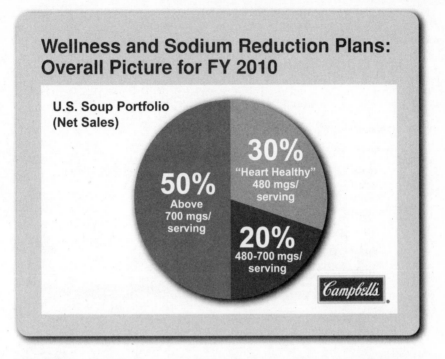

Figure 6.10   Wellness and Sodium Reduction Plans: Overall Picture for FY 2010

Source: Used with Permission by Campbell's Soup Company.

Shanghai alone equal to 60 percent of the entire U.S. soup market. As the company targets international high-potential markets, it expects to gain in revenue and profit, as well as the impacts related to the HIP Categories of Health, Wealth, and Equality.

Campbell's even portrayed its lower risk to analysts in a very creative way, as you see in Figure 6.11. Institutional investors can buy insurance against defaults on bonds, which are known as "credit default swaps." On January 21, 2009, Campbell's calculated that it was a safer investment than most Western European countries and the United States, as indicated by default insurance rates, where lower is better (signifying less risk of default). This indicator shows not only a lower risk for investors, but also a higher degree of quantifiable trust and credibility.

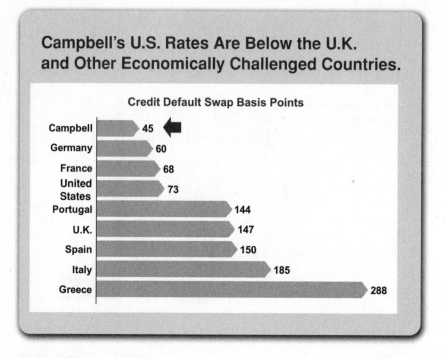

Figure 6.11   Campbell's U.S. Rates Are Below the UK, and Other Economically Challenged Countries

Source: Used with Permission by Campbell's Soup Company.

In addition to generating higher revenue potential and lower risk of default, Campbell's management efforts have ensured long-term benefits including saving operating costs. Dave Stangis, VP of Sustainability and Len Griehs, VP of Investor Relations, shared specific cost savings with investment analysts from the "socially responsible" community at the Social Investment Forum in May, 2009.

Stangis and Griehs reported that Campbell's redesign of heat recovery and water recycling systems has saved 3.5 million gallons of water per day, yielding $4 million directly to the bottom line. The company's largest fuel cell installation in the United States has annual savings that exceed $1 million per year. Right-sizing the Pepperidge Farm Goldfish® carton saved more than 100,000 pounds of material and $900,000 annually (see Figure 6.12). By saving water, substituting energy, and eliminating materials, Campbell's simultaneously realized higher human impact *and* profit.

Operational Sustainability

Manufacturing

- Largest fuel cell installation in the United States
  Annual savings > $1MM.

- Heat recovery and water recycling system redesign
  **Savings—3.5 million gallons/day water
  and $4 million/yr.**

- Increase current 70% waste recycle rate

Packaging

- Right-sizing Pepperidge Farm® Goldfish carton
  saves more than 100,000 pounds of material and $900K.

- Eliminating the paper labels from canned condensed soup
  **eliminates 250,000 lbs. of material and
  saves $550K in one plant alone.**

- Select Harvest labels
  Saving 800 tons of lumber, 2MM gal of water.

- Sustainability Packaging Guidelines

Figure 6.12 Operational Sustainability

Source: Used with Permission by Campbell's Soup Company.

There are very few companies currently communicating these specific messages about quantifiable human impact and how it leads to profit. Campbell's Soup is one of the leaders, by integrating the message into both traditional investor communications and conferences, as well as engaging more deeply with the do-gooder and socially responsible investment communities. For HIP investors, one indicator of a leading company is increased communication of that company's HIP elements (which is also a measure of the HIP Metric of Trust) and how easy it is to find this information.

Investment Analyst Engagement

Engaging the investment community is a "chicken and egg" quandary, says Dave Stangis, currently at Campbell's and formerly of Intel Corp. Stangis managed the investor relations for CSR at Intel, and started holding meetings, both with traditional analysts to educate them about sustainability, and with CSR analysts to update them on the financial side. "You need to manage it as a competitive advantage," Stangis advises.

While annual reports and 10-K documents require disclosure of environmental and other risks, they do not frequently mention the opportunities. At Campbell's, "sustainability" is now one of the seven core business strategies, and it's why Stangis was recruited to join the company.

"Every analyst that covers us gets a whole briefing on environmental aspects and sustainability of the overall business," Stangis says. The CFO and CEO are committed to integrating these elements into investor communications. "Health and wellness is anchored in our presentations," Stangis adds. At Intel and at Campbell's, he has brought both the do-gooder and capitalist investors into the common conversation about business value and sustainability. "Typically, 'mainstream' analysts would not ask about the environment or employees, and some socially responsible investors do not ask deep questions about the financials," Stangis explains. Mary Jane McQuillen, Director of the Socially Aware Investment (SAI) Program at Clear-Bridge Advisors (owned by Legg Mason), is "one of the best advocates and allies of breaking down these barriers," Stangis says, as is Sustainable Asset Management (SAM), an investment and analysis firm based in Switzerland.

"I see investors increasingly integrating both elements of human impact and profit, like HIP does, and thinking in a more strategic way," Stangis concludes. "Business has an impact on the social side, and the social side does on business if it's thought about and constructed strategically."

How to Achieve Truly Sustainable Profits

You should now see that the HIP approach is based on sound fundamentals of traditional finance and next-generation impact evaluation. HIP products generate revenue and add to asset values, while HIP operating processes lower costs and mitigate risks. All of this generates stronger cash flows with lesser risk. When companies measure, manage, and then communicate this to investors, their valuations can benefit, as well. HIP investors are attuned to this sound financial analysis—as well as the leading indicators that drive them. Table 6.2 shows a summary of the HIP drivers of profit and market value covered in this chapter.

Table 6.2 Summary of Selected HIP Drivers of Financial Value

Financial Element	Value Drivers	Change in Financial Value
Income Statement	Higher Revenue	Pricing premiums, like organic milk
		Market share gains, especially new products in old channels, e.g. Clorox GreenWorks
		Product launches, creating new markets
	Lower Costs and Taxes	Labor productivity, from talented staff retained and focused on customers
		Materials, energy, waste, water savings and efficiencies
		Lower facility costs, e.g. green real estate
		Cost of carbon, lower for eco-efficient operations
		Tax incentives, rebates, credits for eco-investments
Balance Sheet	Untapped Assets	Professional talent that adds value from innovation, e.g. Infosys
		Carbon reduction value ($ per GHG ton below market standard)
	Surprise Liabilities & Equity	Lawsuits incurred or avoided related to externalities and human condition (e.g. cigarettes)
		Potential payment for eco-services (reserves for future usage)
		Increased goodwill equity from enhanced HIP value
Market Value	Increased Valuation	Lower cost of equity (or debt) for lower risk enterprises
		Higher demand for stock from sustainable investors

You have now completed Part II, Researching Your HIP Portfolio, covering multiple examples of HIP products and HIP metrics across Health, Wealth, Earth, Equality, and Trust. In addition, the HIP management practices and financial linkages showcase how this approach creates business value—as well as social and environmental benefits.

In Part III, we will demonstrate how to construct a HIP portfolio. Let's show you the tools on how to design one for yourself.

PART
III

DESIGNING YOUR HIP PORTFOLIO

Part III (Chapters 7, 8, and 9) outlines how to integrate the HIP methodology into a portfolio, how HIP can apply to other investment types (like bonds and real estate), and how HIP investors can positively impact their portfolios and their world.

Chapter 7 helps you take your learning from Parts I and II and evaluate any company—or pair of companies in a "face-off" —on their HIP factors. These include the product portfolio and revenue mix, the operating metrics across Health, Wealth, Earth, Equality, and Trust, and the HIP Management Practices. As you compare companies and industries, you will see what role HIP plays in the dynamics of that sector of the economy.

Looking at an entire portfolio, Chapter 8 helps you map a variety of choices—from stocks to bonds to cash to real estate—using a HIP approach. For equities, each company can be assembled into a portfolio that pools their risks, returns, and impacts. By being inclusive, you can seek to capture maximum economic return and human impact, while also diversifying risk. Chapter 8 also describes examples of both investments and investors realizing both human impact and profit from these approaches.

Finally, in Chapter 9, you will read about what a future HIP world looks like. Imagine when all $175 trillion in global capital seeks this transformational investment approach!

Now, let's design a HIP portfolio.

CHAPTER 7

Framing Your Portfolio for Human Impact + Profit

Humans can be quite predictable sometimes. When the media company which owns *The American Lawyer* and the *Minority Law Journal* publishes its annual list of the most- and least-diverse 250 law firms, there are leaders and there are laggards. Each year one law firm ranks low enough in diversity to stimulate action. But by the following year, the firm typically avoids the bottom of the list. Attentive law partners take immediate action after the survey results are made public, by promoting from within and hiring-in ethnically diverse partners. The next year, another law firm laggard takes its place. When each firm being rated feels the pressure to compete, it becomes a race to the top—or in this case, a race from the bottom—and the performance at each institution goes up. The bar is continually raised.

This is a core insight into why most socially responsible investment funds have not lived up to expectations as their main investment tenet has been to screen out firms that are in such negatively viewed sectors such as alcohol, tobacco, and firearms, among others. The firms that are negatively screened-out aren't included on a ranked list—they are simply banished. This exclusionary approach almost never results in those laggards divesting their "negative" businesses (protests against South African apartheid is one shining exception). In fact, those firms with negative businesses continue to produce net-negative impact products (like cigarettes) or pollute the environment. The exclusionary approach of the do-gooders is not really working in either desired sense. It's not dramatically reducing negative impact—and, as an investment, it doesn't consistently outperform financially.

However, as in the law firm example above, when you "name and shame" in a competitive format that includes all firms, human nature takes over. The worst companies typically act to get a little better, and the entire average rises.

Companies are made up of people—and people want to be recognized for doing good work. An inclusive approach can get more results than an exclusionary one. That is the philosophy of a HIP investor. As my mother tells me, "No person is all good or all bad; they are a mix of both." A HIP investor's goal is to increase the overall net positive, while also creating an incentive to reduce the net negative. By constructing a comprehensive framework of the five HIP elements—Health, Wealth, Earth, Equality, and Trust—you, too, can create a "race to the top."

When it works, each company seeks to avoid the bottom and increases their performance every year. Collectively, that results in increases of overall net positive impact—and superior financial performance—in a HIP portfolio.

This approach works at the top of the list as well. "The toughest job isn't getting to number one—it's staying number one," basketball legend Michael Jordan claimed. It's the same in business and investing. Great practices get copied. The race to the top creates a broader critical mass of demand for solutions that deliver environmental, social, and human impact. In turn, this results in even lower costs to implement solutions. For example, renewable energy costs will drop when more buyers emerge, which will make it easier for companies to get more HIP. Inclusiveness leads to competition, which yields critical mass for solutions. That results in lower costs, higher impacts, and more potential profits.

Being Inclusive Can Be More Attractive

One of the concepts profiteers get right is that a full universe of stocks helps to keep your portfolio diversified. Constraining the universe in any way can increase risk or depress your return. It creates a less attractive portfolio because the sector-specific risks may not justify the potential returns—and don't necessarily improve the overall impact, either.

On average, over multiple years, the profiteer indexes, like the S&P, beat the do-gooder indexes. The reason why? The exclusionary approach does not deliver consistently, though do-good funds tend to come out ahead in at least one market phase: they decline less in down markets. The HIP approach takes the best of the profiteers' full universe and applies a data-driven, results-based scorecard by shifting the weightings toward HIP leaders and away from laggards. The HIP approach works because these weights are based on leading indicators that are not yet priced into stock valuations. A company's true value could be lower if added risks were fully accounted for and accurately calculated, and its true value could be higher if the opportunities and improvements were properly foreseen and evaluated.

An index approach can also provide diversification across multiple industry sectors. While a portfolio or mutual fund might contain a smaller number of select companies (from 30 to 50), this approach can involve higher portfolio risk and also requires a strategy of picking winners to generate financial returns. There are funds that are branded socially responsible that use positive social and environmental criteria, but those funds typically pick a small group of winners from a screened universe, which leads to higher risk for the desired returns. A HIP portfolio typically focuses on a broad index of 100 or 500 companies (such as the companies in the S&P 100 and S&P 500) to keep risk lower, be appropriately diversified, and position for attractive returns. It also positions for more human impact, which includes positive contributions in HIP areas from industries perceived to be dirty, like industrials and materials.

As you see in Figure 7.1, the HIP 100 portfolio approach beats the profiteer S&P 100, the do-good Domini 400 index—and even exceeds a mutual fund of companies focusing on controversial products in terms of their negative impact (guns, alcohol, tobacco, defense contractors), called appropriately, the Vice Fund.

A HIP investor's approach is inclusive of all companies, but exercises influence through weightings of actual HIP outcomes—Health, Wealth, Earth, Equality, Trust—not perceptions or policy checkboxes. When all factors are taken into account on a net basis, a portfolio balanced according to the HIP approach should outperform, because HIP scores tend to be leading indicators of profit and lower risk.

HIP is about real results, backed up by data. Each firm gets analyzed and rated for its overall human impact and profit—or rated

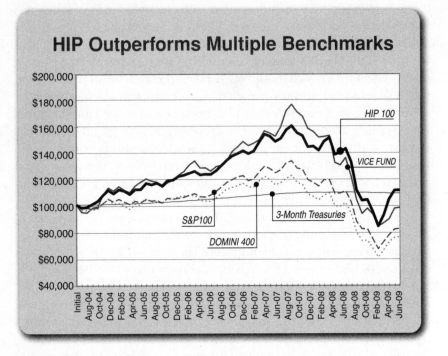

Figure 7.1   HIP Outperforms Multiple Benchmarks

Source: Bloomberg Financial L.P.; HIP Investor analysis.

lower for not reporting at all. How do you compute all of this? You can use the HIP Scorecard. It's actually fun so let's dig in and ask "How HIP Is It?" of big brands and competitors that are everyday names.

How to Complete a HIP Scorecard

Now that you have learned about the HIP methodology, you can create a HIP Scorecard for each company in your portfolio. Based on the share of products that are HIP, the quantitative scores of human impact, and the management practices ratings, you can calculate how much of that stock you want in your portfolio. This is the same process that my firm, HIP Investor Inc., uses to build indexes and portfolios for investors.

Actually, a HIP investor analyzes two or more companies in the same industry at the same time to construct an "industry face-off." You can start with the two largest companies, which in general have the lowest risk due to their size. However, you can face-off any two companies you think have the highest impact to consider for your portfolio. Later in this chapter, you'll see face-offs asking "How HIP Is It?" about companies making products for your medicine cabinet, the fuel for your car, and the computer you use. But before we get started, let's review the components of the HIP approach.

Step 1. Evaluate Products

For each company you evaluate, seek out the products and services that are solving a human need. The goal is to understand the company's offerings for customers. What human need are they serving? How are they creating measurable impact? How much revenue and profit are those products driving relative to the rest of the product lines? Calculate the share of revenue from positive-impact products. Contact the company to ask how it currently reports the revenue linked to positive-impact sectors of its product portfolio—or when it will start doing so.

The *Ratio for HIP Products* is: (a) The value of revenue associated with products creating net positive impact (in the case of GE's ecomagination products, this totals $17 billion for 2008); divided by (b) the total revenues of the company (for GE that year it was $175 billion). So, in this example, we divide $17 billion by $175 billion, and get just under 10 percent. This is the share of revenue from HIP Products. The maximum score is 100 percent, of course—but no public company has hit that magic number yet!

The challenge with this metric is that only a few companies are reporting their numbers this way: PepsiCo's Good-for-You and Better-for-You categories (30 percent of revenue combined); Campbell's Soup's Low-Sodium U.S. soup segment (30 percent of expected 2010 revenue); and DuPont's $8 billion revenue target by 2015 from Non-Depletable Resources are all leading examples.

As a HIP investor, your job is to seek out not just those companies that *do* report, but to encourage firms not yet calculating their own ratios to do so. It's in their best interests to know the upside of being more HIP and the risks to their businesses and valuations of being less HIP.

Step 2. Analyze Human Impact

The goal is to understand how a firm creates positive impact. Read the company's annual report and quarterly earnings statements, investor presentations at shareholder meetings and analyst meetings, and its sustainability scorecards or corporate citizenship reports. Check out third-party sources, like the Carbon Disclosure Project (www.cdproject.net) for greenhouse gas emissions totals, OpenSecrets.org for lobbying information, and Vault.com for employee feedback and pay. (Note: Not all companies fully disclose this information.) Use a common denominator (like revenue or employees) to standardize the comparisons, where appropriate. Go back to Chapter 4 to see typical measures. In addition, the scoring for each metric should generally take into account how each company compares within its industry (for example, carbon emissions for financial companies would be much lower than energy firms or utilities). However there are metrics such as board diversity, women and ethnic employees and certain wealth and health metrics that are not based on industry, and each company should be evaluated on how it compares with cross-industry best practices.

The *Human Impact Score* is a critical measure, because it gauges the true results of a company's impact—which connects directly to how that firm makes money. For example, carbon emissions are a direct product of a company's operations and energy usage. Lowering emissions can result from using less energy or creating more energy efficiencies. For this measure, you can look up the tons of GHG emissions (either from the company or the Carbon Disclosure Project). Then, make sure you understand your units: sometimes the numbers are abbreviated for thousands or for millions. Take the full GHG emissions, like 1,054,749 metric tons for J.P. Morgan Chase in their 2008 CDP report and divide by its revenue ($112 billion, in this example). That ratio of 9.4 GHG per $1 million of revenue compares favorably to Bank of America's slightly higher 12 GHG per $1 million for 2008. Since GHG intensity means fewer emissions per dollar of sales—and contributes to more human impact—it is a useful HIP factor. J.P. Morgan Chase would rate more highly since it has a more advantageous position by being more efficient. Now you can see how face-offs start to take shape, and how a HIP score emerges.

In each Human Impact metric—Health, Wealth, Earth, Equality, Trust—there will be a small set of outcomes, ratios, or other quantitative elements you can research, evaluate, and compare to other companies in the same industry or sector against the best practices in the industry or globally, depending on the metric. As you do, you will discover the leading indicators that a HIP investor uses to reveal a company's hidden value—or liabilities. These values can then be scored from 0 to 100 by each metric. In each HIP category, you can evaluate a few metrics. By weighting companies according to those metrics, you can determine a relative score in each of Health, Wealth, Earth, Equality, and Trust. The sum of each of the five categories can provide an input to the overall HIP rating and weighting.

Step 3. Understand Management Practices

Recurring successes result when there is a methodical and systematic approach. CEOs who cite sustainability as a business strategy, like Jeff Immelt (Ecomagination at GE) or Indra Nooyi (Good-for-You at PepsiCo), are more likely to recruit great talent, impress customers with new products and attract sustainable investors. Live scorecards of sustainability information, like United Technologies' safety and environmental metrics, encourage accountability publicly, as well as internally. The more systematic the management approach, the more likely that firm will gain from sustainable, profitable growth.

To calculate the *HIP Management Practices Rating*, you will need to assess the company on the five characteristics described in Chapter 5. In each of these—vision, metrics, financial alignment, accountability, and decision-making—HIP has constructed five levels of performance. Selecting from five multiple-choice answers (and using a 5-point scale) in each of these five categories, a maximum score of 25 is possible.

For example, in Management Practices, United Technologies rates a 24 out of 25. It achieved the highest rating in four of the five categories (and second-highest in the fifth, aligning financials) for its methodical management approach that continues to create profitable improvements in sustainability—from the energy efficiency of Pratt and Whitney jet engines, to staff skill-building (reimbursement of education expenses). In 2007, Walmart rated an 18 out of 25 for Management Practices; by 2009, Walmart rated a top-notch 23, for accountability, measures, and HIP decision-making. The scores can—and should—improve over time, as companies' management practices become more HIP. High scores tend to correlate with higher Human Impact scores, as you saw in Chapter 6. One challenge here for a HIP investor is learning how specific companies make decisions. It is typically not discussed in public documents. You may need to engage the company directly to ask about how management makes decisions to be more HIP.

Step 4. Calculate the Overall HIP Score

New products that serve growing populations can boost revenue. Implementing energy efficiency in industrial facilities can drop operating costs. Investing in workers can boost productivity. Tapping tax incentives on health care can increase profit. In this step of the analysis, you affirm that the impact measures you selected actually drive financial value—and set up a formula that maps to the profit factors.

Here is where being a HIP investor becomes even more exciting. First you need to decide how much weight should go to the answers in each of the three strategic areas. To begin, you can try 15 percent for Products, 60 percent for HIP measures, and 25 percent for Management Practices. In the HIP metrics, pick the sub-weights each for Health, Wealth, Earth, Equality, and Trust. Then, calculate the *Overall HIP Score* for each company in your portfolio (see Table 7.1).

In the Table 7.1 example, the Overall HIP Score of 51.5 percent would then be used for that company's weighting as you construct your portfolio in the final step.

Step 5. Apply to Your Portfolio

A HIP investor wants a portfolio that gains the highest Human Impact and Profit. By using the methodology here, you can achieve that goal. While a do-good investor has traditionally eliminated companies,

Table 7.1   Calculating the Overall HIP Score for Each Company

HIP Category	Your Choice of Portfolio Weights (total 100%)	Hypothetical HIP Results for Sample Company	Overall HIP Score Components
Products	15% x (multiplied by)	10% =	1.5%
Human Impact	60% x	50% =	30%
Management Practices	25% x	(20 of 25, or) 80% =	20%
		Overall HIP Score =	**51.5%**

Source: From HIP methodology.

the HIP approach is inclusive. A profiteer investor can miss out by not evaluating the proper leading indicators. But the HIP approach brings the best of both—a focus on data-driven results about human impact, and how those results drive profit. In this book so far, you've learned how each element contributes to those goals. When you do the analysis, you can reweight your portfolio accordingly. As you can see in the HIP 100 Top Ten list (see Table 7.2), these leaders all have a HIP Score attached. We use those scores to determine the weights of a large 100-company HIP index (which in the case of the HIP 100, rebalances the companies in the S&P 100 according to HIP scores).

While each company tends to have a unique HIP score, in this case, there are three that ended up with a similar score when calculated to one decimal point. The inputs to that score are different, but sometimes the results work out to be similar.

You can also combine multiple industries to generate a diversified portfolio. This method is similar to stock-index investing that builds portfolios based on leading financial indicators, like Wisdom Tree mutual funds.

Are you ready to see the results of some HIP Scorecard face-offs? Coming up, you'll see scorecards for many big brands that show you the variety in a HIP Portfolio. For simplicity, although we are analyzing the Products, we are not including the Product scores—only the Human Impact and Management Practices scores.

Table 7.2 Weights of Top Ten in the HIP 100 Index

Company (Stock ticker)	HIP Score (of 100)	Weight in the HIP 100 Index
Procter & Gamble (PG)	71.0	1.47%
General Electric (GE)	70.8	1.46%
Intel Corp. (INTC)	70.0	1.45%
United Parcel Service (UPS)	69.5	1.43%
H.J. Heinz Co. (HNZ)	68.8	1.42%
Hewlett Packard (HPQ)	68.8	1.42%
PepsiCo Inc. (PEP)	68.8	1.42%
Int'l Business Machines (IBM)	65.4	1.35%
Nike (NKE)	64.2	1.33%

HIP 100 holdings change over time; these weights were as of summer, 2009.
Source: HIP Investor Inc.

The HIP Scorecard Face-Offs

Building a portfolio of HIP companies is challenging, but can be fun. The HIP Scorecard makes it easier and enlightening. These examples use companies you already know, so they're a great starting point. In each scorecard, you will see:

- Company size and reach—how big are the competitors?
- Products—which products are HIP?
- Human impacts—what metrics produce both impact and profit?
- Management practices—how are HIP decisions made?
- Profit and total shareholder return—how much profit is realized?

Taking the Coke–Pepsi Challenge

Coke and Pepsi have been battling each other for market share for decades. But which is more HIP? While both firms slug it out for what you drink, PepsiCo also has several major food businesses, some of which they call Good-For-You or Better-for-You (totaling 30 percent of revenue, at this book's writing). Over time, Pepsi's stated goal is to grow that Good + Better share to 50 percent, slowly reducing the revenue share of Fun-for-You products like salty snacks. One "good" example is Sun Chips. Made with energy fueled by solar power, the product contains organic corn, and the bag is expected to be fully compostable by 2010. In terms of operations, both Gatorade and Propel sports drinks divisions clean newly manufactured bottles with air instead of water, saving almost 150 million gallons of water per year (PepsiCo Web site "Environmental Efforts").

PepsiCo's CEO Indra Nooyi, a woman of Indian origin who earned internal promotions to eventually lead the company, has a worldly view of Pepsi's mission of "Performance with Purpose." In a 2008 *Fortune* magazine feature, Nooyi says, "Companies today are bigger than many economies. We are little republics. We are engines of efficiency. If companies don't do [responsible] things, who is going to? Why not start making change now?" At the 2008 World Economic Forum in Davos, she told Secretary of State Condoleezza Rice it was critically important that "we use corporations as a productive player in addressing some of the big issues facing the world." But, while Pepsi exhibits many HIP qualities, so does Coca-Cola.

Seeking to invent additional eco-efficient processes and packaging, Scott Vitters, Environmental Manager at Coca-Cola, told consultants from Natural Logic, "First let's figure out the right thing to do for the Earth, then Coke can figure out how to make money doing that" (E-mail interview, Sept 23, 2009). Additionally, Coke is seeking to drop the rate of water—2.47 liters—used to make one liter of Coca-Cola product.

Who wins? In this review (see Table 7.3), Pepsi beats Coke on products, human impact, management practices and financials, and earns a Top 10 spot in the HIP 100 as well.

How HIP Are Your Home Products?

Procter & Gamble, a company nearly 200 years old, is dedicated to pleasing its diverse customer base. P&G has set a 2012 goal to hit $20 billion in cumulative sales of products with low eco-impacts—which would likely qualify as a double-digit revenue share for the $79 billion firm. Coldwater Tide and Cool Clean Ariel require no hot water, which if used nationwide in the U.S. would cut 3 percent from home electricity bills, or "paying for the product itself," says Len Sauers, VP of Global Sustainability in its public reports (P&G Sustainability Report 2007, 29–30 2007; Good Morning America 2008).

P&G is the highest-rated HIP company for many reasons—a product portfolio full of HIP innovations; comprehensive reporting on nearly every HIP metric, strong management practices—all of which lead to strong long-term fundamentals, including shareholder returns.

But Colgate Palmolive has delivered stronger financial performance in the same time frame, building an engine for growth and catching up with P&G's previous international expansions. Colgate has become much more transparent by disclosing more metrics, resulting in its HIP scores leaping significantly in 2009. Its introduction of Palmolive Pure + Clear in 2008 is a major improvement for water supplies, as phosphates and heavy fragrances have been eliminated, saving both money and the Earth. (Colgate Sustainability Web site).

Who wins? P&G remains the strongest, but Colgate Palmolive is gaining fast, with aggressive international growth (see Table 7.4). This is a great example of how owning competitors in close proportion covers your bases as an investor; this is particularly advantageous since both companies are realizing top results across Health, Wealth,

Table 7.3   HIP Industry Face-Off: Beverages

	PepsiCo	Coca-Cola Co.
Overview	Products found in over 200 countries; $43.3 billion revenue, 198,000 employees	Over 3,000 beverage products sold in over 200 countries; $31.9 billion revenue; 92,400 employees
Products	In 2006, 43% of PepsiCo net revenues in North America came from Smart Spot products, and Smart Spot eligible products represented two-thirds of growth in North America; goal of deriving 50% of all U.S. revenues from Smart Spot eligible products by 2010	In 2007, Coke launched 450 new beverage products, including 150 low- and no-calorie options, increasing that share of its product portfolio by 17% from 2006 to 2007; to date, its 700+ low- and no-cal products, account for approximately 23% of their 2007 unit case volume
Human Impact *of 100%*	**62%**	**56%**
Health *of 20%*	**8%** Customer satisfaction in 2008 is 84%. Frito-Lay has 28 sites recognized by OSHA for safety; systematic wellness approach for staff, 60%+ participation rate for eligible employees	**7%** Customer satisfaction in 2008 is 85%; 2.3 per 100 workers safety lost-time incident rate; Coke is expanding its nutrition labeling, but slowly
Wealth *of 20%*	**14%** A majority of employees have access to Pepsi's stock-based compensation program; CEO earned 241-X an average employee's salary	**10%** Employees may contribute 10% or up to $8,000 to the stock option plan; CEO earned 477-X an average employee's salary
Earth *of 20%*	**11%** As of 2006, Frito-Lay achieved a GHG reduction of 8.8% from 2002 baseline and reduction of 16.1% from 1999 baseline In 2007, Pepsi reduced its "absolute distribution footprint" (energy) by 4.3% despite shipping 10.3% more products	**9%** 300 billion liters of water used overall in 2007, a 2% decrease since 2002; 2.47 liters of water/liter of product in 2007; 85% compliance with internal water treatment standards in 2007
Equality *of 20%*	**17%** $1.13B in purchases from minority- and women-owned supplier businesses 7 of 13 Board members are female or ethnic minorities	**16%** $366MM in supplier diversity spending (Increase by 23% from 2006) 4 of 14 Board members are female or ethnic minorities

Table 7.3   (Continued)

	PepsiCo	Coca-Cola Co.
Trust *of 20%*	**12%** LEED certification in some facilities, internal audits; 26 PepsiCo International facilities are ISO 14001 certified	**12%** Coke's system has 146 facilities that are OHSAS 18001 certified, including 37 of Company-owned sites
Mgmt. Practices	**20 of 25** Environmental Sustainability Leadership Team and Environmental Council (2007) Established a leadership team to ensure that environmental impacts are considered in the organization	**20 of 25** In 2008, the company started including sustainability as a tool to evaluate business plans and performance
Profit	**+34.8%** return on equity (2008) **+3.7%** annualized total return, including reinvested dividends (6/2004–6/2009) **+3.8%** annualized total return, including reinvested dividends (6/2006–6/2009)	**+27.5%** return on equity (2008) **+1.8%** annualized total return, including reinvested dividends (6/2004–6/2009) **+6.7%** annualized total return, including reinvested dividends (6/2006–6/2009)

Note: Each Human Impact and Mgmt. Practices score comprises several components, weighted for its link to profit and shareholder value. Examples above are indicative; additional metrics factor into the ultimate scores. Total scores may not sum exactly due to rounding and decimals not shown in impact ratings.
Source: HIP Investor analysis and interviews; company Web sites, American Customer Satisfaction Index (ACSI), Google Finance, Yahoo! Finance, AFLCIO, company sustainability reports, Bloomberg Financial L.P. (Detailed source information is listed in the Bibliography).

Table 7.4   HIP Industry Face-Off: Personal Care Products

	Procter & Gamble	Colgate-Palmolive
Overview	138,000 employees, $79.0 billion in annual revenue	36,600 employees, $15.3 billion in annual revenue
Products	Ariel detergent's sustainability team designed large, seal-tight Polyethylene bags; they are 100% recyclable, require 80% less packaging than boxes and take up 20% less space in transport and storage	Tom's of Maine, acquired by Colgate, who saw an opportunity to also promote oral health globally

(Continued)

Table 7.4   (Continued)

	Procter & Gamble	Colgate-Palmolive
Human Impact of 100%	**70%**	**67%**
Health of 20%	**15%** Safety rating: 0.49% total incident rate	**12%** Safety rating: 1.06% total incident rate
Wealth of 20%	**15%** Encourage employee ownership	**14%** Restricted Stock Awards and stock options granted to some employees
Earth of 20%	**12%** Reduced actual worldwide CO2 emissions from 3,148,000 tons to 2,889,000 tons since 2002. In 2008, P&G produced 81 metric tons of GHG emissions per $1MM in revenue	**11%** Total worldwide GHG emissions of 675,000 metric tons in 2008, or 44 metric tons per $1MM in revenue
Equality of 20%	**17%** 38.9% women management; HRC equality index score is 85%	**15%** 32.9% women management; HRC equality index score is 73%
Trust of 20%	**10%** Sustainability information available on Web site; $4 million lobbying in 2008	**14%** Several products approved by EPA with Design for the Environment Qualification; only $40,000 in lobbying; very comprehensive reporting
Mgmt. Practices	**15 of 25** By 2012, seek to generate at $20B+ in cumulative sales of products with less environmental impact	**10 of 25** Making dramatic strides in sustainability internally, and disclosing new metrics in multiple HIP categories
Profit	**+17.1%** return on equity (2009) **+0.9%** annualized total return, including reinvested dividends (6/2004–6/2009) **−0.5%** annualized total return, including reinvested dividends (6/2006–6/2009)	**+100.7%** return on equity (2008) **+6.2%** annualized total return, including reinvested dividends (6/2004–6/2009) **+8.1%** annualized total return, including reinvested dividends (6/2006–6/2009)

Each Human Impact and Mgmt. Practices score comprises several components, weighted for its link to profit and shareholder value. Examples above are indicative; additional metrics factor into the ultimate scores. Total scores may not sum exactly due to rounding and decimals not shown in impact ratings.
Source: HIP Investor analysis; Company Web sites, ACSI, Google Finance, Yahoo! Finance, CNN Money, Company Sustainability Reports, Bloomberg Financial L.P., Open Secrets, Hoover's Inc, *Fortune, Newsweek* (Detailed source information is listed in the Bibliography).

and Equality. In this case HIP investors should be open to not picking a winner but owning both market leaders in proportion to their HIP Scores.

How HIP Is Your Bank?

As custodians of your money, there's one obvious human need that banks cater to: preserving your wealth. In Fall 2009, seeking to strike a better balance with customers and fearing increased legislation on banking practices, J.P. Morgan Chase, Bank of America, and other banks reduced the amounts and reset the trigger conditions of many fees, like debit card over-limit and checking overdraft charges, that were subtracting wealth from everyday customers. These practices had previously generated billions in fees for banks, cutting into customer income and savings. A more HIP bank aims to avoid unnecessary and over-priced fees for customers, instead seeking to help customers build savings and manage income.

Banks also have an opportunity to underwrite loans that advance human impact. "The Equator Principles" is a common framework for evaluating risk in social and environmental areas. Both Bank of America and J.P. Morgan Chase subscribe to the Equator Principles, which encompasses about 80 percent of global project finance loans made today (Environmental Data Services 2008). However, Bank of America (BofA) was admonished for "green-washing" (or overstating its eco-status) in 2008. The issue? BofA had touted its adherence to the Equator Principles, even though it had not deployed significant capital to them (Reuters, *Free Enterprise* 2008; Bank of America Sustainability Report 2008). Yet J.P. Morgan is quite active in these types of details (J.P. Morgan CSR 2007, 13). This is a lesson to the HIP investor: always check what companies claim, especially about promises or practices. Also remember: Quantitative results are more difficult to obfuscate than policies.

J.P. Morgan Chase and its CEO Jamie Dimon managed to navigate the economic meltdown of 2008 and build a stronger advantage over competitors like Bank of America. The HIP Scorecard (see Table 7.5) shows J.P. Morgan Chase beating Bank of America across all HIP categories—with more HIP products, plus stronger Human Impact and Management Practices scores, which were all factors in its financial outperformance.

Table 7.5   HIP Industry Face-Off: Banking

	J.P. Morgan Chase	Bank of America
Overview	Over 5,000 bank branches in the U.S.; $112.2 billion revenue (2008); 220,255 employees	Over 6,000 locations in the U.S.; $124.1 billion revenue (2008); 283,000 employees
Products	In 2007 and 2008, Chase helped prevent about 330,000 foreclosures, primarily by modifying loan terms; seeking to boost to 650,000 families by the end of 2010	The Brighter Planet Visa card earns EarthSmart™ reward points where every $1,000 spent will fund an estimated ton of carbon offsets – since the card was launched in Nov. 2007, cardholders have offset over 35 million pounds of CO_2
Human Impact of 100%	**60%**	**48%**
Health of 20%	**6%** Customer satisfaction is 73%; Employee retention data not publicly available	**6%** Customer satisfaction is 73%; company retains nearly 90% of its managers
Wealth of 20%	**10%** Part-time employees who work 20 hours per week are eligible to make Roth 401(k) contributions after 90 days of service; CEO compensation is 441 times average employee	**13%** Established qualified retirement plans covering substantially all full-time and certain part-time employees; CEO compensation is 173 times average employee
Earth of 20%	**14%** Bought 127,000 MWh of 2007 vintage Green-e certified wind RECs, representing approx. 5% of U.S. electricity use; 9.4 metric tons of CO_2e emitted per $1MM in revenue in 2008	**8%** 12 metric tons of CO_2e emitted per $1MM in revenue in 2008
Equality of 20%	**17%** 48% women managers; Over $1 billion spent with diverse suppliers, a rapid increase over the past years	**15%** 50% women managers; numerous diversity awards but no quantifiable diversity spending
Trust of 20%	**12%** Comprehensive HIP reporting; spent $48.04 per $1MM in revenue on lobbying activities	**6%** No HIP reporting; Spent $39.36 per $1MM in revenue on lobbying activities

Table 7.5   (Continued)

	J.P. Morgan Chase	Bank of America
Mgmt. Practices	**21 of 25** Established Office of Corporate Responsibility in 2007 to coordinate, align, and articulate positive-impact and socially responsible activities across the firm, led by senior managers	**11 of 25** Established Environmental Council in 2007, composed of senior bank leaders reporting to the CEO; new policies and procedures, aims to help customers take action against global climate change
Profit	**+2.3%** return on equity (2008) **+0.8%** annualized total return, including reinvested dividends (6/2004–6/2009) **−3.7%** annualized total return, including reinvested dividends (6/2006–6/2009)	**+1.8%** return on equity (2008) **−1.7%** annualized total return, including reinvested dividends (6/2004–6/2009) **−17.9%** annualized total return, including reinvested dividends (6/2006–6/2009)

Note: Each Human Impact and Mgmt. Practices score comprises several components, weighted for its link to profit and shareholder value. Examples above are indicative; additional metrics factor into the ultimate scores. Total scores may not sum exactly due to rounding and decimals not shown in impact ratings.
Source: HIP Investor analysis; Company Web sites, ACSI, Google Finance, Yahoo! Finance, AFLCIO, Company Sustainability or CSR Reports, Bloomberg Finance L.P.,,Annual Reports, Diversity Inc. (Detailed source information is listed in the Bibliography).

How HIP Is Your Mobile Phone?

In the United States there are more than 270 million mobile phone user-accounts (CTIA 2009). With customers typically renewing plans every other year, more than 140 million mobile phones are discarded each year—equating to 65,000 tons of electronic-component waste. Only 10 percent of devices are recycled per year, which creates opportunities to both recycle and reconstitute how phones are made. (Sprint, *Wireless Recycling*). In September 2009, Sprint Nextel began marketing the Samsung Reclaim phone, with 40 percent of its materials made from corn-based bio-plastic; what's more, the entire phone is 80 percent recyclable (Sprint, *Meet the Reclaim* 2009).

Both Sprint Nextel and Verizon are making it easier for customers to recycle. All phones, batteries and accessories can be turned into Sprint using free, prepaid envelopes available at its retail stores and with most new phone packages. The company then sells the components for cash, and the proceeds go to charitable community initiatives. Sprint also buys back some phones (those they can recondition and resell) from customers. While phone recycling rates have increased to 18 percent, Sprint's goal is to hit 90 percent of annual phone sales by 2017.

More broadly, Verizon is pursuing two dozen eco-initiatives enterprise-wide to reduce its carbon footprint. In an online video, Paul Tassinari of its Network Services Group notes that Verizon's network accounts for 75 percent of the company's total energy spending. By implementing an "environmentally neutral" engineering policy, the company is seeking to find energy savings within the company for every kilowatt hour added due to growth in the network (Verizon, *Reducing* 2009).

When compared systematically on all HIP aspects, Verizon beats Sprint Nextel on overall human impact scores, management practices and total shareholder return (see Table 7.6).

How HIP Is Your Food-on-the-Go?

"More and more, McDonald's decisions are based on sustainability criteria," says Bob Langert, VP of Corporate Social Responsibility. For example, McDonald's children's marketing featured a nutrition campaign, tied into the *Shrek* movies, resulting in more sales of milk and apples slices. In this case, increased customer Health also enables increased Wealth, due to the chain's reasonable prices.

"The secret story of our success is our suppliers," Langert explains, "Together with them, there are health and nutrition criteria, as well as environmental evaluations, built into our priorities for them." Long-term partnerships, improvements in ingredient quality, and process efficiencies benefit both the supplier and the company's impact and profit (Phone interview, 9/10/08).

Similarly, Starbucks' goal for its supply chain—"By 2015, 100 percent of our coffee will be responsibly grown and ethically traded"—also appeals to its customer base (Starbucks Web site). "The consumer is so well educated and informed that given a choice they will buy from companies that give back to issues they believe in," says CEO Howard Schultz in an online video, "companies need to make deposits on the equity of the brand rather than trying to simply sell the consumer something."

In addition to the fair wages it pays to farmers, Starbucks is also offering farmers incentives to prevent deforestation, a practice that can contribute up to 20 percent of greenhouse gas emissions. Pilot

Table 7.6   HIP Industry Face-Off: Telecommunications

	Verizon	Sprint
Overview	Wireless network serves 87.7 million customers; $97.4 billion revenue (2008), 235,000 employees	40 million customers, $35.6 billion revenue (2008); 56,000 employees
Products	Through HopeLine, collects, refurbishes, and reuses cell phones to provide free phones and service to domestic violence victims; collected more than 1 million cell phones in 2008, up 6% from 2007	The Samsung Reclaim™ is Sprint's first eco-friendly phone designed with 80% recyclable components and 100% recyclable packaging
Human Impact *of 100%*	**51%**	**44%**
Health *of 20%*	**8%** Customer satisfaction is 70%; Verizon spent $3.7B in health care benefits, covering 835K employees, retirees and their dependents	**5%** Customer satisfaction is 56%
Wealth *of 20%*	**13%** CEO's salary is 391 times that of the average employee; long term incentive plan is available to all employees, awarding stock-based compensation	**14%** CEO's salary is 276 times that of the average employee; Employee Stock Purchase Plan available for "eligible" employees
Earth *of 20%*	**7%** Collected over 1.1 million recycled and refurbished phones in 2008	**9%** 20th largest purchaser of green power via EPA's green power partnership for *Fortune* 500 challenge
Equality *of 20%*	**13%** Of 12 directors, 2 are female and 2 are ethnic minorities; 36 percent of Verizon's employees are minorities (2008)	**7%** Of 10 directors, 1 is female
Trust *of 20%*	**10%** Spent $18 million on lobbying activity, but overall reporting transparency is high and detailed, comprehensive and quantitative; nearly 7 times more lobbying spend, while only 3 times higher revenue.	**8%** "Only" $2.6 Million spent on lobbying activity in 2008 but several class action lawsuits for fees; reporting is not sufficiently quantitative.

(Continued)

Table 7.6 (Continued)

	Verizon	Sprint
Mgmt. Practices	**21 of 25** Corporate Responsibility Council establishes benchmarks and goals, assigns and enforces accountability, and measures and tracks results	**11 of 25** Committed to balancing needs of customers and needs of communities in decisions for tower sitting (some poles disguised as flag poles, light poles, pine or palm trees)
Profit	**+13.9%** return on equity (2008) **+2.3%** annualized total return, including reinvested dividends (6/2004–6/2009) **+3.3%** annualized total return, including reinvested dividends (6/2006–6/2009)	**−13.4%** return on equity (2008) **−20.8%** annualized total return, including reinvested dividends (6/2004–6/2009) **+37.6%** annualized total return, including reinvested dividends (6/2006–6/2009)

Note: Each Human Impact and Mgmt. Practices score comprises several components, weighted for its link to profit and shareholder value. Examples above are indicative; additional metrics factor into the ultimate scores. Total scores may not sum exactly due to rounding and decimals not shown in impact ratings.
Source: HIP Investor analysis; Company Web sites, ACSI, Google Finance, Yahoo! Finance, AFLCIO, Company Sustainability and CSR Reports, Bloomberg Financial L.P., Annual Reports, Diversity Inc. (Detailed source information is listed in the Bibliography).

programs are underway in Sumatra, Indonesia, and Chiapas, Mexico. Starbucks also uses its Corporate Treasury funds for loans to farmers seeking expansion. These loans total $12.5 million today, and are expected to grow to $20 million (Starbucks Web site).

In the HIP face-off (see Table 7.7), Starbucks beats McDonald's, based on Health, Wealth and Earth, and edges out a lead in Management Practices. However, McDonald's consistent performance and stock appreciation has exceeded Starbucks. This is another example of covering your bases with both companies, though Starbucks would be allocated slightly more weight in a HIP portfolio.

How HIP Is Your Fuel?

Since at least 2007, Chevron has operated an interactive Web site called "Will You Join Us?" built on assumptions from analysts at *The Economist Group.* Players can select a variety of energy sources to power a simulated city. To begin, you name your city; I called mine "Independence, USA." Then, I started with the most renewable energy

Table 7.7   HIP Industry Face-Off: Consumer Food and Beverage

	McDonald's	Starbucks
Overview	Over 31,000 restaurants in 118 countries; $23.5 billion revenue, 400,000 employees	Over 8,500 company-operated locations in 43 countries, $10.4 billion revenue (FY08); 176,000 employees
Products	Premium salads, fruit and yogurt parfait, and apple dippers in Happy Meal choices; packaging gives customers essential nutrition information in easy-to-understand icon and bar chart format	Sells fair-trade certified coffee, with pioneering Coffee and Farmer Equity Practices (C.A.F.E.) In U.S., spends more on employee health care than coffee bean purchases
Human Impact *of 100%*	**56%**	**64%**
Health *of 20%*	**10%** In 2009 customer satisfaction is 70%; 82% of crew would recommend working at McDonalds to a friend	**14%** Customer satisfaction is 76%; all staff more than 20 hours have health care access
Wealth *of 20%*	**9%** Crew members earn an average of $7.60 per hour; 93% of eligible employees participate in 401(k) plan, made easier by $20 per month auto-deductions	**13%** Baristas earn an average of $8.55 per hour; staff employed for 90 days working 20 hrs. per week eligible for stock purchase plan; up to 10% of base pay toward quarterly common stock purchase at 15% discount;
Earth *of 20%*	**9%** About 82% of the consumer packaging used in its nine largest markets made from renewable materials and 30% of the material comes from recycled fiber. Despite testing of innovative materials, have not yet identified more sustainable packaging materials that are commercially viable	**12%** During fiscal year 2008, 70% of U.S. and Canada locations have recycling programs in place, where company-controlled; In 2007, hot beverage cups made of 10% post-consumer fiber; ultimate goal is to have no waste from cups
Equality *of 20%*	**15%** 37% of all U.S. owner-operators are women and minorities; 26.7% of worldwide leadership are women	**12%** In fiscal year 2008, among managers, 14% are ethnic minorities, 33% are women

(Continued)

Table 7.7   (Continued)

	McDonald's	Starbucks
Trust of 20%	**14%** Guidelines to determine the sustainability of fisheries developed in partnership with Conservation International	**13%** All suppliers that adhere to C.A.F.E. status undergo third-party verification
Mgmt. Practices	**19 of 25** Carefully managing supply chain to control costs and implement sustainability, and developing an environmental scorecard to measure supplier performance	**21 of 25** Sustainability built into business vision, all performance metrics and product development decisions; in fiscal year 2008, Starbucks loaned out $12.5 million to farmers and their communities
Profit	**+30.1%** return on equity (2008) **+20.4%** annualized total return, including reinvested dividends (6/2004–6/2009) **+23.4%** annualized total return, including reinvested dividends (6/2006–6/2009)	**+13.2%** return on equity (2008) **−8.6%** annualized total return, including reinvested dividends (6/2004–6/2009) **−28.3%** annualized total return, including reinvested dividends (6/2006–6/2009)

Note: Each Human Impact and Mgmt. Practices score comprises several components, weighted for its link to profit and shareholder value. Examples above are indicative; additional metrics factor into the ultimate scores. Total scores may not sum exactly due to rounding and decimals not shown in impact ratings.
Source: HIP Investor analysis; Company Web sites, ACSI, Google Finance, Yahoo! Finance, Company Sustainability Reports, Bloomberg Financial L.P., Company CSRs, Glass Door (Detailed source information is listed in the Bibliography).

sources—solar, wind, biomass, geothermal, and hydro. The game calculates overall energy served, and after my choices, Independence was 88 percent powered. However, the game screen blackens to report that "Independence, USA needs oil," while part of the game, the airport, was not running (biofuels for planes are not yet prevalent). But the game missed one essential reduction strategy: energy efficiency solutions, which typically yield 15 percent or more savings. Despite Chevron having a growing, profitable business unit dedicated to that purpose, the game only sought one answer: more oil! This game is not very HIP. It erodes Trust by forcing a fossil fuel solution when many energy needs can be served by renewables or efficiency options. The game would be more powerful if it showed the consequences of alternative choices rather than forcing only one self-serving path.

The game doesn't seem to be consistent with Chevron's leadership in renewable energy, which is a leader in investing in renewables, including geothermal, as well as efficiency services for corporations. While consumers might judge a whole company based on a game like the previous one, a HIP investor takes a more systematic approach as shown in the scorecard below.

Meanwhile, ExxonMobil now seems to see some glimmers of light on renewables, with a $600 million investment in developing a biofuel from algae. In addition, it is partnering with biotech firm Synthetic Genomics to seek out new fuels producible from "sunlight, water and waste carbon dioxide by photosynthetic pond scum" (Howell 2009). This effort seems to finally supersede ExxonMobil's previous strategy on renewable fuels: seeking to sow doubt. In 2007, The UK *Guardian* reported that the American Enterprise Institute (AEI), a think tank partly funded by ExxonMobil, offered $10,000 to each scientist who created more doubt about the prevalence and causes of climate change (Sample 2007). Obviously, this is not a HIP practice, encouraging biases that prejudge the scientific process.

In a HIP face-off (see Table 7.8), Chevron exceeds ExxonMobil on Human Impact and Management Practices but falls short on historical Profit and valuation. since HIP factors are leading indicators, the expectation going forward is that Chevron will outperform. A HIP investor can include both firms in a portfolio, yet consider weighting Chevron higher due to higher rated impacts that drive future profit.

How HIP Is Your Computer?

"Hi, I'm a Mac," the commercial goes. "And I'm a PC." Which will be more HIP?

"A lot of companies publish how green their building is, but it doesn't matter if you're shipping millions of power-hungry products with toxic chemicals in them," said Apple CEO Steve Jobs in an interview with *BusinessWeek*. "It's like asking a cigarette company how green their office is." In September 2009, Apple finally started disclosing more about the lifecycle footprint of its products. For example, we learned that more than half the carbon emissions associated with an iPod are linked to recharging the device. On Apple's MacBook Pro, a smart design eliminated dozens of parts by forging them

Table 7.8   HIP Industry Face-Off: Energy

	Chevron	ExxonMobil
Overview	Chevron-branded products are sold in more than 8,800 retail locations in the United States; $273 billion revenue (2008); 67,000 employees	ExxonMobil products are sold in more than 32,000 retail service stations in the United States; $477.4 billion revenue (2008); 104,700 employees
Products	From 2004 to 2007, Chevron Energy Solutions helped clients reduce energy use at their facilities by nearly 30% on average; unit profitable and growing since 2003	Introduced *Mobil 1 Advanced Fuel Economy*, a lower viscosity motor oil that can improve fuel economy by 2% compared to average motor oil
Human Impact *of 100%*	**52%**	**45%**
Health *of 20%*	**5%** 0.36 TRIR (total recordable incident rate), a measure of safety	**4%** TRIR = 0.42, slightly higher than Chevron
Wealth *of 20%*	**13%** Matches 401(k) one-to-one up to 6%; Chevron invested $160 million in communities around the world in 2008, an increase of $41 million over 2007;	**14%** Matches 401(k) one-to-one up to 5%; In 2008, Exxon Mobil invested $189.1 million in communities around the world
Earth *of 20%*	**11%** In 2008, total GHG emissions were 64.3 million metric tons; that is 236 metric tons per $1 million in revenue	**9%** 137 million metric tons of CO_2e emissions in 2008; that is 287 metric tons per $1 million in revenue
Equality *of 20%*	**12%** In 2008, 24.8% of senior executives were women or minorities; 2009 HRC Score = 100 (the highest score possible for gay-friendly work and management practices)	**9%** In 2008, approximately 20% of officers and managers were women or minorities; 2009 HRC Score = 0 (zero, the lowest score possible for gay-friendly work practices)
Trust *of 20%*	**11%** Nearly $12.8 million spent on lobbying in 2008; that is $47 per $1 million in revenue; accessible and responsive to investor and media interview	**8%** $29 million spent on lobbying in 2008; that is $61 per $1 million in revenue; selectively responds to media channels, sometimes sowing confusion about the facts

Table 7.8   *Continued*

	Chevron	ExxonMobil
Mgmt. Practices	**15 of 25** Sustaining Environmental, Social, and Health Impact Assessment process across global operation; continue using Operational Excellence Management System self-assessment process	**14 of 25** "In such turbulent times, successful companies are those that see business discipline and corporate citizenship as interlinked." Rex W. Tillerson, Chairman and CEO
Profit	**+29.2%** return on equity (2008) **+10.5%** annualized total return, including reinvested dividends (6/2004–6/2009) **+5.4%** annualized total return, including reinvested dividends (6/2006–6/2009)	**+38.5%** return on equity (2008) **+11.7%** annualized total return, including reinvested dividends (6/2004–6/2009) **+6.4%** annualized total return, including reinvested dividends (6/2006–6/2009)

Note: Each Human Impact and Mgmt. Practices score comprises several components, weighted for its link to profit and shareholder value. Examples above are indicative; additional metrics factor into the ultimate scores. Total scores may not sum exactly due to rounding and decimals not shown in impact ratings.
Source: HIP Investor analysis; Company Web sites, Google Finance, Yahoo! Finance, AFLCIO, Company Sustainability and CSR Reports, Bloomberg Financial L.P., Carbon Disclosure Project; Human Rights Campaign (Detailed source information is listed in the Bibliography).

into one, made from recyclable aluminum. Apple's product designs that are "smaller, thinner, and lighter" use less material, saving cost and building profit (Apple, *Environment* Web site). The new operating system (Snow Leopard) expects to save customers 10 percent of electrical usage, or $10 million per year in energy (Environmental Leader, *Apple's New OS* 2009).

Microsoft, too, is integrating power management technologies into its Windows 7 release (Microsoft, *Advancing*). With far more transparency and leadership in several HIP categories, Microsoft beats Apple on Human Impact, Management Practices, and Return on Equity in 2008. Apple's share appreciation was more attractive, and Apple is now more transparent about the entire lifecycle analysis of its products. However, incorporating all that information, Microsoft still wins the face-off (see Table 7.9). Going forward, a HIP investor may choose to invest in both, but would allocate a little bit more to Microsoft.

Table 7.9   HIP Industry Face-Off: Computers

	Microsoft	Apple
Overview	93,000 employees, $58.4 billion in annual revenue	32,000 employees, $32.5 billion in annual revenue
Products	"Virtualization" software approach enables multiple operating systems to run on a single server, reducing energy use by up to 90%	MacBook family designed to be weight, shipping, and energy efficient; on the verge of eliminating lead, arsenic and mercury through use of LCD monitors
Human Impact of 100%	**47%**	**38%**
Health of 20%	**10%** Pays 100% of health care premiums, including dependents; 70% customer satisfaction in 2009; 94% employee retention	**8%** Unclear health coverage; 84% customer satisfaction in 2009; in 2006 claims that its retail store employee staff retention was 80%
Wealth of 20%	**14%** Share purchase plan allows employees to use up to 15% of their gross salary to buy Microsoft stock at a 10% discount	**15%** Employee Stock Purchase Plan allows employees to use up to 10% of their salary to buy Apple stock at a 15% discount
Earth of 20%	**10%** Windows Vista has built-in power management features that can reduce PC energy use by as much as 30%	**3%** Apple was the first in the industry to be able to register to the stricter Energy Star 4.0 standard in 2007.
Equality of 20%	**9%** 3 women or minorities on a Board of 10, equaling 30%	**5%** 1 female on a Board of 7, equaling 14%
Trust of 20%	**4%** Microsoft co-launched with industry peers the Climate Savers Computing Initiative to reduce greenhouse gas emissions from PCs and servers	**6%** Apple is actively engaged with the Electronics Industry Citizenship Coalition (EICC)
Mgmt. Practices	**13 of 25** Seek to increase green computing and drop emissions; via internal measurement, supplier commitments and standard-setting in industry groups	**7 of 25** Until recently, very quiet about its sustainability practices, which are ingrained in Apple's long time breakthrough product innovation approach
Profit	**+38.4%** return on equity (2009) **−0.1%** annualized total return, including reinvested dividends (6/2004–6/2009) **+2.4%** annualized total return, including reinvested dividends (6/2006–6/2009)	**+27.2%** return on equity (2008) **+54.3%** annualized total return, including reinvested dividends (6/2004–6/2009) **+35.5%** annualized total return, including reinvested dividends (6/2006–6/2009)

Note: Each Human Impact and Mgmt. Practices score comprises several components, weighted for its link to profit and shareholder value. Examples above are indicative; additional metrics factor into the ultimate scores. Total scores may not sum exactly due to rounding and decimals not shown in impact ratings.
Source: HIP Investor analysis; Company Web sites, ACSI, Google Finance, Yahoo! Finance, Company Sustainability Reports, Bloomberg Financial L.P., Company CSRs, Ceres (Detailed source information is listed in the Bibliography).

How HIP Is Your Big Retailer?

As I discussed earlier, Walmart has made tremendous strides in boosting the number of its products that are sustainable, reducing waste and increasing renewable energy. It has sold 137 million compact fluorescent light bulbs at Walmart and Sam's Club locations. And 49 percent of the total pounds of seafood (fresh or frozen) sold at Walmart or Sam's Club stores in the United States are certified by the MSC (Marine Stewardship Council) or have ACC certification (Walmart Web site).

Both Target and Walmart offer sustainable choices, like Method cleaning products. Target carries organic cotton bedsheets, and innovations like a cotton blend that also incorporates sustainably raised bamboo.

On the HIP face-off (see Table 7.10), Target beats Walmart on Human Impact, while in Management Practices and Profit, Walmart wins. One important thing to consider is that in the S&P index, Walmart would be weighted at about six times more than Target, based on revenues. In a HIP portfolio, the differential is less pronounced, as both companies are close in ratings.

How HIP Is Your Materials Company?

At Dow, sustainability was woven into goals back in 1996, when the company established 10-year goals on environment, health, and safety, according to Mark Weick, Scott Noesen, and Pete Deal, all part of the Project Management Office for Sustainability. These goals have been updated, and include an energy used per pound of product figure. To help the business units accomplish goals, seven people advise them on how to calculate eight dimensions of sustainability, including the carbon footprint. In addition, "Lifecycle analysis is a management tool of significant proportions" according to Dow. "A lot of the business units have the 'thinking' embedded, but it's not in one place, and not necessarily tied to our goals," said the project management office. The product assessments are designed to be transparent–they're even posted on the corporate Web site, providing full transparency (Interview with Mark Weick, Scott Noesen, and Pete Deal, Dow, Aug. 26, 2008 by phone). Dow also sets targets that link to the Millennium Development Goals (MDGs), which is "very attractive" to the CEO and the company, the Dow sustainability group says (Phone interview, Aug 26, 2008).

Table 7.10 HIP Industry Face-Off: Retail Shopping

	Walmart	Target
Overview	2.1 million employees, 8,100 retail units in 15 countries, $405.6 billion in annual revenue	351,000 employees, 1,684 stores in 48 states, $64.9 billion in annual revenue
Products	Selling products like affordable organic produce, fair trade coffee, and compact fluorescent light bulbs; has specific goals for increasing HIP products in its stores	In 2006, expanded its Archer Farms brand to include affordable organic food products
Human Impact *of 100%*	**51%**	**55%**
Health *of 20%*	**6%** 47.4% of Walmart associates get healthcare coverage from Walmart; Customer satisfaction: 68% to 70% depending on store category	**7%** Target offers full benefits to eligible managers and scaled benefits for hourly workers; customer satisfaction: 77%
Wealth *of 20%*	**8%** $10.76 avg. full-time hourly wage in U.S.; Plans, including 401(k) and profit sharing, may be available to employees after 12 months of employment	**13%** Dollar-for-dollar match for retirement up to 5% of pay with immediate vesting; Since 1946, contributed 5% of annual net income to programs that serve Target communities
Earth *of 20%*	**11%** In 2008, goal to make fleet 25% more efficient was achieved; retrofitted 500 stores with low and medium temp. refrigerated display cases	**8%** 70% of solid-waste materials are now redirected from landfills through various conservation programs for reusing and recycling
Equality *of 20%*	**14%** Score of 40 on the Human Rights Campaign equality index	**16%** Score of 100 on the Human Rights Campaign equality index
Trust *of 20%*	**12%** Despite $6.6 million lobbying, publishing many quantitative metrics and encouraging cross-sector sustainability index to share quantifiable supplier performance	**12%** $2.6 million lobbying (one-third of Walmart's lobbying spend, while firm is one-sixth of Walmart's revenue), some quantifiable metrics published.

Table 7.10 (Continued)

	Walmart	Target
Mgmt. Practices	**23 of 25** Comprehensive goals of zero waste, 100% renewable energy and sustainable products. Launched Sustainability Index across 60,000 suppliers. Front-line to Board accountable for increasing positive impact.	**16 of 25** Seeks to use resources responsibly, minimize its carbon footprint, develop facilities that align environmental, community, and business needs, and influence its vendors and suppliers to embrace sustainable practices
Profit	**+20.4%** return on equity (2009) **−0.1%** annualized total return, including reinvested dividends (6/2004–6/2009) **+2.0%** annualized total return, including reinvested dividends (6/2006–6/2009)	**+15.3%** return on equity (2009) **−0.5%** annualized total return, including reinvested dividends (6/2004–6/2009) **−5.7%** annualized total return, including reinvested dividends (6/2006–6/2009)

Note: Each Human Impact and Mgmt. Practices score comprises several components, weighted for its link to profit and shareholder value. Examples above are indicative; additional metrics factor into the ultimate scores. Total scores may not sum exactly due to rounding and decimals not shown in impact ratings.
Source: HIP Investor analysis; Company Web sites, ACSI, Google Finance, Yahoo! Finance, AFLCIO, Company Sustainability and CSR Reports, Bloomberg Financial L.P., Waddoups Interview, (Detailed source information is listed in the Bibliography).

DuPont is focused on "environmentally smart market opportunities" which it seeks to capture for revenue growth "with direct, quantifiable environmental benefits for our customers and consumers along our value chain" say DuPont's reports. DuPont has targeted R&D spending of $640 million annually by 2015 (DuPont, *Marketplace Goals*). One goal for future revenue is $8 billion from non-depletable resources by that time as well. Another is to boost annual revenue by $2 billion from eco-efficient products. In 2007, $65 million revenue was obtained from products that reduce GHG emissions, which accounted for 55,000 metric tons of GHG emission reductions. Operationally, DuPont expects that 100 percent of its company fleet of vehicles will be the most fuel-efficient; in 2008, 22 percent of U.S. vehicles were hybrid, flex fuel, clean diesel, or E85 octane powered.

In this HIP face-off DuPont edges Dow in Human Impact, and exceeds in financial returns, yet is a point short on Management Practices (see Table 7.11). A HIP Portfolio would weight them close to equally.

Table 7.11   HIP Industry Face-Off: Materials

	Dow	DuPont
Overview	57,903 employees, $57.5 billion in annual revenue	60,000 employees, $31.8 billion in annual revenue
Products	Since 1994, have decreased energy used per pound of product by 22% resulting in $8.6 billion of savings benefiting customers and shareholders	Goal of 1,000 or more products that "protect people" by 2015; seek to double revenues from "non-depletable resources" to $8 billion; in 2007, revenue for these products reached $5.8B
Human Impact of 100%	**49%**	**51%**
Health of 20%	**7%** At the end of the second quarter 2009, the Injury and Illness rate was 0.21 per 200,000 hours of work with a 2015 goal of 0.08	**4%** Between 2006 and 2007 DuPont reduced total recordable injuries by 25% and total incidents by 22%
Wealth of 20%	**13%** About 51% of eligible employees enrolled in discount stock purchase program	**14%** Defined contribution programs cover substantially all U.S. employees; contributes 100% of the first 6% of employee retirement contribution plus another 3% regardless of level of compensation
Earth of 20%	**7%** During 2008, greenhouse gas emissions were 0.602 metric tons per metric ton of production, about a 7% increase in intensity from 2007	**10%** In 2007, 6% of total energy came from renewable sources
Equality of 20%	**11%** Overall workforce is 26.5% female employees	**12%** Overall workforce is 26% female employees
Trust of 20%	**10%** At the end of second quarter, there were 203 Product Safety Assessments (PSAs) posted at www.DowProductSafety.com; the 2015 Goal is to have publicly available PSAs for all applicable Dow products	**10%** In 2008, Environmental Resources Management conducted an evaluation of DuPont's Safety, Health, and Environment Audit Program and concluded that DuPont's Program is generally consistent with, and in some cases, exceeds expectations of the established criteria

Table 7.11 (Continued)

	Dow	DuPont
Mgmt. Practices	**19 of 25** Comprehensive 2015 goals tracker updated quarterly; billion dollar investments need to evaluate sustainability impacts and analyze lifecycle metrics	**18 of 25** Mission is sustainable growth, defined as "creating shareholder and societal value" while reducing company, customer, and supplier environmental footprints
Profit	**+3.5%** return on equity (2008) **−13.4%** annualized total return, including reinvested dividends (6/2004–6/2009) **−21.8%** annualized total return, including reinvested dividends (6/2006–6/2009)	**+22.5%** return on equity (2008) **−7.0%** annualized total return, including reinvested dividends (6/2004–6/2009) **−11.4%** annualized total return, including reinvested dividends (6/2006–6/2009)

Note: Each Human Impact and Mgmt. Practices score comprises several components, weighted for its link to profit and shareholder value. Examples above are indicative; additional metrics factor into the ultimate scores. Total scores may not sum exactly due to rounding and decimals not shown in impact ratings.
Source: HIP Investor analysis; Company Web sites, Google Finance, Yahoo! Finance, Company Sustainability and CSR Reports, Bloomberg Financial L.P., Ceres, Carbon Disclosure Project (Detailed source information is listed in the Bibliography).

How HIP Is Your Defense Contractor?

Lockheed Martin and Raytheon are known for their advanced technologies, but also for their large government contracts, frequently for the military. Can defense contractors be HIP?

In New Jersey, Hawaii, and Spain, Lockheed Martin is testing innovative solutions, like capturing the energy from natural waves in the ocean, converting it to electricity and transferring that electricity to shore. Other investments, given its engineering expertise, include energy storage and climate monitoring (Stevens 2009).

Raytheon reports exploring eco-improvements, including improving its fuel efficiency and use of alterative fuels, both having a positive Earth impact and profit result (Raytheon *Environment*).

Raytheon's Human Impact Score beats Lockheed Martin's, but Lockheed's Management Practices and Profit scores make this one hard to select (see Table 7.12). Depending on your analysis of impact versus management practices, these two may become more equally weighted.

Table 7.12 HIP Industry Face-Off: Industrials

	Raytheon	Lockheed Martin
Overview	73,000 employees, $23.2 billion in annual revenue	146,000 employees, $42.73 billion in annual revenue
Products	Provides systems to the National Weather Service to predict weather, water, and climate conditions; next generation system will use open source software	Environmental Services supports the EPA on multiple contracts such as the Environmental Services Assistant Team, Response Engineering Analytical Team, and the Information Technology Solutions—Environmental Systems Engineering contract
Human Impact of 100%	**48%**	**39%**
Health of 20%	**5%** 0.79 injuries per 200k hours worked in 2008; EHS Today magazine "America's Safest Companies" award; employee satisfaction data is not publicly available	**5%** In 2007, the recordable injury rate fell to 1.45, a 48% improvement since 2003; 69% employee satisfaction with their careers
Wealth of 20%	**12%** 401(k) and Employee Stock Ownership Plan available to most employees on the first day, matching up to 4%. CEO earns 271X an average worker's salary	**10%** 401(k) includes ESOP, limited further details; CEO earns 360X an average worker's salary
Earth of 20%	**10%** 59% of 19,160 tons of solid waste recycled in 2008; 10% reduction in 2008 alone.	**6%** Reduced hazardous waste generation per $1 million in revenue by 30% from 2003 to 2007; similarly non-hazardous waste ratio down by 50%+
Equality of 20%	**13%** 35% of procurement was from small businesses; received 100% Human Rights Campaign score for 5th consecutive year	**10%** Since 2002, more than 50% of entry level hires have been women and minorities
Trust of 20%	**8%** 2007 EnergyStar Partner of the Year, Sustained Excellence Award (2008 and 2009)	**9%** 35 Lockheed Martin facilities have earned ISO 14001 certification (as of 2007, 11 buildings are in the process of being LEED certified)

Table 7.12   (Continued)

	Raytheon	Lockheed Martin
Mgmt. Practices	**15 of 25** Waste metrics are collected monthly and reported quarterly to Board of Directors	**17 of 25** "Target Zero" program to minimize injuries; "Go Green" program to eliminate adverse environmental impact;
Profit	**+15.5%** return on equity (2008) **+6.6%** annualized total return, including reinvested dividends (6/2004–6/2009) **+1.9%** annualized total return, including reinvested dividends (6/2006–6/2009)	**+50.8%** return on equity (2008) **+11.1%** annualized total return, including reinvested dividends (6/2004–6/2009) **+5.9%** annualized total return, including reinvested dividends (6/2006–6/2009)

Note: Each Human Impact and Mgmt. Practices score comprises several components, weighted for its link to profit and shareholder value. Examples above are indicative; additional metrics factor into the ultimate scores. Total scores may not sum exactly due to rounding and decimals not shown in impact ratings.
Source: HIP Investor analysis; Company Web sites, ACSI, Google Finance, Yahoo! Finance, AFLCIO, Company Sustainability and CSR Reports, Bloomberg Financial L.P., Annual Reports, Environmental Protection Agency (Detailed source information is listed in the Bibliography).

What Happens to a HIP Portfolio that Screens Out "Bad" Companies?

The HIP approach is designed to be pragmatic, generating a competitive "race to the top" to sell the most sustainable products, operate with the highest human impact, and embedding those practices in everyday business decisions. However, some investors seek out a "purist" approach, which has been pursued by many "do-gooder" mutual funds. This requires excluding firms based on a judgment of the "bad-ness" of their products and operations.

In Figure 7.2, we compared the HIP 100 to a portfolio that excluded "bad" firms with "negative" products. This reduced portfolio of 75 companies, which we call "HIP 100 Minus Exclusions" yields two insights: (1) by using the HIP methodology and scorecards, this Exclusion-based portfolio outperforms the S&P 100, as it focuses on quantitative results, not just interpretations of policy statements, and (2) this Exclusionary approach still falls short of the inclusionary HIP 100, reinforcing the conclusion that to do well financially you need a more diversified portfolio.

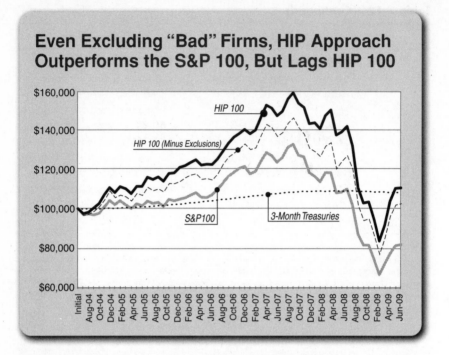

Figure 7.2 Even Excluding "Bad" Firms, a HIP Approach Outperforms the S&P 100, But Lags the Inclusive HIP 100

Source: Bloomberg Financial L.P.; HIP Investor analysis.

You can choose the inclusive HIP approach, or select an exclusionary approach, both of which have outperformed the S&P benchmark. Are you a "pragmatist" or a "purist"? Either way, by using the HIP Scorecard, you can position your portfolio for both more attractive financial performance and a better world.

Build Your Own HIP Scorecard

Now that you have experienced several HIP Scorecards and face-offs, start building some scorecards for your own portfolio. We'll next explore how to use them to assemble a HIP Portfolio in Chapter 8.

Growing a HIP Approach Into Your Entire Portfolio

Can successful investors win Nobel Prizes for Peace? You bet!

Two have in this century for approaches that solve human problems for profit. Muhammad Yunus and the Grameen Bank earned a Nobel in 2006 "for their efforts through microcredit to create economic and social development from below." A fundamental shift in banking to solving the human need first seems to be a radical idea. A citizen takes out a micro-loan of $50 in Bangladesh from Grameen, that entrepreneur creates a career and an income that helps fund education, health care, and savings for their family. These micro-entrepreneurs, 98 percent of whom pay back their loan, then become more positively engaged in society, including voting in elections. The loans that are made to them are profitable to the microfinance institutions that underwrote them. Those loans are aggregated in to large funds that become part of portfolios for large investors, both institutions and high net worth individuals. This Human Impact + Profit approach in microfinance becomes an investable class of assets known as fixed-income, or bonds, and already totals $6.5 billion globally across more than 100 funds, according to CGAP. In 2008, when most traditional corporate fixed-income funds fell about 20 percent in value, microfinance funds typically gained from 2 percent to 7 percent and became a flight to safety for investors.

Another Nobel Prize awardee, former U.S. Vice President Al Gore, has avidly advocated attention to climate change for the past three decades. Since 2006 Gore has built global awareness of the trends leading to increasing carbon emissions, volatile weather, and potential environmental damages through *The Inconvenient Truth* film, book, and PowerPoint slides. The Nobel Committee recognized Gore and the Intergovernmental Panel on Climate Change "for their efforts to build up and disseminate greater knowledge about man-made climate change, and to lay the foundations for the measures that are needed to counteract such change (Nobel Prize Web site 2007). In addition, Gore cofounded an investment firm with the former head of Goldman Sachs' wealth-management business, David Blood. Generation Investment Management (sometimes jokingly called "Blood and Gore") manages more than $5 billion in public equities that provide solutions to human problems, especially those related to climate change (New York Times *Al Gore* 2008). Generation has also partnered with venture capital firm Kleiner Perkins with a $100 million position in the Green Growth fund, which invests in early-stage innovators that develop and sell eco-efficient technologies. Generation's investment performance has exceeded that of its core global benchmarks in both up and down markets so far.

Yunus and Gore have accomplished two world-changing results. First, they are actively solving human needs—poverty alleviation and climate change —with a profit-based model. (While Grameen is a non-profit, its operations are profitable, with revenues exceeding expenses for a "profit" margin of about 10 percent. This economic vitality supports ongoing expansion, with funding from successfully repaid loans.)

Second, these for-profit approaches attract investors seeking choices for multiple asset classes of their portfolios beyond equities, like bonds or venture capital in addition to equities.

You have studied the approach for building an overall HIP portfolio. You have asked the three strategic questions, evaluated the investments, and compared them to each other in face-offs. In constructing your allocations, let's review the tenets of risk and reward in each of your asset choices so that your entire portfolio is diversified.

Evaluating Risk for Your Whole Portfolio

A HIP investor can find human impact and profit potential in every type of investment. Formally, these are called *asset classes*, and you want a mix of them in your portfolio. Each investment category has a different risk and return profile. Choices that have higher risks need to reward investors with higher returns, such as holding equity in a company.

Within public equities, the highest risks are associated with those companies operating internationally in frontier economies, with potential political, economic, and social instability. Companies based in higher-income and more stable economies have lower risks inside the range of equities. The S&P 100 in the United States is a standard benchmark and includes the 100 most valuable companies. These companies tend to be quite stable and most in this group are well-known. The highest potential returns are typically in equities or stocks.

An investment class that has lower risk is bonds. These are loans to companies that are expected to pay back with interest. Again, inside this group, the companies that are less stable have higher risk and must pay higher interest rates to compensate investors for the risk of default. More stable companies, like IBM or Microsoft, with strong cash flows, are seen as lower risks and hence offer lower returns, with stronger likelihood of paying back the principal they borrow.

There are also asset classes in real estate and forestry, gold and commodities, and early-stage companies, such as venture capital. Each of these classes has a risk-reward profile. Each type can be plotted on a grid that has risk on the bottom of the chart (the x axis) and potential return on the left-hand y axis. Figure 8.1 shows this relationship among risk and reward, and is referred to as the "Capital Asset Pricing Model," or CAPM. This figure shows that lower risk investments are expected to earn lower returns, and higher risk investments can yield higher returns. Each type of asset will earn a premium over the risk-free rate, which typically means the interest rate of U.S. Treasury bills over three months, which are backed by the federal government and have the least risk of default.

Each investor has varying tolerance for risk. Portfolios can have a mix of high and low risk, which expect a high or low return. A HIP Portfolio seeks to lower risks, especially those associated with long-term issues like managing health and wellness and ecological sustainability. A HIP Portfolio of equities can also deliver higher than expected returns than the S&P benchmarks. Specifically, the HIP 100 has done well relative to the S&P 100, just by re-weighting the same equities based on sustainability criteria. Hence, with higher returns for the same risk a new, more HIP line can be drawn.

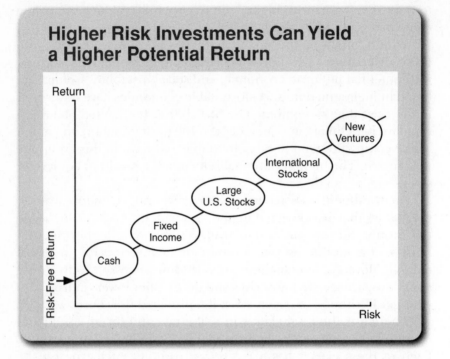

Figure 8.1   Higher Risk Investments Can Yield a Higher Potential Return

In finance terms, this would be more optimal "efficient frontier" of choices for investors. Basically, an investor who assembles portfolios that are "more efficient" can realize more gains or lower risks. In this HIP example, you could also increase your net positive human impact. Figure 8.2 shows how a HIP portfolio, which is designed to yield bigger profits and a better world, could provide more attractive portfolio choices for investors.

What do you do next?

Determining Allocations for Your Portfolio

Throughout this book so far, we have focused on how to evaluate investments for the equity portion of your portfolio. When investing for long-term goals like retirement or your newborn's college tuition, equities tend to deliver the highest returns relative to other choices for your portfolio. Table 8.1 shows the typical risk and return

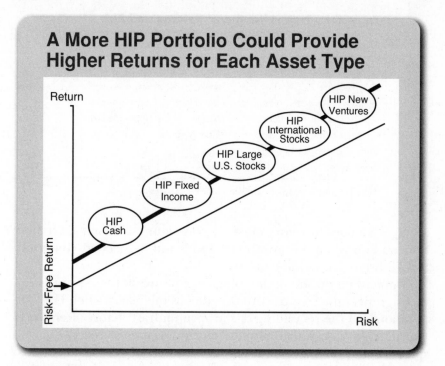

Figure 8.2   A More HIP Portfolio Could Provide Higher Returns for Each Asset Type

ranges of varying asset types including equities, bonds, government Treasuries, and cash.

From 1926 to 2005, Ibboston's database of stocks, bonds and inflation has calculated average annual returns and the annual volatility (risk) realized. Consumer inflation has averaged 3.0 percent, which has mitigated most of the average annual 3.7 percent returns from U.S. Treasury bills. Medium-term government debt (typically 10 years) has averaged 5.3 percent returns, and longer-term government debt (30-year duration) has returned about 5.5 percent annually. Long-term corporate bonds average a return of 5.9 percent over this multi-decade time frame, with slightly lower volatility than U.S. government bonds. The highest returns—and highest risks—come from stocks: large-company stocks have averaged 10.4 percent annually, and small-company stocks have produced 12.6 percent annual returns on average. Any year's returns can vary widely around this

Table 8.1 Typical Ranges of Returns and Risk

Asset Type	Annual Returns	Annual Risk Potential
Consumer goods (inflation)	Low	Low
U.S. Treasury bills	Low	Very Low
Intermediate-term government debt	Medium	Lower Medium
Long-term government debt	Medium	Upper Medium
Long-term corporate bonds	Upper Medium	Medium
Large-company stocks	High	High
Small-company stocks	Higher	Very high

Note: Risk is calculated as the standard deviation around the mean.

average. Hence, investors must be conscientious about their time horizon and when the investment funds will be needed (Ibbotson: Stocks, Bonds, Inflation database).

Depending on the timing of when you invest, these returns can vary significantly. An attractive decade was the 1950s, when U.S. corporations led the rebuilding of European infrastructure after World War II. A "lost" decade for equity returns was the volatile 1970s, with spikes in oil prices and multiple recessions. The year 2008 resulted in much strife among investors as the prices of nearly all types of investments fell at the same time—which is an unusual event for a diversified portfolio. The 2000–2009 decade was not kind to equities either, especially after adjusting for inflation.

While you can't control the performance in each decade, or certainly by year, you can select a diversified HIP approach that seeks to better manage your risks and expected returns, with more positive net impacts of your portfolio.

In the next section, we will examine a comprehensive approach to do good for your portfolio and the world.

Constructing a HIP Equity Portfolio

The first step in your portfolio is to calculate how many assets are going to each type of investment—stocks, bonds, cash, and the like. In calculating the ratio of stocks, aggressive investors like to use the rule "subtract your age from 100" and that is the percentage that should go into stocks. According to that very aggressive approach, at age 25, you would put 75 percent in stocks and age 50, you would put 50 percent in stocks. That rule presumes you want to invest for the very long term, and also that you don't need the funds until a very old age.

However, you likely will want to draw on your portfolio before your retirement, such as for a down payment on a house, tuitions for graduate school for you or college for your children, or simply to save for an emergency. Thus, you should consider a less risky "asset allocation," or how you divide your investment into different types—stocks, bonds, cash, and other elements. Since each investor has unique needs for their money, different time horizons, and a varying tolerance for risk, there is not one unified formula. You can devise the percentage by thinking about your needs and the timing, using an online calculator, or consulting an investment adviser.

Once you have selected the amount you want to invest in each asset type, you can use the HIP methodology to ask the three strategic questions of each investment: How HIP are the products? How does it measure Human Impact + Profit? How is HIP embedded in Management Practices and decision making?

As you read in Chapter 7, based on the answers to those questions you can allocate more to leaders and less to laggards. Some HIP investors will calculate specific scores for each stock, and then weight each stock they include in their portfolio by that percentage of the total scores evaluated.

In equities, there are two types of approaches. One is a small group of selected stocks that I call "picking winners." If you do your homework, then you can feel more comfortable having evaluated a smaller group and allocating a smaller part of your investments to those stocks you think will shine. A more diversified approach is to pick a large group of stocks, like HIP Investor does with the HIP 100 Index, and invest in a broader portfolio. This takes more work, but tends to be more stable and lower risk, as it is more diversified. However, the HIP metrics can be applied to any size portfolio to aid in determining which companies are positioned to deliver higher returns from their long-term, sustainable strategies.

Investors Can Customize to Impact Goals

With the fundamentals you have learned so far, you can build your own HIP index according to your desired impact goals. In the previous chapter, we assumed that each of the Health, Wealth, Earth, Equality, and Trust impacts are equally weighted. However, you can choose to weight some human impact outcomes more heavily, like triple Earth or double Trust.

This is your portfolio so you can design it however you like. You may also know some trends more than others, and have a better sense of how human impact can grow and how that leads to higher profits. You also may have an overall mission for your portfolio to weight more heavily around a particular human impact. For example, individuals may have preferences for higher Earth, Health, or Trust impacts, and weight those HIP metrics higher. Similary, foundations like Environmental Defense Fund might choose an Earth focus, organizations seeking to build transparency in society like the Pew Center might focus more heavily on Trust factors, or health access missions like the Robert Wood Johnson Foundation could focus on Health metrics and products. You can decide to be more specific on particular impacts, or to remain balanced equally among all five impacts of the Human Impact categories. Again, since HIP is built on measures of results, your choices are only weighting preferred outcomes more than another. They are not "screening out" anything unless you choose a zero weight for some reason. The weights express your desired impacts and how you see them relating to profit.

However, investors will not need to pick only one, but can weight the Health, Wealth, Earth, Equality, and Trust factors to match their personal choice. A HIP investor could be balanced equally among all five factors–20 percent each across each element. Or, an investor who's passionate about environmental improvements can choose to weight the Earth factor higher (say, 50 percent), and benefit from cross-industry improvements in natural resource efficiency—while still supporting the other four categories of impact.

This HIP approach allows you as an investor to customize based on quantifiable results, not just investment themes. While mutual funds and exchange-traded funds (ETFs) hone in on only one impact—like a solar-only ETF—this approach can yield higher volatility and risk. A HIP portfolio allows you to create a more diversified portfolio that more closely mirrors your preferences, while seeking a more balanced combination of investments.

How Sector Weights Can Affect Performance

Market valuations are not perfect. Finance theory is helpful to assess the fundamentals of how stock prices can be determined, but finance in practice encounters many imperfections. That's why arbitrage is possible—different beliefs about the same investment's current value, despite any theory of "perfect" pricing.

One of the core tenets of the HIP methodology is that leading indicators are quantifiable and predictive of future performance. Since most of the profiteers are still using market valuation models that ignore these leading indicators, HIP can outperform. Until the profiteer models shift to building a "bottom-up" model on a comprehensive analysis of HIP fundamentals, you as a HIP investor can invest ahead of the pack, and position your portfolio to reap the potential gains of more HIP leaders.

Another element of difference is that market-value-based indexes, including S&P, are held hostage to their own methodology. Because they believe that market values are the most accurate predictors, they force all the indexes into *sector weights* to determine allocations by industry. To be specific, in the energy sector, if the risk of future carbon emissions is not priced into the stocks in that sector, that whole sector can be overvalued in the index, particularly since the energy sector represents both the highest market value and the most carbon risk in the S&P 500. This debate is not new—Wisdom Tree, the financial fundamentals-based family of mutual funds and indexes advocated by Wharton finance professor Jeremy Siegel, has debated John Bogle of Vanguard and his preference for index investing. Essentially, the HIP methodology is supportive of the fundamentals approach, which is designed to generate the profits that end up getting valued by the profiteers when translated into dollars.

While S&P has co-designed a Carbon Efficient Companies index with TruCost, one of the guidelines is that the S&P-calculated market valuations need to govern the proportion of a portfolio going to each industry sector. This allows TruCost's ratings of the best and worst inside those sectors, but risk under-performing due to the sector weights.

HIP allows sector weights to float, based on the exposure of all the companies in that sector based on their core fundamental value driven by human impact, management practices and products delivering impact. This HIP approach leads to *more appropriate valuations* based on fundamentals than the method based on market valuations of each sector.

For HIP, the largest sector weights tend to follow the most HIP companies. As the HIP 100 Portfolio's Top Ten includes Information

Technology sector leaders like Intel, Cisco, IBM, and HP, it has the top sector weight. Consumer Staples and Industrials are the next two largest, as big brand retail companies like Procter & Gamble, and engineering companies like Alcoa, GE, and United Technologies are also top performers.

The differences in sector weights are sometimes called *biases*. This isn't negative, necessarily, but it does distinguish what is common practice from what is new and innovative. HIP has a sector bias toward a more accurate pricing of all the risks and opportunities related to long-term issues, whether currently priced in by profiteers or not.

The HIP approach to your portfolio can be applied to all types of investments (not just publicly listed equities in companies), whether managed by you, your adviser or your employer. Let's look at potential HIP choices to consider for the rest of your portfolio.

Designing the Rest of Your HIP Portfolio

Now you understand how to build a HIP Portfolio of equities. Select a pool of companies, rate and rank them according to the HIP Scorecard, and weight your portfolio by HIP scores. Remember to rebalance quarterly to lock in your gains and reset the balance for the next period. As more and more investors vote with their dollars (both investing and purchasing), companies who are less HIP will get the signal and those companies who are more HIP will be rewarded for their focus on human impact and profit.

What about the rest of your portfolio? Can you make your investments beyond equities more HIP? The next section explores each of the following investment types:

- Cash
- Fixed Income
- Private Equity and Venture Capital
- Real Estate and Forestry
- Commodities
- Currencies
- Tax-Deductible Charity

In the following sections we illustrate the more HIP choices that are available in fixed income, real estate and forestry, venture capital and private equity, gold and commodities, currencies, and

tax-deductible charity. Each section will showcase examples of investment choices that are delivering more attractive human impact and
profit. A HIP investor considers a mix of these types of choices to
best match their risk profile for the goals and objectives for financial
return and human impact for their portfolio.

Investment Choices beyond Public Equities

You have many choices for investing in a HIP way besides how you
allocate among your equity choices. Let's look at some HIP ways
to park your cash, lower your risk with fixed income, and other
emerging options.

Cash

Do you know where the cash in your bank or money market goes?
Most of us do not. Typically, a bank uses your deposits to make
loans to other customers at a higher rate, which is how it can
pay you to "borrow" your money. A money-market fund invests in
low-risk securities ranging from U.S. Treasuries, to lines of credit,
to top-notch corporations that are financing their payroll needs and
inventories. But how do you make your cash more HIP?

More than three decades ago, ShoreBank in Chicago was
founded with the intent to specifically make loans that had positive
human impact in communities where access to capital was difficult.
Many of these communities are low-income and desperate for investments in real estate development that could also support locally
owned businesses. Today, in addition to its customer deposits supporting its original mission, ShoreBank also offers "eco-deposits."
These funds are used to provide the capital for businesses needing
lines of credit and equipment loans for eco-efficient initiatives yielding lower energy usage and expanding renewable power. Total assets
are $2.4 billion.

Self-Help Credit Union in Durham, North Carolina, also provides deposit accounts to customers nationwide, which are then used
to fund the positive impact of small businesses and nonprofits. Self-
Help seeks out opportunities that benefit women, ethnic minorities,
rural residents, and low-wealth families. Deposits earn a market rate
of return, and have impacted 62,288 families, individuals, and organizations, who have benefited from $5.57 billion, as of October 2009.

Simlarly, many credit unions have a community-focused mission and local focus (Self-Help Web site).

Public company Wainwright Bank (WAIN) is based in Boston with $1 billion in assets. Wainwright pays customers an attractive deposit rate so that it can offer reduced-rate equity loans through the Green Loan Fund. Customers with these loans purchase solar panels and wind farms, install energy-efficient windows and "green" roofs that better manage overall energy usage. More than $700 million in loans have generated positive impact so far.

Regional banks like New Resources Bank (assets of over $170 million) and Charter Oak Bank (assets of $131.3 million) in Napa Valley also offer deposits and lend funds that support environmental and energy efficiency improvements (Charter Oak Bank 2008; New Resource Bank 2009).

Ask your bank or money-market provider how the funds generate human impact. If the answer is not sufficient, then explore the banks and credit unions listed here if it's important to you that your cash be more HIP. You can make the same—or better—interest, and help build a better neighborhood.

Fixed Income

There are four fixed-income categories for your portfolio: mutual funds and indexes, pooled loan funds, microfinance funds, and peer-to-peer loans. As with any loans, these are lower risk in comparison to equities, but not immune from risk. There is always a chance of default, which means investors can lose principal.

Mutual Funds and Indexes   The J.P. Morgan Environmental Index featuring the "Carbon Beta" was introduced by J.P. Morgan and Innovest (now RiskMetrics) in 2007 as the first bond index designed to manage the risk exposure related to companies contributing to, or solving, the challenges related to climate change (J.P. Morgan, *Green Bond Index* 2007). It invested in U.S. high-grade corporate bonds, which are increasingly pricing-in the financial risks of carbon emissions by companies, and this index outperformed the standard bond benchmarks. However, the partnership between J.P. Morgan and RiskMetrics was not renewed in May 2009.

Established in 2000, the Domini Social Bond Fund (DSBFX) is a mutual fund of intermediate-term, investment-grade bonds from government and corporations, with the intended human impact to boost home ownership (Domini Social Investments Web site). Hence, the fund holds many Fannie Mae and Freddie Mac loans. In addition, the fund seeks to support corporations serving underserved communities by providing access to banking, improved education and health care or redeveloping deteriorating areas. Up to 10 percent of this fund goes directly to community-focused investments, which may carry higher credit risk and default. Like Domini's equity indexes, this fund has tended to underperform the benchmark in up markets, but do better financially in down markets. While not 100 percent HIP because of this financial performance, each component of the fund is rated for its comprehensive human impact.

Another fixed income mutual fund that allocates a subset of its portfolio to high-impact fixed income, specifically microfinance, is the equity fund Pax World Women's Fund (PXWEX). Up to five percent of the fund goes to microfinance loans that support women entrepreneurs around the world while seeking to generate positive financial return. This is a very HIP approach and adds higher impact and profit for a small fund allocation (Pax World Investments Web site).

The Calvert Social Bond Index (CSIBX) is a mutual fund of bonds that seeks to generate positive impact and profit, and provide investors current income. However, it uses a negative screening approach when selecting investments, like its approach in its equity funds. This exclusionary approach has typically underperformed both the market benchmark and the Domini bond fund described above in financial returns.

Pooled Loan Funds   RSF Social Finance (RSF), based in San Francisco, is a nonprofit financial services organization that offers investing, lending, and giving options for its clients. Its CEO Don Shaffer advocates that today's financial investments, many of which are "complex, opaque, and anonymous," need to move to being "direct, transparent, and personal." Shaffer said in September 2009 that RSF's assets under management increased 10 percent over the previous year, with few redemptions from investors, unlike many other financial management firms (Shaffer 2009).

Among its offerings for investors, RSF manages two loan funds, one is accessible to all investors (RSF Social Investment Fund) and another is mainly targeted at high net worth investors (RSF

Table 8.2 RSF Social Finance Borrower Criteria

Category	Criteria
Product	* Must be socially superior to other existing products; * Product educates consumers at point of sale; * Product packaging and lifecycle demonstrate sustainability.
Production	* Demonstrates principles of green manufacturing/production; * Demonstrates commitment to the local community; * Employs equitable and inclusive HR practices.
Supply chain	* Commitment to local and fair-trade communities; * Demonstrates transparency at all levels; * Adds social and economic value to supply chain partners.

Source: RSF Social Finance.

Mezzanine Fund). As with the banks previously, there is a purposeful drive to make loans to organizations that "improve the well-being of society and the environment." This was the goal of Rudolf Steiner, a renowned long-term systems thinker, who advocated these principles more than a century ago, and whose lectures on economics inspired RSF's founding in 1984. In the loan-process evaluation, RSF highly values firms with sustainable design of products, a fair-trade production system, and even a "capital structure and existing financial partners that reflect commitment to social good and environmental sustainability." (See Table 8.2). Everyday investors can put in as little as $1000 to the Social Investment Fund, and the financial returns have been steady over time with low default rates. Since 1984, the total amount of loans made to enterprises, both for-profit and non-profit, has been approximately $200 million (RSF *Borrower Criteria* Web site).

RSF offers an innovative fund that delivers human impact and profit. The capital invested in its portfolio can vary among debt, warrants, revenue participation streams, and fee notes. The intent is to help growth companies, that are cash-flow positive increase their impact and overall scale. The expected financial return is targeted at double digits (RSF Social Finance *Mezzanine* Web site).

Microfinance Funds Microfinance, which offers loans with interest to micro-entrepreneurs around the world, can be a big financial market that enables positive impact. While approximately $25 billion in capital for microfinance is actively deployed today, Deutsche Bank estimates that the total capital needed to serve all available micro-entrepreneurs to work themselves out of poverty could be $250 billion (Deutsche Bank 2007).

"We believe that microfinance is a financially scalable and sustainable model that can provide both attractive returns for investors, as well as significant social impact by improving the lives of clients it reaches," says Jim Bunch, a director of investments, for eBay founder Pierre Omidyar's investment company, Omidyar Network, which has a core focus in microfinance (interview, November 2009). These quantifiable results include more equal access to capital for women and low-income citizens, the increase in education and literacy among them, and healthier lives lived through increased access to clean water and affordable health care.

Individual investors can access this market through peer-to-peer loans described in the next section. High net worth investors have an increasing number of funds to select from, including those offered by the fixed income and wealth management groups of investment firms like Citigroup, Deutsche Bank, and Morgan Stanley.

A listing of microfinance institutions (MFIs) worldwide can be found at www.MixMarket.org. This information hub tracks the performance details, both financial and social, of microfinance funds worldwide, both for-profit and nonprofit. MixMarket.org also tracks the total number of micro-borrowers and value of microfinance loans around the world. Table 8.3 may surprise you with the large number of borrowers and reasonable average loan amounts.

One of the first microfinance-focused funds for professional investors was developed by BlueOrchard Finance and Dexia (BlueOrchard Web site). In 1998, the partners raised $40 million to reinvest in microfinance institutions in Asia, Africa, and Latin America. Since its launch, the Dexia Micro-Credit Fund (DMCF) has been

Table 8.3   The Microfinance Industry, Leading Countries

Country (# MFIs)	Borrowers	Average Loan	Gross Loan Portfolio*
Indonesia (35 MFIs)	3.7 million	$ 677	$3.56 Billion (US)
Colombia (21 MFIs)	1.8 million	$ 917	$3.43 Billion
Peru (60 MFIs)	2.5 million	$1,145	$2.98 Billion
Mexico (43 MFIs)	3.3 million	$ 358	$2.64 Billion
Vietnam (17 MFIs)	5.8 million	$ 92	$2.20 Billion

*Not all loans are microloans; may be a subset of a larger financial firm's assets.
Source: MixMarket.org, September 2009 (information reported is year-end 2007).

advised by BlueOrchard, based in Geneva and New York. The fund has served 100 microfinance institutions (both for-profit and non-profit) across 34 countries with more than $500 million in loans, and these low-income entrepreneurs pay back 98 percent of the time. Dexia's 3 percent share of the 9 million entrepreneurs supported is estimated at 300,000 people who have built a new income and asset base (BlueOrchard *DMCF* Web site). Today's fund serves borrowers that are 43 percent rural and 52 percent women. The fund's top five countries for loans placed are Bosnia-Herzegovina, Colombia, Ecuador, Ukraine, and Georgia. Annual returns on this fund, which are available in U.S. Dollars, Euros, and Swiss Francs, have ranged from 3 percent to 6 percent annually. But the management fees of 2 percent and potential loads of up to 4 percent offset the financial returns (BlueOrchard 2009). BlueOrchard has partnered with Deutsche Bank, Citigroup, Credit Suisse, and Bank of New York-Mellon on subsequent investment funds, and won a *Financial Times* award in 2008 for the best sustainable investment deal with Morgan Stanley (BlueOrchard, *Morgan Stanley* 2008).

"Microfinance is an ingenious idea because, in a way, it acts as the Federal Reserve for entrepreneurs globally," says Jim Torrey, a professional investment fund manager. "If you look at the numbers, they are really extraordinary—the number of jobs created and people helped. I love the fact that microfinance is not a handout, but enables individuals to take ownership of their lives and become independent and entrepreneurs." Torrey is an investor in microfinance, and also the Board Chair of microfinance fund MicroVest, based in Washington D.C. (Torrey interview, 2009).

MicroVest offers long-term financing to lesser-known but well-run micro-finance institutions (MFI)—39 such institutions across 22 countries as of October 2009—providing access for more than 1,400,000 working poor with loans from these firms (MicroVest phone interview, October 15, 2009). With its MFIs experiencing customer default rates of 1 percent and past-due rates of 2.6 percent in 2008, MicroVest debt holders have been able to realize financial returns in the 4 percent to 6 percent range. Separately, long-term equity holders in MicroVest's fund may seek yields in capital gains from holding until ultimate liquidity or reselling its positions to other investors along the way.

There are a variety of for-profit offerings for investors to seek human impact and profit. Next, we will discuss another fixed-income strategy to be HIP, the world of peer-to-peer loans.

Peer-to-Peer Loans   Have you ever wanted to be your own bank? When banks make loans, they evaluate the person as well as the opportunity, and the likelihood of repayment. Innovative firms have emerged that allow you to do just that, and also provide visibility not only into the impact it creates around the country or the world, but also the repayment activity for your loaned funds.

Prosper Marketplace Inc. (http://www.prosper.com), created by eLoan co-founder Chris Larsen, offers U.S. investors the chance to lend money directly to American borrowers. Since 2006 it has served more than 860,000 members and facilitated $180 million in loans (as of October 2009). Loan-seekers post their names, photos, and purpose for the money, which is limited to $25,000. Individual lenders like you offer capital in amounts as low as $25, which are aggregated among multiple lenders and act as a syndication of that loan. Lenders can view validated credit scores (which need to be above 640) of those borrowers. Prosper uses a range of data to create an additional "Prosper rating" so the marketplace supports informed decisions. Borrowers finance everything from startup ventures, including those with human impact, to the refinancing of school loans, or recovery from financial disasters, including the cost of health care treatments. The yield to investors (the interest rate less the average default rate) in September 2009 ranged from 7 percent to 13 percent, depending on the risks assessed. Prosper lenders can also automate the process by purchasing a portfolio that matches their risk profile, and trade "notes" of previously funded loans. One element that individual lenders need to consider is the risk of default by borrowers. Third-party tools outside Prosper have emerged around the marketplace to create an "ecosystem" of ratings information. An investor can build their own loan portfolio targeting returns to match their own risk profiles (Prosper Web site).

MicroPlace, a subsidiary of eBay Inc., offers everyday investors a unique way to invest in micro-enterprise for as little as $25, at http://www.microplace.com. Also, it is seeking to bring this opportunity to all of eBay's customers, including 84 million auction users, 149 million PayPal payment users, and 300 million Skype users (eBay *History* Web site). Tracey Pettengill Turner founded MicroPlace to enable investors to place loans with microfinance institutions around the world that support micro-entrepreneurs who need a loan that can be "repaid with interest and dignity." (MicroPlace Web site). As seen in Figure 8.3, entrepreneurs are starting electronics repair businesses in Cote d'Ivoire, handmade toys in Guatemala and small cafes in the

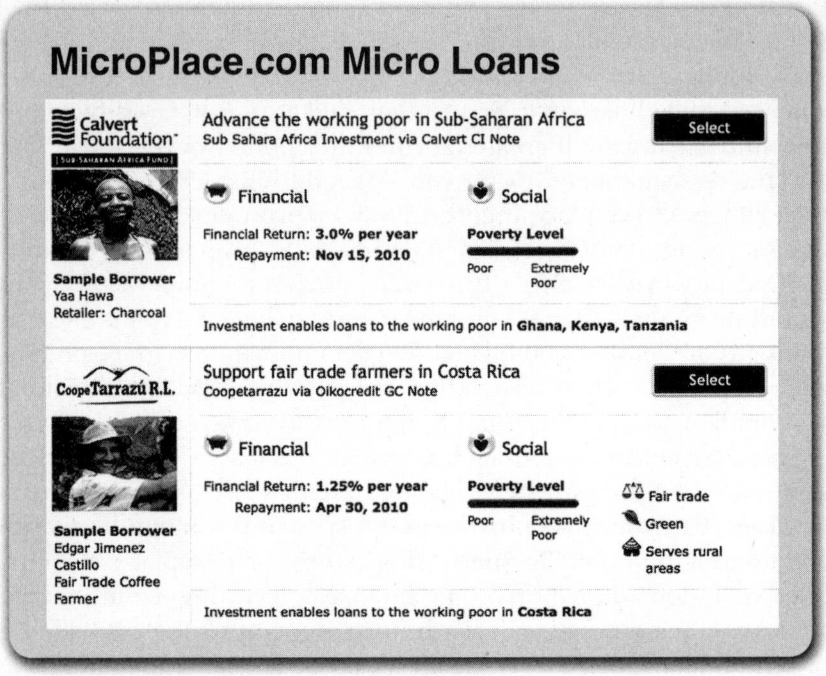

Figure 8.3   MicroPlace.com Micro Loans
Source: www.MicroPlace.com.

rural United States. An investor can select an interest rate ranging from 1 percent to 6 percent, the time to payback from less than a year to more than three years, and a geographic focus. Investors can also specify a particular impact focus, ranging from a focus on women, fair trade, rural areas, and "green" eco-related opportunities. You can also specify "poor, very poor, or extremely poor" as a selection criterion (MicroPlace Web site). As of October 15, 2009, MicroPlace.com had enabled 43,338 loans to the working poor.

Private Equity and Venture Capital

Garage startups are sexy. That's where William Hewlett and David Packard originated what's now known as HP. Google's Larry Page and Sergey Brin followed in that tradition as well. Some new ventures are funded by sweat equity (the founder's time, energy, and sleepless nights) and sometimes financed with credit card debt. High-potential ventures can be funded by third parties; either angels, who fund at the early idea stage, or venture capitalists who typically want to see an early track record of sales, unless the team created a successful firm together previously. Angels put in tens or hundreds of thousands of dollars typically; venture capitalists sometimes put in tens of millions.

Most individual investors do not have access to these deals unless they make $200,000 or more in annual income (or $300,000 if a married couple) or have a net worth of more than a $1 million. The Securities and Exchange Commissions refers to these investors as *accredited* (SEC, n.d.), which also means that these investors are thought to be savvy enough to understand the risks as well as the potential for loss of all their capital. Back in the 1990s, a creative firm called MeVC sought to bring venture capital opportunities to the public, but it closed to new everyday investors after the 2000 stock market crash (Brown 2003).

Individual investors seeking early-stage and high-growth ventures usually gather in angel communities like multi-site networks including the Keiretsu Forum or regional meetings such as the Band of Angels in Silicon Valley, California. In the United States, Investors Circle has become a leading community for accredited investors seeking human impact plus profit. Twice yearly, members gather to hear the investment pitches of for-profit companies also delivering socially beneficial or eco-friendly products and solutions. Since 1992, Investors Circle members have invested more than $130 million in 200 companies (Investors' Circle Web site).

In 2007, Investors Circle supported the launch of the Patient Capital Collaborative, a venture capital fund seeking human impact and profit (Investors' Circle). Led by an experienced venture capitalist, Sky Lance, this fund also taps the expertise of its investors, who perform research, investigate risks, and contribute to the decision of how much to invest. The current portfolio is invested in HIP firms producing nature-based health products, renewable energy, organic food production and green chemistry solutions (Sustainable Resources Ventures Web site).

Similar funds like Funk Ventures seek out early-stage ventures that have a quantifiable and valuable social or environmental impact. According to Fran Seegull and Andy Funk, financial returns are closely tied to higher human impact. One of their portfolio companies, Prolacta Bioscience, is a venture that is pioneering human milk fortification in order to better provide nutrition products to critically ill and premature infants. Cow-milk based formulas are not as effective on premature babies, which can lead to longer stays in the neonatal intensive care units (NICU). This, in turn, increases health system costs. Prolacta's products can reduce the recovery of NICU babies, aligning the impact of improving infant health, reducing the cost burden on the health care system, and generating revenues for the company (Funk Ventures Web site, *Prolacta*).

Other venture firms actively seeking human impact and profit are appropriately named: Triple Bottom Line Capital, seeking positive returns of people, planet and profit, led by Mark Finser and Joe Glorfield; Double Bottom Line Investors, which emerged from a pilot led by Nancy Pfund, a managing principal at JP Morgan; and Good Capital, which also organizes annual Social Capital Markets conferences (TBL and DBL Web sites).

Creative partnerships have been forged among venture investors and corporations too. Wil Rosenzweig, a cofounder of Republic of Tea, created a $30 million early-stage investment firm called Physic Ventures. With Rosenzweig's focus on wellness solutions, as well as healthier consumer food and beverages, he discovered a unique partner. Global consumer products conglomerate Unilever, which also owns Ben and Jerry's Ice Cream, was seeking to invest in these high-growth markets. Unilever offered to become an anchor investor, including sharing corporate experts in these markets, resulting in a $159 million venture fund. Physic's portfolio prioritizes firms pursuing the four "P"s: "prevention, prediction, personalization, or performance" (Calvey 2008).

Silicon Valley legends are also investors in firms that aim to be HIP. Vinod Khosla, who cofounded Sun Microsystems, has focused on technologies and solutions that reduce energy, carbon, and emissions. Khosla Ventures invests $100,000 to $20 million in ventures where they see "innovative bottom up methods solving problems that now seem intractable: from energy to poverty to disease. Science and technology, powered by the fuel of entrepreneurial energy, are the largest multipliers of resources we have to solve our many social problems." Khosla Ventures' Web site also lists white papers like "Breaking the Climate Deadlock: Scalable Electric Power from Solar Energy" and "Think Outside the (Coal) Pits" (Khosla Ventures Web site).

John Doerr is a managing partner at the legendary venture firm Kleiner Perkins Caufield Byers, which funded Google, Amazon,

Intuit, and Sun. The firm has established a $500 million Green Growth Fund to fund growth-phase companies in green technologies, information technology, and life sciences. "We urgently need to advance our green-tech industry at a speed and scale commensurate with the challenges we face," said Doerr in 2008. "We believe green technologies are both the key to solving our energy crisis and a tremendous business opportunity." Former U.S. Vice President Al Gore is also a partner at Kleiner Perkins, and his Generation Investment Management firm exchanged $100 million into the Kleiner Perkins fund, while the venture firm invested in Generation's public equity fund (KPCB Web site).

At Khosla Ventures and Kleiner Perkins, partners made strategic investments in what have become the largest information technology companies. Given their commitment to emerging HIP companies and technologies, you may want to consider investments in private companies or investment funds that are accessible to you.

Real Estate and Forestry

Another potential allocation for a HIP portfolio is investments in real estate and forestry, which can offer interesting opportunities for increased human impact and profit. For many investors, this starts with your house (the asset) and how you finance it (the liability).

If you own a house, you have diversified your portfolio. Historically in the United States, this is one of the best savings and investment vehicles that also benefits from the tax deductibility of mortgage payments. To increase your portfolio's HIP factor, you might consider an energy-efficient mortgage (EEM). Created by President Jimmy Carter's executive order in 1979, these mortgages allow homeowners to take credit for energy savings in the calculation of how much home you can afford, by adding the energy savings onto your income (RESNET and USHUD Web sites). If you are upgrading your home, you might qualify for an Energy Improvement Mortgage (EIM). Both mortgage types require a rating of your home's energy efficiency by a qualified rater. Ask your bank, like Citigroup or Bank of America, or your credit union how you might qualify for an EEM or EIM, which can make your overall portfolio more HIP (Energy Star Web site).

In addition, the green-mortgage program may also facilitate lower-priced improvements through partnerships with contractors specializing in improvements, like installing attic insulation, sealing the air ducts and installing dual-paned windows (Stinson 2009).

As you seek to insure your home's value, HIP investors can also explore house insurance that would rebuild their home to energy-efficient and eco-friendly standards. Fireman's Fund Insurance Company, as well as another two-dozen residential and commercial insurers, offers these types of policies that protect your assets and rebuild a more sustainable home for you if unfortunate damage occurs. If your home is already certified as LEED, you can qualify for a discount, too. Fireman's Fund also announced its "hybrid upgrade" auto insurance in August 2009, which enables owners to purchase a more fuel-efficient auto if they need to replace their vehicle (Rauber 2009).

While you may have the comfort of a home with energy connections provided, much of the world's population does not. Half of wood use worldwide is for subsistence use, specifically energy and cooking, says Peter Mertz, CEO of Global Forest Partners. "We seek to deliver units of wood from much smaller areas and in a sustainable way that is also profitable," he said at a Social Capital Markets conference in San Francisco in September 2009, describing his firm's investment approach. Global Forest Partners (GFP), a forestry-focused investment manager, manages $2.1 billion in assets, where half of its investing is allocated to sustainably cultivating forests in emerging markets. These yield both profit and positive human impact, by creating jobs, building a safety net for the community, and establishing a sustainable foundation for societal advancement.

"We are replacing rural development, like ranching and cattle, with more sustainable development," he says. GFP offers housing for workers, not just managers, as well as showers for daily good hygiene, complete with stocked personal care products. Workers bring their families to the camps on weekends to show off the amenities, he says, continuing: "I was educated as a forester, so I think at a different level of responsibility." This approach requires more investment to achieve the positive impact, but it also results in lower risks, more dedicated workers and an above-market profit. GFP is registered as an investment adviser that offers managed accounts and co-mingled funds to invest in these projects, which have delivered 9 percent annual returns over the past decade.

A real estate investment fund which seeks to deliver human impact is Cherokee Investment Partners, a private investment company in the Southeast, a long-time investor in the redevelopment of "brownfield" sites, which require environmental remediation. Cherokee's unique investment approach acquires these sites, cleans up the damage, builds ecologically efficient buildings, and then operates them sustainably. While Cherokee's profits are private, it manages $2 billion in funds that rehabilitate residential, commercial, and industrial properties across North America and Europe (Cherokee Web site).

Cherokee says that it seeks "financial, environmental, and community benefits, while mitigating risks that challenge them . . . Unlike traditional firms, we look at the whole-system and full lifecycle benefits associated with superior development and design. Our goal is for future generations to benefit from clean land and smart development" (Cherokee Web site). One extreme example is a former metals plant in Charleston, South Carolina, which dumped toxic by-products like lead, arsenic, and mercury in the ground, accumulating more than 6,000 violations of the Clean Water Act. Cherokee's team led the cleanup of the soil, treatment of the groundwater, and dredging. In 18 months, the project addressed 57 years of pollution, enabling the site to be repurposed for intermodal transport, warehouses, and light industry.

Commodities

Did you know you could trade the weather? Actually, you can buy a contract about a weather prediction related to how many cold or hot days there might be in a future month. Utilities purchase these to hedge their risk of making less money due to weather events. It is not technically considered insurance (which covers low-probability events) but rather called a "derivative."

A more tangible example is the trading of commodities like corn, orange juice and coffee. What would you pay for guaranteeing that those food and beverages were raised in a healthy way with no chemicals, or that the farmers were paid a fair wage? Today, that does not yet exist in the commodities or futures markets—but it could with increased information transparency about farming methods. Companies like PepsiCo's Tropicana orange juice unit, Starbucks' coffee purchases and Whole Foods grocery stores might even be active traders of those contracts. Firms that sell jewelry, like Tiffany and Walmart, could trade contracts in metals used in products they sold.

What does exist today is the ability to trade carbon-related emissions. The Chicago Climate Exchange (CCX) is a member-based organization that includes industrial and office-based businesses. CCX's mission is to "apply financial innovation and incentives to advance social, environmental and economic goals," a very HIP aspiration. Companies who join the CCX commit to reduce their carbon equivalents and can trade the financial value of those carbon savings, which have become a new class of assets (Chicago Climate Exchange Web site).

In fall 2009, the price of carbon emissions on the CCX hovered around $2 per ton for U.S. contracts, while those related to the European Carbon Exchange (ECS) ranged in price from 14 euros to 17 euros (US$18 to $20). Given the prices, some investors might consider an investment in carbon credits today that could appreciate in value in the future with demand created from new legislation. The carbon-trading marketplace attracted attention in September 2009, when global bank J.P. Morgan purchased a carbon-credit trading firm, EcoSecurities, for $204 million (Sandle and Szabo 2009).

While it is not yet possible to differentiate commodities by their HIP score today, this is a potential market segmentation that could emerge, just as organic products and eco-efficient materials command different pricing when you buy them as a consumer. There is the opportunity for commodities of different origin, agricultural practices, labor practices and transportation to be priced according to their human, social and environmental impact. Soon, "fair trade" cocoa and "organic" orange juice may have specific pricing and commodity contracts, and be listed as such in *Barron's* and the *Wall Street Journal*.

Currencies

As you diversify globally, how HIP are the practices of the countries where you invest? Does your investing support positive environmental and social impact in China, India, Brazil, and South Africa? While there are stock exchanges of socially beneficial companies in Brazil and South Africa, there is no HIP adjustment for currencies.

However, currency values fluctuate depending on risks linked to political systems (open democracies vs. closed dictatorships) and economic policies (protectionism vs. free trade) among other factors. Most lower-income countries are rated as higher risk also because their quantifiable human impacts are rated lower. Since the U.N. Human Development Index scores the state of human, social, and environmental aspects of a country, might those HDI values be a leading indicator of the volatility of currencies, if not a factor in the future value of the currency?

An initial analysis by HIP does not find any obvious correlations. But if human impact is a leading indicator of profit, which can lead to economic stability, it could be a contributing factor to currency moves.

Tax-Deductible Charity

Can charitable dollars be recycled? In the words of venture capitalist John Doerr, can you "write one $10 million check and have that capital sustain itself?"

To realize that goal takes "earned income," charging for services. Many nonprofits do this already, from hospitals to schools to senior homes. The higher the rate of income to expenses, the fewer dollars the charity needs. When revenue exceeds expenses, you can have a "profitable" nonprofit, as well as delivering positive human impact.

One very HIP example is microfinance institutions. Like a bank, they lend money to low-income clients, who use them to invest in a small business and then pay back the loans. Grameen Bank won a Nobel Prize for this approach, and operates a foundation in the United States to expand the model to low-income citizens there.

Another example is Kiva.org. Launched in 2005 by Matt Flannery and Jessica Jackley, the cofounders wanted to make it easier for borrowers and lenders to find each other. Today, a tax-deductible donation as low as $25 provides capital that is loaned to a micro-entrepreneur that the donor can select, and then when repaid, that capital can be reloaned. This produces an economic and impact multiplier effect that can last for years, which is very HIP. In addition, Kiva.org chose to build trust into its own finances. Donors can choose how much to add on to their donation to support Kiva, which could be zero.

With the simplicity of combining the Internet with donations that reach around the world using a bank card, word of mouth spread fast. Nearly a quarter-million entrepreneurs, more than 80 percent of them women, have borrowed $100 million since Kiva's launch. Covering 185 countries, these loans have been made by more than 500,000 everyday lenders around the world. This person-to-person approach to banking has resulted in payback rates of almost 98 percent, from borrowers to lenders. On average, lenders at Kiva participate in about five loans. (Kiva.org Web site) Kiva's founders have been recognized in Bill Clinton's book, *Giving*, and on *Oprah*.

Beneficiaries of Charitable Giving   In the United States, tax-deductible charitable contributions represent about 1 percent of overall investor dollars that are professionally managed. This $300 billion annually (usagiving.org) totals more than 2 percent of national output (GDP) in 2008. Three of four dollars of this giving is done by individuals like you. Foundations grant about 13 percent of the total, charitable bequests total about 7 percent, and corporate giving represents an estimated 5 percent. Table 8.4 shows where each year's charitable donations go, and what human impacts they help create (Giving USA, 3).

In addition to microfinance, non-profit entrepreneurs create high human impact. In education, the SEED schools, Aspire Public Schools and KIPP Academy all provide a high-quality education that creates the opportunity for teens of all backgrounds and incomes, who apply themselves, to get to college. As JB Schramm of College Summit says, the first kid in a low-income family who goes to college breaks the cycle of poverty in that family forever (Eakin 2003). Also, in the United States, a college graduate exceeds a high-school graduate by earning $1 million more in their lifetime, and saving

Table 8.4   Charitable Giving Received in 2008

Category	2008 Receipts	Share of total	Selected "Human Impact"
Religious congregations and organizations	$106.9 billion	35%	Trust-building in community, access to health services
Education	$40.9 billion	13%	Capacity to increase health, wealth, equality, trust
Foundation receipts	$32.7 billion	11%	(All categories)
Public-society benefit	$23.9 billion	8%	(All categories)
Health organizations	$21.6 billion	7%	Direct increase in health
International affairs	$13.3 billion	4%	Building global trust
Arts, culture, humanities	$12.8 billion	4%	Higher health and trust
Environment/animals	$6.6 billion	2%	Awareness and action in Earth and Health impacts

Source: Giving USA; HIP analysis.

the government $250,000 in welfare payments (Day and Newburger 2002, 3–4).

Is your charitable giving supporting ongoing economic self-sufficiency of the recipient institution? Is that organization generating income consistently (not just collecting donations) and delivering a "return on your charitable donation"? Our problems are so big these days, the challenge is to get higher impact per dollar to solve them more efficiently.

Some charitable models may not lend themselves to economic self-sufficiency. You probably do not want human rights to be a tradable commodity—but rather a set of rights to which we are entitled, like respect and dignity, as well as access to clean water and affordable health care.

Organizations that find, fund, and support these forward-thinking entrepreneurs solving social problems, mainly non-profit and some for-profit, include Ashoka, Echoing Green and the Draper Richards Foundation. They each support the concept of entrepreneurial leaders creating high human impact in a systems-changing and strategic approach.

Some nonprofits achieve this higher level of impact by partnering with corporations. Since 2008, the Environmental Defense Fund has teamed with Kohlberg Kravis Roberts, which owns a portfolio of over 40 firms that can benefit both ecologically and economically (Gunther 2008). Several non-profits have offices in Bentonville, Arkansas, including EDF, NRDC and Conservation International, as Walmart is open to engaging their expertise in becoming more eco-efficient (KKR Web site).

Innovative Financings in the Charitable World   Innovative grant makers, like the Lemelson Foundation, are realizing higher impact by implementing program-related investments (PRIs) of loans or equity, which advance the organizational mission. The Lemelson Foundation, whose eponymous founder has created more than 600 patented inventions, "celebrates and supports inventors and entrepreneurs to strengthen social and economic life" (http://www .lemelson.org). PRIs increase the multiplier effect of social impact for the same tax-advantaged grant money (Lemelson Web site).

Lemelson has applied PRIs in its grant making since 2003. According to Senior Program Officer Patrick Maloney, the foundation is using them for about 20 percent of grant making, but expects that rate to drift to half of its grants over time. "That split will be driven by where we find the highest impact for our funding," Maloney says. This translates into new risk-taking capital for ventures like Emergence BioEnergy, founded by Dr. Iqbal Quadir, who also started Grameenphone. The firm will provide heat and power solutions for Bangladesh villages, 70 percent of which are unconnected to the electricity grid. Root Capital is also an investee of this type, which has provided funding for small farmers needing to finance working capital for their water-efficient coffee plantation.

Lemelson invested in these ventures, given its high impact and innovation. But unlike traditional investors, Lemelson is willing and able, as a foundation, to be more patient in waiting for payback. "We can be more flexible in waiting for exits, or can structure revenue-share as the venture scales," Maloney says. This type of tax-deductible investing, where the returns go back to the foundation for regranting, is acceptable to the IRS if documented as to its ultimate impact and connection to the foundation's mission. Maloney says that means meticulous documentation is required in pursuing this innovative investment approach.

Because PRIs encourage financial accountability through repayment, the culture of management teams of nonprofits is important. "It feels different than a grant," Maloney says. It's also critical to know your co-investors. For Lemelson, these have included Gray Matters Capital, RSF Social Finance, and Calvert. "You need to understand why everyone is in the deal, talk through the conditions under which you would sell your position, and ensure everyone has similar expectations," Maloney advises.

A HIP investor seeks high human impact in every investment, including tax-deductible charitable contributions. Measuring "return on investment" is possible for nonprofits too. The HIP framework enables you to select a range of human impacts to realize—Health, Wealth, Earth, Equality, Trust—and apply your donations and overall investing to those that are most meaningful to you—or those of you who work through a donor advised fund or foundation.

Planning for a More HIP World

Now you have an overview and description of the HIP methodology, tools and approach. This book has demonstrated how you can evaluate any investment by asking "How HIP is it?" The three detailed questions focus on an investment's products and revenue, how it measures human impact and links it to profit, and embeds HIP management practices for ongoing value. You now have the tools and approach at your command.

You can start anytime with your portfolio—easygoing with cash at a more HIP bank, or taking the time to build your own HIP index. You may want to engage an investment adviser to help (or even get them a copy of this book).

The final chapter of this book describes a more HIP world, and how companies can evolve, investors can manage their portfolios, and each discipline can tackle tough issues together. A more profitable portfolio and a better world are near.

How to Make a Future HIP World

I s a more HIP world possible in our lifetime? Bigger profits and a better world for all? The quest to land on the moon was declared in 1961 and achieved in 1969. Facebook was launched in 2003 and had transformed communication by 2008, connecting 300 million people worldwide via computers and phones, as of October 2009 (Facebook Web site). So it is possible in a short time.

Life expectancies worldwide continue to climb, in general, through better health and wellness. Access to capital is expanding through micro-loans and entrepreneurship. Renewable energy and clean water technologies will help release the strain on our natural world. HIP companies and investors will reap bigger profits by building a better world—and this can actually be realized over the next five to ten years.

As we move closer to a HIP world, how will your choices as a HIP consumer, employee, and citizen make a difference to the world of business, investing, and society? There are four major evolutions underway that you have the power to impact:

1. Corporations competing to attract HIP investors
2. HIP investing tools and information in widespread use
3. Diverse types of investors allocating their assets using a HIP approach
4. An integrated, multi-disciplinary approach to solving problems

The HIP framework provides a financially attractive and socially beneficial path. Ultimately, the corporate and financial worlds will look much different when they become more HIP. With $175 trillion of value in global financial assets, the investors who build portfolios yielding both impact and profit will lead the way toward a better world—and can reap the rewards.

A Competitive Race-to-the-Top by Corporations

As corporations worldwide re-evaluate how to maintain competitive advantage, they must re-evaluate their overall mission. PepsiCo's CEO Indra Nooyi shifted the company mission to Performance with Purpose, seeking to sell products that are Good- and Better-for-You alongside their traditional Fun-for-You product lines (ICMR Case Studies in Business 2009). GE's Jeff Immelt has built upon the success of the ecomagination business strategy to create a healthymagination strategy, with the goal of increasing health care quality and wellness (Schmid 2009). The core goals of a HIP corporation will explicitly specify its role in society—and the natural benefits for shareholders.

"HIP changed the way I think about the business and its impacts," says Dave Stangis, VP of Sustainability at Campbell's Soup, "I challenge anyone I run into: what is the quantifiable impact of your work and why are you not measuring it up front? This thinking leads to key business strategies."

As corporations seek to expand their human impact and profit across all products, operations, and management practices, these four strategies are likely to emerge:

1. Multi-impact conglomerates
2. High-impact product components
3. Measurement standards that index human impact
4. Open access to breakthrough innovations

These will accelerate the pace of competition and expand the spread of human impact across society.

Multi-Impact Conglomerates

To create the highest human impact for society, corporations could choose to compete on multiple fronts. A corporation could use its core business structure across all the elements—Health, Wealth,

Earth, Equality, and Trust—and seek positive benefits in each of the HIP categories. A leading example of a multi-impact company is McGraw-Hill. While its affiliation with textbooks is well known, McGraw-Hill (a multi-generational family-controlled public company) owns several lines of business that generate positive impacts for customers and society across every HIP category (The Denver Channel Web site).

- **Health**: *Harrison's Practice* is a mobile resource that provides doctors and nurses with the latest medical advances and knowledge via online and handheld devices, making information more accessible than it is in books. This improves patients' health outcomes and also improves the timeliness and efficacy of delivering care.
- **Wealth**: Standard and Poor's, author of the S&P 500 and other indexes, tracks daily changes in stock prices around the world, supplying investors with timely information about the state of their portfolios. This service makes it easy to diversify and provides the platform for managing wealth via portfolios that balance risk and return.
- **Earth**: *Platts'* energy commodities price assessments now incorporate information about emerging emissions, biofuels, and liquid natural gas markets, increasing customers' ability to make smart, long-term energy choices. McGraw-Hill's construction industry media, product information, market trends, and forecasts also include green and sustainable building projects, highlighting how this approach can yield higher rents and occupancies.
- **Equality**: iSpeak is an MP3 player that transforms into a portable translation device, allowing more timely cross-cultural communication. *Acuity* is an accountability-testing program for public schools, which highlights opportunities for special learning needs and can identify resources that will boost student performance.
- **Trust**: Customer satisfaction surveyer (and adviser) J.D. Power and Associates creates a deeper understanding of what customers want—and showcases it with awards that increase transparency about the top performers. Increases in customer satisfaction scores also correlate with higher revenue growth,

profit growth and shareholder value (The McGraw-Hill Companies Web site).

Today's corporations with multiple business units, like Dow, DuPont, Johnson Controls, and Honeywell, have portfolios of products that deliver multiple impacts, similar to the McGraw-Hill diverse suite of products. As investors reward HIP approaches, those companies are upping the competitive game. Their wide range of offerings gives HIP investors the opportunity to achieve a full spectrum of Human Impact, across Health, Wealth, Earth, Equality, and Trust.

High-Impact Product Components

Semiconductors and microprocessors are part of nearly all the electronics you use today–from your personal phone or laptop to the servers that form the backbone of the Internet. The total lifetime cost of energy—and equivalent emissions—for some of these devices exceeds the equipment cost. In 2006 AMD, an innovator in semiconductors and computer infrastructure, introduced a lower energy-use chip (AMD 2006). The product gained fast market share, and PC makers were eager to embed the new chip in their product, increasing the advantage their computers offered to customers. Intel, the market leader, quickly followed suit and today, the industry focuses as much on energy efficiency as it does on speed.

In addition to the energy savings, Intel's micro-controllers are inherently structured to generate Human Impact. "Anti-lock brakes (with micro-controllers) save a child from getting hit," says Suzanne Fallender, Intel's Corporate Responsibility Communications Manager. "Micro-controllers are integrated into modern windmill energy," adds Gary Niekirk, director of global citizenship. This leads to high business value and competitive advantage for Intel's customers and, as Niekirk says: "Corporate social responsibility results are getting to be regular business."

Corporations that become the source of "ingredients" for high human-impact solutions ensure their leadership across the industry. HIP investors can capitalize on these leaders by evaluating how they integrate with their business customers and the opportunities for increased impact and profit.

Measurement Standards that Index Impact

For many corporations, especially big brands, supplier competition is fierce. One strategy to accelerate human impact is a supplier scorecard. Since customers are increasingly adding sustainability and other HIP factors to their buying criteria, companies that lead the way can gain increased sales and market share.

An excellent example is the Sustainability Index that Walmart pioneered for its 60,000 suppliers (which HIP Investor helped to design). The world's largest retailer shifted what was initially a company-specific initiative to a cross-industry, multiple-sector consortium approach. Walmart took the lead on the design and first year's rollout of a baseline scorecard. Now the consortium also includes large companies who compete with each other, like Procter & Gamble and Colgate-Palmolive, as well as General Mills and Unilever. These firms are teaming together to ensure the consistency of measurements (Walmart Stores "Walmart Announces..." 2009). Four areas of impact are covered:

1. Energy and climate
2. Material efficiency
3. Natural resources
4. People and community

Walmart's consortium approach also includes academic institutions like Arizona State University, government representatives like the U.S. Environmental Protection Agency, and NGOs like the Environmental Defense Fund. This collaborative design will spread expertise faster across multiple companies, building capability to increase quantifiable impact over a range of products, more efficiently and with lower costs than if developed independently (The Sustainability Consortium Web site).

Open Access to Breakthrough Innovations

A future HIP world will also test the boundaries of managing intellectual property protection. Historically, most scientific breakthroughs generating a competitive advantage are highly guarded and secured with patents or trade secret agreements. Inventing new processes and materials can be expensive. Generating revenue from those breakthroughs also requires capital and the talent to maximize their potential.

But NIKE has a different attitude when it comes to creating positive impact. There is "too much duplication of effort in sustainability," according to Kelly Lauber, a director in the Sustainability unit. "Companies face very similar sets of sustainability challenges—how to reduce resource consumption and achieve greater efficiency—but few companies are designed to share the learning and solutions developed to solve those challenges."

That's where the Green Exchange (GX), founded by NIKE and other corporate partners, comes in. Companies seeking a high-impact and profitable solution can combine their purchasing power to create a larger market that entrepreneurs and inventors can tap into to sell early-stage offerings. The entrepreneurs can then go to investors with demand-driven proof that larger companies will buy enough to support a "return on investment" of equity and debt.

In addition, participating corporations can open up their banks of intellectual property and license it to other corporations, potentially generating new revenue from an increasing breadth of innovations across many industries. Lauber says the Green Exchange makes it "easy and legal to share—while making sure that credit is given where it is due."

NIKE is making a serious commitment to the GX, by first putting the majority of its approximately 700 "utility" patents into the Freedom to Research section of the database. Initially, access to these innovations will be restricted to non-competitors and licensing costs will be based on the purpose (free for research purposes of academics and nonprofits and scaled pricing for products designed for the developing world). This initial step opens up the potential for high-investment innovations to reach billion-person markets that might otherwise wait years for access to innovative products. The inventor can set the price of how far and wide they desire their innovation to spread.

The Green Exchange platform itself is designed as "not just another database for intellectual property, but a destination for sustainability," says Lauber. "We want each innovation to have quantifiable metrics."

The overall benefits of the GX are very attractive, Lauber adds. For example, "inventing ecologically sensitive 'green rubber' was really expensive," she explains. "Recouping a percentage of that helps our return on investment—and anyone who licenses it." On the cost side, eliminating redundant innovation is another benefit. "Do we need new R and D for grinding our shoes?" Lauber asks. "It should be out there already."

Finally, people involved in the process may become more inspired to innovate, knowing that multiple applications of the new technology are possible, and could represent a new source of talented innovators who were previously undiscovered.

NIKE's CEO Mark Parker and Sustainability VP Hannah Jones presented this groundbreaking concept to the World Economic Forum in Davos in 2009, to push for a shift in thinking of patents—especially those related to sustainability solutions—as "investable assets" instead of defensive assets. This transformation opens up the path to new products, incremental revenues at lower costs, and an increased awareness of the inventor's brand. It also enriches the environment with less waste and lower-polluting approaches. Table 9.1 shows the financial benefits of this open innovation approach.

"Isn't this a risky approach for a large corporation built on trade secrets and premium-priced innovation?" a traditional profiteer might ask. "To be honest with you, our Board of Directors was skeptical for a short time while we introduced this revolutionary idea," says Lauber, a sustainability director. "Intellectual property

Table 9.1 Financial Benefits of Open Innovation

Category	Financial Benefits
Higher revenues	New revenue from existing intellectual property
	Faster new product launches built from common intellectual property
	Innovator branding potential with opportunity to contribute to wider impact could open the door for premium pricing
Lower costs	Recoup research and development expenses from new sources
	Share development expenses across a wider group of funders; avoid "recreating the wheel" in multiple organizations
	Link "closed-loop" systems across industry lines more easily through eco-efficient technologies serving the whole lifecycle of a product
	Lower-cost sourcing for inventors and entrepreneurs
Optimal taxes	Future tax reduction potential if new levies on carbon, waste, or water emerge.
	Some technologies (e.g. renewable energy) could be extended to new locations globally for tax credits or government grants

Source: NIKE; Creative Commons; HIP interview and analysis (August 2009).

online is a conditional license," says John Wilbanks of Creative Commons, Nike's legal partner on the GX. "As long as you follow the terms of attribution and fees, then the system works well. If you fail to give credit or neglect to pay the fee, then the licensee is in breach, and you follow the traditional remedies."

Overall, this approach provides licensing at a lower cost. The licenses come in three flavors: "lawyer readable" for the details, "human readable" for the layperson, and "machine readable" for maximum transparency. The electronic approach to licensing more easily enables online searching, the potential for voting by participants on ease of use, the sharing of impact information on the results in the marketplace, and the tracking of usage—where and how products are sold, and at what price.

The Green Exchange is "wholly HIP." The outcomes of this new platform not only seek to increase transparency and trust, but the resulting products will boost equality and access to population segments worldwide, support eco-efficient innovations that are seeking larger markets, create a path to wealth for entrepreneurs and inventors around the globe, contribute to improved health and wellness results and generate profit for all parties. These higher levels of both Human Impact + Profit shift business toward a more open-source model, similar to what is evolving today with Linux, Mozilla, and other technology innovations. With increased transparency and open solutions available for billion-citizen markets, the benefits of a more HIP approach worldwide become widespread.

Expanded Tools for HIP Investors

As companies compete to deliver more Human Impact + Profit, investors need the tools to determine which firms are leading and which are lagging. The tools of a HIP investor's world will include:

- Scorecards, Ratings, and Rankings
- Investor Databases that Include Impact Data
- Portfolios Personalized to Your Desired Impacts
- A New Metric: Net Positive Impact

How will these innovative new tools be used? Comparative scorecards, ratings, and rankings can distill HIP comparisons so investors can build company face-offs for human impact and profit. Investor databases provide new information for portfolios to be customized around impact. New metrics become positive success indicators that build a better world. This information can then be customized as desired, by individual investors to achieve their own investment goals. Let's examine each of them in more detail, and give investors access to source information on a timely basis.

Scorecards, Ratings, and Rankings

Public rankings stimulate competition between companies, while raising awareness among investors. *Fortune* magazine's famous lists track companies, including the iconic *Fortune* 500, by revenue, but also look beyond financials, to the "100 Best Companies to Work For" and "World's Most Admired Companies." Wharton School professor Alex Edmans has calculated that investors can generate returns 4 percent above the standard market benchmark by investing in public companies named among the "100 Best Companies to Work For." Mutual fund company Parnassus offers a Workplace Fund with this strategy.

Fast Company magazine has published the HIP Scorecard since 2007, featuring a rating and ranking of large public companies based on their quantifiable performance in products, operational metrics and management practices. A HIP portfolio like the HIP 100 has realized outperformance beyond the S&P 100 benchmark by 4 percent on an annual basis from mid-2004 to mid-2009.

Mass-audience media outlets have initiated rankings, like *Newsweek*'s Green Ratings for 500 large firms in 2009, while specialist media lists, like *Diversity Inc.*'s Top 50, have ranked the performance of corporations on their ethnic inclusiveness. The public recognition and competitive tension that these comparisons encourage creates a dynamic "race to the top" among companies. When they are associated with financial outperformance, they become an investor tool as well.

Investor Databases Include Impact Data

Many everyday investors look for information on sites like Yahoo! Finance and Google Finance. More detailed information is included, for premium pricing, on sites like Morningstar. Free corporate filings with the SEC are found at EDGAR online, and SeekingAlpha.com provides access to quarterly earnings report transcripts.

To date, there is no easily accessible clearinghouse of comparative information for HIP data. The majority of sustainability information is tied up in high-priced databases provided by Asset4 or KLD.

Bloomberg, a financial information provider, has licensed the Carbon Disclosure Project's data on greenhouse gas emissions, expanding access to leading indicators of HIP performance (see Figure 9.1). In addition to the detail about sources of emissions by type and geography, Bloomberg also shows the emissions ratio relative to revenue and profit. An investor can use this information to assess risk or construct a more HIP portfolio.

The *Wall Street Journal* or *Barron's* could take a lesson from what *USA Today* and *Sporting News* did for baseball box scores. They might provide basic information free to the public, while offering richer detail on "how the game was played" for a premium price. This approach could apply, for example, to offering a broader set

Bloomberg's Investor Database Now Includes the Carbon Disclosure Project

Equity CED

BHP BILLITON LTD			
Total Global Emissions (Metric Tons)		Intensity (Metric Tons/Million US$)	
Scope 1 Activity Emissions Globally	21,394,070	Scope 1/Sales	520
Scope 1 Activity Emissions Annex B	13,912,390	Scope 1/EBITDA	1,010
Scope 2 Activity Emissions Globally	30,626,090	Scope 2/EBITDA	1,450
Scope 2 Activity Emissions Annex B	4,058,350		
Emissions from Disposal of Services	329,993,000	Emissions by Country (Metric Tons)	
Emissions from Distribution/Logistics	N.A.	● Scope 1 ○ Scope 2	
Emissions from Employee Business Travel	172,450	Australia	12,565,660
Company Supply Chain	N.A.	South Africa	4,544,870
		USA	1,162,430
Electricity Purchases (Megawatt Hours)		Mozambique	933,480
Global Electricity Use	33,973,690	Colombia	668,160
Global Electricity Use Annex B	5,039,900	Chile	431,740
Electricity from Renewables	1,717,300	EU Emissions Trading (Metric Tons)	
Electricity from Renewables - Annex B	735,020		
Total Costs of Energy Consumption (US$)*	2,570	2005	306,165	333,193
% of Total Operating Costs	18	2005	306,165	333,193
% Energy Costs from Renewables	3	2006	415,652	332,522
		2006	415,652	332,522
		2007	415,652	323,020

Metric Ton is in CO2 Equivalent
* In Millions

Figure 9.1   Bloomberg's Investor Database Now Includes Carbon Disclosure Project Data

Source: Bloomberg Financial L.P.

of fundamental metrics and leading indicators, such as employee satisfaction and overall diversity.

Portfolios Personalized to Impact

Today, you can select among mutual funds and ETFs by specific geography or industry—and even gamble on whether the stock market, or a commodity like oil, will go up or down. Though there are more than 200 mutual funds that have do-good as a theme or strategy, many are not specific to quantifiable impact. With a data-driven approach that is specific to human impacts like Health, Wealth, Earth, Equality, or Trust, investors could choose one of two strategies. You could opt for an impact-specific approach, similar to the Pax Women's Equity mutual fund that evaluates companies on their gender equality. Or, you could build a personal rating by human impact according to your preferences and where you see the most opportunity. For example, you could establish Earth's weighting at 60 percent or double the Trust element to 40 percent, or specify 20 percent ratings equally across five impact categories of the portfolio.

Investment advisers today ask about your appetite for risk and your desired investment goals. Some even ask about specific parameters, such as companies that may be off limits—often the case with the do-good approach. In the perfect HIP scenario, investment advisers would customize portfolios based on investors' impact preferences to yield a portfolio with bigger profits and a better world.

A New Metric: Net Positive Human Impact

Measures of human impact could total several dozen metrics in a future world. However, what matters in a portfolio is how meaningful those metrics are to successful companies, and how they contribute to profit. The HIP score is one way of consolidating diverse metrics that drive value. A single value that synthesizes how all the dimensions of impact drive profit could be a new metric for investors. In a future HIP world, not only will investors rate companies on this factor, but companies themselves could report a single number.

Discounted cash flows and net present values underlie the valuation of an enterprise. These are estimated financial flows based on assumptions of future performance. Investors could use an impact score to quantify the leading indicators of companies in their portfolios, providing a weighting tool for future returns that also create an improved society.

Just as announcements of new products and customers trigger an uptick in stocks, so could the release of higher employee satisfaction or lower emissions data. Today, there tends to be a lag of at least six months before these new fundamentals are factored into valuations by investors.

In addition, companies are seeking to boost their position in ratings and rankings on sustainability. Because everyday customers and forward-looking investors are voting with their dollars, the leading firms are competing to show up as high as possible, including in the HIP Scorecard.

More Investors Allocating with a HIP Approach

With new investor tools and corporations racing to the top, the number and types of HIP investors will continue to grow. And they won't all be individuals. A few pensions and endowments are already pursuing a high-impact investment approach, while corporate investors and foundations are beginning to experiment. Let's look at how some innovators are leading the way.

Individual Investors

Individual investors are pioneering new investment approaches. There are no investment committees required to approve a new way of thinking, just your drive and imagination. Want to change how you invest? Just start practicing today, using this book as your guide.

Pierre Omidyar discovered that microfinance investing fit his vision of "every person has the power to make a difference." The matching of buyers and entrepreneurial sellers in the electronic eBay marketplace mirrored the matching of everyday people seeking micro-loans to create a new life for their families. This approach to human impact has been able to generate profit for Omidyar and his investment company, as well as to grow his anchor contribution to Tufts University's Microfinance Fund.

Jeff Skoll's motivation to build a better world—ever since his teen years—became a core element of his investing across a "full spectrum" of opportunities. Skoll has pursued investments that seek impact and profit in his personal portfolio. His production company, Participant Media, has created Oscar-winning movies and achieved box-office success, focusing on topics that have a strong human-impact component. Online networks at Skoll-backed SocialEdge.net and Participate.net encourage individuals to tackle new human challenges together.

Charly Kleissner, a high-tech executive, formerly at HP and Ariba and author of two patents, has asked his investment adviser to build a portfolio seeking positive human impact and profit. This covers equities, stocks, real estate, and other investable assets.

Lili Stiefel, president of the Stiefel Foundation, sees money as one of several possible resources to tackle a human need, such as renewable energy and women's rights in the Arab world. When the problem is beyond an individual investor's sole ability or requires public policy, it may need a partner to help. However, Stiefel explains, she chooses grants in response to urgent humanitarian needs, but in longer-term projects investments are often more appropriate. "They allow the project to scale faster and sometimes they're necessary to incentivize the people involved," Stiefel says. "Plus the returns on our investments allow us to make more grants and investments and thus have a greater impact overall."

Bonny Meyer of Meyer Family Enterprises seeks out ventures poised to realize high human impact as well as profit. Some are led by quantitatively driven entrepreneurs, like Jeff Dlott of Sure Harvest. MFE's CEO Patrick Gleeson seeks impact metrics from investees.

Your portfolio is only waiting for your initiative. You can choose to start implementing a new HIP approach today. You can request more options from your company's retirement plan or 401(k) that deliver impact and profit. You can also ask your investment adviser to help you find opportunities. The more of us who do, the faster we can transform our profits—and our world.

Corporate Investors

Corporations are not only creating human impact and profit through their products and operations, but also through their investments. At Starbucks, the Corporate Treasury function of the Finance group has allocated about $10 million in investments to expand the capacity of its company's small suppliers. Starbucks has committed that by 2015, 100 percent of its coffee will be grown responsibly and traded at a fair price for growers. Root Capital, a non-profit investment fund, is the facilitator of these loans. Since 1999, Root has loaned $150 million to more than 250 small businesses involving more than 370,000 people in 30 countries across Africa and Latin America.

These loans to farmers have a 99 percent repayment rate, and investors have been compensated for the money they have loaned, plus interest.

"Starbucks' growing investment in Root Capital's fund will help to strengthen and stabilize our supply chain and ultimately help improve farmer livelihoods," says Ben Packard, VP of Global Responsibility at the coffee company. The program is creating positive human impact in Health, Wealth, and Equality.

"In 2005, we were selling one kilogram of coffee for 1000 shillings," says one of Root Capital's customers, Shiwahiade Munuo, a member of Kilicafe in Moshi, Tanzania. "After acquiring the coffee washing station, we now earn 1900 shillings. Also, our kids no longer have to help us with work, so they have time to sit down and study for school."

Starbucks expects these types of investments to increase to $20 million by 2015. Root Capital was recognized in 2009 by the *Financial Times* and the International Finance Corp. for an "achievement in banking at the bottom of the pyramid."

Starbucks is not alone in this endeavor—other companies, such as Whole Foods Markets, are following a similar approach by investing in their suppliers to secure long-term supply and new avenues for revenue.

To cultivate its expansion of U.S. suppliers, Whole Foods' $10 million Local Producer Loan Program (LPLP) is another innovative corporate fund. "Because we believe in supporting local farmers and producers," says Whole Foods' Web site, "We want to make it easier for them to grow their businesses and bring more local products to market. That's good for us and it's good for you." As of October 2009, the loan amounts ranged from $1000 to $100,000 and interest rates range from 5 percent to 9 percent. Whole Foods encourages existing suppliers with good working relationships to apply for capital to expand their business.

In Florida, a supplier of honey and bee-related products, Buzzn Bee, took a loan to purchase a freezer, so that owner-beekeeper David Rukin could expand to produce "creamed" honey. In the state of Georgia, supplier Via Elisa secured a loan for an oxygen analyzer and pasta cutting machine to expand its all-natural Italian foods line, which uses organic flour and free-range eggs. These healthy products benefit customers' wellness, while earning an operating profit for Whole Foods. The program profitably expands the potential for higher human impact.

Foundation Investors

Charitable foundations exist to make investments that realize positive human impact. But guess what? Many foundations invest their sizeable endowments with a traditional robber-baron approach. Adopting a HIP approach gives foundations the opportunity to invest their assets in leading companies that deliver human impact similar to what they fund with their grants–all while generating profit to fund more grants!

A leader down this path is the Lemelson Foundation, whose namesake was an inventor of more than 600 patents, including components for computers, faxes, and bank machines. The foundation's goal is to spread products that improve the lives of the billions in poverty worldwide. Lemelson's corpus is targeting 5 percent of its for-profit investments to yield explicit societal benefits, which it has called "human-related investing." The portfolio allocation so far has focused on clean energy and technologies mitigating climate change, which will affect people in lower-income countries to a greater degree. "The key is to encourage a continued holistic view for our investments," says executive director Julia Novy-Hildesley.

Leading individual investors are also aligning their foundation corpus or endowment investing with a focus on generating high positive impact as well as profit. Skoll and Omidyar, as well as Stiefel, Meyer and Kleissner, look across the entire spectrum of organizations they manage to be more HIP. Some community foundations also offer investment options for donor-advised funds to seek out positive, profitable human impact. A better world emerges when foundations that fund positive impacts put the weight of their entire investment portfolio to work in a HIP way.

Influential Institutional Investors

State pension funds cover a variety of employees and retirees, including teachers, public agencies, and of course, state workers. California's state pension fund, CalPERS, controlled over $200 billion in assets as of late 2009, and is responsible for 1.6 million people's health care and retirement funds. It wields great influence as an institutional investor, typically initiating higher ethics and accountability among its investments. For example, CalPERS's criteria for allocating funds to emerging markets include transparency, political stability, fair labor practices, and overall corporate responsibility—all factors that increase Health, Wealth, Earth, Equality, and Trust.

On the East Coast, the New York State Common Retirement Fund is licensing clean-technology investment index Impax, so it can benchmark $100 million worth of assets to the index as part of its clean-tech allocation.

These new approaches are taking hold internationally as well, including among them sovereign wealth funds, which were estimated to have holdings totaling $2.5 trillion by *Foreign Policy* magazine, in December, 2007. (www.foreignpolicy.com/story/cms.php?story_id=4056) Abu Dhabi is allocating $15 billion of its $600 billion fund to build an entire city, called Masdar, with 100 percent renewable energy and zero waste. Norway is investing $4 billion of its $400 billion fund in sustainable projects, including renewable energy. Interestingly, both these countries are rich in fossil fuels. So, these forward-looking investments are signs that they seek to continue energy leadership over the long term.

At universities, the Responsible Endowments Coalition supports student initiatives on 95 campuses, encouraging responsible investing (www.endowmentethics.org). As trends toward more transparency and the push for good take hold, university endowments will face increased pressure to invest for high impact and profit.

Profiteer-style investment approaches put these large institutional investors at risk in the meltdown of 2008. As they see that building a better world can yield bigger profits, these large investors will shift their portfolios.

An Integrated Multi-Disciplinary Society, Solving Problems Collaboratively

Finally, in the HIP future, the business, social and government sectors can evolve to adopt one meta-approach that encompasses finance, human behavior, and science—reflecting more accurately how life really happens.

One intersection, understanding the human behavior behind finance, continues to gain momentum, particularly in the design of investment choices. For example, setting the default for employee retirement plans to "automatic sign-up" yields more than 90 percent participation rates, whereas requiring employees to proactively "opt in" only captures about a third of the potential pool. This increases opportunities for long-term wealth creation.

Multi-Disciplinary Learning

An interconnected society was the worldview of Joseph Wharton, an industrialist inventor who was friends with Thomas Edison and Cornelius Vanderbilt, and the founder of the eponymous school of business and finance (my alma mater). As a Quaker, honesty, integrity, and trust were endemic to Wharton's life. In founding the Wharton School in 1881, he sought to establish a training ground for professionals from all sectors—business, social, and government—and required ethics in all coursework. He expected "sound financial morality" in all students so they could become leaders in any sector and serve "faithfully in offices of trust" (Yates, 206).

A variety of forward-looking multi-disciplinary approaches that encourage a comprehensive, lifecycle view of the world and business are taking shape in today's academic programs, according to the Aspen Institute and Net Impact:

- The Simmons School of Management in Boston has integrated sustainability and social entrepreneurship into its core curriculum for MBAs, undergraduates, certificate programs, and executive education. Thirty-five percent of its full-time faculty are researching topics of corporate responsibility and innovations.
- Full-fledged graduate degrees that embed sustainability expertise in management, finance, marketing, and business specialties, are proliferating. These "green" MBAs can be earned at the Presidio School of Management, Dominican University, and the Bainbridge Graduate Institute.
- Joint degrees integrating disciplines across programs are a more traditional way of building a multi-sector expertise. Yale University students can combine an MBA from its School of Management and a master's in environment from its School of Forestry and Environmental Studies.
- Certificate programs and concentrations in sustainability and social entrepreneurship are blended into traditional programs, such as Stanford University's Certificate in Public Management, and Duke University's concentration in

social entrepreneurship, offered through its Center for the Advancement of Social Entrepreneurship (CASE).

- Sustainability centers and institutes are growing as well, typically to provide services to corporations. The Center for Responsible Business at the University of California, Berkeley, is one example. Also, the Erb Institute at the University of Michigan fosters global sustainable enterprise through interdisciplinary research and education initiatives.
- Elective courses focused on evaluating and solving environmental and social issues have increased 20 percent, according to the Aspen Institute.

Newly established social entrepreneurship institutions, like Babson College's Lewis Center, seek to grow new enterprises to solve compelling global problems and "create societal value in the areas of education, health care, communications and infrastructure, poverty, economic development, security, sustainability, energy, the environment, and quality of life," as the college states on its Web site.

The first undergraduate major in social entrepreneuring has been established by Belmont University, focusing on "alleviating social problems through sound business efforts," according to the university's description. It is attracting young talent who see business as a force for change. This is "exactly what I want to study in order to lead a fulfilling life while benefiting and working for my fellow human beings," said incoming freshman Paul Malone in September, 2009.

Cross-Sector Partnerships

Corporations, including Dow, have funded a Sustainability Products and Services center at the University of California at Berkeley. The company committed $10 million over five years to seed this cross-disciplinary center of expertise, which connects the Business and Chemistry schools. A key goal is "students who think more broadly and deeply in terms of sustainability," says Tony Kingsbury, the Dow executive-in-residence at the program.

Each of these programs is developing Renaissance like problem solvers, drawing on multiple disciplines of expertise to find solutions that balance all aspects of society—and preparing the workforce and next-generation leaders of tomorrow.

$175 Trillion of Profitable Investments that Build a Better World

The pinnacle of a better world is that all its resources—human, eco-logical, and financial—are put to productive and beneficial use. This book has provided a guide for you as an investor, fiduciary, and citizen. It's also highlighted how you can influence companies and the world as a customer, employee, and supplier. Your portfolio can benefit from the trends toward building a better world.

Going forward, how can investors manage their risks, seek higher returns and advance society? The profiteer path has become rick-ety, the safety valves unmonitored. The do-gooder path, while well-intentioned, needs a more focused methodology to be economically attractive. More than $175 trillion in global financial assets certainly provides a sufficient supply of capital to solve human needs.

This book has shown that a revolutionary new path to investing, a HIP way, can generate higher profits by building a better world. I hope you've learned that the trends of new consumers worldwide, the boundaries of finite resources, the increase in transparency of all information connected by social networks, and the booming demand for "good" products make for timely action.

The best-managed corporations are bringing new products and solutions to market to solve a variety of human needs—in Health, Wealth, Earth, Equality, and Trust. These products are serving multi-billion-dollar markets, with the leaders capturing new revenues, higher shareholder value, and competitive advantage. The ability to quantify human, social, and environmental impacts across the entire enterprise, from customer to employee to supplier, is a critical skill. When business understands the value of these leading indicators, it can boost overall profit while simultaneously creating more good. The leading companies embed this approach in all that they do.

Investors who recognize these winning practices, and identify and rank companies according to this new framework, position them-selves for greater good and gain. Any investor can participate. And every investment has the potential for human impact, if your eyes are open to it. Assemble a portfolio of HIP investments—whether in stocks, real estate, or other assets—and your entire portfolio presents the next wave of opportunities. Importantly, this can all be achieved with a compelling purpose: an improved society for everyone, globally.

The future is waiting for you to act. You can achieve higher human impact and profit. You can make bigger profits by building a better world. So which will you be . . .

- A traditional investor waiting for "proof"?
- A socially responsible investor stuck in the old approach?
- Or a new breed of investor who sees the trends, quantifies these new approaches to human needs, and builds a portfolio around these emerging rules that value human impact and profit?

After reading this book, you are hereby invited to become a HIP investor.

Bibliography

3M. "3M US: Company Information – Who We Are." 3M. http://solutions.3m
.com/wps/portal/3M/en_US/our/company/information/about-us.

Abbott Laboratories. "2008 Global Citizenship Report." Abbott Laboratories.
http://www.abbott.com/en_US/content/document/gc_report_2008.pdf.

Abbott Laboratories. "Abbott 2008 Global Citizenship Report." Abbott Laboratories. http://www.abbott.com/global/url/content/en_US/40.40:40/general_
content/General_Content_00274.htm.

Abbott Laboratories. "Abbott and Government of Brazil Sign Kaletra® (lopinavir/
ritonavir) Supply Agreement." Abbott Laboratories. http://www.abbott.com/
global/url/pressRelease/en_US/60.5:5/Press_Release_0491.htm.

ACT-1. "If these women did it, so can' you! (excerpt)." ACT-1. http://www
.act-1.com/media/essence.asp.

Agilent Technologies. "Service Values and Benefits." Agilent Technologies. http://www.chem.agilent.com/EN-US/PRODUCTS/ SERVICES/Pages/
gp12993.aspx.

AK Steel. "Markets and Products: agION Antimicrobial Coated Steel." AK Steel.
http://www.aksteel.com/markets_products/agion.aspx.

Alcoa Group. "Sustainability and Alcoa: Case Studies: Alcoa Vision and Strategy."
Alcoa Group. http://www.alcoa.com/global/en/about_alcoa/sustainability/
home_vision_and_strategy.asp.

Alcoa, Inc. "Sustainability Approach: 2020 Framework." Alcoa, Inc. http://www
.alcoa.com/global/en/about_alcoa/sustainability/2020_Framework.asp.

Alibaba. " IMF Raises US 2010 GDP Forecast, Warns on Debt." Alibaba, October
9, 2009. http://news.alibaba.com/article/detail/markets/100181453-1-imf-
raises-us-2010-gdp.html.

Allen, Derek R., and Morris Wilburn. *Linking Customer and Employee Satisfaction to the
Bottom Line.* Wisconsin: ASQ Quality Press, 2002.

Allen, Elizabeth, in discussion with the author. 7 August 2009.

Altria Group, Inc. "About PMI: Our Strengths and Goals." PMI. http://www.docs
.i-version.com/construct/download.aspx?id=F5TYFWKJ5&page=2.

Altria Group, Inc. "Our History—Altria Group Story." Altria Group, Inc.
http://www.altria.com/about_altria/1_6_1_altriastory.asp.

Altria Group. "About Altria—Altria Group—Our Missions and Goals." Altria Group.
http://www.altria.com/about_altria/1_1_1_missionandgoals.asp.

AMD. "50x15." AMD. http://50x15.amd.com/en-us.

AMD. "AMD Drives Next Generation of Energy-Efficient Computing with 65nm Technology Transition." AMD, December 5, 2006. http://www.amd .com/us/press-releases/Pages/Press_Release_114609.aspx.

AMD. "The Future." AMD, 2007. http://50x15.amd.com/en-us/docs/50x15_ brochure.pdf.

American Customer Satisfaction Index. "ACSI Scores and Commentary." ACSI. http://www.theacsi.org.

American Customer Satisfaction Index. "Frequently Asked Questions." ACSI. http://www.theacsi.org/index.php?option=com_content&task=view&id=46 &Itemid=43#whos_behind.

American Customer Satisfaction Index. "Apple." ACSI. http://www.theacsi.org/ index.php?option=com_content&task=view&id=149&Itemid=157&c=Apple.

American Customer Satisfaction Index. "Coca-Cola." ACSI. http://www.theacsi .org/index.php?option=com_content&task=view&id=149&Itemid=157&c= Coca-Cola.

American Customer Satisfaction Index. "McDonald's." ACSI. http://www .theacsi.org/index.php?option=com_content&task=view&id=149&Itemid= 157&c=McDonald%27s.

American Customer Satisfaction Index. "Microsoft." ACSI. http://www.theacsi .org/index.php?option=com_content&task=view&id=149&Itemid=157&c= Microsoft.

American Customer Satisfaction Index. "PepsiCo." ACSI. http://www.theacsi .org/index.php?option=com_content&task=view&id=149&Itemid=157&c= PepsiCo.

American Customer Satisfaction Index. "Sprint Nextel." ACSI. http://www.theacsi .org/index.php?option=com_content&task=view&id=149&Itemid=157&c= Sprint+Nextel.

American Customer Satisfaction Index. "Starbucks." ACSI. http://www.theacsi .org/index.php?option=com_content&task=view&id=149&Itemid=157&c= Starbucks&i=Limited+Service+Restaurants.

American Customer Satisfaction Index. "Walmart Supermarkets." ACSI. http:// www.theacsi.org/index.php?option=com_content&task=view&id=149&Itemid =157&c=Wal-Mart+Stores&i=Supermarkets.

American Federation of Labor—Congress of Industrial Organizations. "Executive Paywatch Database—Bank of America." American Federation of Labor— Congress of Industrial Organizations. http://www.aflcio.org/corporatewatch/ paywatch/ceou/database.cfm?tkr=BAC&pg=1.

American Federation of Labor—Congress of Industrial Organizations. "Executive Paywatch Database—JP Morgan." American Federation of Labor—Congress of Industrial Organizations. http://www.aflcio.org/corporatewatch/paywatch/ ceou/database.cfm?tkr=JPM&pg=1.

American Federation of Labor—Congress of Industrial Organizations. "Executive Paywatch Database—PepsiCo." American Federation of Labor—Congress of Industrial Organizations. http://www.aflcio.org/corporatewatch/paywatch/ ceou/database.cfm?tkr=PEP&pg=1.

American Federation of Labor—Congress of Industrial Organizations. "Executive Paywatch Database—Raytheon." American Federation of Labor—Congress of Industrial Organizations. http://www.aflcio.org/corporatewatch/paywatch/ceou/database.cfm?tkr=RTN&pg=1.

American Federation of Labor—Congress of Industrial Organizations. "Executive Paywatch Database—Sprint." American Federation of Labor—Congress of Industrial Organizations. http://www.aflcio.org/corporatewatch/paywatch/ceou/database.cfm?tkr=S&pg=1.

American Formula for Growth—Foreign Policy & the Entrepreneurial Economy, 1958–1998. 2002. National Commission on Entrepreneurship. http://www.publicforuminstitute.org/nde/sources/reports/americanformula.pdf.

American Society of Pharmacognosy. "Taxol." *American Society of Pharmacognosy.* http://www.phcog.org/Taxus/Taxus_Web.html.

American Wind Energy Association. "AWEA 2008 Annual Rankings Report." AWEA, April 2008. http://www.awea.org/AWEA_Annual_Rankings_Report.pdf.

Anderson, Ray, in discussion with the author. January 2007.

Apple. "Board of Directors." Apple. http://www.apple.com/pr/bios/bod.html.

Apple. "Form 10-K: Apple." Apple, 2008. http://phx.corporate-ir.net/phoenix.zhtml?c=107357&p=irol-sec.

Apple. "A Greener Apple." Apple. http://www.apple.com/hotnews/agreenerapple/.

Apple. "Environment Reports." Apple. http://www.apple.com/environment/reports.

Apple. "Supplier Responsibility." Apple. http://www.apple.com/supplierresponsibility.

Ashland. "Integrated Resource Management (IRM)." Ashland, 2009. http://www.ashland.com/pdfs/EnvironmentalServices-IntegratedResourceManagementIRMLineCard.pdf.

Autodesk. "Sustainability Strategy." Autodesk, 2008. http://images.autodesk.com/adsk/files/sustainability_report_book_1_strategy.pdf.

Ayres, R.U, and A.V. Kneese. "Externalities, Economics, & Thermodynamics," in *Economy and Ecology: Towards Sustainable Development,* ed. Franco Archibugi and Peter Nijkamp, 109–117. Netherlands: Kluweracademie Pubs, 1989.

Babson College. "Babson College Receives $10.8 Million Gift To Establish Lewis Institute For Social Entrepreneurship." Babson College, October 10, 2008. http://www3.babson.edu/Newsroom/Releases/lewisannouncement.cfm.

Bain & Company. "One number to grow." Bain & Company: Results Brief Newsletter, February 24, 2004. http://www.bain.com/bainweb/publications/publications_detail.asp?id=15302&menu_url=publications_results.asp.

Ball Corporation. "Environmental Sustainability." Ball Corporation. http://www.ballcorporate.com/page.jsp?page=190.

Ball Corporation. "GRI Context Index—Social Performance." Ball Corporation. http://www.ballcorporate.com/page.jsp?page=187.

Bank of America. "Our Commitment toward Sustainable Business." Bank of America. http://environment.bankofamerica.com/commitment.jsp.

Bank of America. "Annual Report." Bank of America (2007). http://media.corporate-ir.net/media_files/irol/71/71595/reports/2007_AR.pdf.

Bank of America. "Bank of America Initiatives: Bank Products that Reward our Customers for Rewarding the Environment." Bank of America. http://environment.bankofamerica.com/article.jsp?articleId=Brighter-Planet.

Bank of America. "Sustainability Report 2007-8." Bank of America. http://environment.bankofamerica.com/articles/OUR-COMMITMENT/2007-2008_GRI_Report.pdf.

Bank of America. "Workforce Data." Bank of America. http://careers.bankofamerica.com/learnmore/workforce.asp.

Barletta, Marti. *Prime Time Women: How to Win the Hearts, Minds, and Business of Boomer Big Spenders,.*USA: Kaplan Business, 2007.

Barron, James. "A Less-Colorful Seal of Approval." The N.Y. Times City Room Blog, January 2, 2009. http://cityroom.blogs.nytimes.com/2009/01/02/a-less-colorful-seal-of-approval.

Baue, Bill. "Blue Funds to Invest in Companies that Support Democrats." Social Funds, October 13, 2006. http://www.socialfunds.com/news/article.cgi/2134.html.

Bauer, Krista, in discussion with the author. 29 September 2009.

Baxter. "2008 Annual Report." Baxter. http://www.baxter.com/about_baxter/investor_information/annual_report/2008/PDF_files/BaxterAR_2008.pdf.

Becker, David. "It's the Sustainability, Stupid." *Friend of the Farmer*, September 24, 2009. http://friendofthefarmer.com/2009/09/walmart-starbucks-on-sustainability.

Best Buy Inc. "Corporate Responsibility 2009." Best Buy Inc.http://www.bestbuyinc.com/assets/corporate_reponsibility/08_report/CSR_2009_Final.pdf.

Beyond Grey Pinstripes. "Preparing MBAs for Social and Environmental Stewardship." Beyond Grey Pinstripes, 2008. http://www.beyondgreypinstripes.org/rankings/bgp_2007_2008.pdf.

Bialik, Carl. "Unhealthy Accounting of Uninsured." *Wall Street Journal*, June 24, 2009. http://online.wsj.com/article/SB124579852347944191.html.

Bigelow, Bruce V. "Qualcomm's Don Jones and the Year of Inflection for Wireless Health." Xconomy Inc., June 18. 2009. http://www.xconomy.com/san-diego/2009/06/18/qualcomms-don-jones-and-the-year-of-inflection-for-wireless-health.

Billion Dollar Roundtable, Inc. "Members." Billion Dollar Roundtable. http://www.bdrusa.org/members.php.

Billion Dollar Roundtable, Inc. "Our Vision Statement." Billion Dollar Roundtable. http://www.bdrusa.org/vision_statement.php.

Bio Medicine. "Together Rx Access(R) Program Enrolls More Than 1.5 Million Americans Without Prescription Drug Coverage." *Bio Medicine*, May 19. 2008. http://www.bio-medicine.org/medicine-news-1/Together-Rx-Access-28R-29-Program-Enrolls-More-Than-1-5-Million-Americans-Without-Prescription-Drug-Coverage-19773-4.

Black Enterprise. "BE 100s – The Nation's Largest Black Businesses." Black Enterprise. http://www.blackenterprise.com/wp-content/themes/b-e/img/be100s/pdfs/industrial-service.pdf.

Black Enterprise. "BE Industrial/Service Companies." Black Enterprise. http://www.blackenterprise.com/wp-content/themes/b-e/img/be100s/pdfs/industrial-service.pdf.

Bloomberg Finance L.P. "PBG: US Pepsi Bottling Group Inc." Bloomberg Finance L.P. http://www.bloomberg.com/apps/quote?ticker=PBG%3AUS.

Bloomberg Finance L.P. "VZ: US Verizon Communications Inc." Bloomberg Finance L.P. http://www.bloomberg.com/apps/quote?ticker=VZ%3AUS.

Bloomberg Finance L.P. "XOM: Exxon Mobil Corp." Bloomberg Finance L.P. http://www.bloomberg.com/apps/quote?ticker=XOM%3AUS.

BlueOrchard. "Dexia Micro Credit Fund." BlueOrchard. http://www.blueorchard.com/jahia/Jahia/Products_1/pid/190.

BlueOrchard. "BlueOrchard and Morgan Stanley's BOLD 2 Obtains FT's Sustainable Deal of the Year Award." BlueOrchard, June 4, 2008. http://www.blueorchard.com/jahia/Jahia/Products_1/pid/201.

BlueOrchard. "Dexia Micro-Credit Fund (DMCF)." BlueOrchard. http://www.blueorchard.com/jahia/Jahia/site/blueorchard/pid/190.

BlueOrchard. "Dexia Micro-Credit Fund August 2009 Investors' Update." BlueOrchard, September 2, 2009. http://www.blueorchard.com/jahia/webdav/site/blueorchard/shared/Products/Dexia/Newsletter/090907_DMCF_Monthly_update_August_2009%5D.pdf.

Bonini, Sheila M. J., Kerrin McKillop and Lenny T. Mendonca. "The Trust Gap Between Consumers and Corporations." *McKinsey Quarterly*, May, 2007. http://www.mckinseyquarterly.com/The_trust_gap_between_consumers_and_corporations_1985.

Bornstein, David. *How to Change the World: Social Entrepreneurs and the Power of New Ideas.* USA: Oxford University Press, 2004.

Bornstein, David and Susan Davis. *Social Entrepreneurship: What Everyone Needs to Know.* USA: Oxford University Press, 2010.

Bristol-Myers-Squibb. "Product Stewardship." Bristol Meyers-Squibb. http://www.bms.com/sustainability/environmental_performance/Pages/product_stewardship.aspx.

Bristol-Myers-Squibb. "Bristol-Myers-Squibb Sustainability- Employees." Bristol Myers-Squibb. http://www.ifex.com/static/ehs/perfor/data/employ.html.

Bristol-Myers Squibb. "Executive Summary." Bristol-Meyers Squibb. http://www.bms.com/Documents/sustainability/downloads/exec_summary.pdf.

Brown, Erika. "Unfit For Public Consumption." *Forbes*, August 11, 2003. http://www.forbes.com/forbes/2003/0811/064.html.

Bureau of Economic Analysis. "Gross Domestic Product by Industry Accounts." Bureau of Economic Analysis, April 23, 2009. http://www.bea.gov/industry/gpotables/gpo_action.cfm?anon=101186&table_id=24753&format_type=0.

Bureau of Labor Statistics. "Table 1: Mean hourly earnings and weekly hours for selected worker and establishment characteristics." National Compensation Survey, Dec. 2007 to January 2009 (average July 2008). http://www.bls.gov/ncs/ocs/sp/nctb0715.pdf.

Bureau of Transportation Statistics. "Table 1-11: Number of U.S. Aircraft, Vehicles, Vessels, and Other Conveyances." Research and Innovative Technology Administration. http://www.bts.gov/publications/national_transportation_statistics/html/table_01_11.html.

Burns, Jenny. "Belmont opens social entrepreneur center." *Nashville Business Journal*, September 24, 2009. http://nashville.bizjournals.com/nashville/stories/2009/09/21/daily36.html.

Burr, Andrew C. "CoStar Study Finds Energy Star, LEED Bldgs. Outperform Peers." CoStar, Inc. March 26, 2008. http://www.costar.com/News/Article .aspx?id=D968F1E0DCF73712B03A099E0E99C679.

Burrows, Peter. "Apple Launches Major Green Effort." *BusinessWeek.* 24 September 2009. http://www.businessweek.com/magazine/content/09_40/ b4149068698190.htm.

Business Planning Solutions Global Insight Advisory Services Division. "The Price Impact of Walmart: An Update Through 2006." *Global Insight*, September 4, 2007. http://www.livebetterindex.com/2007GlobReport.pdf.

Business Wire. "Bank of America, Citibank, Wells Fargo Top Vividence Customer Experience Rankings; Vividence Study Highlights Striking Changes and Challenges in Online Banking." BNET. http://findarticles.com/p/articles/ mi_m0EIN/is_2003_Sept_24/ai_108088792.

BusinessWeek. "Abbott." *BusinessWeek.* http://investing.businessweek.com/research/ stocks/financials/financials.asp?ric=ABT.

BusinessWeek. "Businessweek Top 50 Companies: Gilead." *BusinessWeek.* http://images.businessweek.com/ss/09/03/0326_bw50/51.htm.

BusinessWeek. "Maggie Wilderotter: Executive Profile & Biography." *BusinessWeek.* http://investing.businessweek.com/businessweek/research/stocks/people/ person.asp?personId=235419&ric=CZN.TO.

BusinessWeek. "Merck." *BusinessWeek.* http://investing.businessweek.com/research/ stocks/financials/financials.asp?ric=MRK.

BusinessWeek. "What Price Reputation?" *BusinessWeek*, July 9 2007. http://www .businessweek.com/magazine/content/07_28/b4042050.htm.

BusinessWeek. "What Price Reputation?" *BusinessWeek*, July 9, 2007. http:// www.businessweek.com/magazine/content/07_28/b4042050.htm.

Butschli, Jim. "'Nutrition' label reveals Timberland's footprint." *Packing World Magazine*, March 2006, http://www.packworld.com/package-20533.

CalPERS. "Emerging Equity Markets Principles." CalPERS. November 13, 2007. http://www.calpers.ca.gov/eip-.docs/investments/policies/inv-asset-classes/ equity/ext-equity/emerging-eqty-market-prinicples.pdf.

Calvey, Mark. "Physic Raises $159M in its First Fund." *San Francisco Business Times*, July 14, 2008. http://www.physicventures.com/news/physic-raises-159m-its-first-fund.

Campbell's Soup Company. "2009 CAGNY Presentation PPT" Consumer Analyst Group of New York Food, Beverage, Tobacco, and Household Products Conference, February 18, 2009.

Capital E. "Capital E." Capital E. http://www.cap-e.com.

Captain, Lori. "DuPont Selected Among Top Companies for Female Leaders." DuPont, March 23, 2009. http://www2.dupont.com/Media_Center/en_ CA/pressrelease20090323.html.

Carbon Disclosure Project. "About Us." Carbon Disclosure Project. https://www .cdproject.net/aboutus.asp.

Carbon Disclosure Project. "Carbon Disclosure Project 2009 Global 500 Report." Carbon Disclosure Project. https://www.cdproject.net/CDPResults/67_329_ 143_CDP%20Global%20500%20Report%202008.pdf.

Carlson School of Management. "The Summit 2002: Summit Newsletter." Carlson School of Management. http://www.carlsonschool.umn.edu/Page5384.aspx.

Carpenter, Dave. "Tracking Infections." *Hospitals & Health Magazine,* February 2006. http://www.hhnmag.com/hhnmag_app/jsp/articledisplay.jsp?dcrpath= HHNMAG/PubsNewsArticle/data/0602HHN_FEA_InfectionControl&domain =HHNMAG.

Catalyst, Inc. "The Bottom Line: Corporate Performance and Women's Representation on Boards." Catalyst.org, 2007. http://www.catalyst.org/file/139/bottom %20line%202.pdf.

Center for Responsive Politics. "Bank of America." Open Secrets. http://www .opensecrets.org/lobby/clientsum.php?year=2008&lname=Bank+of+America &id=.

Center for Responsive Politics. "Chevron Corp. Total Lobbying Expenditures, 2008." Open Secrets. http://www.opensecrets.org/lobby/clientsum.php? year=2008&lname=Chevron+Corp&id=.

Center for Responsive Politics. "Colgate-Palmolive." Open Secrets. http://www .opensecrets.org/lobby/clientsum.php?lname=Colgate-Palmolive+Co&year= 2009.

Center for Responsive Politics. "ExxonMobil." Open Secrets. http://www.open secrets.org/lobby/clientsum.php?year=2008&lname=Exxon+Mobil&id=.

Center for Responsive Politics. "JP Morgan Chase." Open Secrets. http://www .opensecrets.org/lobby/clientsum.php?year=2008&lname=JPMorgan+Chase +%26+Co&id=.

Center for Responsive Politics. "Procter & Gamble." Open Secrets. http://www .opensecrets.org/lobby/clientsum.php?lname=Procter+%26+Gamble&year= 2009.

Center for Responsive Politics. "Sprint Nextel." Open Secrets. http://www.open secrets.org/lobby/clientsum.php?year=2008&lname=Sprint+Nextel&id=.

Center for Responsive Politics. "Top All-Time Donors – 1989–2010 Summary." Open Secrets. http://www.opensecrets.org/orgs/list.php.

Center for Responsive Politics. "Verizon Communications." Open Secrets. http://www.opensecrets.org/orgs/summary.php?id=D000000079.

Central Intelligence Agency. "The World Factbook – Kenya." Central Intelligence Agency. https://www.cia.gov/library/publications/the-world-factbook/ geos/ke.html.

Ceres. "Corporate Governance and Climate Change: Consumer and Technology Companies." Ceres. http://www.ceres.org/Document.Doc?id=394.

Ceres. "Global Reporting Initiative." Ceres. http://www.ceres.org//Page.aspx?pid= 435.

CF Industries. "Products." CF Industries. http://www.cfindustries.com/Products .htm.

CGAP. "Microfinance Funds Continue to Grow Despite the Crisis." CGAP Brief, April 2009. http://www.cgap.org/gm/document-1.9.34437/CGAP% 20Brief_MIV_FinancialCrisis.pdf.

Charles Schwab Corporation "The Charles Schwab Corporation." Charles Schwab Corporation. http://www.aboutschwab.com/community/financial- literacy/index.html.

Charter Oak Bank. "Charter Oak Bank Reports Strong 3rd Quarter, 2008." Charter Oak Bank, October 2, 2008. http://www.charteroakbank.com/OCTOBER-2,- 2008.aspx.

Cherokee. "Company." Cherokee. http://www.cherokeefund.com/company.htm.

Cherokee. "Portfolio." Cherokee. http://www.cherokeefund.com/portfolio.htm.

Chevron. "2008 Corporate Responsibility Report." Chevron. http://www.chevron.com/globalissues/corporateresponsibility/2008/documents/Chevron_CR_Report_2008.pdf.

Chevron. "Charts & Tables." Chevron. http://www.chevron.com/globalissues/corporateresponsibility/2007/chartstables/#b3.

Chevron. "Priorities, Progress & Plans." Chevron. http://www.chevron.com/globalissues/corporateresponsibility/2007/priorityprogressplans.

Chevron. "United States: Highlights of Operations." Chevron. http://www.chevron.com/countries/usa.

Cheyney, Tom. "BP Solar to install, operate 2.42MW PV rooftop system on FedEx hub in New Jersey." *PV-tech.org*, July 30, 2009. http://www.pv-tech.org/news/_a/bp_solar_to_install_operate_2.42mw_pv_rooftop_system_on_fedex_hub_in_new_je/.

Chicago Climate Exchange. "Chicago ClimateX." Chicago Climate Exchange. http://www.chicagoclimatex.com/

Choney, Suzanne. "Let's market PCs like it's 1959." *MSNBC*, May 14, 2009. http://www.msnbc.msn.com/id/30709961.

Cisco EcoBoard. "A letter from the Cisco EcoBoard." Cisco Systems. http://www.cisco.com/web/about/ac227/ac333/the-environment/ecoboard-letter. html.

Cisco Systems. "Cisco Aims to Reduce Greenhouse Gas Emissions 25% by 2012." Cisco Systems, June 24, 2008. http://www.cisco.com/cisco/web/UK/news/archive/2008/062408.html.

Cisco Systems. "Cisco and the Environment – CSR Report 2008." Cisco Systems. http://www.cisco.com/web/about/ac227/csr2008/the-environment/index.html.

Cisco Systems. "To Our Shareholders – Annual Report 2008." Cisco Systems. http://www.cisco.com/web/about/ac49/ac20/ac19/ar2008/letter_to_shareholders/index.html.

Citi. "Microfinance Banana Skins." Citi (formerly Citibank). http://www.citibank.com/citi/microfinance/data/initiatives.pdf.

City Data. "Bentonville AR: Walmart Home Office Sign." City-Data. http://www.city-data.com/picfilesv/picv33542.php.

Climate Savers Computing Initiative. "2007-2008 Annual Report." Climate Savers Computing Initiative. http://www.climatesaverscomputing.org/docs/Climate_Savers_Computing_2008_Annual_%20Report.pdf.

CNN Money. "Exxon-Mobil merger done." CNN Money. http://money.cnn.com/1999/11/30/deals/exxonmobil.

CNN Money. "Colgate Palmolive." CNN Money. http://money.cnn.com/quote/snapshot/snapshot.html?symb=CL.

CNN Money. "Sprint." CNN Money. http://money.cnn.com/quote/snapshot/snapshot.html?symb=S.

Coca-Cola Company. "2007/2008 Sustainability Review." The Coca-Cola Company. http://www.thecoca-colacompany.com/citizenship/pdf/2007-2008_sustainability_review.pdf.

Coca-Cola Company. "Board of Directors." The Coca-Cola Company. http://www.thecoca-colacompany.com/ourcompany/board_kent.html.

Coca-Cola Company. "Our Company." The Coca-Cola Company. http://www.thecoca-colacompany.com/ourcompany/index.html.

Coca-Cola Company. "Product Variety." The Coca-Cola Company. http://www.thecoca-colacompany.com/citizenship/products.html.

Coffey, Valerie. "DLP technology aims at emerging applications." Laser Focus World, August 15, 2008. http://www.laserfocusworld.com/articles/article_display.html?id=337111.

Cohen, Adam. *The Perfect Score: Inside eBay*. Boston: Little, Brown and Company, 2002.

Colborn, Kate, and Christine Heinrichs. "GE Africa Project improves healthcare in Ghana." Diversity Careers. http://www.diversitycareers.com/articles/college/06-winspr/reaching_geafrica.htm.

Colgate-Palmolive. "2008 Corporate Responsibility Report." Colgate-Palmolive. http://www.colgate.com/app/Colgate/US/Corp/LivingOurValues/Sustainability/HomePage.cvsp.

Colgate-Palmolive. "Colgate Purchasing Tom's of Maine; Enters Fast-Growing Natural Products Segment." Colgate. http://investor.colgate.com/ReleaseDetail.cfm?ReleaseID=190765&ReleaseType=Company&header=&ReleaseDate={ts%20%272006-03-21%2000:00:00%27}&Archive=Yes.

Colgate-Palmolive. "Form 10-K: Colgate-Palmolive Company." Colgate.http://investor.colgate.com/secfiling.cfm?filingID=1193125-08-41526.

Colgate-Palmolive. "Sustainability." Colgate. http://www.colgate.com/app/Colgate/US/Corp/LivingOurValues/Sustainability/HomePage.cvsp.

Colgate-Palmolive. "Sustainable Cleaning Initiatives." Colgate. http://www.colgate.com/app/Colgate/US/Corp/LivingOurValues/Sustainability/RespectForOurPlanet/SustainableCleaningInitiatives.cvsp.

Company Pay. "Executive Compensations – CEO Salaries, Stock Options, Bonuses, Compensations for Executives." Company Pay. http://www.companypay.com.

Computerworld Inc. "Special Report: 100 Best Places to Work in IT 2008." Computerworld. http://www.computerworld.com/spring/bp/detail/64.

Cone Inc. "2007 Cone Cause Evolution & Environmental Survey." Cone Inc. http://www.coneinc.com/files/2007ConeSurveyReport.pdf.

Connors, Devin, Steve Seguin, Humphrey Cheung and Marcus Yam. "IDF: Barrett Says It's Not About Money." Tom's Hardware, August 19, 2008. http://www.tomshardware.com/news/IDF-Barrett-Intel-WiMax,6188.html.

Constellation Energy Group. "Constellation Energy Recognized as One of the Best Places to Launch a Career." Constellation Energy Group, November 14, 2007. http://ir.constellation.com/releasedetail.cfm?releaseid=31786.9.

Corning Inc. "Global Career Opportunities." Corning Inc. http://www.corning.com/careers/global_opportunities.aspx.

Corporate Library. "The Corporate Library." The Corporate Library. http://www.thecorporatelibrary.com.

CPI Financial. "Impax and New York State Common Retirement Fund in index deal." CPI Financial, September 07, 2009. http://www.cpifinancial.net/v2/news.aspx?v=1&aid=3272&sec=Alternative%20Investments.

CTIA – The Wireless Association. "Background on CTIA's Semi-Annual Wireless Industry Survey." CTIA, 2009. http://files.ctia.org/pdf/CTIA_Survey_Midyear_2009_Graphics.pdf.

Databeans, Inc. "2008 Medical Semiconductors." Databeans, Inc. http://www
.databeans.net/reports/2008_php_files/08IND_Medical.php.

Day, Jennifer Cheeseman and Eric C. Newburger. "The Big Payoff: Educational
Attainment and Synthetic Estimates of Work-Life Earnings." Current Popula-
tionReports. U.S. Census Bureau, July 2002. www.census.gov/prod/2002pubs/
p23-210.pdf.

DBL Investors. "About DBL Investors." DBL Investors. http://www
.dblinvestors.com.

DDB. "United Technologies Wins Best Corporate Advertising by IR Magazine Collaboration with DDB Wins Industry Recognition." DDB, June 20,
2007. http://www.ddb.com/pdf/press/current/6-20-07_United_Technologies_
Wins_Best_Corporate_Advertising.pdf.

De Grasse, Robert, in discussion with the author. July 2009.

Definity Health. "Whirlpool Offers Employees New Consumer-Driven Health
Benefit From Definity Health." Definity Health. http://www.definityhealth
.com/marketing/newsroom/pressreleases/2003/whirlpool.pdf.

Denove, Chris and James D. Power IV. *Satisfaction; How Every Great Company Listens
to the Voice of the Customer Portfolio.* Macmillan Publishing (NOTE: now called
Portfolio Hardcover on Amazon), 2006.

Denver Channel. "Who is McGraw Hill?" *The Denver Channel.* http://www
.thedenverchannel.com/denvers7/214051/detail.html.

Deutsche Bank. "Microfinance: An emerging investment opportunity." December
19, 2007. http://www.dbresearch.com/PROD/DBR_INTERNET_DE-PROD/
PROD0000000000219174.PDF.

Dimitri, Carolyn and Kathryn Venezia. "Retail and Consumer Aspects of the Organic Milk Market." Economic Research Service, USDA, May 2007. http://www
.ers.usda.gov/publications/LDP/2007/05May/LDPM15501/ldpm15501.pdf

Diversity Inc. "JP Morgan Chase." Diversity Inc. http://www.diversityinc.com/
content/1757/article/5502/?No_15_JPMorgan_Chase.

Diversity Inc. "2007 Top 50 Profiles: No 1. Bank of America." Diversity Inc.
http://www.diversityinc.com/public/1786.cfm.

Diversity Inc. "No. 14: Procter & Gamble." Diversity Inc. http://www.diversityinc
.com/public/1816.cfm.

Domini Social Investments. "Domini Social Bond Fund Overview." Domini Social
Investments. http://www.domini.com.

Dow Chemical Company. "2015 Sustainability Goals Report 2Q 2009." Dow.
http://www.dow.com/commitments/pdf/2015_SustainRep_2Q09.pdf.

Dow Chemical Company. "Dow 2008 GRI report." Dow. http://www.dow
.com/commitments/pdf/GRI_71409.pdf.

Dow Chemical Company. "2008 10-K and Stockholder Summary." Dow. http://
www.dow.com/financial/pdfs/161-00720.pdf.

Dow Chemical Company. "2008 Corporate Report." Dow. http://www.dow.com/
financial/pdfs/161-00722.pdf.

Dow Chemical Company. "2015 Sustainability Goals Update—4Q 2008."
Dow. http://www.dow.com/commitments/pdf/4Q_2015_SustainabilityReport_
021009.pdf.

Duggan, Kelli M. "MedMined on fire with infection 'smoke alarm.'" *Birmingham Business Journal,* March 31, 2006. http://birmingham.bizjournals.com/birmingham/stories/2006/04/03/focus4.html.

Duke Energy. "Energy Sustainability Report." Duke Energy. (2009), www.duke-energy.com/pdfs/sar09-01-complete-report.pdf.

DuPont. "10-K 2008." DuPont. http://media.corporate-ir.net/media_files/irol/73/73320/BOP72619BOP005_BITS_N_1519.pdf.

DuPont. "2008 Sustainability Report." DuPont. http://www2.dupont.com/Sustainability/en_US/assets/downloads/DuPont_2008_Sustainability_Progess_Report.pdf.

DuPont. "Marketplace Goals." DuPont. http://www2.dupont.com/Sustainability/en_US/Marketplace_Goals/index.html.

DuPont. "Reducing DuPont's Footprint." DuPont. http://www2.dupont.com/Sustainability/en_US/Footprint/index.html.

DuPont. "Summary of Progress Toward 2015 Goals." Du Pont, 2008. http://www2.dupont.com/Sustainability/en_US/assets/downloads/DuPont_2008_Sustainability_Progess_Report.pdf.

DuPont. "Third Party Evaluation." DuPont. http://www2.dupont.com/Sustainability/en_US/Performance_Reporting/thirdparty.html.

DuPont. "Our Company." DuPont. http://www2.dupont.com/Our_Company/en_US/.

DuPont. "Sustainability – How DuPont is Transforming Food and Agriculture." DuPont. http://www2.dupont.com/Sustainability/en_US/Marketplace/Ag_Nutrition/food_safety.html.

Dvorak, Phred, Joann S. Lublin and Cari Tuna. "Motorola Co-CEO Tops Pay Survey." *The Wall Street Journal,* April 3, 2009. http://online.wsj.com/article/SB123870806394084045.html#project%3DPROXYPRIMER0902%26articleTabs%3Darticle.

Eakin, Emily. "How to Save the World? Treat It Like a Business." *New York Times,* December 20, 2003. http://www.nytimes.com/2003/12/20/arts/how-to-save-the-world-treat-it-like-a-business.html.

Eastman Kodak Company. "Global Sustainability: Eastman Kodak Company Annual Report 2008." Eastman Kodak Company. http://www.kodak.com/US/plugins/acrobat/en/corp/environment/08CorpEnviroRpt/Global_Sustain Rept_2008.pdf.

Eaton Corporation. "Green Building Services: LEED Certification." Eaton Corporation. http://www.eaton.com/EatonCom/Markets/Electrical/Sustainability/EatonsGreenProductsandServices/index.htm.

eBay, Inc. "New Study Reveals 724,000 Americans Rely on eBay Sales for Income." eBay, Inc. July 21, 2005. http://investor.ebay.com/releasedetail.cfm?releaseid=170073.

eBay, Inc. "Who We Are." eBay, Inc. http://www.ebayinc.com/who.

eBay, Inc. "eBay Inc. Reports Second Quarter 2009 Results." eBay Ink blog, July 22, 2009. http://ebayinkblog.com/wp-content/uploads/2009/07/Q209-Earnings-Release.pdf.

eBay, Inc. "eBay Inc.: A Short History." eBay. http://news.ebay.com/about.cfm.

EcoLab. "Compensation and Benefits." EcoLab. http://www.ecolab.com/Publications/SustainabilityReport/SupportingAssociates.pdf.

EcoLabelling.org "EcoLabelling.org—Who's Deciding What's Green?" EcoLabelling.org. http://ecolabelling.org.

The Economist. "Trucking in Cameroon: The road to hell is unpaved." The Economist, December 19, 2002. http://www.economist.com/displayStory.cfm?Story_ID=1487583.

Edmans, Alex. "Does the Stock Market Fully Value Intangibles? Employee Satisfaction and Equity Prices." August 12, 2009. http://ssrn.com/abstract=985735.

Edwards, Melanie, in conversation with author. January 2009.

Elliott, Stuart. "Dueling Brands Pick Up Where Politicians Leave Off." *New York Times*, November 3, 2008. http://www.nytimes.com/2008/11/04/business/media/04adco.html.

Energy Information Administration. "World Consumption of Primary Energy by Energy Type and Selected Country Groups, 1980-2004" (XLS). Energy Information Administration, U.S. Department of Energy, July 31 2006. http://www.eia.doe.gov/pub/international/iealf/table18.xls.

Energy Star. "Data Center Report to Congress – FINAL 7-25-0." Energy Star, August 2, 2007. http://www.energystar.gov/ia/partners/prod_development/downloads/EPA_Datacenter_Report_Congress_Final1.pdf.

Energy Star. "What is an Energy Efficient Mortgage?" Energy Star. http://www.energystar.gov/index.cfm?c=bldrs_lenders_raters.energy_efficient_mortgage.

Eni. "Eni Sustainability Report 2006." Eni. https://www.eni.it/en_IT/attachments/publications/corporate-responsability/general/eni_sustainability_report_2006_rev.pdf_rev.pdf.

ENS Economic Bureau. "HLL fires at P&G, offers shampoo freebie." *Indian Express*, March 24 2004. http://www.indianexpress.com/oldStory/43033.

Entergy. "Operations Information." Entergy. http://www.entergy.com/operations_information.

Environmental Data Services. "ENDS Agenda." Equator Principles, 2008. http://www.equator-principles.com/documents/ENDSReport12-08English.pdf.

Environmental Defense Fund. "KKR and EDF Partnership Helps Companies Save Over $16 Million While Reducing Emissions and Waste." Environmental Defense Fund, February 18, 2009. http://www.edf.org/pressrelease.cfm?contentID=9269.

Environmental Leader. "Apple's New OS Could Save $10M Annually in Energy." Environmental Leader, September 4, 2009. http://www.environmentalleader.com/2009/09/04/apples-new-os-could-save-10-million-annually-in-energy.

Environmental Leader. "GRI Touts 46% Increased Use of GRI Guidelines In Sustainability Reporting." Environmental Leader, July 16, 2009. http://www.environmentalleader.com/2009/07/16/gri-touts-46-increase-use-of-gri-guidelines-in-sustainability-reporting/[0].

Environmental Leader. "KKR Partners With EDF On 'Green Portfolio' Project." Environmental Leader, May 2, 2008. http://www.environmentalleader.com/2008/05/02/kkr-partners-with-edf-on-green-portfolio-project.

Environmental Leader. "Nymex Launches Green Exchange For Taking Carbon Credits." Environmental Leader, December 12, 2007. http://www

.environmentalleader.com/2007/12/12/nymex-launches-green-exchange-for-trading-carbon-credits.

Environmental Leader. "Office Depot Helps Large Customers Understand 'Greenness' of Purchases." September 23, 2009. http://www.environmentalleader.com/2009/09/23/office-depot-helps-large-customers-understand-greenness-of-purchases.

Environmental Protection Agency. "2008 Plug-in Partner Accomplishments." Environmental Protection Agency. http://www.epa.gov/epawaste/partnerships/plugin/activ-08.htm.

Environmental Protection Agency. "Green Power and Renewable Energy." EPA. http://www.epa.gov/oaintrnt/greenpower/index.htm.

Environmental Protection Agency. "Seize the Moment: Opportunities for Green Chemistry and Green Engineering in the Pharmaceutical Industry." Environmental Protection Agency, September 27, 2007. http://www.epa.gov/Region2/p2/seizethemoment_summary_final.pdf.

Equity Green Blog. "Green REITs Part II (Hines REIT + Liberty Property Trust)." March 11, 2007. http://equitygreen.typepad.com/blog/2007/03/green_reits_par.html.

Equity Market Partners. "2009 Annual Report." Patterson Companies, Inc. http://equitymarketpartners.com/PDCO/annuals/PDCOWEBAR2009.pdf.

Erica L. Plambeck. "The Greening of Walmart's Supply Chain." *Supply Chain Management Review,* July 1, 2007, http://www.scmr.com/article/CA6457969.html.

Estee Lauder Companies Inc. "The Estee Lauder Companies Inc. Corporate Social Responsibility Report 2007." The Estee Lauder Companies Inc. http://www.elcompanies.com/csr2007/enviro_beauty.html.

ExxonMobil. "2008 Corporate Citizenship Report." ExxonMobil. http://www.exxonmobil.com/Corporate/Imports/ccr2008/pdf/community_ccr_2008.pdf.

ExxonMobil. "A long-term vision: A letter from Rex W. Tillerson, Chairman and CEO." ExxonMobil. http://www.exxonmobil.com/Corporate/community_ccr_ceo.aspx.

ExxonMobil. "Corporate Citizenship Report 2007." ExxonMobil. http://www.exxonmobil.com/Corporate/files/Corporate/community_ccr_2007.pdf.

Facebook. "Facebook Statistics." Facebook. http://www.facebook.com/press/info.php?statistics.

Fast Company. "Valero Energy." Fast Company. http://www.fastcompany.com/investing/2008/valero-energy.html.

FedEx. "Sun Shines on FedEx Facilities." FedEx. http://fedex.com/ gb/about/enews/articles/0508article4.html.

Feldman, Matan, and Arkady Libman. *Crash Course in Accounting and Financial Statement Analysis.* Hoboken: Wiley, 2007.

Fielding, Stanley. "ISO 14001 Brings Change and Delivers Profits." Quality Digest, November 2000. http://www.qualitydigest.com/nov00/html/iso14000.html.

Finkle, Jim. "Intuit buys personal finance site Mint.com." Reuters, September 15, 2009. http://www.reuters.com/article/smallBusinessNews/idUSTRE58E37620090915.

First Energy Corp. "Benefits." First Energy Corp. http://www.firstenergycorp.com/career_center/why_firstenergy/benefits/index.html.

Fisman, Ray, Geoffrey Heal and Vinay B. Nair. "Corporate Social Responsibility: Doing well by doing good?" *Northwestern University*, 2006. http://www.kellogg .northwestern. edu/research/fordcenter/conferences/ethics06/heal.pdf.

Fontecchio, Mark. "Sun's data center consolidation reduces space, servers." *Data Center News*, August 20, 2007. http://searchdatacenter.techtarget.com/ news/article/0,289142,sid80_gci1268825,00.html.

Fortune. "100 Best Companies to Work for 2007." CNN Money. http://money .cnn.com/magazines/fortune/bestcompanies/2007/snapshots/83.html.

Fortune. "100 Best Companies to Work For 2008: 86. Microsoft." CNN Money. http://money.cnn.com/magazines/fortune/bestcompanies/2008/snapshots/ 86.html.

Fortune. "100 Best Companies to Work For: Yahoo 2008 snapshot." CNN Money. http://money.cnn.com/magazines/fortune/bestcompanies/2008/snapshots/ 87.html.

Fortune. "David Blood and Al Gore. Talking 'bout their Generation." CNN Money. http://money.cnn.com/2007/11/11/news/newsmakers/david_blood_ generation.fortune/index.htm.

Fortune. "*Fortune* Global 500 – 2006: Cisco Systems." CNN Money, 2006. http:// money.cnn.com/magazines/fortune/global500/2006/snapshots/307.html.

Fortune. "Global 500: 79. Procter & Gamble." CNN Money. http://money.cnn .com/magazines/fortune/global500/2008/snapshots/334.html.

Framework: CR. "Where Sustainability Lives." Framework: CR, July 2008. http:// frameworkcr.com/wp-content/uploads/2009/07/Where-sustainability-lives .pdf.

Friedman, Stew. *Total Leadership: Be a Better Leader, Have a Richer Life.* Boston: Harvard Business School Press, 2008.

Friend, Gil, in discussion with the author, 30 August 2009.

Funk Ventures. "Home." Funk Ventures. http://www.funkventures.com/index.aspx.

Funk Ventures. "Portfolio: Prolacta Bioscience." Funk Ventures. http://www .funkventures.com/portfolioprolacta.aspx.

Funk, Andy, and Fran Seegull, in discussion with Napoleon Wallace on behalf of author. 12 December 2008.

Gap Inc. "Goals and Progress: Employees—Data." Gap Inc. http://www.gapinc .com/GapIncSubSites/csr/Goals/Employees/Data/Em_Health_Safety_Data .shtml.

Gap Inc. "Governance and Nominating Committee." Gap Inc. http://www.gapinc .com/public/Investors/inv_govern_board_governance.shtml.

GE. "Annual Report 2008." GE. http://www.ge.com/ar2008/pdf/ge_ar_2008.pdf.

GE. "GE 2008 Annual Report: Financial Section." GE. http://www.ge.com/ ar2008/pdf/ge_ar_2008_financial_section.pdf.

GE. "GE 2008 Ecomagination Fact Sheet." GE Ecomagination. http://ge .ecomagination.com/annual-reports/ecomagination-fact-sheet.html).

GE. "GE Healthcare Accelerates Growth of Compact Ultrasound and Expands Use of Emerging Patient Applications: New Editions Designed Specifically for Emergency Medicine and Anesthesia Delivery." GE, January 10, 2007. http:// www.genewscenter.com/content/detail.aspx?releaseid=2885&newsareaid=2& download=true.

General Mills. "Corporate Social Responsibility 2008." General Mills. http://www.generalmills.com/corporate/commitment/NEW_CSR_2008.pdf.

Geodata Group. "Geodata Group." Geodata Group. www.geodata.com.

Gereffi, Gary, and M. Christian. "A Global Value Chain Approach to Food, Healthy Diets, and Childhood Obesity." *Duke University*, Nov 12, 2007. http://www.cggc.duke.edu/pdfs/GlobalHealth/Gereffi_Christian_GVCs_childhoodobesity_WHOpaper_22Oct2007a.pdf.

Gilead. "Partnerships." Gilead. http://www.gilead.com/access_partnerships.

Giving USA, a publication of Giving USA Foundation™, researched and written by the Center on Philanthropy at Indiana University. http://www.philanthropy.iupui.edu/News/2009/docs/GivingReaches300billion_06102009.pdf.

Glass Door. "McDonald's Crew Member Hourly Pay." Glass Door. http://www.glassdoor.com/Hourly-Pay/McDonald-s-Crew-Member-Hourly-Pay-E432_D_KO11,22.htm.

Glass Door. "Starbucks Barista Hourly Pay." Glass Door. http://www.glassdoor.com/Hourly-Pay/Starbucks-Barista-Hourly-Pay-E2202_D_KO10,17.htm.

GlaxoSmithKline plc. "Materials Efficiency." GlaxoSmithKline plc. http://www.gsk.com/responsibility/materials-efficiency.htm.

Global Environmental Management Initiative. "GEMI Publications." Global Environmental Management Initiative. http://www.gemi.org/GEMIPublications.aspx.

Global Forest Partners LP. "Experience." GFP. http://www.gfplp.com/experience.shtml.

Global Giving. "India – Safe Water." Global Giving. http://www.globalgiving.com/projects/india-safe-water.

Goldman Sachs, Inc., "Introducing GS Sustain." UN Global Compact, June 22, 2007. http://www.unglobalcompact.org/docs/summit2007/gs_esg_embargoed_until030707pdf.pdf.

Goleman, Daniel, Annie McKee and Richard E. Boyatzis. *Primal Leadership: Realizing the Power of Emotional Intelligence.* Boston: Harvard Business Press, 2002.

Good Guide. "About." Good Guide. http://www.goodguide.com/about.

Good Housekeeping. "Good Housekeeping Seal – Good Housekeeping Approved Products." Good Housekeeping. http://www.goodhousekeeping.com/product-testing/seal-holders/about-good-housekeeping-seal.

Goodyear Tire & Rubber Company. "Goodyear Corporate Responsibility Report 2007." The Goodyear Tire & Rubber Company. http://www.goodyear.com/corporate/about/responsibility/pdf/gy_corpresp_en07.pdf.

Google Finance. "Dow." Google Finance. http://www.google.com/finance?q=dow.

Google Finance. "The Coca-Cola Company." Google Finance. http://www.google.com/finance?q=NYSE:KO.

Google Finance. "CF Industries Holdings, Inc." Google Finance. http://www.google.com/finance?q=NYSE:CF.

Google Finance. "Cisco Systems." Google Finance. http://www.google.com/finance?q=NASDAQ:CSCO&fstype=ii.

Google Finance. "Devon Energy." Google Finance. http://www.google.com/finance?q=NYSE:DVN&fstype=ii.

Google Finance. "Salesforce.com" Google Finance. http://www.google.com/finance?q=NYSE:CRM&fstype=ii.

Google Finance. "McDonald's Corporation." Google Finance. http://www.google
    .com/finance?q=NYSE%3AMCD.

Google Finance. "Raytheon Company." Google Finance. http://www.google.com/
    finance?q=NYSE%3ARTN.

Google Finance. "Starbucks Corporation." Google Finance. http://www.google
    .com/finance?q=NASDAQ%3ASBUX.

Google Finance. "Bank of America Corporation." Google Finance. http://www
    .google.com/finance?q=NYSE%3ABAC.

Google Finance. "JPMorgan Chase & Co." Google Finance. http://www.google
    .com/finance?q=INDEXNYSE%3AAMJ.SO.

Google Finance. "Lockheed Martin Corporation." Google Finance. http://www
    .google.com/finance?q=NYSE%3ALMT.

Google Finance. "Chevron Corporation." Google Finance. http://www.google
    .com/finance?q=NYSE%3ACVX.

Google Finance. "E.I. du Pont de Nemours & Company." Google Finance. http://
    www.google.com/finance?q=DD.

Google Finance. "Microsoft Corporation." Google Finance. http://www.google
    .com/finance?q=NASDAQ%3AMSFT.

Google Finance. "Sprint Nextel Corporation." Google Finance. http://www
    .google.com/finance?q=NYSE%3AS.

Google Finance. "Walmart Stores, Inc." Google Finance. http://www.google
    .com/finance?q=walmart.

Green Planet Solar Energy. "The Advantages of Fossil Fuels—what are they?" Green
    Planet Solar Energy. http://www.green-planet-solar-energy.com/advantages-of-
    fossil-fuels.html.

Green Power Partnership. "Top 20 On-Site Green Power Partnership." The
    Environmental Protection Agency. http://www.epa.gov/greenpower/toplists/
    top20onsite.htm.

Green@work. "Special Section: Truth & Transparency." Green@work, January/
    February 2003. http://www.greenatworkmag.com/gwsubaccess/03janfeb/
    truth.html.

Greene, M.V. "Billion Dollar Roundtable 2008 Policy Paper Opening Opportunities
    for Diverse Suppliers in Advertising/Marketing." Billion Dollar Roundtable
    USA, 2008. http://www.bdrusa.org/pdf/BDR_paper_2008.pdf.

Gross National Happiness. "Gross National Happiness." Gross National Happiness.
    http://www.grossnationalhappiness.com.

Gross, Matt. "Packing the Right Credit Card." *NY Times* Frugal Traveler Blog, Jan-
    uary 27, 2009. http://frugaltraveler.blogs.nytimes.com/2009/01/27/packing-
    the-right-credit-card.

Gunther, Marc. "Private equity goes green." *Fortune*, May 1, 2008. http://money
    .cnn.com/2008/05/01/technology/KKR_EDF.fortune/index.htm.

Halter, J., in discussion with the author. July 2008.

Hammonds, Keith, in discussion with the author. December 2006.

Hannaford. "About Hannaford." Hannaford. http://www.hannaford.com/
    Contents/Our_Company/About/index.shtml?lid=mb.

Hannaford. "Food we rate." Hannaford. http://www.hannaford.com/Contents/
    Healthy_Living/Guiding_Stars/foods_we_rate.shtml.

Hannaford. "Grocery Shoppers Follow Hannaford's 'Guiding Stars' to More Nutritious Food Choices." News Infusion. http://newsinfusion.com/video_details.php?videoId=92.

Hannaford. "Guiding Stars Basics." Hannaford. http://www.hannaford.com/Contents/Healthy_Living/Guiding_Stars/faqs.shtml.

Harrison's Practice. "About." Harrison's Practice. http://www.harrisonspractice.com/practice/ub?cmd=about.

Hasbro. "Waste Reduction and Recycling." Hasbro. http://www.hasbro.com/corporate/corporate-social-responsibility/environment-health-and-safety-recycle.cfm.

Hawken, Paul. *The Ecology of Commerce: A Declaration of Sustainability.* New York: HarperCollins Publishing, 1993.

Hess Corporation. "Corporate Sustainability Report 2007." Hess Corporation. http://www.hess.com/downloads/reports/EHS/US/2007/2007.pdf.

Hewlett Packard. "HP Extends Environmental Leadership with New Technology to Save Customers Money." Hewlett Packard, June 2, 2009. http://www.hp.com/hpinfo/newsroom/press/2009/090602xa.html

Hewlett Packard. "HP Global Citizenship Report: Employee Diversity." Hewlett Packard. http://www.hp.com/hpinfo/globalcitizenship/gcreport/employees/diversity.html.

Holmes, Tamara E. "Bridgewater Interior closes $400 million deal." *Black Enterprise.* http://www.blackenterprise.com/magazine/2005/01/01/bridgewater-interiors-closes-400m-deal.

Honeywell International. "2006 Annual Report and 10-K." Honeywell International. http://library.corporate-ir.net/library/94/947/94774/items/235263/HON06ARa.pdf.

Hoover's Inc. "JPMorgan Chase – Company Description." Hoover's. http://www.hoovers.com/jpmorgan-chase/–ID__10322–/free-co-profile.xhtml.

Hoovers. "Hoovers: Sprint Nextel Corporation." Hoovers. http://www.hoovers.com/sprint-nextel/–ID__103483–/free-co-factsheet.xhtml.

Howell, Katie. "Exxon Sinks $600M Into Algae-Based Biofuels in Major Strategy Shift." *New York Times,* July 14, 2009. http://www.nytimes.com/gwire/2009/07/14/14greenwire-exxon-sinks-600m-into-algae-based-biofuels-in-33562.html.

Hromadka, Erik. "Indiana Manufacturers Turn Green." *Indiana Business* magazine, May 1, 2008, http://www.encyclopedia.com/doc/1G1-179569937.html.

Human Rights Campaign. "Corporate Equality Index 2006 – A Report Card on Lesbian, Gay, Bisexual, and Transgender Equality in Corporate America, 2006." The Human Rights Campaign Foundation. http://www.hrc.org/documents/HRCCorporateEqualityIndex2006.pdf.

Human Rights Campaign. "Corporate Equality Index 2009 – A Report Card on Lesbian, Gay, Bisexual, and Transgender Equality in Corporate America, 2009." The Human Rights Campaign Foundation. http://www.hrc.org/documents/HRC_Corporate_Equality_Index_2009.pdf.

Human Rights Campaign. "Corporate Equality Index 2009 – A Report Card on Lesbian, Gay, Bisexual, and Transgender Equality in Corporate America." Human Rights Campaign Foundation, 2008.http://www.hrc.org/documents/HRC_Corporate_Equality_Index_2008.pdf.

Human Rights Campaign. "2002 Human Rights Campaign Corporate Equality Index 2002." The Human Rights Campaign Foundation. http://www.hrc.org/documents/cei2002.pdf.

Human Rights Campaign. "Corporate Equality Index: Rating Criteria 3.0 (2011-)." The Human Rights Campaign Foundation. http://www.hrc.org/issues/workplace/cei_criteria_new.html.

Human Rights Campaign. "Walmart Stores Inc." Human Rights Campaign Foundation. http://www.hrc.org/issues/8990.htm.

Ibbotson, Roger G., and William N. Goetzmann. *The Equity Risk Premium: Essays and Explorations.* New York: Oxford University Press, 2006. Permission granted from Ibbotson, owned by Morningstar.

ICMR Case Studies in Business, Management. "Leadership – The Indra Nooyi Way." ICMR Case Studies in Business, 2009. http://www.icmrindia.org/casestudies/catalogue/Leadership%20and%20Entrepreneurship/LDEN058.htm.

Ifo Apple Store. "New Stores, New Design." Ifo Apple Store, September 13, 2006. http://www.ifoapplestore.com/db/2006/09/13/new-stores-new-design/.

iLike. "iLike Challenge App Now Available on App Store." iLike, August 12, 2009. http://blog.ilike.com/ilike_press_releases.

Infosys. "Annual Report 2009." Infosys. http://www.infosys.com/investors/reports-filings/annual-report/annual/Infosys-AR-09.pdf.

Innovations-Report. "Cornell to Show Off its 100-mpg Car-in-Progress at New York State Fair." Innovations-Report, August 21, 2008. http://www.innovations-report.com/html/reports/automotive/cornell_show_100_mpg_car_progress_york_state_fair_116490.html.

Institute of Food Technologists. "Disney Consumer Products and Institute of Food Technologists Student Association Announce Winners of the 'Nutritious Food for Kids' Competition." January 25, 2009. http://www.ift.org/cms/?pid=1002084.

Intel. "Intel Corporate Responsibility Report 2008." Intel. http://download.intel.com/intel/cr/gcr/pdf/Intel_CSR_Report_2008.pdf.

Intercontinental Exchange. "About ICE." Intercontinental Exchange. https://www.theice.com/history.jhtml.

Interface Europe. "Mission Zero, Sustainability, About InterfaceFLOR." Interface Europe. http://www.interfaceflor.eu/internet/web.nsf/webpages/528_EU.html.

Interface Global. "Climate Change Means Business." Interface Global. http://www.interfaceflor.eu/Internet/web.nsf/webpages/571520075_EN.html.

Interface Global. "Ecometrics." Interface Global. http://www.interfaceglobal.com/Media-Center/Ecometrics.aspx.

Interface Global. "Our Journey." Interface Global. http://www.interfaceglobal.com/Sustainability/Our-Journey.aspx.

Interface Global. "Interface Global EcoMetrics." Interface Global. http://www.interfaceglobal.com/getdoc/7e96b54e-ad49-4eff-9877-38a55df0396d/Global-EcoMetrics.aspx.

Internal Revenue Service. "The American Recovery and Reinvestment Act of 2009: Information Center." Internal Revenue Service. http://www.irs.gov/newsroom/article/0,,id=204335,00.html.

International Finance Corporation. "World's Financial Institutions Take Responsible Investing to Next Level." Innovations in Emerging Markets blog. July 13, 2006. http://ifcblog.ifc.org/emergingmarketsifc/2006/07/44_global_banks.html.

Intuit. "Intuit Careers." Intuit. http://www.intuitcareers.com.

Invesco. "Benefits." Invesco. http://careers.invesco.co.uk/portal/site/ipcareers/benefits/financialbenefits.

Investors' Circle. "IC Funds." Investors' Circle. http://www.investorscircle.net/about-us/ic-funds.

Investors' Circle. "Patient Capital for a Sustainable Future." Investors' Circle. http://www.investorscircle.net.

Investors' Circle. "What Does Investors' Circle Do?" Investors' Circle. http://www.investorscircle.net/for_entrepreneurs/entrepreneur-help/faq/what-does-investors-circle-do.

Ito, Aki. "IMF Raises China 2010 Growth Forecast, Trims India." Bloomberg, October 1, 2009. http://www.bloomberg.com/apps/news?pid=20601089&sid=aFHAbQp7Scx4.

Jackson, Mitch, in discussion with the author. 7 August 2009.

Jacobs Engineering Group Inc. "2008 Annual Report." Jacobs Engineering Group Inc. http://media.corporate-ir.net/media_files/irol/11/117895/JEC_08AR_final.pdf.

Jobnob. "Jobnob." Jobnob. http://www.jobnob.com.

John Deere. "Deere & Company 2007 Global Citizenship Report." John Deere. http://www.deere.com/en_US/compinfo/media/pdf/csr/report/2007_gcreport_en.pdf.

John Deere. "Tobacco Cessation." John Deere. http://www.deere.com/healthy directions/wellness/programs/stopsmoking.html.

Johnson & Johnson. "Johnson & Johnson 2007 Sustainability Report." Johnson & Johnson. http://www.jnj.com/connect/pdf/publications-pdf/2007-sustainability-report.pdf.

Johnson Controls, Inc. "Our Visions, Our Values." Johnson Controls, Inc. http://www.johnsoncontrols.com/publish/us/en/about/vision.html.

Jones Lang LaSalle Incorporated. "Q1 2009 Earnings Call Transcript." Seeking Alpha, April 29. 2009. http://seekingalpha.com/article/134031-jones-lang-lasalle-incorporated-q1-2009-earnings-call-transcript.

Jones Lang LaSalle Incorporated. "Perspectives on Sustainability." Jones Lang LaSalle, October 2008. http://www.joneslanglasalle.com/ResearchLevel1/JLL_Sustainability_-_Perspectives_on_Sustainability_October_2008.pdf.

Jones, Del. "Women business founders rising, but slowly." USA Today, April 22, 2008. http://www.usatoday.com/money/companies/management/2008-04-22-women-founders-success_N.htm.

JPMorgan Chase & Co. "Corporate Responsibility Report 2007." JPMorgan. http://www.jpmorganchase.com/pdfdoc/jpmc/corpresp/jpmc_crr07.pdf.

JPMorgan Chase & Co. "Environmental Indicators—United States." JPMorgan. http://www.jpmorgan.com/pages/jpmc/community/env/indicators_us.

JPMorgan Chase & Co. "Corporate Responsibility Update." JPMorgan. http://eurocareers.jpmorgan.com/directdoc/jpmorgan/careers/goodventure/csr/report.

JPMorgan Chase & Co. "JPMorgan and Innovest launch green bond index." JPMorgan, February 27, 2007. http://www.jpmorgan.com/pages/jpmorgan/news/JENIlaunch_Feb07.

Kaplan, Robert S., and David P. Norton. *The Balanced Scorecard: Translating Strategy into Action.* Boston: Harvard Business School Press, 1996.

Katz, Jonathon. "Paccar's Hybrids: Building a Heavy-Duty Supply Chain: Special Report: Anatomy of a Product." *Industry Week,* December 1, 2008. http://www.industryweek.com/articles/paccars_hybrids_building_a_heavy-duty_supply_chain_special_report_anatomy_of_a_product_17760.aspx?Page=3.

Katz, Randy H. "Tech Titans Building Boom." *IEEE Spectrum Magazine,* February 2009. http://www.spectrum.ieee.org/green-tech/buildings/tech-titans-building-boom.

Katz, Rob. "Pop!Tech: MobileMetrix Makes the Base of the Pyramid Visible Again." *Next Billion,* November 6, 2009. http://www.nextbillion.net/blog/pop-tech-mobilemetrix-makes-the-base-of-the-pyramid-visible-agai.

Kennedy, Robert F. "Remarks" Speech, University of Kansas, Kansas, 18 March, 1968. John F. Kennedy Presidential Library and Museum. http://www.jfklibrary.org/historical+resources/archives/reference+desk/speeches/rfk/rfkspeech68mar18ukansas.htm.

Kenworth Truck Company. "Kenworth Earns 2009 J.D. Power and Associates Customer Satisfaction Awards." Yahoo! Finance, August 3, 2009. http://finance.yahoo.com/news/Kenworth-Earns-2009-JD-Power-bw-3261079654.html?x=0&.v=1.

Khosla Ventures. "Home." Khosla Ventures. http://www.khoslaventures.com/.

Khosla Ventures. "What we are looking for." Khosla Ventures. http://www.khoslaventures.com/look.html.

Kimberly-Clark. "2007 Sustainability Report." Kimberly-Clark. http://www.kimberly-clark.com/PDFs/2007SustainabilityReport_ExecutiveSummary.pdf.

King, Thomas, in discussion with the author. 29 January 2007.

Kiva. "Lend." Kiva. http://www.kiva.org/app.php?page=businesses.

KLA-Tencor. "2006 Programs for US Employees." KLA-Tencor. https://ktcareers.kla-tencor.com/ps/KT_Benefits.pdf.

Kleiner Perkins Caufield & Byers. "Kleiner Perkins Caufield & Byers Launches Green Growth Fund." KPCB, May 1, 2008. http://www.kpcb.com/news/articles/2008_05_00.html.

Kohlberg Kravis Roberts & Co. "Green Savings Program." Kohlberg Kravis Roberts & Co. http://greensavings.kkr.com/home/kkr_edf_partnership.htm.

Kohlberg Kravis Roberts & Co. "Overview." KKR. http://www.kkr.com/company/company_overview.cfm.

Krause, Thomas. *Leading with Safety.* Hoboken, NJ: John Wiley & Sons, Inc., 2005.

Kumar, V., J. Andrew Petersen, and Robert P. Leone. "How Valuable is Word of Mouth?" Harvard Business Publishing, October 2007. http://hbr.harvardbusiness.org/2007/10/how-valuable-is-word-of-mouth/ar/1.

Langert, Bob, in discussion with the author. 10 September 2008.

Lauber, Kelly, in discussion with the author. 6 August 2009.

Leimsider, Rich and Nancy McGaw. "Sustainability Trends in MBA Education." Webinar, Aspen Institute, August 25, 2009.

Lemelson Foundation. "Home." The Lemelson Foundation. http://www
    .lemelson.org.

Les Blumenthal McClatchy Newspapers "Nuclear sites fear being the alternative
    to Yucca," *Richmond Times Dispatch*, September 26, 2009. http://www2.times
    dispatch.com/rtd/lifestyles/health_med_fit/article/I-NUKE0901_20090924-
    231810/295414/.

Little, Amanda Griscom. "Walmart CEO explains his green creed." Msnbc.com,
    April 14, 2006. http://www.msnbc.msn.com/id/12316725.

Lockheed Martin. "2008 Annual Report." Lockheed Martin. http://www
    .lockheedmartin.com/data/assets/corporate/documents/ir/2008-Annual-
    Report.pdf.

Lockheed Martin. "Corporate Social Responsibility." Lockheed Martin. http://
    www.lockheedmartin.com/aboutus/culture/csr.html.

Lockheed Martin. "Lockheed Martin Go Green." Lockheed Martin. http://
    lockheedmartinjobs.com/learnaboutus_green.asp.

Lockheed Martin. "Making Progress on Our Commitment to Equal Opportu-
    nity and Affirmative Action." Lockheed Martin. http://www.lockheedmartin
    .com/aboutus/diversity/commitment.html.

Lockheed Martin. "Energy, Environment, Safety & Health Sustainability Re-
    port 2007." Lockheed Martin. http://www.lockheedmartin.com/data/assets/
    corporate/documents/environment/LM-Sustainability-2007.pdf.

Lockheed Martin. "Environmental Services." Lockheed Martin. http://www
    .lockheedmartin.com/products/environmental-services/index.html.

Love Earth. "About Responsible Jewelry." Love Earth. http://www.loveearthinfo
    .com/About_Responsible_Jewlery.htm.

Love Earth. "Home." Love Earth. http://www.loveearthinfo.com/.

Lowery, Kevin, in discussion with the author. 26 January 2007.

Maloney, Patrick, in discussion with the author. July 2009.

Mantero, Frank, in discussion with the author. January 2007.

Marathon. "Living Our Values, 2008 Corporate Social Responsibility Report."
    Marathon. http://www.marathon.com/lov2008/content-id17.shtml.

Marriott International, Inc. "Diversity Fact Sheet." Marriott International, Inc.
    http://www.marriott.com / Multimedia / PDF / Corporate / DiversityFactSheet
    .pdf.

Marriott. "Committed to Diversity Ownership." Marriott. http://www.marriott
    .com/marriott.mi?page=diversity_ownership.

Martin, Lauralee, in discussion with the author. July 8, 2009.

Maslow, Abraham. "A Theory of Human Motivation." *Psychological Review* 50(1943):
    370–396.

McDonald's Corporation. "Balanced, Active Lifestyles." McDonald's. http://www
    .mcdonalds.com/usa/good/balanced_active_lifestyles.html.

McDonald's Corporation. "Corporate Careers." McDonald's. http://www
    .aboutmcdonalds.com/mcd/careers.html.

McDonald's Corporation. "Values in Practice: Welcome." McDonald's Corporate
    Responsibility. http://www.crmcdonalds.com/publish/csr/home.html.

McDonald's Corporation. "2008 Build-Your-Own Report: Responsible Food for
    a Sustainable Future." McDonald's Corporate Responsibility. http://www

.crmcdonalds.com/publish/csr/home/report/sustainable_supply_chain.print report.html.

McDonald's Corporation. "A Filet-O-Fish you can feel good about." McDonald's Corporate Responsibility. http://www.aboutmcdonalds.com/mcd/csr/ report/sustainable_supply_chain/resource_conservation/sustainable_fisheries .html.

McDonald's Corporation. "At the front counter – Engaged and committed employees." McDonald's Corporate Responsibility. http://www.crmcdonalds .com/publish/csr/home/report/employment_experience/employment_value_ proposition.html.

McDonald's Corporation. "Diversity." McDonald's. http://www.mcdonalds.com/ usa/work/diversity.html.

McDonald's Corporation. "Worldwide Corporate Responsibility Report." McDonald's Corporate Responsibility, 2008. http://www.crmcdonalds.com/ publish/etc/medialib/mcdonalds_media_library/report/docs/minireport.Par .0001.File.MCD037_Minireport.pdf.

McGraw-Hill Companies. "Home." The McGraw-Hill Companies. http://www .mcgraw-hill.com/index.html.

McKinsey & Company and Boston College Center for Corporate Citizenship. "How Virtue Creates Value for Business and Society." Boston College Center for Corporate Citizenship, April 2009. http://commdev.org/files/ 2426_file_ Boston_College_McKinsey_31909.pdf.

McKinsey Global Institute. "Entering a New Era." McKinsey Global Institute, 2009. http://www.mckinsey.com/mgi/reports/pdfs/gcm_sixth_annual_report/gcm_ sixth_annual_report_full_report.pdf.

McKinsey Global. "The McKinsey Global Survey of Business Executives: Business and Society." *McKinsey Quarterly*, January 2006. http://www.mckinseyquarterly .com/The_McKinsey_Global_Survey_of_Business_Executives__Business_and_ Society_1741.

McKinsey Global. "What Customers Expect." McKinsey Global. www.mckinsey .com/clientservice/ccsi/pdf/What_Consumers_Expect.pdf.

McKinsey Quarterly. "The McKinsey Global Survey of Business Executives Confidence Index." *McKinsey Quarterly*, January 2006. http://www.mckinseyquarterly .com/The_McKinsey_Global_Survey_of_Business_Executives__Confidence_ Index_January_2006_1740.

Medco.com®. "Career Opportunities." Medco.com®. http://www.medco.com/ medco/corporate/home.jsp?articleID=CorpCareers.

Melaver, Inc. "Sorting Through Green Building Myths and Facts." *Sustainable Land Development Today Magazine* via Melaver, Inc., October 2008. http://www .melaver.com/news/sorting-through-green-building-myths-and-facts.html.

Mendez, Angel, in discussion with the author. Summer 2007.

Merck. "Merck Receives Presidential Green Chemistry Challenge Award." Merck. http://www.merck.com/about/feature_story/08032005_challenge_award.html.

Meredith. "National Media Brands – Magazines." Meredith. http://www.meredith .com/media_portfolio/magazines.html.

Micron. "Micron Environmental Awards." Micron. http://www.micron.com/ quality/environment/awards.

MicroPlace. "Community." MicroPlace. https://www.microplace.com/community.

MicroPlace. "How Microfinance Works." MicroPlace. https://www.microplace.com/learn_more/microfinancehowitworks.

Microsoft. "Microsoft Board of Directors." Microsoft. http://www.microsoft.com/presspass/bod/bod.aspx.

Microsoft. "Advancing Power Management with Windows 7!" Microsoft. http://www.microsoft.com/environment/windows7.aspx.

Microsoft. "Environment." Microsoft. http://www.microsoft.com/environment/.

Microsoft. "Form 10-K: Microsoft Corporation." Microsoft.www.microsoft.com/msft/download/FY08/10K%20FY2008.doc.

Microsoft. "Green IT is good for your bottom line." Microsoft. http://www.microsoft.com/environment/greenit.

MicroVest. "Annual Report 2008: MicroVest I, LP." MicroVest, p. 16. http://www.microvestfund.com/docs/2008-06-30-15.pdf.

MicroVest. "Investor Profile: Omidyar Network." MicroVest. http://www.microvestfund.com/omidyarprofile.html.

Miller, Mark. "Heinz Splat!" Brandchannel, August 3, 2009. http://www.brandchannel.com/features_webwatch.asp?ww_id=443.

Mind Tools, Ltd. "The McKinsey 7S Framework." Mind Tools, Ltd. http://www.mindtools.com/pages/article/newSTR_91.htm.

Mininni, Ted. "Cutting Packaging Down to Size." Point-of-Purchase Online Network. http://www.popon.net/ted_mininni.asp.

Minority Law Journal. "Diversity Scorecard." Law.com. http://www.law.com/jsp/mlj/diversityScorecard.jsp.

Minute Clinic. "Our History." Minute Clinic. http://www.minuteclinic.com/en/USA/About/History.aspx.

Money Management News. "Generation Outperforms Benchmark." Money Management. http://www.moneymanagement.com.au/article/Generation-Global-Sustainability-Fund-outperforms-benchmark-in-its-first-year/428774.aspx.

Monnery, Laurence. "Women on European Boards." Egon Zehnder International. http://www.egonzehnder.com/global/thoughtleadership/hottopic/id/78402633/article/id/11900485.

Montgomery, David B., and Catherine A. Ramus. "Including corporate social responsibility, environmental sustainability, and ethics in calibrating MBA job preferences." *Graduate School of Business*, Stanford University, 2007. https://gsbapps.stanford.edu/researchpapers/library/RP1981.pdf.

Morgan Stanley. "Morgan Stanley Diversity. Morgan Stanley." http://www.morganstanley.com/global/commitment-to-environment.html.

Morningstar Document Research. "Form 11-K Wal-Mart Stores Inc – WMT." Morningstar Document Research, filed July 29, 2009. http://ccbn.10kwizard.com/xml/download.php?repo=tenk&ipage=6436612&format=PDF.

Morris, Betsy. "The Pepsi Challenge." *Fortune*, February 19, 2008, http://money.cnn.com/2008/02/18/news/companies/morris_nooyi.fortune/index3.htm.

Mui, Chunka and Paul B. Carroll. *Billion Dollar Lessons: What You Can Learn from the Most Inexcusable Business Failures of the Last 25 Years*. USA: Portfolio Hardcover, 2008.

Mullen, Michael, in discussion with the author. August 2009.

Murph, Darren. "Tata's $2,000 Nano car to hit Indian streets in July." Engadget, March 23, 2009. http://www.engadget.com/2009/03/23/tatas-2-000-nano-car-to-hit-indian-streets-in-july.

Mydans, Seth. "Recalculating Happiness in a Himalayan Kingdom." *New York Times*, May 6, 2009. http://www.nytimes.com/2009/05/07/world/asia/07bhutan.html.

Nasdaq. "PACCAR, Inc. Profile." Nasdaq, 2009. http://www.nasdaq.com/MorningStarProfileReports/PCAR_USA.pdf.

National Association of Attorneys General. "Tobacco Master Settlement Agreement." National Association of Attorneys General. http://www.naag.org/backpages/naag/tobacco/msa/msa-pdf/1109185724_1032468605_cigmsa.pdf.

National Cancer Institute. "Success Story: Taxol." National Cancer Institute. http://dtp.nci.nih.gov/timeline/flash/success_stories/S2_Taxol.htm.

National Consumers League. "American Consumers' Definition of the Socially Responsible Company Runs Counter to Established Beliefs." *National Consumers League*, May 31, 2006. http://www.nclnet.org/news/2006/csr_05312006.htm.

National Geographic News. "Global Warming Fast Facts." *National Geographic*, June 14, 2007. http://news.nationalgeographic.com/news/2004/12/1206_041206_global_warming_2.html.

National Health Plan Collaborative. "United HealthCare: Developing an Asian In-Language Provider Directory." Robert Wood Johnson Foundation. http://www.rwjf.org/qualityequality/product.jsp?id=34025.

National Public Radio. "Cutting Health Costs: Discounts for the Healthy?" National Public Radio, October 7, 2009. http://www.npr.org/templates/story/story.php?storyId=113549864.

National Semiconductor. "Annual Report 2008." National Semiconductor. http://annualreport.national.com/invest/2008annual/national_AnnualRpt_2008.pdf.

NetApp. "Careers – Benefits." NetApp. http://www.netapp.com/au/careers/your-career/benefits-new.html.

New Resource Bank. "New Resource Bank Appoints Vincent Siciliano as CEO." New Resource Bank, April 15, 2009. http://www.newresourcebank.com/pdf/04-15-09_Appoints_Vincent_Siciliano_CEO.pdf.

New York Times. "Al Gore's fund to close after attracting $5 billion." *New York Times*, March 1, 2008, Business section, Online edition. http://www.nytimes.com/2008/03/11/business/worldbusiness/11iht-gore.4.10942634.html.

Newsweek. "Newsweek: Green Rankings, 2009." *Newsweek*. http://greenrankings.newsweek.com/companies/view/colgate-palmolive.

Nicholson, Ann H.S., in discussion with the author. 29 April 2009.

Niekirk, Gary, in discussion with the author. Phone interview Aug 21 2008.

Niemann, Thomas, in discussion with the author. September 2008.

Nike. "Corporate Responsibility Governance." Nikebiz. http://www.nikebiz.com/responsibility/cr_governance.html.

Nixon, Bonnie, in discussion with the author. 4 September 2009.

Nobel Prize. "The Nobel Peace Prize 2007." Nobel Prize. http://nobelprize.org/nobel_prizes/peace/laureates/2007.

Nofsinger, John. "Opt-in and Opt-out Pension Design." *Psychology Today*, Mind on My Money Blog, August 30, 2009. http://www.psychologytoday.com/blog/mind-my-money/200908/opt-in-and-opt-out-pension-design.

Nordstrom, Inc. "Diversity Affairs." Nordstrom, Inc. http://about.nordstrom .com/aboutus/diversity/our_people.asp.

Northrop Grumman. "Annual Report 2007." Northrop Grumman. http://www .northropgrumman.com/corporate-responsibility/pdf/2007-corporate-social-responsibility-report.pdf, http://www.rockwellcollins.com/content/pdf/pdf_2318.pdf.

Novy-Hildesley, Julia, in discussion with the author. 14 July 2009.

O'Neill, Paul. "The Summit 2002: Summit Newsletter." Carlson School of Management. http://www.carlsonschool.umn.edu/Page5384.aspx.

O'Sullivan D. and J. McCallig. "Does Customer Satisfaction Influence the Relationship Between Earnings and Firm Value?" *The University of Queensland Business School*, September 11 2009. http://www.business.uq.edu.au/download/attachments/14483973/dosullivan-paper.pdf.

Office Depot. "Corporate Citizenship." Office Depot. http://www.officedepot .cc/corporate-citizenship-report/buy_green.asp.

Office Depot. "Office Depot Joins U.S. EPA SmartWay[SM] Transport Partnership; Becomes First Office Products Reseller to Support Nationwide Effort Focused on Energy Efficiency and Lowering Greenhouse Gases from Shipping Operations." Office Depot, May 08, 2006 http://mediarelations.officedepot .com/phoenix.zhtml?c=140162&p=irol-newsArticle&ID=853454&highlight=.

Office Depot. "Taking Care of Business, People and the Planet." Office Depot. http://www.officedepot.cc/corporate-citizenship-report/downloads/OD-Corporate-Citizenship-Report-2009.pdf.

Office of Aviation Enforcement and Proceedings. "Air Travel Consumer Report, February 2008." http://airconsumer.dot.gov/reports/2009/February/200902ATCR.PDF.

Olmstead, Gary. "Wellness: The New EHS Frontier." *Academy of Industrial Hygiene newsletter*, Fall 2006. http://www.aiha.org/1documents/aih/Diplo06-3 .pdf.

One Laptop Per Child. "Frequently Asked Questions." One Laptop Per Child. http://laptop.org/en/vision/mission/faq.shtml.

Organic Facts. "Organic Farming in India." Organic Facts. http://www.organic facts.net/organic-cultivation/organic-farming/organic-farming-in-india.html.

Pallarito, Karen. "The Pepsi challenge: Sustaining employee participation in wellness." *All Business*, November 1 2008. http://www.allbusiness.com/medicine-health/diseases-disorders-obesity/11706610-1.html.

Palmisano, Samuel J. "The Globally Integrated Enterprise," *Foreign Affairs*. The Council on Foreign Relations, May/June 2006. http://www.foreignaffairs .com/articles/61713/samuel-j-palmisano/the-globally-integrated-enterprise.

Park, Esther. "RSF's Lending Process As Inspired by Rudolf Steiner." RSF Finance, July 6, 2006. http://rsfsocialfinance.org/2009/07/rsfs-lending-process-as-inspired-by-rudolf-steiner.

Parker Hannifin. "Parker Hannifin EHSE Performance Report 2007/2008." Parker Hannifin. http://www.parker.com/parkerimages/Parker.com/Literature/Parker%20Hannifin_EHSE_Performance_Report_2008.pdf.

PATH. "Durability Doctor." PATH. http://www.pathnet.org/durability_doctor/

Patnaik, Priti. "Norway's Sovereign Wealth Fund To Spend 1% Of Its Funds On Green Projects." *Business Insider*, September 4, 2009. http://www.businessinsider.com/green-investments-by-norways-swf-2009-9.

Pax World Investments. "Community." Pax World Investments. http://www.paxworld.com.

PayScale. "PayScale." Payscale. http://www.payscale.com.

PepsiCo. "2007 Corporate Sustainability Report." PepsiCo. http://www.pepsico.com/Purpose/Sustainability/Sustainability-Report.html.

PepsiCo. "Board of Directors and Committees." PepsiCo. http://www.pepsico.com/Company/Board-of-Directors.html#block_Shona%20L.%20Brown.

PepsiCo. "Children's Food and Beverage Advertising Initiative Pledge of Pepsico, Inc." PepsiCo. http://www.pepsico.com/Purpose/Health-and-Wellness/Responsible-Marketing.html.

PepsiCo. "Energy." PepsiCo. http://www.pepsico.com/Purpose/Environment/Energy.html.

PepsiCo. "Environmental Efforts." PepsiCo. http://www.pepsico.com/Brands/Gatorade-Brands.html.

PepsiCo. "PepsiCo Joins with America's YMCAs to help Americans Live Healthier Lives." YMCA, March 8, 2006. http://www.ymca.net/about_the_ymca/press_release_20060308_pepsico.html.

PepsiCo. "Providing a Safe and Healthy Work Environment." PepsiCo. http://www.pepsico.com/Purpose/Sustainability/Talent-Sustainability.html.

PepsiCo. "Talent Sustainability: Extending Talent Sustainability Principles to our Supplier Community." PepsiCo. http://www.pepsico.com/Purpose/Sustainability/Talent-Sustainability.html.

PepsiCo. "Monitoring." PepsiCo. http://www.pepsico.com/Purpose/Sustainability/Environmental-Sustainability.html.

PepsiCo. "Our History." PepsiCo. http://www.pepsico.com/Company/Our-History.html#block_2008.

PepsiCo. "Performance with Purpose: Corporate Sustainability Report: 2006-2007." PepsiCo.

Peterbilt. "Peterbilt Green Technologies." Peterbilt. http://www.peterbilt.com/eco/ReadyTrucks-SmartWayTrucks.htm.

PG&E. "2008 Renewables." PG&E. http://www.pge.com/b2b/energysupply/wholesaleelectricsuppliersolicitation/renewables2008.

Physic Ventures. "Physic Ventures Investing Landscape." Physic Ventures. http://www.physicventures.com.

Pica, Maria, in discussion with the author. 22 October 2007.

Plum Creek. "Sustainable Forestry." Plum Creek. http://www.plumcreek.com/Environment/nbspSustainableForestrySFI/tabid/149/Default.aspx.

Prahalad, C. K. *The* Fortune *at the Bottom of the Pyramid*. New Jersey: Wharton School Publishing, 2006.

Procter & Gamble. "2006 Global Sustainability and Philanthropy Report." P&G. http://www.scienceinthebox.com/en_UK/pdf/sustainability_report_2007.pdf.

Procter & Gamble. "2007 Global Sustainability Report." P&G. http://www.pg.com/company/our_commitment/pdfs/gsr07_Web.pdf.

Procter & Gamble. "P&G Lauded for Sustainable Package Designs at 21st DuPont Innovation Awards." P&G, May 28, 2009. http://www.pg.com/news/sustainability.shtml.

Progressive Insurance Company. "Company Introduction." Progressive Insurance Company. http://www.progressive.com/progressive-insurance/company-introduction.aspx.

Project Finance. "Dealogic Global Project Finance Review—Full Year 2008." *Project Finance*, April 2009. http://www.projectfinancemagazine.com/default.asp?page=7&PubID=4&ISS=25371&SID=720127.

ProLogis. "2008 Sustainability Report." ProLogis. http://pld.client.shareholder .com/common/download/download.cfm?companyid=PLD&fileid=294140& filekey=E521CE83-BBC2-456F-ADAA-BAF6AB2BE70B&filename=ProLogis_Sustainability_Report.pdf.

Prologis. "Investor Fact Sheet – Second Quarter 2009." Prologis. http://files .shareholder.com/downloads/PLD/708397584x0x100467/a5235797-036f-4d88-a621-7e060331da56/Factsheet.pdf.

Prosper. "Company Overview." Prosper. http://www.prosper.com/about/.

Prosper. "Marketplace Performance." Prosper. http://www.prosper.com/welcome/marketplace.aspx.

Qualcomm. "Every Body on the Net." Qualcomm. http://www.qualcomm.com/common/documents/brochures/QCOM_WirelessHealth.pdf [O28].

Rauber, Elizabeth. "Fireman's Fund to sell 'hybrid upgrade' insurance." *San Francisco Business Times*, August 12, 2009. http://www.firemansfund.com/servlet/dcms?c=about&rkey=1791.

Ravilious, Kate. "Antarctic Oceans Absorbing Less CO2, Experts Say." *National Geographic*, May 17 2007. http://news.nationalgeographic.com/news/2007/05/070517-carbon-oceans.html.

Rawlins, Kiley, in discussion with the author. 26 January 2009.

Raytheon. "Annual report 2008." Raytheon. http://phx.corporate-ir.net/External.File?item=UGFyZW50SUQ9MjY0NXxDaGlsZElEPS0xfFR5cGU9Mw===&t=1.

Raytheon. "2007 Stewardship Report." Social Funds. http://www.socialfunds .com/shared/reports/1213716934_Raytheon_2007_Stewardship_Report.pdf.

Raytheon. "Capabilities." Raytheon. http://raytheon.com/capabilities/.

Raytheon. "Corporate Responsibility Report 2008." Raytheon. http://media .corporate-ir.net/media_files/irol/84/84193/CRR_09/HTML/pdfs/raytheon_crr_2008.pdf.

Raytheon. "Environment." Raytheon. http://www.raytheon.com/responsibility/stewardship/sustainability/environment.

Regional Greenhouse Gas Initiative. "Regional Greenhouse Gas Initiative." Regional Greenhouse Gas Initiative. http://www.rggi.org.

Regional Greenhouse Gas Initiative. "RGGI Benefits." The Regional Greenhouse Gas Initiative. http://www.rggi.org/about/benefits.

Reichheld, Frederick F., and James Allen. "One Number to Grow." Results Brief newsletter. February 2004. http://www.loyaltyrules.com/loyaltyrules/library_articles_details.asp?id=15302&menu_url=library%5Farticles%2Easp.

Rental Equipment Register. "Contractor Partners with Climate Earth to Reduce Greenhouse Gas Emissions from Construction Projects." *Rental Equipment Register Magazine*, April 17, 2009. http://rermag.com/trends_analysis/rer_the_environment/climate-earth-webcor-builders-042009.

Republic Services, Inc. "CREDIT SUISSE – Environmental and Industrial Services Conference." Republic Services, Inc., May 2009. http://phx.corporate-ir.net/External.File?item=UGFyZW50SUQ9NjkzMXxDaGlsZElEPS0xfFR5cGU9Mw===&t=1.

Residential Energy Services Network. "Energy Efficient Mortgage: Energy Efficiency Financing Overview." RESNET. http://www.natresnet.org/lender/lhandbook/overview.htm.

Resnick, Andrea Shaw. "Coach Inc. 2007—Declined to Participate." Carbon Disclosure Project, May 21 2007. https://www.cdproject.net/en-US/Pages/CDPAdvancedSearchResults.aspx?k=coach.

Reuters UK. "CFTC's Chilton to say carbon markets will soar." *Reuters UK*, June 25, 2008. http://uk.reuters.com/article/idUKN2537034520080625.

Reuters. "Free Enterprise Action Fund Demands Bank of America Disclose Its Green-Washing Activities." *Reuters*, April 22, 8008. http://www.reuters.com/article/pressRelease/idUS173399+22-Apr-2008+PRN20080422.

Rizzo, Jack, in discussion with the author. 8 August 2009, phone interview.

Roach, John. "Global Warming 'Very Likely' Caused by Humans, World Climate Experts Say." *National Geographic*, February 2, 2007. http://news.nationalgeographic.com/news/2007/02/070202-global-warming.html.

Robert Wood Johnson Foundation. "Evidence-Based Hospital Design Improves Healthcare Outcomes For Patients, Families and Staff." Robert Wood Johnson Foundation, June 7, 2004. http://www.rwjf.org/programareas/resources/product.jsp?id=21765&pid=1142.

Root Capital. "Spring 2009 Newsletter." Root Capital. http://www.rootcapital.org/newsdocs/nl_2009Spring.html.

Root Capital. "Starbucks to Invest Additional $2 Million in Root Capital." Root Capital, September 1, 2009. http://www.rootcapital.org/newsdocs/pr_20090903.pdf.

RSF Social Finance. "Borrower Criteria." RSF Finance. http://rsfsocialfinance.org/services/lending/borrower-criteria.

RSF Social Finance. "Mezzanine Fund." RSF Finance. http://rsfsocialfinance.org/services/investing/mezzanine.

Rushe, Dominic. "Walmart aspires to be jolly green giant." *Times Online,* April 19, 2009. http://business.timesonline.co.uk/tol/business/industry_sectors/retailing/article6122371.ece.

Safeway Inc. "Form 10-K." United States Securities and Exchange Commission, 2007. http://www.sec.gov/Archives/edgar/data/86144/000119312508038856/d10k.htm.

Safeway Inc. "The Heart of Safeway: 2008 Corporate Social Responsibility Report." Safeway, Inc. http://www.safeway.com/CMS/includes/docs/2008%20CSR%20Report.pdf.

Salesforce Foundation. "2008 Annual Report." Salesforce Foundation. http://www.salesforcefoundation.org/files/SalesforceFoundation_2008AnnualReport-sm4.pdf.

Salesforce Foundation. "Volunteers of the Year—2007." Salesforce Foundation. http://www.salesforcefoundation.org/VOY2007#amar.

Salesforce.com. "Salesforce.com Achieves Outstanding Customer Satisfaction" Salesforce.com, 2009. http://www.salesforce.com/company/news-press/press-releases/2009/04/090407.jsp.

Sample, Ian. "Scientists offered cash to dispute climate study." *The Guardian*, February 2, 2007. http://www.guardian.co.uk/environment/2007/feb/02/frontpagenews.climatechange.

Sandle, Paul, and Michael Szabo. "JPMorgan to buy EcoSecurities for $204 million." Reuters, September 14, 2009. http://www.reuters.com/article/GCA-GreenBusiness/idUSTRE58D37020090914.

Sauers, Len. "Sustainable Innovation Products." The Procter & Gamble Company, 2008. http://www.gmaonline.org/events/2008/sustainability/Presentations/Len%20Sauers%201-11_Sustainable%20Innovation%20Products.pdf.

SCE. "Workforce Diversity." SCE. http://www.sce.com/Sc3/Templates/EndContent Flexible2Col.aspx?NRMODE=Published&NRNODEGUID={0CE300DE-0E0A-49B1-A0D9-D2F6D7DAB6BE}&NRORIGINALURL=%2fsc3%2fCommunity andRecreation%2fDiversity%2fWorkforceDiversity%2f&NRCACHEHINT= Guest#payroll.

Schevitz, Tanya. "Cal given $10 million by Dow Chemical to work on sustainability." *San Francisco Chronicle*, October 31, 2007. http://www.sfgate.com/cgi-bin/article.cgi?f=/c/a/2007/10/31/BA67T2UHH.DTL.

Schmid, John. "GE's 'healthymagination' born from green challenge." *Journal Sentinel Inc.*, June 29, 2009. http://www.jsonline.com/business/49466327.html.

Self-Help. "Impact: Total Investment." Self-Help. http://www.self-help.org.

Shaffer, Don. "It's Happening Right Now." RSF Finance, August 3, 2009. http://rsfsocialfinance.org/2009/08/its-happening-right-now.

Sherwin-Williams. "Retirement Plans." Sherwin-Williams. http://www.sherwin-williams.com/about/careers/benefits/retirement/index.jsp.

ShoreBank Corporation of America. "About ShoreBank: Corporate Information." ShoreBank. http://www.shorebankcorp.com.

Simmons School of Management. "A Message from the Dean." Simmons School of Management. http://www.simmons.edu/som/about/dean/3143.shtml.

Simply Hired. "Simply Hired." Simply Hired. http://simplyhired.com.

Sims, Peter. *Little Bets*. USA: Simon & Schuster, Free Press, 2011.

Social Investment Forum. "Executive Summary: 2007 Report on Socially Responsible Investing Trends in the United States." Social Investment Forum. http://www.socialinvest.org/resources/pubs/documents/FINALExecSummary_2007_SIF_Trends_wlinks.pdf.

Solmonese, Joe. Introduction to Corporate Equality Index 2009—A Report Card on Lesbian, Gay, Bisexual, and Transgender Equality in Corporate America. The Human Rights Campaign Foundation, 2008.

Sprint Nextel Corporation. "Benefits." Sprint. http://about.sprint.com/careers/content.do?lookupKey=benefits/wealth.

Sprint Nextel Corporation. "Directors." Sprint. http://www.sprint.com/gover nance/board.

Sprint Nextel Corporation. "2007 Corporate Social Responsibility Report." Sprint. http://www.sprint.com/responsibility/environment/docs/csr_report.pdf, pg. 21.

Sprint. "Meet the Reclaim." Sprint. http://green.sprint.com/reclaim.php?&id9= Ad_2009q3_green_reclaim_bird_300x250.

Sprint. "Wireless Recycling." Sprint. http://www.sprint.com/responsibility/communities_across/index.html.

Staff of World Resources Program. "The Value of Eco System Services." *Stewardship*, May 29, 2009. http://www.stewardship.co.za/index.php?option=com_content&view=article&id=69:the-value-of-eco-system-services&catid=1:latest-news&Itemid=50.

Staff of World Resources Program. "World Resources 1998–1999: Valuing Ecosystem Services." World Resources Institute. http://earthtrends.wri.org/features/view_feature.php?theme=4&fid=15.

Stangis, Dave, in discussion with the author. 9 July 2009, and throughout 2007–2009.

Stanley Reed, Miriam Elder. "BP's Russian Joint Venture Falters." *Business-Week*, July 31, 2008, http://www.businessweek.com/magazine/content/08_32/b4095050383376.htm?chan=globalbiz_europe+index+page_energy+%2Bamp%3B+environment.

Starbucks Coffee Company. "Ethical Sourcing: Verification and Transparency." Starbucks. http://www.starbucks.com/SharedPlanet/ethicalInternal.aspx?story=verification.

Starbucks Coffee Company. "FY2008 Global Responsibility Report." Starbucks. http://www.starbucks.com/sharedplanet/customGRPage.aspx.

Starbucks Coffee Company. "Our Goals and Progress: Ethical Sourcing Goal." Starbucks. http://www.starbucks.com/sharedplanet/customGRPage.aspx.

Starbucks Coffee Company. "Our Responsibility: Our Collaborators." Starbucks. http://www.starbucks.com/SHAREDPLANET/ourPartnerships.aspx.

Starbucks Coffee Company. "Recycling: Store Recycling." Starbucks. http://www.starbucks.com/SHAREDPLANET/customGRPage.aspx.

Starbucks Coffee Company. "Starbucks Corporate Social Responsibility 2007." Starbucks. http://www.starbucks.com/aboutus/csrreport/Starbucks_CSR_FY2007.pdf.

Starbucks Coffee Company. "Your Special Blend." Starbucks. http://www.starbucks.com/aboutus/SB-YSB-US-HR.pdf.

Starbucks Coffee Company. "C.A.F.E. Practices (Coffee and Farmer Equity Practices)." Starbucks. http://www.starbucks.ca/en-ca/_Social+Responsibility/C.A.F.E.+Practices.htm.

Starbucks Coffee Company. "Company Fact Sheet." Starbucks. http://www.starbucks.com/aboutus/Company_Factsheet.pdf.

Starbucks Coffee Company. "Frequently Asked Questions." Starbucks Coffee. Company. http://www.starbucks.com/customer/faq_qanda.asp?name=jobs.

Starbucks Coffee Company. "Frequently Asked Questions: Jobs at Starbucks." Starbucks. http://www.starbucks.com/customer/faq_qanda.asp?name=jobs.

Starbucks Coffee Company. "Mission Statement." Starbucks Coffee Company. http://www.starbucks.com/mission/default.asp.

Starbucks Coffee Company. "Our Goals." Starbucks Coffee Company. http://www.starbucks.com/SHAREDPLANET/ourGoals.aspx.

Starbucks Media Relations, in discussion with the author. 2007.

Stevens, Suzanne. "Lockheed Martin dips into wave energy technology." *The Deal*, October 14, 2009. http://www.thedeal.com/corporatedealmaker/2009/10/lockheed_martin_dips_into_wave.php.

Stinson, Sonya. "Green mortgages save on energy, loan costs." Bankrate.com, March 30, 2009. http://www.bankrate.com/finance/mortgages/green-mortgages-save-on-energy-loan-costs-3.aspx.

Supermarket & Retailer. "Safeway extends its private label brands to SA." *Supermarket & Retailer*, May 26, 2009. http://www.supermarket.co.za/news_detail.asp?ID=1510.

Supermarket News. "Safeway Employees Compete in Healthy Lifestyle Contest." *Supermarket News*. http://supermarketnews.com/news/safeway_healthy_0722/.

Sustainability Consortium. "Sustainability Consortium." The Sustainability Consortium. http://www.sustainabilityconsortium.org.

Sustainable Life Media. "92% of New Grads Say They Want to Work for a Green Company." *Sustainable Life Media*, October 11, 2007. http://www.sustainablelifemedia.com/content/story/strategy/10112007.

Sustainable Resources Ventures. "Founder." Sustainable Resources Ventures. http://www.sustainvc.com/Founder.html.

Sustainable Resources Ventures. "Our Portfolio Companies." Sustainable Resources Ventures. http://www.sustainvc.com/Portfolio.html.

Sweetman, Kate. "Norway's Boards: Two Years Later, What Difference Do Women Make?" *Fast Company*, July 13, 2009. http://www.fastcompany.com/blog/kate-sweetman/decoding-leadership/norway-s-boards-two-years-later-what-difference-do-women-make.

Takahashi, Toshio. "Toyota to License Hybrid Patents For Use by Ford." *Wall Street Journal*, March 9, 2004. http://online.wsj.com/article/SB107880303676250060.html.

Target Corporation. "Careers – Benefits." Target Corporation. http://sites.target.com/site/en/company/page.jsp?contentId=WCMP04-031455.

Target Corporation. "Fast Facts." Target Corporation. http://pressroom.target.com/pr/news/target-stores/fastfacts.aspx.

Target Corporation. "Target Archer Farms Food Brand Eliminates Added Trans Fats." Target Corporation Pressroom. http://pressroom.target.com/pr/news/consumables/af-eliminates-trans-fat.aspx.

Target Corporation. "Target Corporate Responsibility Report 2008." Target Corporation. http://target.com/responsibilityreport2008.

Target Corporation. "Working at Target: Wealth." Target Corporation. http://sites.target.com/site/en/company/page.jsp?contentId=WCMP04-031458.

Target. "2008 Corporate Responsibility Report." Target. http://target.com/responsibilityreport2008.

TBL Capital. "About Us." TBL Capital http://www.tblcapital.com/.

TechCrunch. "Mint." TechCrunch. http://www.techcrunch.com/tag/mint.

Texas Instruments. "2008 Corporate Citizenship Report—Sustainable Product Design." Texas Instruments, 2008. http://www.ti.com/corp/docs/csr/prodstewardship/SustainableProductDesign.shtml.

Thayer, Ann M. "Sustainable Synthesis." *Chemical and Engineering News* 87, no.23 (June 8, 2009): 13–22.

Timberland®. "CSR—Environmental Stewardship." Timberland®. http://www .timberland.com/corp/index.jsp?page=csr_green_index.

Timberland®. "Introducing the Green Index(tm) Rating." Timberland®. http:// www.timberland.com/corp/index.jsp?page=csr_green_index.

Timberland®. "What Kind of Footprint Will You Leave?" Timberland®. http:// www.timberland.com/shop/ad4.jsp.

Torrey, Jim, in discussion with the author. October 2009.

Transparency International. "Corruption Perception Index 2007." Transparency International. http://www.transparency.org/policy_research/surveys_ indices/cpi/2007.

Transparency International. "Corruption Perception Index 2008." Transparency International. http://www.transparency.org/policy_research/surveys_ indices/cpi/2008.

Treille, Teri, in discussion with the author. October 2009.

Tronche, John-Laurent. "Water recycling debate has many sides." *Fort Worth Business Press*, March 24, 2008. http://www.fwbusinesspress.com/display.php?id= 7232.

Tufts e-news. "$100 Million Puts Tufts On Cutting Edge." Tufts University, November 7, 2005. http://enews.tufts.edu/stories/374/2005/11/07/ $100MillionPutsTuftsOnCuttingEdge.

U.S. Census Bureau. "Hispanics in the U.S." U.S. Census Bureau, 2006. http://www.census.gov/population/www/socdemo/hispanic/files/Internet_ Hispanic_in_US_2006.pdf.

U.S. Census Bureau. "Overview of Race and Hispanic Origin Census Brief." U.S. Census Bureau, 2000. http://www.census.gov/prod/2001pubs/c2kbr01-1.pdf.

U.S. Census Bureau. "We the People: Women and Men in the United States." U.S. Census Bureau, 2005. http://www.census.gov/prod/2005pubs/censr-20.pdf.

U.S. Department of Housing and Urban Development. "Energy Efficient Mortgage Home Owner Guide." Housing & Communities. http://www.hud.gov/ offices/hsg/sfh/eem/eemhog96.cfm.

U.S. Department of Labor, Bureau of Labor Statistics. Employment and Earnings, 2008 Annual Averages and the Monthly Labor Review, November 2007. http://www.dol.gov/wb/stats/main.htm.

U.S. Equal Employment Opportunity Commission. "The Civil Rights Act of 1991." The U.S. Equal Employment Opportunity Commission. http://www .eeoc.gov/policy/cra91.html.

U.S. Equal Employment Opportunity Commission. "The Equal Pay Act of 1963." The U.S. Equal Employment Opportunity Commission. http://www .eeoc.gov/policy/vii.html.

U.S. Environmental Protection Agency. "2007 ENERGY STAR Award Recipients." Energy Star. https://www.energystar.gov/index.cfm?c=industry.bus_ award_recipients_2007.

U.S. Environmental Protection Agency. "2008 ENERGY STAR Award Recipients." Energy Star. http://www.energystar.gov/index.cfm?c=industry.bus_award_ recipients_2008.

U.S. Environmental Protection Agency. "*Fortune* 500 Challenge." U.S. Environmental Protection Agency. http://www.epa.gov/grnpower/toplists/fortune500.htm.

U.S. Securities and Exchange Commission. "Accredited Investors." U.S. Securities and Exchange Commission. http://www.sec.gov/answers/accred.htm.

United for a Fair Economy and Institute for Policy Studies. "Executive Excess Reports." United for a Fair Economy. http://www.faireconomy.org/executive_excess_reports.

United Nations Development Programme. "Statistics – HDI Trends." Human Development Reports. http://hdr.undp.org/en/statistics/data/trends.

United Technologies Corporation. "2008 Annual Report." United Technologies Corporation. http://utc.com/utc/about_utc/company_reports/2008_annual_report.html.

US Biofuels Exchange. "Home." US Biofuels Exchange. http://www.us-bx.com/.

Venture Beat. "Kleiner Perkins creates $700M new fund, plus $500M for green investments." *Venture Beat*, May 1, 2008, Deals & More section. http://deals.venturebeat.com/2008/05/01/kleiner-perkins-creates-700m-new-fund-plus-500m-for-green-investments.

Verizon Communications Inc. "Board of Directors." Verizon. http://investor.verizon.com/corp_gov/board_directors.aspx.

Verizon Communications Inc. "Form 10-K." Verizon. http://investor.verizon.com/sec/sec_frame.aspx?FilingID=6435582.

Verizon Communications Inc. "08/09 Corporate Responsibility Report." Verizon. http://responsibility.verizon.com/images/vz_uploads/verizon_cr_report_2008-2009.pdf.

Verizon Communications Inc. "Verizon Fact Sheet." Verizon. http://newscenter.verizon.com/kit/vcorp/factsheet.html.

VerizonCSR videos. "Video: Reducing our Carbon Footprint." YouTube. http://www.youtube.com/watch?v=tETxFdHh0LM&feature=channel_page.

Vestal, Christine. "Gay marriage legal in six states." Stateline.org. http://www.stateline.org/live/details/story?contentId=347390.

Viegas, Jennifer. *The Founder of eBay*. New York: The Rosen Publishing Group, 2007.

Villalobos, Alejandra, in discussion with the author. 25 September 2009.

Virtual World News. "WeeWorld Grows to 30 Million WeeMees." *Virtual World News*, September 22, 2009. http://www.virtualworldsnews.com/2009/09/weeworld-grows-to-30-million-weemees.html.

Vitters, Scott, in discussion with the author. 23 September 2009.

Waddoups, Rand, in discussion with the author. 21 September 2009.

Wainwright Bank & Trust Company. "2008 Annual Report." Wainwright Bank. https://www.wainwrightbank.com/html/about/financials/reports/wbtar2008.pdf.

Walgreens. "Walgreens to Harness Power of Sun." *FYPower*, January 11, 2001. http://www.fypower.org/pdf/Walgreens_PV.pdf.

Walker, Brian, in discussion with the author. 31 January 2007.

Wall Street Journal. "Sarkozy Adds to Calls for GDP Alternative." *Wall Street Journal*, September 14, 2009. http://blogs.wsj.com/economics/2009/09/14/sarkozy-adds-to-calls-for-gdp-alternative.

Wall Street Journal. "Where the Grass Is Made Greener." *Wall Street Journal*, August 19, 2009, http://online.wsj.com/article/SB1000 142405297020404420457436055268425027 2.html.

Walmart Stores, Inc. "Greenhouse Gas Emissions Fact Sheet—September 2009." Walmart Stores, Inc. walmartstores.com/download/2311.pdf.

Walmart Stores, Inc. "Sustainability Report 2007—Associate Wages." Walmart Stores, Inc. http://walmartstores.com/sites/sustainabilityreport/2007/ associatesWages.html.

Walmart Stores, Inc. "Where Do Walmart Associates Get Their Health Care Coverage?" Walmart Stores, Inc. 2007. www.walmartfacts.com/Media/ 128129402428782500.pdf.

Walmart Stores, Inc. "Agriculture and Seafood" Walmart Stores, Inc. http:// walmartstores.com/Sustainability/9173.aspx.

Walmart Stores, Inc. "Investors." Walmart, Stores Inc. http://walmartstores .com/Investors.

Walmart Stores, Inc. "Live Better Index." Walmart Stores, Inc. http://www .livebetterindex.com/savemore.html.

Walmart Stores, Inc. "Saving Money and Energy with CFLs." Walmart Stores, Inc., 2007. walmartstores.com/download/2303.pdf.

Walmart Stores, Inc. "Sustainability." Walmart Stores, Inc. http://walmartstores .com/Sustainability/7672.aspx.

Walmart Stores, Inc. "Sustainability: Products." Walmart Stores, Inc. http:// walmartstores.com/Sustainability/7772.aspx.

Walmart Stores, Inc. "Walmart 2009 Sustainability Report." Walmart Stores, Inc. http://walmartstores.com/sites/sustainabilityreport/2009/en_threeKeyGoals .html.

Walmart Stores, Inc. "Walmart Announces Sustainable Product Index." Walmart Stores, Inc. http://walmartstores.com/FactsNews/NewsRoom/9277.aspx.

Walmart Stores, Inc. "Walmart's Health Care Benefits are Competitive in the Retail Sector." Walmart Stores, Inc., http://walmartstores.com/ FactsNews/NewsRoom/5575.aspx.

Walmart Stores, Inc. "Waste Fact Sheet—September 2009." Walmart Stores, Inc. http://walmartstores.com/download/2323.pdf.

Walmart Stores. "Global Corporate Responsibility Report 2009." Walmart Stores, Inc. http://www.socialfunds.com/shared/reports/1245090485_Wal-Mart_2009_Sustainability_Report.pdf.

Wang, Ucilia. "Masdar Breaks Ground on $230M Solar Factory." GreenTech Media, August 21, 2008. http://www.greentechmedia.com/articles/read/masdar-breaks-ground-on-230m-solar-factory-1307.

Washington Post Company. "Officers." The Washington Post Company. http://www .washpostco.com/phoenix.zhtml?c=62487&p=irol-govHistOfficers.

Waste Management Inc. "Social Responsibility Report 2006." Waste Management Inc. http://www.wm.com/wm/WM_SRR_2006.pdf.

Water.Org. "Learn About the Water Crisis." Water.org. http://water.org/learn-about-the-water-crisis/billion.

Wedin, Randy. "Sustainability and Green Chemistry—Not Just Buzzwords" *Chemistry*, Winter 2006, 40-41.

Wells Fargo. "2008 Annual Report." Wells Fargo. https://www.wellsfargo.com/downloads/pdf/invest_relations/wf2008annualreport.pdf.

Wells Fargo. "Environmental Affairs." Wells Fargo. https://www.wellsfargo.com/about/csr/ea.

Wells Fargo. "Executive Officers—Patricia Callahan." Wells Fargo. https://www.wellsfargo.com/about/corporate/executive_officers/callahan.

Wells, John, in discussion with the author. 19 January 2007.

White, Vince, in discussion with the author. 11 February 2009.

Whole Foods Market, Inc. "Form 10-K." Whole Foods Market, Inc. http://www.wholefoodsmarket.com/company/pdfs/2007_10K.pdf.

Whole Foods Market, Inc. "Whole Foods Market Benefits." Whole Foods Market, Inc. http://www.wholefoodsmarket.com/careers/benefits_us.php.

Wood, Chris. "Platinum Power." *MultiFamily Executive*, June 1, 2007. http://www.docstoc.com/docs/3540507/multifamily-executive-magazine.

Xerox Corporation. "Diversity: Making all the Difference." Xerox Corporation. http://www.xerox.com/go/xrx/template/009.jsp?view=Feature&Xcntry=USA&Xlang=en_US&ed_name=Careers_Diversity&metrics=Diversity_Vanity.

Xigi. "Charly Kleissner." Xigi. http://www.xigi.net/index.php?person=458.

XL Capital, Ltd. "About us." XL Capital, Ltd. http://www.xlcapital.com/xlc/xlc/about_detail_template.jsp?propid=xlc_about_exec_profiles#board.

Yahoo! Finance. " Bank of America." Yahoo! Finance. http://finance.yahoo.com/q?s=BAC.

Yahoo! Finance. "Colgate-Palmolive." Yahoo! Finance. http://finance.yahoo.com/q?s=CL.

Yahoo! Finance. "Chevron Corp." Yahoo! Finance. http://finance.yahoo.com/q?s=CVX.

Yahoo! Finance. "Dow." Yahoo! Finance. http://finance.yahoo.com/q/pr?s=Dow.

Yahoo! Finance. "Exxon Mobil CP." Yahoo! Finance. http://finance.yahoo.com/q?s=XOM&.yficrumb=OWslLvE6muY.

Yahoo! Finance. "Intercontinental Exchange." Yahoo! Finance. http://finance.yahoo.com/q/is?s=ICE&annual.

Yahoo! Finance. " J.P. Morgan Chase Co." Yahoo! Finance. http://finance.yahoo.com/q?s=jpm.

Yahoo! Finance. "Johnson and Johnson." Yahoo! http://finance.yahoo.com/q?s=jnj.

Yahoo! Finance. "Kroger Annual Revenue." Yahoo! Finance. http://finance.yahoo.com/q/is?s=KR&annual.

Yahoo! Finance. "Sealed Air Income Statement." Yahoo! Finance. http://finance.yahoo.com/q/is?s=SEE&annual.

Yahoo! Finance. "Lockheed Martin CP." Yahoo! Finance. http://finance.yahoo.com/q?s=LMT&.yficrumb=OWslLvE6muY.

Yahoo! Finance. "McDonalds CP." Yahoo! Finance. http://finance.yahoo.com/q?s=MCD&.yficrumb=OWslLvE6muY.

Yahoo! Finance. "Procter and Gamble." Yahoo! Finance. http://finance.yahoo.com/q?s=Pg.

Yahoo! Finance. "Raytheon Co." Yahoo! Finance. http://finance.yahoo.com/q?s=RTN.

Yahoo! Finance. "Starbucks Corporation." Yahoo! Finance. http://finance.yahoo
.com/q?s=SBUX&.yficrumb=OWslLvE6muY.

Yates, Willard Ross. *Joseph Wharton: Quaker Industrial Pioneer.* Bethlehem: Lehigh
University Press, 1987.

Yelland, Alex, in discussion with the author. 22 October 2007.

Yerema, Richard. "Chosen as one of Canada's Top 100 Employers, Manitoba's Top
Employers and Canada's Top Family-Friendly Employers for 2009." Eluta Inc.
http://www.eluta.ca/top-employer-monsanto.

Yucknut, Steve, in discussion with the author. 12 September 2008.

Yum! Brands. "Serving the World: Corporate Social Responsibility Report." Yum!
Brands, 2008. http://www.yum.com/responsibility/pdf/yum08csrrpt.pdf.

Acknowledgments

Producing a book is akin to building a house—this "dream home" is the result of a multitude of passionate, committed and optimistic people. While the foundation of my daily inspiration—and superbly edited prose—is my soul mate, best friend, and wife, Gayle Keck, the encouraging "push" for communicating HIP through a book came from my friend David Bornstein, author of several books, including *How to Change the World*. The architecture of this work greatly benefited from my business partner, Jessica Skylar, and her ongoing sculpting of the logic, flow, and friendly style. Jessica's talent to find, select, and manage more than 50 high-quality researchers, analysts, and associates has enabled HIP to take shape, helping to make this "house" sound and solid.

The first blueprint, published as the HIP Scorecard in *Fast Company* magazine, came to life with Cheryl Dahle's entrepreneurial insights and Keith Hammonds' wisdom and guidance, joined by the pioneering Sara Olsen and tenacious Brett Galimidi of SVT Group. The second HIP analysis for *Fast Company*, on Big Oil, was fostered by editors Bob Safian and Denise Martin, and enhanced by the thoughtful, innovative analysis of Jenny Harms, with researchers Ashok Kamal, Aparna Darisipudi, Jenna Carl, Javier Flores, Greg Noce, Pierette Imbriano, and Barbara Berska.

Whether on-site or virtual, the co-builders of the HIP Indexes are many. William Reinhardt, who trained and mentored scores of researchers, and Tom Willis, who drove the HIP Scorecards in Chapter 7, helped build the foundation of the HIP 100, with Mike Manzano and Todd Feiler. Financial whizzes Will Finkelstein, Vivek Kumar, Napoleon Wallace, Velvet Voelz, Joselle Deocampo, Eileen McInerney, and Abha Thakur affirmed that HIP portfolios could be fruitful. The HIP 500 benefited from a very large team: Fulbright scholar Michael Reading, Lee Coker, Jamie Chomas, Preston Sharp, Adam Jagelewski, Susie Heller, Mara Ludmer, Sasha Mironov, Jillian McCoy, Line Moisan, Gina Wu, Robin Connell, Soma Parui, Varun Parmar, Nick Gower, Jared Alaqua, Ajay Gopalan, Stephanie Parent, Peter Hadar, Navneet Gautam, and Muhammad Safdari. Multiple HIPsters helped spread the word and build the community: Stephanie Gerson, Debra Langley, Dina Beigelman, Lisa Giarretto, Maureen Loftus, Sylvia Gibson, Sonia Talati, Bailey Stoler, Avary Kent, Mandy Gamarra, Anne Kim Ho, Waymond Ngai, Kevin Christopher, Melina Wyatt, Nyambura Gichohi, and the collegial Wil Keenan.

All the rooms of the HIP "house" have unique touches from leaders of their disciplines who shared their valuable insights: Rand Waddoups and Matt Kistler of Walmart; sustainability advisers from BluSkye Consulting, including John Whelan and Dave Sherman; Kelly Lauber and Ziba Cranmer of NIKE; Dave Stangis of Campbell's; Bob Langert of McDonald's; Ben Packard of Starbucks; Bonnie Nixon of H-P; and Teri Treille and Kirsten Uttam of Cisco.

The community of forward-thinking optimists is strong, and it has accelerated the spread of HIP. Empowering Professor Ed Rubesch and the multi-talented Pattraporn Yamla-or of Thammasat University in Bangkok are partners in spreading HIP globally, as are Liz Maw, Dara Kosberg and Coree Brown of Net Impact. Continuously supportive of HIP are Deb Parsons, Matt Lombardi and Molly Deringer of Investors, Circle; KoAnn Vikoren Skrzyniarz of Sustainable Life Media; Nikki Pava of ecoTuesday, Jonathan Lewis of the Opportunity Collaboration; Bruno Giussani of TED; Robert Rubenstein of Triple Bottom Line Investing; and Kevin Jones, Tim Freundlich and Joy Anderson of Social Capital Markets. I am grateful for the faculty and future leaders of the Green MBA at Dominican University, the Presidio MBA, the Bainbridge Graduate Institute, and all entrepreneurship programs integrating a full-world view.

The HIP home could not have been as strong or advanced without our core advisors and supporters: the brainy Divesh Makan, the masterful Joan Varrone and Joe Catalano, the visionary Lili and Marie Stiefel, the superb Anne Marie Burgoyne, entrepreneurs Ramesh Parameswaran and Digvijay Chauhan, as well as Mike Mohr, Tim Sarhatt, Gwen Edwards, Perla Ni, Scott Smith, Todd Johnson, Terry Mollner, Suzanne Biegel, Andrew Horowitz, Brian Dunn, Shaula Massena, Keith Jardine, Michi Nishimura, Marie Trexler, Jonathan De Yoe, Sylvia Ventura, Francine Gordon and Lisa and Bob Skylar.

In addition, HIP has benefited from the analytical minds of Lloyd Kurtz, Liz MacMillan, Patrick Malone, Joe Glorfield, Kathy Brozek, Mark Jamison, Eric Steinhofer, Rahilla Zafar, Leslie Berliant, Jessica Margolin, Danny Bradbury, Trevor Curwin, and Dale Wannen—and of course the "perfect CEO," Evan Siegel. The coaching from authors David Bank, Peter Sims, Fred Krupp, Heather McLeod Grant, Jennie Fields, Tyler Colman, and Chunka Mui—and the spirit of Frank Herbert—enlightened me as to how to navigate the construction process for this book.

No dream home is complete without family and friends. I wouldn't be who I am if it weren't for my loving, compassionate mother, Alice, and my logic-fanatic, yet inventive father, Ross. My sister Mary was a meticulous editor and kept me laughing and my spirits bright, especially during the final deadlines, and taught me everything I know about belly-buttons. My mother-in-law, Sue Ann—and my late father-in-law, Gordon—have always been continuously curious and ready to celebrate! My decades-long friendships with Abbey Linfert, Rob Holtz, David Gordon, Greg Back, Dana Hoffman, Alistair Goodman, Mary Doan, Cathy Grisham, Lauren Azuma, Jill Totenberg, Frederick Doner, Bruce McKenzie, and Christopher Hall join the newer but no-less-enthusiastic Vittorio and Ann Mischi (welcome Alexander!), Cassandra and Nigel Lake (and my godson William), Seth Bindernagel, Scott Beale, Ben Smilowitz, and John McWalter in supporting my penchant for new ideas and keeping the fires of world-changing initiatives stoked.

Apprentices become masters over time by learning from the experienced elders. I am especially grateful for the patience of my mentors in forging the professional I have become today: Les Silverman, Paul Jansen, Jim Hine, Jeff Rubin, Jim Kennedy, Leo Redmond, and the late Jeffrey Walker. At Ashoka, Leslie Crutchfield and Bill Drayton get due credit for enlightening my path along social entrepreneurship, while Doug Solomon and Pierre Omidyar have illuminated my craft of impact investing.

Who made sure the welcome wagon arrived? This "dream home" would not have opened its doors without a world-class quality inspector, permit acquirer and metaphor-appreciator, the Olympian Nina Jacinto. The "interior design" of the HIP visuals in the book, the web site, and brand identity are the product of a late-night "dream team" (thanks, Grish!): the fantastic Kelly J. Smith, David Maloney, Brian Leland, Bradley Charbonneau and Adrian Preuss. The online and social media presence is due to the diligent planning and creativity of Dana Roytenberg and Darcy Villere.

Even in tough times, getting a "dream home" to market can be difficult. It looked easy, due to the wisdom of generous and connected author Connie Hale, the leadership of Wharton professor Stew Friedman, and the commitment and expertise of my agent, James Levine, and his associate, Kerry Evans, both of Levine Greenberg.

I am deeply appreciative for our publisher's leadership, trust, and enthusiasm—the foresight and thought leadership of Editor Debra Englander, the cultivating style of Kelly O'Connor, the production excellence of Kevin Holm, and the always-supportive Adrianna Johnson, of John Wiley & Sons. Their design team did an excellent job of "painting" our exterior and their sales and marketing team will ensure that this HIP work is accessible to all who seek a better world.

About the Author

R. Paul Herman was trained in finance at the Wharton School of the University of Pennsylvania. His multisector experience includes consulting to top *Fortune* 500 firms at McKinsey & Company and CSC Index; creating and entrepreneuring the first online permission-based debit-card system for teens, kids, and parents; and financing entrepreneurs delivering human impact and profit while serving as an investment strategist for eBay founder Pierre Omidyar's impact investing firm. Herman also advised business entrepreneurs on how to donate to—and invest in—social entrepreneurs, while at Ashoka.org.

Herman created the HIP (Human Impact + Profit) methodology as the foundation for a new way of investing producing both good and profit. In growing HIP Investor Inc. since its incorporation in 2006, Herman and his team have evaluated more than 500 companies, examining the relationship between shareholder returns and human impact. Herman pioneered "The HIP Scorecard^{SM}" for *Fast Company* magazine, rating and ranking companies in multiple industries. With collaborators, he also conducted an in-depth evaluation of the global energy industry for *Fast Company*. (Both can be found at www.fastcompany.com/investing.) Nobel Peace Prize winner Muhammad Yunus made note of HIP Investor's innovative scorecard as a "new yardstick for business", in his recent book, *Creating a World without Poverty: Social Business and the Future of Capitalism* (Public Affairs, 2008).

Comprehensive analysis of the 500 largest U.S.-based companies by Herman and his team has led to the launch of the HIP 100 and HIP 500 investment indexes. HIP's portfolios for clients—serving individual, family, foundation and institutional investors as an investment adviser—seek to make bigger profits by building a better world. Herman is a sought-after speaker for conferences, a guest lecturer at universities, and often serves as a media source. He has been quoted in the *Wall Street Journal, Fortune, Forbes, BusinessWeek, CNN's Crossfire,* and *CNBC.*

Herman has also advised leading companies, including Walmart, Nike, Cisco, and Charles Schwab, on strategic sustainability, how to measure it and how it drives business value. Herman is an advisor and lifetime member of Net Impact, the association for business people and students seeking to use the power of business for good.

Born in Chicago, Herman has traveled to 40 countries and has lived in Philadelphia, Washington D.C., New York City, Mexico City, and Sydney, Australia. He now resides in his adopted city of San Francisco, with his wife Gayle Keck, an award-winning travel and food writer and branding expert.

Index